Anne Frank

Reflections on Her Life and Legacy

Edited by
Hyman Aaron Enzer and Sandra Solotaroff-Enzer

Foreword by Bernd Elias

University of Illinois Press
Urbana and Chicago

Publication acknowledgments on pages 261–65 are an extension of the
copyright page.

Library of Congress Cataloging-in-Publication Data
Anne Frank : reflections on her life and legacy / edited by Hyman Aaron
Enzer and Sandra Solotaroff-Enzer; foreword by Bernd Elias.
  p.   cm.
Includes bibliographical references (p.) and index.
ISBN 0-252-02472-9 (alk. paper)
ISBN 0-252-06823-8 (pbk. : alk. paper)
1. Frank, Anne, 1929–1945. Achterhuis. 2. Frank, Anne, 1929–1945.
3. Holocaust, Jewish (1939–1945)—Netherlands—Amsterdam.
4. Jewish children in the Holocaust—Netherlands—Amsterdam.
5. Holocaust, Jewish (1939–1945)—Influence. I. Enzer, Hyman Aaron,
1916–   . II. Solotaroff-Enzer, Sandra, 1933–   .
DS135.N6F73   2000
940.53'18'092—dc21   99-6291
[B]
CIP

1 2 3 4 5 C P 5 4 3 2 1

For our granddaughter, Aethena-Rose,
and our mothers, Rivka and Rosie

This is my letter to the World
That never wrote to Me—
—Emily Dickinson

Contents

Foreword

Bernd Elias

Even after more than fifty years, I can still hardly believe what became of my little cousin Anne, the boisterous, funny, and beloved playmate of my childhood. Did I realize her talent for writing when we played with my puppet theater the last time Anne, her sister, Margot, and her father, Otto, visited us in Switzerland before the war? Of course not. And not even her letters to us when Holland was already invaded and occupied by Germany revealed what was to move millions of people in times to come.

Her last letter for my seventeenth birthday, which I still have and cherish, is the epistle of a teenager that then showed little of her great talent. That was one month before the family went into hiding.

And then silence. No contact, no letters, no idea where the family was. Three years later came the dreadful news that Anne, Margot, and their mother, Edith, like millions of others, had perished, victims of intolerance, of a murderous fascist regime.

About the end of 1945 Uncle Otto, the only survivor of the family, sent the first pages of Anne's diary, translated into German, to us in Switzerland. We were stunned. We saw a new Anne, one we didn't know. Otto told us it was her dream and hope that something she would write would be published after the war. And he also told us that he had found a publisher.

But not even then, even after her diary came out in Holland, did I have the faintest idea that this heritage of Anne's would become, as someone has said, the most read book after the Bible. Translated into fifty-eight languages, it has sold about 26 million copies.

Anne, my little cousin, your dream has come true, better than you had ever hoped. I'm proud of you!

Preface
and Acknowledgments

Although we had assigned Anne Frank's diary in our respective college courses, the idea for this anthology came to us from two prominent figures in its history. The first was Philip Roth, whose roman à clef, *The Ghost Writer,* produced an astonishing reincarnation of Anne Frank. The moral and aesthetic dilemmas provoked by Roth led us to consider how different interpretations influenced public perceptions of the diary.

The second was B. M. Mooyaart-Doubleday, whose intriguing, ambiguous name appeared as translator of the 1952 English edition. We assumed a son or daughter of the Doubleday publishing family had been handpicked for the task. The translator, however, turned out to be unrelated. She was Barbara Mary Doubleday, who, as a young English war bride, had gone to live in Holland with her Dutch aviator husband, Eduard Mooyaart. Vallentine Mitchell, the British publisher, chose her over older, professional translators because of her fluent re-capturing of Anne Frank's style. When we visited her in Amersfoort in 1994, she showed us a trove of memorabilia from Otto Frank and her unique experience of reliving the life of the young diarist.

So inspired, we began tracing the voluminous intellectual and personal reactions to Anne Frank's diary since it was first published in 1947. We acknowledge our thanks to all the writers and publishers who have made this collection possible, especially the translators Susan Massotty and Alfred J. Pomerans, and the editors Judith McCulloh, Peter Kracht, and Rob Williams.

Ted Solotaroff, Marcia Posner, and Laureen Nussbaum read various drafts of the manuscript and helped us avoid many pitfalls of diction and interpretation. We are grateful to Lawrence Graver, Sylvia P. Iskander, Alex Sagan, Phyllis B.

Maguire, William McBrien, and Carola Gouse for stimulating exchanges of ideas and suggestions; to David Barnouw and Gerrold van der Stroom, editors of *The Diary of Anne Frank: The Critical Edition,* for their textual corrections and guidance; and for notes from H. J. J. Hardy, who prepared the forensic science report for the Netherlands Institute of War Documentation.

Sir Jack Polak, chairman emeritus of the Anne Frank Center USA, and his wife, Ina, were especially helpful. Vincent Frank-Steiner and Bernd Elias, past and present presidents, respectively, of the Anne Frank-Fonds in Basel, provided support and encouragement. Grayson Covil, executive director of the Anne Frank Center USA, and her staff members supplied valuable documents and services as did staff members of the Anne Frank House in Amsterdam, especially Yt Stoker, Dineke Stam, and Menno Metselaar.

Translations from Dutch, French, and German sources were provided by Rita Landman Greene, Lt. Col. John Greene, Marie-Rose Myron, and Ethan Izak Enzer. Lisa Enzer-Mahler and Robert Mahler gave emergency computer help. Marion Pritchard gave us information on Lin Jaldati and her husband. Esther Markman Enzer obtained rare materials for us in Hebrew and Yiddish. Milton Teichman and Sharon Leder shared their experience of editing their Holocaust collection, *Truth and Lamentation,* and Wendy Kesselman gave us valuable insights about the writing and staging of the 1997–98 adaptation of *The Diary of Anne Frank.* Jack Nusan Porter guided us to helpful sociological sources. Angelika Gausmann found and translated pertinent German tapes and articles for us, and Christoph Möllman located the Anne-Frank-Shoah-Bibliothek in Leipzig.

We are grateful for the support of President James M. Shuart and Provost Herman Berliner of Hofstra University and for grants from the Louis Posner family and an anonymous donor. Librarians at Hofstra University were generous with their time and expertise, particularly Martha Kriesel, Maureen Brown, Elena Cevallos, Maureen Howe, Beatrice Thompson, and Janet Wagner. We also are grateful to our respective departmental secretaries, printing staff, and editorial service personnel, especially Kim Alvarez, Ernest Angiulo, Doris Brown, Phyllis Droessler, Linda Ann Merklin, Carolann Parrino, Jennifer Stern, and Barbara Warburton at Hofstra, and Ethel Zamurut and her staff at Nassau Community College.

Major Identifications

Diary Names	Real Names

The Eight Jews in Hiding

Diary Names	Real Names
Anne M(arie)(Mary) Frank	Anneliese Marie Frank
Margot Frank	Margot Betti Frank
Pim, Daddy	Otto Heinrich Frank
Mumsie, Mummy	Edith Holländer Frank
Petronella Van Daan, Kerli	Auguste Van Pels
Herman Van Daan, Putti	Hermann Van Pels
Peter Van Daan	Peter Van Pels
Dr. Dussel, Mr. Dussel	Fritz Pfeffer

Business Names and Employees

Diary Names	Real Names
Travies	Opekta
Kolen & Co.	Gies & Co.
Mr. Koophuis	Johannes Kleiman
Mr. Kraler	Victor Gustav Kugler
Elli Vossen	Elisabeth (Bep) Voskuijl
Dirk	Bertus (Bep's boyfriend)
Mr. Vossen	Mr. Voskuijl (Bep's father)
Miep Van Santen	Miep Gies
Henk Van Santen	Jan A. Gies

Diary Names	Real Names
Mr. Van Dijk, Mr. Van B.	Mr. Broks
Mr. Sleegers	Mr. Slagter
V.M.	W. G. van Maaren

Anne's Friends and Acquaintances

Lies Goosens, Hannali	Hannah Elisabeth Pick-Goslar
Jopie de Wal	Jacqueline (Jaques) van Maarsen
Sanne Houtman	Sanne Ledermann
Peter Wessel	Peter (Petel) Schiff
Harry Goldberg	Helmuth (Hello) Silberberg
Fanny	Ursul, Ursula
Wilma	Eva
Corry Koophuis	Jopie Kleiman
Karel Samson	Sally (Sol) Kimmel
Mr. Goudsmit	Mr. Goldschmith (or Goldschmidt)
Mr. Keptor	Mr. Keesing
Mrs. K.	Mrs. Kuperus

The Diary Versions

Anne's first diary entry was dated June 12, 1942, and was written in the red and white checkered autograph album she had received from her father for her thirteenth birthday. The entries continued in this book until December 5, 1942. Anne wrote further entries in another diary between December 6, 1942, and December 21, 1943, but they have been lost. All of these entries are known as the *a* version of the diary.

A black covered exercise book contains the entries beginning on December 22, 1943, and continuing through April 17, 1944. Margot tore pages from a chemistry exercise book and gave them to Anne for her next diary, which had a green and gold speckled cover. The entries in that diary begin on April 17, 1944, and end with one dated August 1, 1944.

On March 28, 1944, Gerrit Bolkestein, the minister of education, art, and science in the Dutch government-in-exile in London, made an appeal over Radio Oranje to the Dutch people to keep diaries, letters, and other "ordinary" documents as firsthand evidence of what happened to them during the war years.

On March 29 Anne recorded that the news prompted everyone "to make a rush at my diary immediately." This entry marks the first explicit reference to her imagining that her diary might be published after the war.

On May 11 she wrote that her "greatest wish" was to be a journalist, "and later on, a famous writer." Then she added: "After the war I'd like to publish a book called *Het Achterhuis*." On May 20 Anne recorded that she had begun rewriting the diary: "At long last after a great deal of reflection I have started my 'Achterhuis,' in my head it is as good as finished, although it won't go as quickly as that really, if it ever comes off at all."

The rewritten entries of her diary form the *b* version and were recorded on loose sheets and also on pages she had left blank in her checkered diary. In effect, all her rewriting was done in about ten weeks, from May 20 to her last known revision on August 1. The secret annex was raided on August 4. The first date entered in her rewritten diary (June 20, 1942) marks the first time she addresses her diary as "dearest Kitty." The last of the rewritten entries was dated March 29, 1944, and thus incorporates all of the original entries now lost—those between December 6, 1942, and December 21, 1943. While she was rewriting and editing almost two years of previous entries, she continued to write new entries. The entries recorded between December 22, 1943, and August 1, 1944, in her exercise books were never revised by Anne.

The published diary, known as the *c* version, was prepared by Otto Frank, in collaboration with the Dutch publisher, based upon the *a* and *b* versions. He ignored much of Anne's editing in the *b* version, restored material she had cut from the *a* version, and cut further entries himself.

The publication in 1986 of *The Diary of Anne Frank: The Critical Edition* brought together for the first time all three versions of the diary for comparison.

Chronology

May 12, 1889	Otto Frank is born in Frankfurt am Main, Germany
January 16, 1900	Edith Holländer is born in Aachen, Germany
May 12, 1925	Otto Frank and Edith Holländer are married in Aachen
February 16, 1926	Margot Betti Frank is born in Frankfurt am Main
June 12, 1929	Anneliese (Anne) Marie Frank is born in Frankfurt am Main
January 30, 1933	Adolf Hitler and the Nazi party take control of Germany
March 20, 1933	Dachau, one of the first concentration camps, is established near Munich
Summer 1933	Edith, Margot, and Anne go to Aachen to stay with their grandmother, Rosa Holländer-Stern
September 15, 1933	Otto starts Opekta Works in Amsterdam; his righthand man is Victor Gustav Kugler; Hermine (Miep) Santrouschitz joins the staff and eventually becomes Otto's chief secretary
October 1933	Otto's mother, Alice Frank-Stern, moves from Frankfurt to Basel, Switzerland, to live with Otto's sister Helene and her husband, Erich Elias
December 5, 1933	Edith and Margot move from Aachen to 37 Merwedeplein in Amsterdam
March 1934	Anne is taken from Aachen to join her family and is enrolled in the nearby Montessori school

March 12, 1938	Nazi troops enter Vienna, beginning the Austrian *Anschluss* with Germany
June 1, 1938	Otto Frank establishes his second company, Pectacon N.V.; Johannes Kleiman is named "supervising director" and bookkeeper for both companies; Hermann Van Pels, who fled from Osnabruck, Germany, in 1937 with his wife and son, becomes the herbal specialist for Pectacon N.V.
November 9–10, 1938	*Kristallnacht* leads to the destruction of synagogues and Jewish property in Germany and the deportation of thousands of Jews to the camps
November 16, 1938	Official decree bars Jewish children from German schools
December 8, 1938	Fritz Pfeffer flees Germany to Holland
March 1, 1939	Edith Frank's mother moves to Amsterdam
September 1, 1939	Germany attacks Poland; England and France declare war on Germany two days later
May 10, 1940	Holland, stormed by German paratroopers, surrenders in five days; the Dutch royal family flees and sets up a government-in-exile in England
June 1940	Kugler, as a non-Jew, is given proxy as director of Pectacon N.V.
October 22, 1940	Dr. Arthur Seyss-Inquart, chief of the Nazi occupation, issues the decree of *Entjudung* (de-Judification) of all Dutch businesses
October 23, 1940	A new company, La Synthese N.V., is formed with two Aryans in charge: Kugler, managing director, and Jan A. Gies, supervisory director
December 1, 1940	The joint company moves to 263 Prinsengracht in Amsterdam, in whose annex Anne Frank would write her diary
Fall 1941	Margot, Anne, and other Jewish children are forced out of Dutch schools to attend segregated Jewish schools in Amsterdam
December 7, 1941	The Japanese bomb Pearl Harbor; the United States enters the war against Japan and Germany a few days later
January 1942	Edith Frank's mother dies
January 20, 1942	Top Nazi officials meet at Wannsee, a Berlin suburb,

	to devise the Final Solution (extermination) to the "Jewish question"
June 12, 1942	On Anne's thirteenth birthday she receives the diary with its red and white checkered cover and makes her first entry
June 20, 1942	This is the date of the first entry in her rewritten diary (the *b* version), which she began on May 20, 1944
July 5, 1942	Margot receives a "call up" to report to a "labor camp"
July 6, 1942	The Frank family goes into hiding in the secret annex at 263 Prinsengracht early Monday morning; Anne describes her father's secret plan to go into hiding (diary entries of July 8, 9, 10, and 11)
July 13, 1942	The Van Pels family joins the Franks in the secret annex
November 16, 1942	Fritz Pfeffer, Miep's dentist, moves in with the Franks and the Van Pelses
March 29, 1944	Anne refers to a report on Radio Oranje that diaries and letters should be collected after the war
May 20, 1944	Anne writes: "I have started my 'Achterhuis,'" the *b* version of her diary
June 6, 1944	D day: Allied Forces land at Normandy; Anne writes, "It gives us fresh courage"
August 4, 1944	The Dutch Nazi police raid the secret annex
August 5, 1944	Miep Gies and Bep Voskuijl recover the diary and loose pages strewn on the floor of the attic before the Green Police return
August 8, 1944	The Franks, the Van Pelses, and Fritz Pfeffer are moved from the Gestapo prison in Amsterdam to Westerbork
September 3, 1944	The prisoners are sent on the last transport to Auschwitz; they arrive September 6; Hermann Van Pels dies there a few weeks later
October 1944	Anne and Margot are sent to Bergen-Belsen in northwestern Germany
December 20, 1944	Fritz Pfeffer dies in Neuengamme camp, north of Bergen-Belsen
January 6, 1945	Edith Frank dies in Auschwitz
January 27, 1945	Otto Frank, barely alive, is freed when Russian troops capture Auschwitz

February-March 1945	Margot, then Anne, die in Bergen-Belsen, two weeks before British troops liberate that camp
Spring 1945	Auguste Van Pels dies in Theresienstadt, in northern Czechoslovakia
May 5, 1945	Peter Van Pels dies in Mauthausen, in northern Austria
June 3, 1945	Otto Frank returns to Amsterdam and is taken in by Miep Gies and her husband
Summer 1945	Otto learns of the deaths of his daughters; Miep then gives him Anne's diary, which he translates into German for his mother in Basel
Summer 1947	The diary of Anne Frank edited by Otto is published in Dutch, then in French, German, and English between 1950 and 1952
November 11, 1950	Janet Flanner's "Letter from Paris" in the *New Yorker* and Meyer Levin's report in *Congress Weekly* call attention to *Le Journal de Anne Frank,* the French translation of the diary
May 1952	Vallentine Mitchell publishes the English translation in Great Britain
June 1952	Doubleday publishes the British version in the United States
June 15, 1952	The *New York Times* publishes Meyer Levin's review of the diary; by the next day the entire first printing is sold out; theater, film, and television producers rush to obtain rights to the diary
Fall 1952	Otto moves to Basel, Switzerland, to join his mother
November 1953	Otto marries Elfriede Markovitz Geiringer (aka Fritzi), who, with her daughter, Eva (Anne's age), also survived Auschwitz
October 5, 1955	The play *The Diary of Anne Frank* by Frances Goodrich and Albert Hackett opens at the Cort Theater in New York, later winning a Tony, the New York Critics Circle Award, and the Pulitzer Prize
1956	Levin charges Goodrich and Hackett with plagiarizing his script, beginning protracted legal challenges against Otto Frank and others
November 9–11, 1957	The first of many neo-Nazi attacks on the authenticity of the diary, claiming Meyer Levin was the "real" author, is made in Sweden

1959	The Hollywood film version of *The Diary of Anne Frank,* produced and directed by George Stevens, opens in movie theatres throughout the United States. Shelley Winters wins an Oscar for her performance as Mrs. Van Daan.
May 3, 1960	The Anne Frank House officially opens and the Anne Frank Foundation begins international campaigns against bigotry and hatred
November 1966	Levin's stage version of the diary in Hebrew is performed at the Soldiers Theater in Tel Aviv; it is withdrawn after fifty performances
Spring 1973	Levin publishes the story of his twenty-year legal battles in *Obsession*
August 19, 1980	Otto Frank dies in Birsfelden, near Basel, at age ninety-one
June 1986	*The Diary of Anne Frank: The Critical Edition* is published in Dutch by the Netherlands State Institute for War Documentation; the English translation is published in 1989
March 1995	On the fiftieth anniversary of Anne Frank's death, *The Diary of a Young Girl: The Definitive Edition* is published in English
June 5, 1995	*Anne Frank Remembered* has its premiere; it wins the Academy Award as best documentary film the following year
December 4, 1997	Wendy Kesselman's adaptation of *The Diary of Anne Frank* opens on Broadway

Note to the Reader

Except for minor editing, a dozen selections in this anthology are complete; the rest are excerpts of other works. Because commentaries about the Frank family and their friends restate or revise "the facts," some repetition and discrepancies may be found in this collection. Wherever possible, redundant material has been omitted. Abridgements are indicated by ellipsis points. Some footnotes that appeared in the original essays have been edited or eliminated to avoid duplication. In addition, minor stylistic changes have been made in the essays to give consistency to the volume. Because the contributors used various versions and translations of the diary, some quotations will differ from the diary passages familiar to American readers. In most cases the diary entries are identified by date only, and we have referred to Anne Frank's work merely as "the diary" throughout instead of using its various titles. To each contribution we have added an epigraph from the 1995 American edition of the diary translated by Susan Massotty, unless otherwise noted.

In anticipation of publishing her diary, Anne Frank had assigned pseudonyms to the people mentioned in her diary. When the diary was originally published, Otto Frank employed Anne's scheme, so most readers are familiar with the fictional names. Because the real identities were revealed over time, some contributors in this collection used only the fictional names in their original essays, some used only the real, while others used a combination of the real and the fictional. To avoid confusion, except where the characters of the play and film are being discussed, only the real names have been used in this collection.

Anne Frank:
Reflections on Her Life and Legacy

Introduction

Of all the memoirs that convey the human devastation of Hitler's Final Solution, Anne Frank's *The Diary of a Young Girl* is by far the most popular and influential. Yet the diary did not record any horrors. Only by reading recollections of survivors who saw Anne Frank during her final seven months do we learn what happened to her at Westerbork, Auschwitz, and Bergen-Belsen.

Although she died more than fifty years ago, the young girl who wrote about eight Jews hiding in an attic for two years has left a haunting reminder of a generation that was almost totally snuffed out. Even though this diary is just one of thousands recorded during the war, Anne's is the only report of what her contemporaries saw and experienced in the ghettos of Europe "to have captured and conquered the hearts and imagination of the wider public," as the Nobel Laureate Elie Wiesel has remarked.[1] But why did Anne Frank's voice become the one most widely identified with the Holocaust?

Since its first publication in Holland in 1947, the diary has been translated into more than fifty languages, reprinted in millions of copies, and transformed into plays, films, teaching guides, and political tracts. Hundreds of commentaries and very active Anne Frank organizations also keep her memory alive and reiterate the "lessons" of her life and death. As one reader of our manuscript wrote: "The more I think of it, the more the diary comes to seem like *the* book of the past half-century in its paradigmatic account of innocence confronting political evil—the story of much of this era."

In spite of all the contending attempts to reveal the "real" Anne Frank and her legacy, no single work has gathered the disparate facts and interpretations into a compact volume for the general reader. For this anthology we have examined many articles and memoirs to find those we believe are most relevant for understanding the significance of her experiences and legacy. We have organized these materials around the following questions and their implications:

1. What are the facts about Anne Frank's life and the writing of the diary?

2. What are the major critical assessments of Anne Frank as a writer and the bases for her reputation?

3. How have controversies over the stage and film versions of the diary altered Anne Frank's original intentions?

4. How have interpreters of Jewish experiences in World War II defined Anne Frank's significance for understanding and memorializing the Holocaust?

Rereading Anne's words in all their versions and hearing others' impressions of her do not diminish the emotional intensity of our first encounter with her. She is still the same amusing, often outrageous girl who evolved from an acutely sensitive child into a wise, reflective young woman. But after a half-century of interpretations the distinctive selves that constituted the "bundle of contradictions," as she described herself, have been separated. Once, Anne turned herself inside out to discover who she was. Now others tell us they know who she "really" was. Like the witnesses in the Japanese film *Rashomon,* many of her interpreters have reconstituted Anne Frank from their often righteous self-interests or their misreading of her words. Anne Frank has become an intricate play of shadows. True or false as they may be, these portrayals blend in and out of each other. A protean Anne Frank slips from the grasp of devotees and antagonists in this anthology.

History, Biography, and Authenticity

During the two years she was writing in relative safety, Anne's uninhibited, often witty diary evolved naturally into a drama of eight Jewish characters in search of positive meaning in a world that wanted to destroy them. She reveals their lives as if the front of the annex on the Prinsengracht was sheared off and the interior projected on the screen of history. What she wrote privately has now been interpreted by so many admirers and emulators that the bright, saucy Anne Frank has become a blur of images. She is no longer just a young girl budding into womanhood, writing to make sense out of a cruel confinement, but has become a patron saint of adolescence, an ardent feminist, a literary prodigy, a champion of religious and racial equality, and an embattled literary property.

Despite epochal social and cultural changes that have diminished the words of most writers of her time, Anne's diary continues to have lasting appeal. Readers of all ages identify with her enthusiasms and fears because they can readily recognize their own adolescences in her words and because she writes without affectation. The diary has endured also because it continues to provoke new controversies about what she did or did not intend to write, what her father did or did not excise, and what writers such as Meyer Levin, John Berryman, and Philip Roth conceived to be the "real" Anne Frank.

Most of these disputes seemed to have been resolved with the publication of the virtually unedited text—*The Diary of Anne Frank: The Critical Edition*—by the Netherlands State Institute for War Documentation in 1986. However, even that seemingly definitive document was brought into question by the discovery in 1998 that Otto Frank removed five pages of the diary just before his death in 1980 and gave them to his friend Cornelius Suijk (known as Cor). Three of these pages contain Anne's observation that Otto lacked passion for his wife, Edith. A footnote on page 482 in the critical edition for the entry on February 8, 1944, indicated that "in the 47 lines omitted here Anne Frank gave an extremely unkind and partly unfair picture of her parents' marriage. At the request of the Frank family this passage has been deleted." Since no revision of this section was found—because it was held by Otto Frank and then put into Suijk's care—other members of the Frank family may have believed Anne had willfully excluded this material, so they agreed to the deletion in the published version. Because we now have the missing pages we know that Anne expanded these forty-seven lines into seventy-four lines during her revisions three months after writing the February 8, 1944, entry.[2]

Even with this startling revelation, the 700-page critical edition remains authoritative in documenting Anne Frank's work on the diary. By ingenious reconstruction of her entries in the original red-checkered diary and other writings in booklets and scraps of paper, the Dutch editors made it possible to compare her private first draft with the more crafted revision she hoped to publish. Then, with the addition of the third version compiled by Otto Frank and others after the war, most changes in the ur-text could be traced and the controversy surrounding the authenticity of the work could be ended; the evidence, like a Rosetta stone, was laid out so that all contenders for Anne's "true" intentions could "quote scripture" to justify their claims. In addition, the editors filled in gaps in the history of the Franks and their friends.

In this anthology we present many views of the residents of the secret annex. After Laureen Nussbaum recounts the history of Anne Frank's life and the publication of various versions of her diary, Harry Paape details the betrayal and arrest of the eight Jews in hiding and Ernst Schnabel reconstructs their night in Gestapo headquarters. Although we cannot hear directly from Anne or her sister, Margot, about their days in the concentration camps, we do have Hannah Elisabeth Pick-Goslar and Lin Jaldati to tell us what they witnessed. These accounts are rounded out by Miep Gies's report of finding and saving the diary and Simon Wiesenthal's success at identifying the policeman who led the raid on the secret annex.

Beyond the personal history of the Franks, the other Jews in hiding, and their protectors is the larger history of the Jews during World War II. Only within the context of the *Shoah,* the Hebrew term for the Holocaust, can we locate the main reasons for the diary's significance. First of all, without knowing about Anne's fate in Auschwitz, the story of a young girl hiding in a secret annex would be relatively unremarkable. It is our knowledge of the calculated destruction of the Jews in Europe, and Anne and almost all of her family in particular, that throws a pall over the simplest events in her diary. When Anne says that being in hiding is like a great adventure, her momentary euphoria fills us with the foreboding that she herself constantly recognizes. We cannot throw off the sense of doom even as she vividly describes the rainy July morning in 1942 when she and her family, in heavy layers of clothing—"as if we were going to the North Pole"—walked fearfully to their secret refuge. Grateful as she was to Miep Gies, her father's secretary, and her other protectors, we know, as she could not, that the overflow of her feelings for the Dutch was only half justified: Holland had at once almost the worst and almost the best record of rescuing Jews in Europe.

Anne Frank was one of 34,000 German Jews who fled to Holland when Hitler seized power in 1933. Her father, Otto, moved his family and his fruit pectin company to the country where Jews had been allowed to live in relative freedom for over three hundred years. The Dutch also accepted refugees in numbers far beyond most other nations, including the very restrictive United States. However, when the Germans invaded neutral Holland in 1940 and were supported by Dutch Nazi collaborators, most of the 140,000 Jews, both natives and refugees, found that the historic sanctuary was an illusion.

Nevertheless, despite great personal risks, many Dutch citizens resisted Nazi controls and managed to hide more than 24,000 native and refugee Jews. Over 16,000 survived, an extraordinary record compared with those in other occupied countries. In contrast, nearly 107,000 German and Dutch Jews were deported, of whom all but 5 percent died, the highest Jewish death toll in a western European country. These extremes have generated conflicting myths about Dutch resistance and complicity. Anne's justifiable trust in Miep Gies and her grateful references to other Dutch protectors have led many readers to believe most Dutch people were solidly against the German occupiers. But Anne's personal judgment is not tenable, considering Holland's wartime record.[3]

The diary's importance in the context of the *Shoah* also rests on its use in introducing audiences, especially school-age readers, to the political and social events leading up to and through the Holocaust. It was the first document about the Holocaust to stir the consciousness and conscience of Europeans, particularly the young. In the United States, in which the havoc of the war was not felt as it was in Europe, younger generations have acquired more information about the direct experiences of the war from history texts and less and less from memoirs. Today, teachers rely on the diary to build a bridge to the past and make the Holocaust meaningful for students now several generations removed from the horrors that shocked their elders.

Because Anne Frank had not yet been subjected to the worst horror of the war, her diary alone is not sufficient to teach about the Holocaust, however. Richard D. Western and Karen Shawn, among others, point out that young readers of the diary with insufficient background or reading skills may not be able to grasp what they are reading, so teachers must be prepared to introduce students to historical events and data.[4] Although valuable guides have been developed for this purpose, serious obstacles may still block readers' understanding.[5] A number of American schools have been confronted with political antagonism to the diary. For example, a reference guide to banned books indicates that some parents and administrators have objected to Anne's egalitarian ideas and boldness in describing her sexual development.[6] These attempts to exclude the diary from classrooms and libraries are linked to movements to deny the authenticity of the diary as well as the Holocaust.

Despite such limitations, teachers actually receive a double benefit from its classroom use: not only is it effective as an introduction to the Holocaust for history and social studies but also students are stimulated to use it as a model for writing about their own lives. Two of the most famous emulators are Zlata Filopovic of Sarajevo and Raimonda Kopelnitsky of Chernobyl. *Zlata's Diary* became a bestseller and inspired even more students to become diarists.[7]

Writer and Rewriter

Whatever claims are made to justify the diary's popularity, more than anything, the quality of Anne Frank's writing has gained her universal acclaim. Frank's artistry was instantly recognized by the Dutch historian Jan Romein when he read a typescript of her diary in 1946: "The Netherlands State Institute for War Documentation already holds some two hundred similar diaries, but I should be very much surprised if there were another as lucid, intelligent, [and] at the same time as natural."[8] His tribute has been reiterated by schoolchildren and politicians, popular and scholarly writers, and notable writers and survivors of the Holocaust, such as Elie Wiesel and Primo Levi.

Most essays devoted to her writing style have focused on her spare, insightful descriptions of events and relationships. A handful, like G. B. Stern in her introduction to a collection of Anne's tales included in this volume, center on the development of Anne's writing skills and the potential she demonstrates in her tales and diary. A few have concentrated on her rhetorical skills or on sources influencing her content and style, as does Sylvia P. Iskander in her essay in this volume.[9] Others, like Rachel Feldhay Brenner and Henry F. Pommer in their pieces, have stressed her literary significance rather than her political or social relevance.

Brenner, a Judaica scholar, equates Anne's writing with the act of self-assertion. In her essay, subtitled "Anne Frank's Self-Portrait as a Young Artist," Brenner evokes the self-searching themes of James Joyce's hero, Stephen Dedalus. Pommer, a Milton scholar, describes the maturity of Frank's ideas and her ability to reveal her multiple selves, but remarks as well on her ability to enchant us: "Sometimes our delight is simply in her charm, as in 'Daddy always says I'm prudish and vain but that's not true. I'm just simply vain.'" The critics Ann Birstein and Alfred Kazin, commenting on her varied writings, distinguish between her realistic and her imaginative writing: for the real events in her diary "her subjects chose her" whereas in her tales, fables, and essays, "she chose her subjects."[10]

Other scholars are more concerned with the content than with the form or style of her writing. Unlike those who focus on Anne's diary as a document to introduce the Holocaust, Lawrence L. Langer and Alvin H. Rosenfeld in their essays in this volume attribute the diary's appeal for teenage females to Anne's curiosity about her anatomy and her adolescent *Sturm und Drang*. Similarly, James E. Young and Pommer allude to her "drama of puberty," a subject prominent in the numerous juvenile adaptations of the diary and emphasized in essays by the psychologist Carol Gilligan and the feminist critic Katherine Dalsimer.[11] Indeed, John Berryman in his essay regards the diary as "the most remarkable account of *normal* human adolescent maturation" he has ever read, and in his opinion, for that, first and foremost, instead of anything else, it should be valued. Berryman's psycholiterary tribute to Anne's seriousness was one of the first to emphasize the maturity of her thinking and her writing.

More recently, Anne's sophistication has been especially noted by feminist writers. Catherine A. Bernard, for example, claims that Anne Frank's qualities as a serious writer had been largely ignored or discounted because editors and critics had relegated her to childhood.[12] One reason this stereotype of childlike innocence persists is that many readers are familiar only with the edited version of her diary that Otto Frank published and assume that an overprotective father censored her indelicate entries. More complex is the truth, as the comparisons of the versions of the diary in the critical edition demonstrate. It was Anne herself, increasingly conscious of cultural pressures "to be nice," who deleted the explicit descriptions of her sexual development and most of the critical remarks about her mother.

Berteke Waaldijk in her essay in this anthology has also substantiated Anne's conscious moderation of her language by delineating Anne's deletions made out of a sense of propriety, but emphasizing changes she made in the revised version of the diary that were for literary effect. Waaldijk argues that Anne consciously strove to turn her diary into a publishable work and was influenced by the many books and genres she read. Waaldijk notes that, like other female writers, Anne had to find a way to write about her life that seemed truthful to her experiences. In upsetting conventional expectations about mother-daughter relationships in her acerbic, witty, and conflicting viewpoints, Anne's bold example has stimulated feminist scholars to examine a vast, but largely ignored treasury of women's writings about the Holocaust. The roles of young and old women, mothers and children hidden below the surface of male-dominated or genderless literature of the period are being uncovered or examined anew.[13]

Scholars' focus on the diary as a work of art rather than a document of World War II leads Harry Mulisch, one of Holland's outstanding novelists and the winner of the first Anne Frank Prize in 1957, to raise fundamental questions about the nature of Holocaust "literature." By treating the diary as a "creative" work, Mulisch fears he might give credence to claims by neo-Nazis that the diary was a fabrication, that it was ghostwritten, or that Anne Frank is a diarist's literary creation. But by ignoring its power, he realizes he diminishes its ability to reach millions of people who need to be educated or reminded about the lessons of the Holocaust. In the end, after being profoundly moved by reading the diary and visiting the secret annex, Mulisch is torn between the world described in the diary, the fate of the Jews hiding in the secret annex, and the lives of his own family members who perished in the camps. He cannot determine the meaning—or deny the power—of any of these experiences.

Anne Frank on Stage and Screen

As she was being transformed into the star of a popular play in 1955 and of George Stevens's 1959 film, the young girl of the diary was thrust into a courtroom conflict between Meyer Levin and her father. Levin, a novelist who had vowed to avenge the horrors he saw at Buchenwald, found in the diary the "voice from the mass grave" he was looking for. Overwhelmed when he read the diary in French in 1950, he wrote Otto Frank for permission to bring it to wider public attention by finding an American publisher for it and by writing a play based upon it. Levin wrote a script that was never authorized—for disputed reasons—and launched a bitter tirade against the producers, directors, and playwrights of the successful stage version as well as Otto Frank. The story of his winning Otto's support, losing it, and struggling to regain it has the aura of tragedy. For more than thirty years until his death in 1981 Levin maintained that Frances Goodrich and Albert Hackett, whose script was awarded a Pulitzer Prize, plagiarized the structure and material from his version. At least four books (two by Levin himself) and many articles have been written about the dispute. In this collection, Lawrence Graver recounts the long, painful conflict between the two men who were Anne Frank's most devoted advocates.

Levin's legal battles and the transformation of the diary into a Broadway play and a Hollywood movie created a whole set of claimants to the Anne Frank legacy. Levin attacked those associated with the play not only for depriving him of his rights to the story but also for minimizing the Jewish and tragic qualities of the diary. In 1955 when the play opened, public attitudes toward the victims of the Holocaust and Jews in general were becoming more sympathetic, but they were also complicated by the politics of the cold war. Levin bitterly resented Lillian Hellman's involvement in the production of the play because he believed her support for Stalinism, which promoted anti-Jewish policies, was responsible for the removal of the Jewish elements in the diary from the Goodrich-Hackett play. Regardless of whether Hellman did or did not exercise that kind of control, Judith Doneson, a film historian, reports in her contribution in this anthology that during a time of investigating communists—who were strongly linked with Jews—Hollywood writers such as Goodrich and Hackett and directors such as Garson Kanin consciously avoided making their characters or situations "too Jewish" or "too ethnic." The "cleansing" of material in Hollywood meant, in this case, "universalizing" Jews and minimizing their "particularistic" religious or ethnic traits. Doneson writes: "Within this context of the quest for universal meaning in American society, *The Diary of Anne Frank* becomes a universal symbol."

Most criticism for the homogenizing of Anne Frank's work begins with the end of the play, where Goodrich and Hackett twice quote—out of context—her best-known sentence: "In spite of everything, I still believe that people are really good at heart." As part of a gloomy passage about approaching doom, where Anne had originally written them, those fourteen words express hope in the midst of despair. But bravely intoned by the stage Anne, on the verge of being betrayed to her enemies, they sound like a saintly benediction projecting optimism to Americans and absolution to Germans. Because this line was taken out of context, many people wrongly condemn Anne as a character and as a person for making a tenderhearted remark instead of cursing the cruelty of her circumstances.

Dramatically intensified by the play and repeatedly invoked by critics, these words in their uplifting context have obscured the "formidable" Anne Frank, as John Berryman described her. Like a one-line paraphrase of a Shakespearean tragedy, this mantra has been pounced on by audiences to substitute for the inherent complexities of her original work. This overly simplistic view of Anne was evident to Algene Ballif when she reviewed the original stage play. Unlike the Anne of the diary, the stage Anne in her eyes was merely "another image of that fixed

American idea of the adolescent, the central imperative of which is that this species of creature is not to be taken seriously." In her review reprinted here, she heavily criticized the stage version of the diary for taking away from the real Anne Frank what is, to Ballif, her most remarkable quality: "the way in which she is able to command our deepest seriousness about everything she is going through—the way she makes us forget she is an adolescent and makes us wish that this way of experiencing life were not so soon lost by some of us, and much sooner found by most of us."

Other audience members saw a different version of Anne on the stage, one that more closely corresponded with Barbara Epstein's view, for example. Epstein commented that since in the diary Anne "was a normal, in many ways still conventional, girl," the stage version had captured "Anne Frank's remarkable spirit, whose main quality, as she herself so often and so sensibly remarked, was its wholeness." Such conflicting views, combined with Levin's continued efforts to reclaim his rights to the play and his particular version of the story, led to acrimonious debate.

In Germany the reception of the diary was even more complex. Before the play opened in Berlin and six other German cities in 1956, no one anticipated the response in the country responsible for the extermination camps. Kenneth Tynan, a British critic and playwright who had been "vaguely perturbed" by the play in New York, was caught up with the Berlin audience in "the most drastic emotional experience the theater has ever given me." The stunned reaction that first night, which he recounts in this volume, was repeated through more than two thousand performances in Germany. This response, other changes in Germans' attitudes toward Jews, and their growing interest in the Holocaust prompted the art critic Alfred Werner to analyze the psychohistory of German "self-flagellation." Although, as he remarks in his piece in this volume, he believes the feelings of identification with Anne are genuine, he is skeptical about how they will be used.

The philosopher Hannah Arendt is less charitable in her assessment of this reaction, describing the evidence of German guilt about the Holocaust as "phony."[14] Theodor Adorno, the Frankfurt psychiatrist, was strongly tempted to agree, but found any change in feeling good enough: "I once heard the story of a woman who, after attending a performance of the dramatization of *The Diary of Anne Frank*, said in a shaken voice: 'Yes, but really, at least *that* girl ought to have been allowed to live.' Surely, even this was to be welcomed as a first step toward insight."[15]

Alex Sagan, who has analyzed the cultural implications of Anne's famous sentence, enlarged on Adorno's position: "It would be anachronistic and unduly dismissive to deny the positive role of the play and the film, especially insofar as audiences developed empathy for Anne Frank. Though such empathy may have been limited or ill-informed, I am convinced, as Adorno was, that such emotions constituted an early step in the process of coming to terms with the legacy of the mass murder of European Jewry."[16]

Similarly, David Barnouw in his essay in this anthology, while acknowledging that the 1959 George Stevens film converted Anne Frank into a celebrity, denies that the Hollywood "dream machine" exploited or trivialized her story or the lessons of the Holocaust. Like Adorno and Sagan, Barnouw believes that the first Anne Frank movie as well as subsequent Holocaust films awakened public consciousness to the buried horrors of the Nazi era, an issue that has taken on a new polemical life with the publication in 1996 of Daniel Jonah Goldhagen's *Hitler's Willing Executioners* and its subsequent critiques.[17]

And the debate continues. In the decades since the play and film first appeared, the diary has been reincarnated as abridgements for young readers, comic books, video reenactments, and adolescent playlets. Miep Gies has been portrayed in a TV film, *The Attic,* and a 1985 musical by Enid Futterman and Michael Cohen, *Yours, Anne,* is the source for new cassette and CD versions of the story. The Academy Award–winning two-hour film *Anne Frank Remembered,* written and produced by Jon Blair in 1995, is perhaps the most significant and all-encompassing of these latter-day productions. It not only recapitulates the ambivalent history of Dutch resistance to the Nazis and Dutch complicity in the persecution of Jews in Holland but also avoids the polemics that have afflicted other versions of Anne Frank's story. G. Jan Colijn, in his review reprinted in this volume, demonstrates how Blair's film corrects the dehistoricized and "de-Judaized" portrayals of Anne Frank. In effect, Colijn writes, this "masterpiece" manages "to normalize Anne's life without belittling her legacy in the slightest way."

But the controversy that seemed settled with the reception of this film was short-lived. Questions were raised anew in the last months of 1997 when Anne Frank became the subject of a new Broadway play adapted by Wendy Kesselman from the Goodrich-Hackett version, extensive reviews, detailed analyses and critiques by critics and historians, and at least five new books for general and specialized readers. Suddenly, Anne Frank was on several stages at once and beset on all sides.

Cynthia Ozick staked out her territory in the *New Yorker* when she lashed out at the playwrights, producers, and director of the original Broadway play for Anne Frank's "evisceration by fame, by shame, by blame." Ozick supported a major argument made by Ralph Melnick in *The Stolen Legacy of Anne Frank* and by Meyer Levin that Anne's diary was "falsified" by her father as well as by Lillian Hellman and others.[18] Ozick found herself caught in a crossfire of corrective letters, including one by Barbara Epstein, editor of the 1952 American edition, and another by Laureen Nussbaum, an author and a personal friend of the Franks.

Ian Buruma, the Dutch historian, also loosed a few barbs at Ozick in his review of the Kesselman play and books by Melnick and Lawrence Graver. Although he agreed with Ozick's thesis that "everyone wants his own Anne," he disliked her stridency. His comments provoked her defense and his retort.[19] Despite these skirmishes, a watershed was reached in the Levin saga. In her version Kesselman sought to emphasize the Holocaust and moderate the sentimentality of the Goodrich-Hackett play. According to Buruma, of the three theatrical versions of the diary, Kesselman's "strikes the fewest false notes," a view seconded by Ben Brantley in his review reprinted here. Brantley refers to the "unwieldy load of polemical baggage" carried by the new production, but credits Kesselman with going a "long way in redressing" the imperfections of the original. A less favorable opinion of the new play, with a succinct review of the Levin-Frank controversy, is presented by Molly Magid Hoagland in her *Commentary* review.[20]

After so many decades of debate and analysis, so many schools of critics and interpreters, so many attacks and counterattacks over more than half a century, finding fresh perspectives, like those offered by Wendy Kesselman and Jon Blair, is difficult. In a world of seemingly endless dialogue about the Holocaust, Anne of the little red checkered diary has been almost lost.

Memorializing the Holocaust

To determine how all the dramatizations and documentaries have reflected or distorted images of Anne Frank requires that we know the interplay between the history of the Holocaust and these recreated images and interpretations. Anne's diary, of course, differs from most tales of Holocaust victims because we do not hear directly about the worst of her suffering. While in hiding, the Jews had only the news on the radio and rumors from her protectors, which she noted in her diary. She did not lack insight into her desperate situation, however, because on at least two occasions she tells a prescient dream about her friend Lies, emaciated and in rags, as she herself eventually was seen by Lies in Bergen-Belsen.

The limitations of her story have led many critics to question the use of the diary as a document of the Holocaust. Lawrence L. Langer, for example, finds her diary does not meet his strict definition of "Holocaust literature," which requires "a view of the apocalypse" that goes beyond the palliatives of heroic dignity or redeeming truth, as he states in one of his contributions in this anthology. Though Anne writes (May 3, 1944), "there's in people simply an urge to destroy, an urge to kill, to murder and rage," Langer finds that the diary as well as the plays lack the full horror of the Holocaust; they appeal to audiences because they give only "the bearable part of the story" before Auschwitz and Bergen-Belsen.

Langer's view is reinforced by other scholars, including Alvin H. Rosenfeld, who has written extensively on Frank's reputation. Rosenfeld maintains that "the image of Anne Frank that has evolved over the years has been largely sanitized of any realistic sense of her life and death." In his essay in this volume he remarks that the continuing popularity of the diary in all its versions results from our imperfect knowledge of her suffering. Separated from the facts of her death, her story reflects in dramatic form the common teenage fantasies of desire and dread and "renders the worst aspects of the Holocaust in grossly understated terms."

Other critics, in contrast, have focused not on the audience's perceptions of the Holocaust as seen—or not seen—through Anne's eyes but rather on what she was able to transmit about her experiences during the war. In her essay in this collection, Denise de Costa defends Anne Frank's intuitive sense of history and politics against conventional beliefs that women were not expected to be knowledgeable about such matters. The Dutch literary scholar Sem Dresden and the American scholar Robert Alter are among those who blame Frank for not writing about the war or the barbarity of nazism, positions that de Costa diplomatically, but forcefully, finds lacking in credibility.[21]

Critics like Alter who dismiss Anne's ideas as having "the banality one would expect from a 14–year-old" are guilty, in de Costa's terms, of applying age- or sex-based stereotypes. De Costa finds many correspondences between Anne Frank and her older contemporary, Etty Hillesum, in their acute sensitivity to the foreboding evil of the Holocaust. Instead of erasing or sanitizing the Holocaust, as Rosenfeld and Langer claim, de Costa suggests that Anne's awareness of her feminism has helped make visible the distinctive experience of women of the Holocaust, as writers or subjects.[22]

Harsher critiques than Langer's and Rosenfeld's came from other sources. Bruno Bettelheim, who was incarcerated in Dachau and Buchenwald for a year before the outbreak of the war, openly challenged the almost universal admiration of Frank as well as the reputation of her father. Bettelheim argues in his essay in this volume that the acclaim for Anne Frank results from the sentimental belief that people can live a nearly normal life even in abnormal times, as the Franks and their friends attempted to do. Those who glorify Anne overlook the erosion of their personal autonomy in the all-powerful modern state and the potential tyranny of power in highly developed industrial civilizations. His thesis has implications beyond what happened to Jews during the Holocaust, as Zygmunt Bauman has suggested:

> The Holocaust did not just, mysteriously, avoid clashing with the social norms and institutions of modernity. It was these norms and institutions that made the Holocaust feasible. Without modern civilization and its most central essential achievements, there would be no Holocaust. . . . When it came to mass murder, the victims found themselves alone. Not only had they been fooled by an apparently

peaceful and humane, legalistic, and orderly society—their sense of security became a most powerful factor of their fall.[23]

In contrast, Jehuda Bauer finds Bauman's thesis simplistic because modern society did not have the same effect in other countries.[24] Bettelheim's insensitivity to the painful circumstances of the Frank family and of Jews in the camps, however, has prevented his central message from having wider currency and has brought him severe condemnation and only limited support.[25]

Despite Bettelheim's criticisms, it is only because of the tragic failure of Otto Frank's plan that Anne Frank's words inspire so much hope in the face of adversity. If Anne had lived she would not be as available to the imagination and hence to the posthumous uses made of her life and diary. Anne Frank, as a character, has transcended reality in the minds of many of her readers. Indeed, some believe they are her reincarnation or that she never existed.[26] One high school senior from Long Island, New York, who visited the Anne Frank House in Amsterdam in 1996 told his mother in amazement, "When I read the diary in school, I never thought she was real."

Anne Frank's idealism, blended with innocence and terror, has had profound, unanticipated consequences. When Otto Frank first circulated his daughter's manuscript among his family and friends, he did not realize how deeply people would be touched. The overwhelming response in Holland and France, and even in Germany, to the initial publication of the diary convinced him to establish an international foundation. The Anne Frank Stichting in Amsterdam, Holland, operates the Anne Frank House, which James E. Young has dubbed "the preeminent Dutch war shrine." In his essay in this volume Young suggests that the diarist may be the patron saint of Holland because there are now so many buildings and public places named after her, but she is equally a reminder to the Dutch that "even though they harbored her, they also betrayed her in the end." It is this mixture of pride and shame, claims Young, that adds to the fascination with the building where Anne and the other Jews were hiding.

More than half a million people visit the back quarters at 263 Prinsengracht every year, and a comparable number attend the special Anne Frank exhibits that tour cities throughout the world. Hundreds of volunteers, Holocaust survivors, scholars, and young people are constantly involved in these large-scale traveling exhibitions. One of these volunteers, Anna Cook, a fifteen-year-old docent who was instructed by Sir Jack Polak, chairman emeritus of the Anne Frank Center USA and a survivor of Bergen-Belsen, described her month's service with the exhibit "Anne Frank in the World," in Holland, Michigan, in October 1995: "One thing stuck out in my mind. What you have to remember is that the horror is *behind* the pictures. This exhibit is not full of pictures of dead corpses. There are pictures of smiling people and happy, healthy children. The horror is that most of these people did not live to finish their stories. Each face has a story as wrenching as Anne's—stories that were brought to abrupt ends by one man's twisted dream. We know Anne's because she was the one who wrote the story down for all of us to read."[27]

The Anne Frank-Fonds, based in Basel, as well as the Ann Frank Stichting are dedicated to Anne's ideals of justice and social harmony, but are constantly battling the lack of historical knowledge in young minds as well as the inevitable erosion of memory among the old. Furthermore, they have to contend with the overt opposition of groups who resent the use of Anne Frank's name for political causes and a more subtle danger that Geoffrey Hartman has called the "mechanics of commemoration."[28] Referring to the ceremony attended by President Ronald Reagan and Chancellor Helmut Kohl for German SS troops interred in the Bitburg military cemetery, Hartman suggested that the proliferation of memorials for victims of the Holocaust might "construct" forgetfulness about catastrophic events.

Some groups are working actively to do more than construct such forgetfulness. Several essays in this collection illustrate the difficulty in viewing the diary free of the smoke screens thrown up by so-called revisionists. Deborah Lipstadt in particular has documented revisionists' attempts to undermine the diary. Recognizing its magnetic effect on young readers, the neo-Nazis struck at the diary to hide their much larger goal: to prove the Holocaust itself was a fraud. Lipstadt summarizes the questions about the diary's provenance, the claim that the diary is too sophisticated to have been written by a teenage girl, and the assumption that Meyer Levin was its ghostwriter. She turns in particular to the evidence put forth in the critical edition, which was ostensibly issued to end questions about the diary's authenticity, but at the same time served to redress Dutch sensitivity about their collaboration with the Germans and what many historians perceived as Dutch neglect of that famous book.

The myriad possibilities for missing, undermining, distorting, or amplifying the educational lessons of the diary have not deterred Anne Frank's advocates from trying to preserve her legacy. The rites of memorialization—unveiling monuments and instituting new calendar days of remembrance—may indeed become routinized, but Yad Vashem, the Anne Frank House, and other Holocaust museums guarantee that personal and collective memories will be kept alive.

But the reality embedded in so many different memories of Anne Frank blends in and out of the world of the imagination, as Philip Roth has so boldly dared to do in *The Ghost Writer*. Conjuring with the possibility that Frank may have survived the Holocaust, Roth creates the mysterious "Amy Bellette," an aspiring writer who in 1955 could be Anne Frank had she not died of starvation and typhus in Bergen-Belsen ten years earlier.

Roth's "reincarnation" of Anne allows him to interweave major elements of her story within the narrative of Nathan Zuckerman, who is alienated from his family and who fancies that he could gain an awesome stature by marrying the icon of Jewish martyrdom. By fictionalizing the real Anne Frank, Roth alienated some readers, who considered his treatment of "the saintly Anne" exploitation and blasphemy.[29]

Roth's "Femme Fatale," reprinted here, is an imaginative reconstruction of the diary and its history by a writer whose "seriousness," like that of Anne Frank herself, has often been questioned or abused. Roth's concern about Jews, the Holocaust, and Anne Frank is revealed in his response to an interviewer's question about another novel, *The Anatomy Lesson*. In that story, when asked for her name, Zuckerman's dying mother instead writes *Holocaust* on a slip of paper. Her doctor holds on to the paper and cannot throw it away. Roth is asked why neither the doctor nor Zuckerman can throw it away, to which he replies: "Who can? Who has? . . . Without this word there would be no Nathan Zuckerman. . . . There'd of course be no Amy Bellette the young woman in *The Ghost Writer* who he likes to think could have been Anne Frank." When asked later whether the Holocaust is the subject of his books, Roth says of course not. But he then qualifies his remark: "For most reflective American Jews . . . it [the Holocaust] is simply there, hidden, submerged, emerging, disappearing, unforgotten. You don't make use of it—it makes use of you. It certainly makes use of Zuckerman."[30]

And it certainly makes use of Anne Frank.

Notes

1. Elie Wiesel, introduction (trans. Euan Cameron) to Anne Frank, *The Diary of a Young Girl: The Definitive Edition*, ed. Otto Frank and Mirjam Pressler, trans. Susan Massotty (London: Penguin, 1997), vii–xi.

2. Melissa Müller, *Anne Frank: The Biography,* trans. Rita Kimber and Robert Kimber (New York: Henry Holt, 1998), 204–13; Ralph Blumenthal, "Five Precious Pages Renew Wrangling over Anne Frank," *New York Times*, Sept. 10, 1998, A1, A6.

3. See, for example, Jacob Presser, *The Destruction of the Dutch Jews: A Definitive Account of the Holocaust in the Netherlands*, trans. Arnold Pomerans (New York: E. P. Dutton, 1969); Louis de Jong, *Het Koningrijk der Nederlanden in de Tweede Wereldoorlog* [The History of the Kingdom of the Netherlands in the Second World War], 12 vols. (The Hague: Nijhoff, 1966–88); Judith Miller, *One, by One, by One: Facing the Holocaust* (New York: Simon and Schuster, 1990); and Jack Polak, "Anne Frank's Dream Came True," letter in *Forward*, Apr. 7, 1995, 36.

4. See Richard D. Western, "The Case for *Anne Frank: The Diary of a Young Girl*," in *Celebrating Censored Books*, ed. Nicholas Karolides and Lee Burress (Racine: Wisconsin Council of Teachers of English, 1985), 12–14; and Karen Shawn, *The End of Innocence: Anne Frank and the Holocaust*, 2d ed. (New York: Anti-Defamation League, 1994).

5. *Readers' Companion to Anne Frank: The Diary of a Young Girl: The Definitive Edition* (New York: Doubleday, 1995).

6. Herbert N. Foerstel, *Banned in the U.S.A.: A Reference Guide to Book Censorship in Schools and Public Libraries* (Westport, Conn.: Greenwood Press, 1994); see also Karolides and Burress, *Celebrating Censored Books*.

7. Zlata Filopovic, *Zlata's Diary: A Child's Life in Sarajevo*, trans. Christina Pribechevich (New York: Viking, 1994); and Raimonda Kopelnitsky, with Kelly Pryor, *No Words to Say Goodbye* (New York: Hyperion, 1994). The contagious effects in a California school are demonstrated by a young teacher, Erin Gruwell, in a collection of essays by her "freedom writers," "An American Diary: Voices of an Undeclared War," manuscript by 150 Freedom Writers, Woodrow Wilson High School, Long Beach, Calif., 1998.

8. Jan Romein, *Het Parool*, Apr. 23, 1946, 1.

9. See Hyman A. Enzer, "Art and/or Blasphemy: Philip Roth's *The Ghost Writer* and the Literary De-Con-Struction of Reality," paper presented at the Fourteenth Annual Conference on Social Theory, Politics, and the Arts, American University, Washington, D.C., Oct. 30, 1988; and Hyman A. Enzer, "For and Against Interpretation: Moral and Aesthetic Dilemmas in Holocaust Literature (with an Analysis of the Art of Anne Frank)," paper presented at the Fifteenth Annual Conference on Social Theory, Politics, and the Arts, Glendon College, York University, Toronto, Oct. 8, 1989.

10. Ann Birstein and Alfred Kazin, eds., introduction to *The Works of Anne Frank* (New York: Doubleday, 1959), 12.

11. See Carol Gilligan, "Joining the Resistance: Psychology, Politics, Girls, and Women," *Michigan Quarterly Review* 29 (Fall 1990): 501–33; and Katherine Dalsimer, *Female Adolescence: Psychoanalytic Reflections on Works of Literature* (New Haven: Yale University Press, 1986).

12. Catherine A. Bernard, "'Tell Him That I': Women Writing the Holocaust," Stanford University Department of Modern Thought and Literature, honors thesis, 1995, 80.

13. See, for example, Charlotte Salomon, *Charlotte: A Diary in Pictures* (New York: Harcourt, Brace, and World, 1963), and *Charlotte: Life or Theater?: An Autobiographical Play*, trans. Leila Vennewitz (New York: Viking, 1981); Vera Laska, ed., *Women in the Resistance and the Holocaust: The Voices of Eyewitnesses* (Westport, Conn.: Greenwood Press, 1983); Yasmine Ergas, "Growing Up Banished: A Reading of Anne Frank and Etty Hillesum," in *Behind the Lines: Gender and the Two World Wars*, ed. Margaret R. Higonnet, Jane Jenson, Sonya Michel, and Margaret Collins Weitz (New Haven: Yale University Press, 1987), 84–95; Carol Rittner and John K. Roth, eds., *Different Voices: Women and the Holocaust* (New York: Paragon House, 1993); Ellen S. Fine, "Women Writers and the Holocaust: Strategies for Survival," in *Reflections of the Holocaust in Art and Literature*, ed. Randolph L. Braham (New York: Columbia University Press, 1990), 79–95; and Mary Lowenthal Felstiner, *To Paint Her Life: Charlotte Salomon in the Nazi Era* (New York: HarperCollins, 1994).

14. Hannah Arendt, "Comment," *Midstream* 8 (Sept. 1962): 85.

15. Theodor W. Adorno, "What Does Coming to Terms with the Past Mean?" in *Bitburg in Moral and Political Perspective,* ed. Geoffrey H. Hartman (Bloomington: Indiana University Press, 1986), 127.

16. Alex Sagan, "An Optimistic Icon: Anne Frank's Canonization in Postwar Culture," *German Politics and Society* 13 (Fall 1995): 104–5.

17. Daniel Jonah Goldhagen, *Hitler's Willing Executioners: Ordinary Germans and the Holocaust* (New York: Alfred A. Knopf, 1996).

18. Cynthia Ozick, "A Critic At Large: Who Owns Anne Frank?" *New Yorker,* Oct. 6, 1997, 87; Ralph Melnick, *The Stolen Legacy of Anne Frank: Meyer Levin, Lillian Hellman, and the Staging of the Diary* (New Haven: Yale University Press, 1997).

19. Ian Buruma, "The Afterlife of Anne Frank," *New York Review of Books,* Feb. 19, 1998, 79–80; see also the exchange of letters between Cynthia Ozick and Buruma in "Anne Frank's Afterlife," *New York Review of Books,* Apr. 9, 1998, 79, and between Ralph Melnick and Buruma in "Anne Frank's Afterlife, Cont'd," *New York Review of Books,* May 28, 1999, 53–54.

20. Molly Magid Hoagland, "Anne Frank On and Off Broadway," *Commentary,* Mar. 1998, 58–63.

21. Sem Dresden, *Vervolging, Vernietiging, Literatuur* (Persecution, Extermination, Literature) (Amsterdam: Meulenhoff, 1991); Robert Alter, "The View from the Attic: An Obsession with Anne Frank: Meyer Levin and the Diary by Lawrence Graver/The Diary of a Young Girl by Anne Frank, edited by Otto H. Frank and Mirjam Pressler and translated by Susan Massotty," *New Republic,* Dec. 4, 1995, 38–42.

22. Alter, "View from the Attic," 41. For women's views on the Holocaust, see, for example, Milton Teichman and Sharon Leder, eds., *Truth and Lamentation: Stories and Poems on the Holocaust* (Urbana: University of Illinois Press, 1994), 11.

23. Zygmunt Bauman, *Modernity and the Holocaust* (Ithaca: Cornell University Press, 1991), 87–88.

24. Jehuda Bauer, "Daniel J. Goldhagen's View of the Holocaust," in *Hyping the Holocaust: Scholars Answer Goldhagen,* ed. Franklin H. Littell (Marion Station, Pa.: Merion Westfield Press International, 1997), 63.

25. Jacob Robinson, *Psychoanalysis in a Vacuum: Bruno Bettelheim and the Holocaust* (New York: Yad Vashem Yivo Documentary Projects, 1970), 3–36; Helen Fein, "Beyond the Heroic Ethic," review of Bruno Bettelheim's *Surviving and Other Essays, Transaction* 17 (Mar.–Apr. 1980): 81–86; and Arendt, "Comment."

26. See, for example, "Barbro Karlén und Anne Frank," *Der Europäer* (Basel), Aug. 1997, 56.

27. Anna Cook, "Following Anne Frank through the Holocaust," *Holland (Michigan) Historical Trust Volunteer Update* (Dec. 1995): 2.

28. Mark Segal, "The Second Agony of Anne Frank," *Jerusalem Post,* June 17, 1977, magazine section; Hartman, *Bitburg,* 1.

29. For more than one hundred critical reactions to *The Ghost Writer,* see Bernard F. Rodgers Jr., ed., *Philip Roth: A Bibliography,* 2d ed. (Metuchen, N.J.: Scarecrow Press,

1984). See also the detailed commentary by Sander Gilman in "The Dead Child Speaks: Reading *The Diary of Anne Frank*," *Studies in American Jewish Literature* 7 (Spring 1988): 9–25.

30. Philip Roth, "Interview with *The London Sunday Times*," *Reading Myself and Others* (New York: Viking Penguin, 1985), 135–36.

Part 1

History, Biography, and Authenticity

1

Anne Frank

Laureen Nussbaum

Sometimes I think God is trying to test me, both now and in the future.
Who else but me is ever going to read these letters?
—*November 7, 1942*

On May 11, 1944, after almost two years of hiding in the secret back quarters of an Amsterdam canal house, Anne Frank wrote to her imaginary friend Kitty: "You have known for quite a while now that it is my fondest wish to become a journalist and eventually a famous writer. It remains to be seen, whether I can ever make good on these grandiose ambitions (or delusions!) but so far, I have plenty of topics. In any case, once the war is over, I want to publish a book under the title 'Het Achterhuis' ('The Back Quarters'). Who knows, whether I can bring it off, but it can be based on my diary[. . .]."* It was the posthumous publication of this epistolary diary that has made Anne Frank probably the best known Dutch writer in the world.

Anne (Anneliese Marie) Frank was born June 12, 1929, in Frankfurt am Main, Germany, the second and youngest child of an upper-middle-class family. Her grandparents were bankers and manufacturers, her parents, Edith and Otto Frank, culture-loving, well-assimilated Germans of Jewish descent. At the time Anne was born, Otto's father had long since died and Otto, together with his younger brother Herbert and his brother-in-law Erich Elias, ran what was left of the family bank after the staggering inflation of the early 1920s. In subsequent years, during the Great Depression, the partners scattered: Herbert went to Paris and the Eliases to Basel, where Erich opened the Swiss branch of Opekta, manufacturers and distributors of pectin. Otto finally closed the family bank in the spring of 1933, just after the Nazis had assumed power in Germany, and soon thereafter, he moved his family to Amsterdam. For years, Otto Frank had maintained busi-

*Editors' note: Translations of the diary and other materials are by Laureen Nussbaum.

ness relations in Amsterdam, which he had frequently visited in the twenties. There, thanks to Elias, Frank was able to establish a Dutch branch of Opekta, which provided the family a reasonable standard of living, especially after Hermann Van Pels joined the business and added a new line in the form of spices, necessary for the production of sausages. Anne and her sister, Margot, who was three years her elder, grew up in a brand new neighborhood of three- to four-story apartment buildings at the southern edge of Amsterdam, where many Jewish refugee families from Germany had settled starting in 1933. Thus, there were numerous neighbors who shared their fate and, typically, parents would compare notes in German. The children, however, soon adapted themselves completely to their Dutch surroundings, especially those who had come as young as Anne, who was to receive all her schooling in the new country.

By the spring of 1940, Anne was a lively fifth grader, well liked and well adjusted to life in what was called the "river district" of Amsterdam. Then, May 10, disaster struck. Within five days, Hitler's troops occupied the Netherlands. Very few people could escape to England; everybody else had to submit to the occupational regime of the Nazis with its discriminatory laws against Jews. Anne was still able to finish her elementary grades in the Montessori school (Niersstraat), which is now named for her. But in the fall of 1941, all youngsters from Jewish families had to attend separate Jewish schools—just one of many new restrictions that regulated Jewish life. By May 1942, all Jews had to wear the invidious yellow star with JOOD ("Jew") on it, and on July 5, just as the school year ended, thousands of Jewish men and women between the ages of 16 and 40 were called up to report for forced labor. Margot Frank was among them.

At this point, Otto Frank was already in the process of preparing a hiding place for both his family and that of Van Pels in the back rooms and attic of the partners' business premises at 263 Prinsengracht. The summons for Margot caused them all to cut short their preparations and go immediately into hiding. Anne had just turned thirteen a few weeks earlier and her most treasured birthday present had been a diary in a red and white checkered cover. It was to be her steady companion and a great source of comfort as she experienced accelerated puberty in the hothouse atmosphere of the hideout. Forewarned by what happened to Jewish firms in Germany, Otto Frank had made sure that Opekta was no longer officially in his hands. Trusted non-Jewish business associates and the office personnel ran the firm for him and Van Pels. Henceforth, these same people took care of the two hiding families, who were soon joined by a Jewish dentist. They provided for all the needs of eight persons as well as they possibly could under very trying circumstances. Many details of their loving care are known from entries in Anne's diary. Miep Gies, the firm's executive secretary, was the main lifeline for the hiders. She was also the one who salvaged Anne's diaries. The last cattle train from the Netherlands with destination Auschwitz, Poland, departed on September 3, 1944, from camp Westerbork. The eight hiders from 263 Prinsengracht were among the 1,019 Jews of this last shipment.

Liberated in Auschwitz by Soviet troops, Otto Frank already knew that his wife had died from exhaustion in that notorious death camp. When he returned via Odessa and Marseille to Amsterdam in early June 1945 he was anticipating being reunited with his two daughters, who, together with other young women, had been sent from Auschwitz to camp Bergen-Belsen in northwest Germany. Since the latter was not an extermination camp, Otto had great hopes for their survival. But by the time the girls arrived there, around November 1, 1944, the place was so overcrowded and hygiene and food supplies were at such a dismal low that typhoid fever soon spread like wildfire and killed tens of thousands. As survivors trickled back from Bergen-Belsen, Otto would ask them about his girls only to learn, after weeks of agony, from women who had known his daughters, that in March both girls had succumbed, first Margot and shortly afterwards Anne. Eventually Otto had to resign himself to the bitter fact that of the eight deported hiders, he was the only survivor. It was then that Miep, who together with her husband had lovingly taken him in, handed Otto his daughter's diaries and loose sheets of notepaper, which she had kept away in hopes of returning them to Anne.

At first, Otto Frank had no intentions of publishing his daughter's diaries. Understandably, he was deeply moved by her entries and decided to copy what he deemed the "essential" passages in order to share them with relatives and friends. For the benefit of his mother and other close relatives in Basel, who did not read Dutch, he translated his excerpts into German. Subsequently, he went about typing a more complete transcript, partly basing it on Anne's original diaries, partly on her own revisions and on her vignettes of life in the "back quarters." This typescript, corrected for language errors by some of Otto's Dutch friends, was allowed to circulate among a somewhat wider circle of acquaintances, which included Dr. Kurt Baschwitz, also a German refugee, at the time lecturer and later professor of journalism and psychology of mass media at Amsterdam City University. Baschwitz was deeply impressed by the typescript of Anne's journal. In a letter to one of his daughters, dated February 10, 1946, he commented: "It is the most moving document of our time I know, also from a literary standpoint a surprising masterpiece. It deals with the inner experiences of a maturing girl, her impressions in the close confinement together with her father, whom she adores, her mother, with whom she runs into conflicts, her sister, in whom she discovers a friend, with the other family sharing the hide-out, and with their son, with whom she is beginning to fall in love. I think it ought to appear in print."

Others shared his sentiment, particularly the eminent Dutch historian Jan Romein, who, after reading the typescript, published an article in the daily *Het*

Parool (April 3, 1946) in which he praised Anne's writing not only for its documentary value but also for the way she handled the language, for her insight into human nature, for her sense of humor and her empathy. On the strength and persuasiveness of this article, several publishers expressed interest in Anne's diary and before long, the Amsterdam publishing house Contact secured the rights.

Thus, Anne Frank's *Het Achterhuis: Dagboekbrieven 12 Juni 1942–1 Augustus 1944* ("The Back Quarters: Diary-Letters June 12, 1942–August 1, 1944") first appeared in June 1947 with an introduction by Annie Romein-Verschoor, the wife of Jan Romein and herself a historian. Comparing Anne's diary to *The Journal of a Young Artist,* also an autobiographical work by a very young woman (Marie Bashkirtseff) which had shaken up Paris in the 1880s, Romein-Verschoor points out that Anne's text happily lacks the self-consciousness that marks the reflections of the earlier, very ambitious child prodigy. While granting Anne Frank "the one important characteristic of a great writer: an open mind, untouched by complacency and prejudice," Romein-Verschoor emphasizes the young author's "direct, non-literal and therefore often excellent" descriptions that have a natural purity devoid of extraneous admixtures.[1] But in fact she overstated the natural, nonliterary quality of Anne's diary. [. . .]

In a radio broadcast from London (via the clandestine Dutch station Radio Oranje) on March 28, 1944, Gerrit Bolkestein, the education secretary of the Dutch cabinet in exile, announced that after the war, diaries and letters written in the occupied Netherlands would be collected as firsthand documentation. Few people realize that soon after his broadcast, Anne very consciously started rewriting her diary on loose sheets of paper with an eye to postwar publication. "At last," she writes on May 20 of that year, "after considerable deliberations, I started working on my 'Achterhuis.' In my mind I have already finished it as far as I can, but in reality it won't get done all that fast if, indeed it will ever get finished." As pointed out, Otto Frank had picked and chosen from Anne's extant diary versions when assembling the typescript on which the original (1947) Dutch edition and the subsequent translations into dozens of languages would be based. He had added some of the vignettes she had written separately about life in the back quarters, made several rearrangements and corrections, while omitting some passages which he deemed either too irrelevant or too personal to include. In other words, Otto Frank had edited his daughter's diary, to which he had, of course, a perfect right; a prefatory note to this effect, however, would have saved him many future problems. To make matters worse, the Dutch publishing house labored under some constraints regarding the length of the book. Moreover, it rather prudishly insisted that some of Anne's references to her own maturing body be left out. Since the publishers of the German and English translations went back to Otto Frank's typescript and did not feel compelled to exclude certain entries or passages, these versions are actually more complete than the original Dutch. All this led to a great deal of confusion, which is meticulously explained and sorted out in the critical edition [of the diary].

The publication of *Het Achterhuis* gave Otto Frank a great sense of satisfaction. He had been able to fulfill his daughter's most cherished wish and, as the Dutch reviews were unanimously favorable, he was sure that he had done the right thing. When the American edition, graced with a preface by Eleanor Roosevelt, was published in 1952, the *New Times Book Review* carried a glowing review by Meyer Levin, which aroused widespread interest in the book. [. . .]

From the beginning, Meyer Levin championed the idea that Anne Frank's diary should be made into a play and a film. With Otto Frank's blessing, he tried his hand at a play script and felt deeply hurt when, eventually, Frank gave the rights to Frances Goodrich and Albert Hackett. A most painful lawsuit followed and Levin remained obsessed with the affair for twenty years, claiming that his version of the play had been rejected because it was deemed too Jewish. [. . .] Undoubtedly, the Goodrich-Hackett dramatization of *The Diary of Anne Frank* was an overwhelming stage success. It premiered in New York, on October 5, 1955, with Susan Strasberg as Anne and Joseph Schildkraut as Otto Frank and won various awards including the 1955 Pulitzer Prize for drama. When in 1959 a film based on [the play] proved equally successful, Anne Frank's story conquered the world.

[In 1957], the Anne Frank Foundation was established. It was charged with the upkeep of the house at 263 Prinsengracht, especially its back quarters, and with the dissemination of Anne's ideals of religious tolerance and interracial cooperation. About half a million visitors file through the premises every year. Moreover, schools and streets are named for her all over the world. For countless people, Anne Frank has become a symbol of the six million Jews murdered by the Nazis, not a symbol in an abstract sense, but somebody very real and endearing, because of her youth and the directness of her words. What made her story so powerful is the fact that it brought home the genocide of European Jewry. Small wonder then, that from 1957 on, Neo-Nazis and revisionist historians from Scandinavia via Germany to Austria and from France via Britain to the United States had a vested interest in attacking the authenticity of Anne Frank's diary. [. . .]

✦ ✦ ✦

The original diary with the red and white checkered cover, Anne's most cherished birthday present, opens with a full page picture of herself and spans the period from June 12 until December 5, 1942. The early entries in this book (version *a*) are juvenilia of a zestful teenager, telling about her thirteenth birthday and her ping-pong club and focusing on her girlfriends and admirers as well as on school events.

On June 15–16, Anne gives a thumbnail sketch of each of her classmates. Suddenly, she realizes that she had better tell her own life story, which she does succinctly on the next page, so as to lay the foundation for her diary. Once the Frank family had gone into hiding, Anne's life changed drastically. After her account of the day they left home and moved into the secret back quarters, she appears rather overwhelmed by her new experiences. Quite understandably, Anne found it difficult to sort out her very mixed feelings, so at first she left large gaps to be filled in later. Then, after about ten weeks in hiding, there is a marked shift toward introspection. Henceforth, the diary is going to take an important place in Anne's new life. On September 21 she decides to write her entries in the form of letters, addressing them to a variety of girls, mostly characters from her favorite series of juvenile books by Cissy Van Marxveldt. Kitty is just one of these characters. A week later Anne begins to fill some of the empty spaces in her diary with small annotated photographs of herself and her closest kin and a very large one of her beloved father preceded by a charming letter from him. She reflects about her looks and about her earlier entries, is dissatisfied with what she wrote before, and explains somewhat apologetically: "I see things differently now but I cannot very well tear pages out of my diary, and I hope nobody will reproach me later for poor penmanship in those days, since that is not what it was. Rather, I just did not feel like writing into my diary because I found it quite hard to do so" (September 28, 1942).

Subsequent entries dealing with life in the back quarters include occasional squabbles between the hiding families and tensions between Anne and her mother. There is the schoolwork, which Anne takes quite seriously so as not to fall behind, great appreciation for what their helpers are doing for the hiders, and deep worries about their many friends and acquaintances who could not go into hiding and are now being sent to Poland. Anne also indulges in a curious daydream: she and her darling father somehow make it to Switzerland and then share a room at their relatives' home. He gives her enough money to go and buy herself a new wardrobe, which she does immediately with Bernd, her cousin. A shopping list is attached. A week later she fantasizes that she is attending eighth grade in Switzerland. She quickly picks up French and German and is popular in school. One of her new friends is Kitty. Bernd teaches her figure skating and the two of them become very successful ice skating partners and are eventually filmed. She sketches the movie scenes, which also include her father.

When in the spring of 1944 Anne revised her diary with an eye to possible publication, she omitted much of what she had entered in her first journal and tightened the rest as she rewrote it on loose sheets of paper (version *b*). The first entry now is dated June 20, 1942. Anne, putting herself in her state of mind of two weeks before she went into hiding, explains why, despite all her popularity, she feels lonely and in need of a true friend to whom she can direct her outpourings. That friend she decides to call Kitty and after a terse version of her original autobiographical sketch, she proceeds immediately to write her first "Dear Kitty" epistle. In just four letters she summarizes both her school and her social life of the spring of 1942 and ends with a beautiful transition: an evening stroll with her father, during which he broaches to her the subject of hiding and all the drastic changes which that move will entail.

After an entry about the July 3 graduation exercises in the Jewish Theater— soon to be the roundup place for tens of thousands of Amsterdam Jews—Anne gives a gripping description of her consternation when Margot received her call to report for a labor camp and of the family's quick decision to go into hiding right then and there. Otto Frank made only very minor changes in this captivating account for the printed version of the diary (version *c*), but he substituted the conversational term *onderduiken* ("to duck under [water]") for the rather stilted *schuilen* ("to take shelter"). Moreover, in this entry (as, indeed, throughout *c*), he systematically replaced people's real names by pseudonyms, most of which Anne had devised herself for eventual publication.

In revising her original diary (version *a*) Anne cut out [. . .] entries which in retrospect she may have deemed somewhat frivolous and set about consolidating and focusing her writing with amazing insight and skill. Anne's new version was apparently too sparse for her father, for he reinstated some early entries, e.g., Anne's description of her thirteenth birthday and a passage of October 3, 1942, in which Anne reports her father's admonition to show more forbearance toward her mother. The fascinating process of revising can only be followed until December 5, 1942. Then there is a year's gap since Anne's original second journal has never been found. Hence, for that period, we have only her revised manuscript *b* on loose sheets and Anne's vignettes about life in the back quarters, the vast majority of which were written during the same year. Anne had assigned some of them to both her version *b* of the diary and her very special "Book of Tales," while others were to appear only in the latter. Otto Frank augmented Anne's version *b* by including some of the vignettes Anne had not intended for the [published] diary. In doing so, he extended Anne's attempt to sketch a complete and at times humorous picture of the hiders' daily life under steadily worsening circumstances. [. . .] Cooped up under these dismal conditions, Anne continues her studies, her readings and her writings, and her valiant efforts to make sense of life and to become her own person.

The new diary, a black notebook, which Anne started December 22, 1943, has been preserved; so from that date there exist again three versions—the original (*a*), Anne's rewriting (*b*), and the amalgamated version her father published (*c*)—but only until March 29, 1944. Sadly, Anne had not gotten beyond that date with her revisions by August 4, the fateful day the hideout was raided by the authorities.

On Christmas Eve 1943, Anne draws up a balance sheet of her one and half years in hiding: there is on the one hand her gratitude for still being alive and on the other her despondency at being cheated out of a normal adolescence. In her original version she writes how she is longing to do things other teenagers do: "*fietsen, dansen, flirten*" ("to bike, to dance, to flirt") but in her sterner revised version she apparently changed that into "*fietsen, dansen, fluiten*" ("to bike, to dance, to whistle")—if indeed, her usually very regular and legible handwriting has not been misread. But there cannot be any doubt that when revising her black notebook during the late spring and early summer of 1944, only a few months after she had originally filled it with her outpourings, Anne had become very critical of her in-fatuation with Peter Van Pels and of her repeated *de profundis* calls on God and on the memory of her beloved grandmother. In the *b* manuscript she eliminates most of her more effusive entries of that emotional period, their essence having been sublimated in two of her tales of fiction. Otto Frank reinstated the bulk of those eliminations. Did he think that this mixed version made better reading in connection with the unrevised last part of Anne's diary? Or did he want to pre-serve a stormy stage in the development of his beloved little Anne rather than al-low her to present herself as the more objective and self-contained young writer she had become at such a precocious age? One can only speculate.

As it is, the middle part of Anne's diary, i.e., the year 1943, stands out for the balanced expository quality of her revised version. By contrast, the mixed ver-sion *c* of late December 1943 through March 1944 and the unrevised text of the last four months tell the reader a great deal about her roller coaster emotions during that fateful period of hope and despair both in her most intimate life and with regard to the progress of the war, on which her chance of survival depended. Some of the most famous Anne Frank passages are from these last seven months, including the one expressing her faith in the intrinsic goodness of human beings, which is now written in her handwriting on the outside of the wall of her former elementary school.

The diary has captivated a worldwide readership of all ages since it deals with the struggle for survival and growth under dismal circumstances. Moreover, it offers a rare glimpse into the development of a most promising woman writer whose life, like that of the millions for whom she stands, was snuffed out so tragi-cally and wantonly.

✦ ✦ ✦

I knew Anne Frank. My sisters and I grew up just like Anne and Margot as im-migrant children in Amsterdam's "river district." In Frankfurt our parents had belonged to the same liberal Jewish congregation, and especially during the first years of the German occupation, the Frank girls would frequently visit our apartment in Amsterdam. In 1947, Otto Frank, the only survivor of the Frank family, was my husband's best man at our wedding.

That was the year Anne's *Achterhuis* was published for the first time. For quite a while, the book's most important contribution seemed to me the fact that it was the spontaneous expression of a young person, a girl, who despite the oppressiveness and the anxieties of living underground, was trying to develop herself. [. . .] For all I knew, there was only one version of Anne's diary, and although there were minor discrepancies in the subsequent English and German editions, I always believed Otto Frank's assertion that he had published "all that was essential."

In 1986, six years after the death of Mr. Frank, when the Netherlands State Institute for War Documentation issued the integral, critical version of Anne Frank's diaries [. . .] my eyes were at last opened. [. . .] Anne had decided to rewrite her spontaneous entries with an eye to publication after the war. On May 20, 1944, the almost fifteen-year-old started her thoroughgoing version, of which she had written 324 pages when she and the seven other hiders were arrested by the Nazi authorities two and a half months later. [. . .]

In a review of the 1986 critical edition, Mr. C. Blom, former director of Contact Publishers, who had brought out the first edition of Anne Frank's *Diary* forty years earlier, calls for "the definitive edition of *Het Achterhuis* . . . the complete publication of the final text as Anne Frank herself, had she been allowed to live, or her editor would most likely have handed it in."[2] Yet, in the anniversary year of 1995, fifty years after the end of World War II, Anne Frank's final text, the one she intended for publication, still has not seen the light of day.

In the United States, the remembrance of the liberation of the Bergen-Belsen concentration camp, where Anne Frank had died miserably fifty years ago, was the occasion to put the American translation of the new Otto Frank–Mirjam Pressler edition of *Het Achterhuis* (subtitled *The Definitive Edition*) on the market.

There is, in fact, nothing "definitive" about this new edition of Anne's diary-letters. Sadly, it is a hotchpotch of Anne's revised texts, stitched together with bits and pieces of her original entries and offset by larger passages from the *a* version, many of which Anne had rejected and eliminated in her astute and careful revision. Actually, this new edition does even less justice to Anne's intention than the original *c* version published under the aegis of her father. Most objectionable, though, is the fact that in her introduction Mirjam Pressler perpetuates the myth that Otto Frank had omitted mostly sexual themes and scathing remarks made by Anne about her mother.

Since Anne revised her original text with insight and skill, she would have been indignant had she known how she is being used as a symbol onto which millions of people can project their feelings of guilt and of compassion. She would feel deeply hurt by the fact that fifty years after her death, her intentions and her work as a writer still have not been taken seriously, despite her dedicated efforts.

A reader pouring over the *b* version will find it hard not to look at the parallel printed *a* version in order to make comparisons. In doing so, *this* reader could not help but be impressed with the amount of self-criticism and literary insight the barely fifteen-year-old Anne brought to bear upon her revision, omitting whole sections, reshuffling others, and adding supplementary information so as to create a most interesting and readable text. In the process, she must have used all her writing talent and the know-how gleaned from her extensive reading.

While revising her text, Anne eliminated most of the bursts of anger formerly directed against her mother. In the light of the prevailing myth, it is interesting that Otto Frank reinstated the *c* version, for example, in the entry of October 3, 1942, [which had] some nasty comments Anne herself had omitted in her revision. The same holds true for Anne's remarks about her longing for her first menstruation. She elided this remark in her rewrite, but father Frank included it in the *c* version of the October 29, 1942, entry.

The long entry of January 5–6, omitted by Anne, was also reinstated by Otto Frank. It tells about the psychological wound inflicted to Anne by her mother years ago. This is true for the text of March 2, 1944. In the process of rewriting, Anne left out criticism of her elders in the house, especially of her mother. Otto Frank reinserted most of these remarks in his *c* version. In the light of the prevailing myth, it is even more curious that father Frank reinstated Anne's spontaneous remarks about her developing body, her menstruation, and her "terrible urge" to touch her breasts at night, while Anne had elided those passages in her revision.

It is difficult to reconstruct what principles or ideas might have guided father Frank in the editing of the *c* version. Most notably in the case of the text of the first months of 1944, he selected time and again the more emotional passages of Anne's *a* version, some of which Anne had dispensed of, while she had reworked others into fictional stories. By the time she was rewriting her entries of the beginning of 1944, Anne had gone through a great deal of inner development. Father Frank ignored all of that evidence of growth. Apparently, he had a need to preserve the image of his beloved, tempestuous little Anne and didn't quite know what to do with the more mature, objective, and autonomous young writer.

Only when I started concentrating on Anne Frank's writing did it become clear to me that the history of the publication of Anne Frank's diary is an anomaly. My conclusion: readers who appreciate a well-written book, but who are not necessarily into women's studies or literary criticism, have the right to read Frank's wartime story in a form as close as possible to the author's own final version.

Conversely, we owe it to Anne Frank that at long last she be taken seriously as the writer she really was, before the Disney people market her as their next popular heroine, Pocahontas-style.

Notes

1. Annie Romein-Verschoor, Introduction to *Het: Achterhuis: Dagboekbrieven 12 Juni 1942–1 Augustus 1944* (Amsterdam: Contact, 1947), v–ix.

2. C. Blom, op-ed page, *NRC Handelsblad,* May 14, 1988.

2

The Arrest

Harry Paape

I get frightened myself when I think of close friends who are now at the mercy of the cruelest monsters ever to stalk the earth. And all because we are Jews.
—*November 19, 1942*

Friday, August 4, 1944. The great Allied offensive, which was to lead to the liberation of almost all France and Belgium within a month, had begun at the end of July. The major breakthrough had come nearly two months after the landings on the Normandy coast. Every day Radio Oranje and the BBC marveled at the astonishing advance of U.S. General Patton's tanks. The whole of occupied western Europe was filled with joyful expectation. Otto Frank and his family had spent two years and thirty days in the so-called secret annex.

The account we are about to give of the events at 263 Prinsengracht is entirely based on reports, oral and written, by people personally involved in them. The violent emotions to which they were all exposed, and their awareness at the time they made their statements of the subsequent fate of the deported, easily account for the fact that their respective memories of August 4 differed at times, and that some of them, questioned more than once, failed to use exactly the same words when repeating their observations. In the circumstances, we can do no better than try—on the basis of their statements—to give as faithful as possible a reconstruction of the events, fully realizing that there may well have been discrepancies in the details of sequences recalled.

It was a pleasant, warm summer's day, and the doors of the warehouse in the Prinsengracht stood wide open. The two warehousemen, W. G. van Maaren and L. Hartog, were busy at their work. Between ten o'clock and half past ten a German car drew up. A uniformed German and several[1] Dutchmen in civilian clothes got out of the car and ran into the building. One of them asked van Maaren a question. "Upstairs," van Maaren replied, pointing with his thumb. While one of the men stayed behind in the warehouse, the German and the rest went up to the offices on the next floor.[2]

One of them opened the door to the main office. There he found Miep Gies, Bep Voskuijl, and [Johannes] Kleiman.[3] This man, Miep reported many years later, "was holding a pistol which he pointed at us, saying: 'Just sit there quietly and don't go away.' From the noise in the corridor, I could tell there were others in the building."[4]

And Bep: "He had a long, dried-up, yellowish face. [. . .] I heard Mrs. Gies say: 'Bep, we've had it.' We sat there petrified."[5] The man went out again.

[Victor Gustav] Kugler, [Otto Frank's righthand man,] who emigrated to Canada in 1955, was officially questioned after the war about these events. Ernst Schnabel quotes a letter addressed to him by Kugler (probably written in 1957):

> Suddenly a staff-sergeant of the "Green Police" and three Dutch civilians entered my office and asked me for the owner of the house. I gave them the name and address of our landlord. No, they said to me, we want the person who is in charge here. That is myself, I replied. Then, "Come along," they ordered.
>
> The police wanted to see the storerooms in the front part of the building, and I opened the doors for them. All will be well if they don't want to see anything else, I thought. But after the sergeant had looked at everything, he went out in the corridor, ordering me again to come along. At the end of the corridor they drew their revolvers all at once and the sergeant ordered me to push aside the bookcase at the head of the corridor and to open the door behind it. I said: "But there's only a bookcase there!" At that he turned nasty, for he knew everything. He took hold of the bookcase and pulled at it; it yielded and the secret door was exposed. Perhaps the hooks had not been properly fastened. They opened the door, and I had to precede them up the steps. The policemen followed me; I could feel their pistols in my back. But since the steps were only wide enough for a single person, I was the first to enter the Franks' room. Mrs. Frank was standing at the table.[6]

Of those in hiding in the annex, Otto Frank was the only one left able to tell the story of the arrest after the war. Couched in the official language of the Dutch detective examining him, it read as follows:

> In the morning—it was about 10:30—I was in the Van Pels boy's room [. . .] giving him an English lesson. At the said time a civilian I did not know came into the said room. He was holding a pistol and he aimed it at us. He made us put our hands in the air and searched us for weapons. This man appeared to be a Dutch official of the German *Sicherheitsdienst* [Security Service, or SD] in Amsterdam. Then he ordered us to go downstairs. He followed us with his pistol drawn. First we entered the room of the Van Pels family where I saw Mr. and Mrs. Van Pels and also Mr. Pfeffer, all of them standing with their hands up. There was a man in civilian clothes

there, too, not known to me, also with a drawn pistol. Then we were all made to go down one floor to where I lived with my family. There I saw my wife and my two daughters standing with their hands up. I believe Mr. Kugler was also in our room but I am not sure. It may well have been Mr. Kleiman. At the same time I saw a man in a green uniform, not known to me, who had also drawn his pistol. This man's name, I learned later, was Silberbauer. He ordered me in a curt, barrack-room tone of voice to show him where we kept our money and jewelry. I pointed out where they were. Then he picked up a briefcase in which my daughter Anne kept her papers, including her diary notes. He shook the briefcase out onto the floor and then put our jewelry and our money into it.[7]

The German's accomplices continued to search the annex for money and valuables. Those who had been arrested were allowed to pack some clothes and toilet articles. One of the SD men then went downstairs to telephone for transport for the large group of prisoners. It took some time before the transport arrived.

The German, Karl Silberbauer, meanwhile walked about in the Franks' room. His eye fell on the old army footlocker belonging to Otto Frank, on which the latter's name and rank in the German army were printed. In answer to Silberbauer's question, Otto Frank confirmed that he had been a German reserve lieutenant during World War I. "At once, Silberbauer's attitude changed. He even looked for a moment as if he was going to snap to attention in front of me. Then he asked why I had not reported this fact before, since I would then have been sent to the labor camp at Theresienstadt. He stopped insisting that we hurry, and told us and his subordinates to take our time."[8] Silberbauer was obviously impressed by Otto Frank's military rank. During his examination many years later by the Austrian police, in the presence of a detective from Amsterdam, he mentioned his conversation with Otto Frank as "proof" that he had not behaved discourteously to the prisoners. Otto Frank, who had been "a German Reserve officer during the First World War, also told me," remembered Silberbauer, "that he and his family, including his daughter Anne, had spent a good two years in the hiding place. When I refused to believe him, he pointed to the marks that had been made on the doorpost, showing how much Anne had grown since they had gone into hiding."[9]

Eventually—no transport having arrived—Silberbauer went downstairs.

On the floor where the offices were something else was happening meanwhile. Quite some time after Kugler had been ordered by the SD men to show them the hiding place, they had fetched Kleiman from the front office and had questioned him in the room at the back. Then they told him to hand over the keys of the building to Miep, who was apparently not under suspicion.[10]

Kleiman made use of this opportunity to give Bep his briefcase with the request that she take it straight to a friendly pharmacist on the Leliegracht and ask him to pass it on to Mrs. Kleiman. Then he told Miep: "Make sure you stay out of this. You can't save us, so try to save what you can here." Then he returned to the back room where the SD men were waiting for him.[11] [. . .]

At about one o'clock the transport finally arrived. "A closed truck," Otto Frank later described it.[12] The eight who had been in hiding, together with Kugler and Kleiman, were led down the stairs and into the truck. Jan Gies and Kleiman's brother, whom he had gone to warn, watched the scene from across the canal.[13] The truck made off toward the school building in Euterpestraat used as the head-quarters of the Aussenstelle Amsterdam des Befehlshabers der Sicherheitspolizei und des SD (Amsterdam Bureau of the Commander of the Security Police and Security Service). No one paid any further attention to Miep Gies.

Notes

1. The number of Dutch SD men mentioned by the various witnesses ranges from three to eight. The most probable number is four or five. [Editors' note: In March 1995 David Barnouw discovered in the archives of the Netherlands State Institute for War Documentation (NIOD) the names of two of the four Dutch police officers who raided the annex. Willem Grootendorst, a member of the Dutch Nazi party who worked at the Jewish Affairs station and hunted down hidden Jews, received an extra allowance for this work as did his colleague, Gezinus Gringhuis, who was also a party member. They were both jailed for some years after World War II.]

2. Examination of W. G. van Maaren, Oct. 6, 1964, State Criminal Investigation Department, Amsterdam, Doc. 1, K. J. Silberbauer, NIOD Archives.

3. Hermine (Miep) Gies-Santrouschitz, Feb. 19, 1985, NIOD Archives.

4. Examination of Hermine (Miep) Gies-Santrouschitz, Dec. 23, 1963, State Criminal Investigation Department, Amsterdam, Doc. 1, K. J. Silberbauer, NIOD Archives.

5. Examination of Elisabeth (Bep) van Wijk-Voskuijl, Dec. 13, 1963, State Criminal Investigation Department, Amsterdam, Doc. 1, K. J. Silberbauer, NIOD Archives.

6. Ernst Schnabel, *The Footsteps of Anne Frank,* trans. Richard Winston and Clara Winston (London: Longmans Green, 1959), 99–100. The original letter has never been found. Compare Kugler's statement in "The Reminiscences of Victor Kugler—the 'Mr. Kraler' of Anne Frank's Diary, as Told to Eda Shapiro," *Yad Vashem Studies* 13 (1979): 357–59.

7. Examination of Otto Heinrich Frank, Dec. 2, 1963, State Criminal Investigation Department, Amsterdam, Doc. 1, K. J. Silberbauer, NIOD Archives.

8. Ibid. Theresienstadt was a camp in Czechoslovakia, originally described as an *Altersghetto* (Old-Age Ghetto) by the Nazis, and used as a camp for "privileged" Jews. The chances of survival in that camp were appreciably greater than those in such camps as Auschwitz.

9. Examination of Karl Silberbauer, Mar. 4, 1964, State Criminal Investigation Department, Amsterdam, Doc. 1, K. J. Silberbauer, NIOD Archives.

10. Hermine (Miep) Gies-Santrouschitz, Apr. 5, 1984, NIOD Archives.

11. Declaration made by Hermine (Miep) Gies-Santrouschitz on June 5, 1974, before A. J. Dragt, notary in Amsterdam, Anne Frank Collection, 1 d, NIOD Archives. According to her statement of April 18, 1985, this did not happen until after her husband arrived.

12. Examination of Otto Heinrich Frank, Dec. 20, 1963, State Criminal Investigation Department, Amsterdam, Doc. 1, K. J. Silberbauer, NIOD Archives.

13. J. A. Gies, Apr. 5, 1984, NIOD Archives.

3

The Betrayal

Harry Paape

A deathly, oppressive silence hangs over the house and clings to me as if it were
going to drag me into the deepest depths of the underworld.
—*October 29, 1943*

Following more than two years of pressure, worry, and strain, and in particular
following the last few months of growing hope and increasing confidence that
liberation was just around the corner, what now prevailed at 263 Prinsengracht
were desperate feelings of anguish and distress concerning the fate of those who
had been taken away.

It was not long before the painful question had to be faced of how the SD [se-
curity service] could possibly have learned that Jews had been hiding in the house.
How had they known about the access door, which had been so cleverly camouflaged behind the bookcase?

Of the more than 25,000 Jews who went into hiding in the Netherlands in the
years 1940 to 1945 in order to escape deportation, some 8,000 to 9,000 fell into
German hands.[1] The causes were various but can be grouped under four head-
ings: organized mass raids by the Germans and their Dutch accomplices; chance;
carelessness on the part of those in hiding or of their "protectors"; and betrayal.
The last two causes often coincided. There were countless letters and telephone
calls to the SD or the Dutch police: "Dear Sir, I have noticed that . . ." or "I have
heard that . . ."

The protectors of those hidden in the annex realized immediately after the raid
of August 4 that in this case betrayal was the only explanation, possibly as a consequence of carelessness. Kleiman—after his return in October*—also took this

*Editors' note: Kleiman had been taken and detained in the prison in Amstelveenseweg
and then was transferred to Weteringschans prison. He was released on September 18,
following a gastric hemorrhage that made him unfit for work, and finally returned to work
at Opekta at the end of October.

view. The SD had after all come directly to this address, and this address only. There could thus be no question of chance.[2]

Outside the small circle of protectors, no one knew that the Frank family had gone into hiding: the story that the Franks had escaped to Switzerland via Limburg had gone the rounds most successfully.[3] The Van Pels family and [Fritz] Pfeffer had also been able to obliterate their traces completely in 1942. Naturally, it was possible someone in the immediate neighborhood might have been made suspicious by a noise, a chink of light through one of the annex windows, or a shadow behind a window elsewhere in the building during the evening or at weekends, when those in hiding were able to leave their cramped quarters for a short while. It was also possible that someone had noticed the unusually large daily supply of food—enough, after all, for eight people—that came to the building. Each of these factors might have explained an SD raid after three or six months. But after more than two years? It seemed improbable. The precautionary measures and vigilance of those in hiding and of their protectors had never flagged; on the contrary, their routine, if only through long experience, had greatly improved, albeit there had been some carelessness.

No, there must have been some other explanation, those left behind believed, and after a little while their suspicions fell on the warehouseman, W. G. van Maaren.

Van Maaren had been hired after the old head warehouseman, Voskuijl (Bep's father), had been taken to the hospital in the spring of 1943, and the new man, as Miep continued to insist many years after the war, "was a very capable storeman."[4] However, his conduct quickly began to cause annoyance and even concern for some time: petty thefts of sugar, potato flour, and spices from the store had been discovered, and van Maaren seemed to show curiosity about things that were kept from him. The protectors of those in the annex grew increasingly worried and tense: with every step they took, they felt that they had to reckon with the presence of the dubious van Maaren.[5]

The inmates of the annex were informed of these developments. The need to be even more careful than before was impressed upon them. Anne, too, mentioned the suspicions against van Maaren and various careless acts several times in her diary.[6]

Suspicion was increased even further when it appeared that in the evenings, before he went home, van Maaren would set small traps in the warehouse: a pencil at the extreme edge of a table, where it could easily be knocked off; a sprinkling of potato flour on the floor in which footprints could be seen. To the protectors, this seemed to indicate that he suspected someone was hiding in the building and was trying to make sure.[7]

Then there was the even more important question of the door keys. As early as the spring of 1945, Kleiman wrote: "The keys of the business were [. . .] handed to v. M. on August 4 and he was informed that he was answerable for everything. He was told to expect further orders, but these never came." In a statement to the Amsterdam police in 1948, Miep Gies declared: "When one of the SD men saw the name Gies on my identity card and remembered that the name of Gies was also connected with the business, the keys were taken away from me and handed to Van Maaren."[8] [. . .]

And finally there was also the suspicion that van Maaren was involved with the SD. Miep declared in 1948: "When it looked at first as if I too would be taken away by the SD, Van Maaren boasted to me that he was on good terms with the SD and that I need not fear they would arrest me. He would go to the SD himself. When I paid a visit to Silberbauer later, his words suggested that Van Maaren had indeed been to see him to put in a good word for me."[9] [. . .]

During the first two months after August 4 there was little change in the situation. Business went on as usual. Van Maaren continued to do his normal work although he sometimes behaved as if he were in charge. Miep clearly accepted this state of affairs. She looked on van Maaren's supposed status as *Verwalter* as a means of keeping the company in business. Thus she had asked him to accompany her to the annex at the end of the afternoon of August 4; again, when the removal firm had arrived to clear the annex, she had asked him to go upstairs with them and to bring her any parts of Anne's diary he might come across.

On Kleiman's return the situation changed. He took charge of the business and van Maaren accepted his demotion to his old status. The thefts continued; indeed the amounts that went missing increased. On one occasion—in December—goods were found to be missing from a hiding place kept secret from van Maaren. Kleiman went to the police. A search of van Maaren's home by detectives proved abortive. Afraid of van Maaren's assumed links with the SD, Kleiman took no further action. Their relationship, however, became increasingly fraught. Shortly after the liberation, van Maaren was dismissed, having once again been caught in the act of stealing (this time pectin, salt, and soda).[10]

Meanwhile the questions raised by the raid on August 4 continued increasingly to exercise Kleiman and the other protectors, and suspicions against van Maaren grew. Very soon after the liberation, Kleiman wrote a letter, undated and without an address but intended for the POD (Politieke Opsporings Dienst, the Political Criminal Investigation Department). In it he gave a detailed account of the thefts and other breaches of trust attributed to van Maaren. [. . .]

Not until 1947 did things begin to move. The initiative was probably taken by Otto Frank. In July 1947, Kleiman referred, in a letter to the PRA (Politieke Recherche Afdeling, the Political Investigation Branch) of the Amsterdam police, to a visit Otto Frank had paid them "a few weeks ago," and enclosed a copy of the letter he had written in 1945.[11]

Slowly the wheels now began to turn. On January 12, 1948, Kleiman was finally examined by the PRA. He had nothing to add to what he had written in 1945 concerning his suspicions. About the actual arrest of those hidden in the annex, however, he now made a very important statement. Speaking of Silberbauer and his assistants, he declared: "They seemed to know precisely what they were doing, for they went straight to the hiding place and arrested all eight persons present there."[12] This statement implied not only that the SD knew that Jews were hidden in the building but that they also knew the location of the hiding place and also perhaps about the entrance to the annex, the bookcase built by Voskuijl. The conclusion must be that the traitor was someone well acquainted with all the arrangements. [. . .]

Miep Gies, too, who was examined the same day by the PRA, was unable to add many concrete details. She again mentioned the suspicions against van Maaren arising from his curiosity, his questions about Otto Frank, the way he would check whether anything had been removed or shifted in the warehouse or the office at night or on weekends, the business with the keys, his relationship with the SD, his petty thefts. "When Van Maaren got his hands on the keys after the raid, it became perfectly obvious that he was extremely pleased about it," she added.[13] [. . .]

The last to be examined was the suspect, who had, evidently in answer to questions put to him, previously lodged a written deposition.[14] In this, he had described himself as holding a position of trust in the business. He denied having had any prior knowledge that Jews were hidden in the building. As for the thefts, he tried to throw suspicion on Bep Voskuijl and her father (in fact already hospitalized by the time van Maaren joined the company), whom he had once, he said, surprised in the building after office hours, one carrying a shopping bag and the other a parcel. The rest of the deposition also contained statements that could be considered as veiled accusations (especially against Miep Gies). [. . .]

Van Maaren alleged in the same written deposition that when he was shown the secret entrance to the annex he was "dumbfounded by its technical ingenuity" and had expressed the opinion that "the SD would never have been able to find out anything about this secret door without inside information." As for the raid on August 4, 1944: "I was told that on their arrival the SD went straight upstairs to the bookcase and opened the door." He was not asked for the source of this information.

His examination on March 31, 1948, was short (the official report covered less than one page) and full of denials and explanations of his strange behavior. Thus "in the course of 1943–1944" he had "suspected that something peculiar was going on in the building, without, however, hidden Jews ever coming to mind," because the baker, the milkman, and the greengrocer kept supplying so much food.

As for the business with the pencils and the potato flour, he gave a simple explanation which nobody could challenge, and which at the same time was intended to clear him of the theft charges:

> Now and then goods were also stolen from the warehouse. That is why—with Mr. Kugler's full knowledge—I placed some bottles on the floor in such a way that you'd be able to tell immediately if anyone had been on the premises after closing time. And occasionally I would also [put down] a pencil for the same reason. I can't remember anything about scattering stuff around[. . .] . I did what I did only because every so often goods were stolen and they suspected me. If I could show that people had been in the premises after hours, I would no longer be under suspicion." [. . .]15

Five days later the district judge delivered his verdict. He considered that treason had not been proven. Van Maaren had been cleared. [. . .] In response to the tracing by Simon Wiesenthal of the SD officer Silberbauer, who had been in charge of the raid on the annex, the case was reopened. [. . .]

It was not until November 1964 that van Maaren was examined again. He admitted the thefts although he tried to minimize them. The footprints in the warehouse, he claimed, together with Kugler's evasive reaction when his attention had been drawn to them, had indeed aroused his suspicions, as had the ample supply of provisions. He denied having scraped the paint off the window that overlooked the back of the building, but admitted that he had seen the house at the back when he (and Kugler) had been on the roof to repair a leak; however, he denied that he knew that Jews were hidden there.16 [. . .]

The van Maaren file was closed by the State Criminal Investigation Department on November 4, 1964. Two days later it was sent to the public prosecutor. In an accompanying letter signed by the two detectives concerned, we can read "that the inquiry did not lead to any concrete results."17

Van Maaren was left alone from that time on. He died in 1971, at the age of seventy-six, at his home in Amsterdam. [. . .]

Though we have dwelled at length on the evidence produced by the protectors, their original statements were little more than justifications of their suspicions and gave the detectives few concrete facts to go on. [. . .]

All we can say with any conviction is that van Maaren must have known that Jews were hidden in the building, where they were, as well as how to get there: he must have put two and two together—his general observations, the statements made to him, his "discovery" (both from the roof and also when he scraped off the paint on the back window) of the house at the back, and the position of the bookcase. We can, however, again draw no conclusions from this about his alleged treachery.

There are, as we have said, scores of other possible explanations of the raid.

Perhaps van Maaren was only an indirect link. He was a loudmouth and a boaster, and he undoubtedly mentioned his suspicions and growing knowledge of what was going on in the building to others—to [his assistant, L.] Hartog, and to the warehouseman of the firm next door. There was Hartog's wife's indiscretion. There were others who must have known or suspected something: the merchant in chemical supplies a few buildings up the street, the tradespeople who took provisions to 263 Prinsengracht. How good were they at keeping their own counsel? There is a story about an NSB [Dutch Nazi party] man who lived in the Westermarkt, diagonally behind 263 Prinsengracht, and who made inquiries of his neighbors about what was going on in the building—he died in 1943, but how many others in the block knew too much and did not keep quiet? There is a letter from a man who, when he was eight years old, climbed into the back of the warehouse one evening with a friend to see what they could find. They were frightened by the flushing of a lavatory in the building above them, and ran away. He never told anyone about this incident, as he informed us by letter in 1981 when confessing to his minor break-in.[18]

How many kept what they knew to themselves? How fast did the rumors grow, the stories in the neighborhood about what was happening at the back of 263 Prinsengracht? It took a good two years before someone picked up the telephone and called the SD. That this someone was van Maaren does not strike us as an impossibility. To what length could not frustration and rancor drive a man? That it could have been someone else, however, is, we feel, at least as likely. It is no longer possible to reconstruct exactly what happened.

[Editors' postscript: Paape's last two sentences were reinforced in 1998 by Melissa Müller in her biography of Anne Frank (*Anne Frank: The Biography,* trans. Rita Kimber and Robert Kimber [New York: Henry Holt, 1998]). Lena van Bladeren Hartog, the wife of van Maaren's assistant in the warehouse, is identified as a prime suspect. Müller provides strong but not conclusive evidence that Hartog was the most likely person to have called the Gestapo on August 4, 1944, because according to rumors, a woman made the call (230). Hartog, a cleaning woman in the offices of Opekta, was in a position to observe any unusual activities at 263 Prinsengracht.

Her responses during her interrogation in 1948 by the political investigation branch of the Amsterdam police (283–84) gave explicit grounds for suspecting her role in the betrayal, but evidently those clues were never pursued. Hartog died in 1963, a few months before the case was reopened. Müller quotes Miep Gies as saying the police could have been more diligent had they asked Bep [Voskuijl] to clear up the inconsistencies in Hartog's testimony (301). Without definitive evidence, van Maaren, Hartog, or someone still unknown might have been the betrayer.]

Notes

1. Louis de Jong, *Het Koninkrijk der Nederlanden in de Tweede Wereldoorlog,* vol. 7 (The Hague: Nijhoff, 1978), 441.

2. Statement by K. J. Silberbauer, Aug. 21, 1963. Doc. 1, K. J. Silberbauer, Netherlands State Institute for War Documentation Archives (hereafter NIOD Archives).

3. Anne wrote of this in her diary; see also Ernst Schnabel, *The Footsteps of Anne Frank,* trans. Richard Winston and Clara Winston (London: Longmans Green, 1959), 99.

4. Examination of Hermine (Miep) Gies-Santrouschitz, Dec. 23, 1963, State Criminal Investigation Department, Amsterdam, Doc. 1, K. J. Silberbauer, NIOD Archives.

5. Ibid.; examination of Elisabeth (Bep) van Wijk-Voskuijl, Dec. 13, 1963, State Criminal Investigation Department, Amsterdam, Doc. 1, K. J. Silberbauer, NIOD Archives; examination of Johannes Kleiman by Amsterdam police, Jan. 12, 1948, Ministry of Justice, W. G. van Maaren dossier, NIOD Archives.

6. Diary entries on Sept. 16, 1943, Oct. 17, 1943, Apr. 15, 1944, Apr. 18, 1944, Apr. 21, 1944, and Apr. 25, 1944.

7. Examination of Kleiman by Amsterdam police.

8. Examination of Hermine (Miep) Gies-Santrouschitz by Amsterdam police, Jan. 14, 1948, Ministry of Justice, W. G. van Maaren dossier, NIOD Archives.

9. Ibid.

10. Johannes Kleiman, [1945], Ministry of Justice, W. G. van Maaren dossier, NIOD Archives; examination of W. G. van Maaren by the State Criminal Investigation Department, Amsterdam, Oct. 6, 1964, Doc. 1, K. J. Silberbauer, NIOD Archives.

11. N. V. Nederlandsche Opekta Maatschappij (signed by Johannes Kleiman), July 16, 1947, to PRA, Amsterdam, Ministry of Justice, W. G. van Maaren dossier, NIOD Archives.

12. Examination of Kleiman by Amsterdam police.

13. Examination of Gies-Santrouschitz by Amsterdam police.

14. W. G. van Maaren, Feb. 2, 1948, to Political Investigation Branch, Amsterdam police, Ministry of Justice, W. G. van Maaren dossier, NIOD Archives.

15. Examination of W. G. van Maaren by Amsterdam police, Mar. 31, 1948, Ministry of Justice, W. G. van Maaren dossier, NIOD Archives.

16. Examination of W. G. van Maaren by the State Criminal Investigation Department, Amsterdam, Oct. 6, 1964, Doc. 1, K. J. Silberbauer, NIOD Archives.

17. Report of the State Criminal Investigation Department, Amsterdam, 1964, 35–36, Doc. 1, K. J. Silberbauer, NIOD Archives.

18. Telephone call from H. Weinberg, Schiedam, Oct. 13, 1981, Netherlands State Institute for War Documentation Archives. He also informed us in writing that the boys must have broken in on March 25, 1943, one of the dates mentioned in Anne's diary.

4

Visiting Hours after 9 A.M.

Ernst Schnabel

That day I walked to Gestapo headquarters. The red-and-black swastika flew
from the flagpole. Uniformed Germans were everywhere. It was a well-known
fact that people who entered this building did not always leave it again.
—*Miep Gies and Alison Leslie Gold,* Anne Frank Remembered

The events that followed were played out in several different theaters.

The ten prisoners were taken to Gestapo headquarters and locked in a room
already containing other arrested persons. [Pfeffer] sat in numbed silence. The
children whispered to one another. [Kleiman] sat on the bench beside Mr. Frank,
who whispered to him:

"You can't imagine how I feel, [Kleiman]. To think that you are sitting here
among us, that we are to blame . . ."

[Kleiman] replied dryly:

"Don't give it another thought. It was up to me, and I wouldn't have done it
differently."

The interrogation was brief. Horror can develop a routine which on the surface seems identical with standard procedure. Moreover, the case of the ten prisoners was quite clear. [Kleiman] and [Kugler] did not attempt to defend themselves; they remained silent, and the officials evidently did not think it worthwhile
forcing them to talk. Mr. [Kugler] recalls that the Gestapo man remarked to his
stenographer: "Today was a good day!"

And [Kugler] thought: Yes, there on the desk he has the gold from [Pfeffer's]
dental stock, and our radio, and everything they found, and the ten of us to boot.

They were taken away.

Fortunately for [Kleiman] and [Kugler], the year was 1944, not 1943 or 1942.
The outcome of the war had already been decided, and although this fact scarcely
induced the Gestapo to feel any greater respect for human lives, the future was
no longer quite so clear, and in the minds of these officials first gleams of insecu-

rity were beginning to flicker. They were now rather inclined to stay within the confines of standing orders, instead of making their own decisions. And in cases like those of [Kugler] and [Kleiman] the regulations were not entirely clear; an on-the-spot decision was necessary. Therefore when an international welfare organization intervened on behalf of [Kleiman] and pointed out that he was ill, he was released for medical care after a few weeks of imprisonment.

[Kugler], too, was not sent to the death camp of Mauthausen, a procedure that would have been virtually automatic only a year earlier. Instead, he went to a camp near Amersfoort in Holland, and thence to a forced-labor camp in Zwolle. In March 1945 the inmates of the Zwolle camp were supposed to be removed to Germany. Four hundred men were marched under guard along the highway from Arnhem to Zevenaar. During the march the column was strafed by planes, and in the confusion [Kugler] and a man from Rotterdam succeeded in escaping. They crawled off into the underbrush, and when the firing stopped they slipped into a house.

After an hour they ventured out again and hid with a farmer for two days. Traveling by night over back roads [Kugler] made his way to Hilversum, where his relatives lived.

As far as the eight Jewish prisoners were concerned, the regulations were completely unequivocal. Their money and valuables had already been taken from them. There was an attempt to make Mr. Frank reveal the addresses of other Jews in hiding. He replied that during his twenty-five months in the secret annex he had lost all contact with friends and acquaintances, and therefore knew nothing. This explanation seemed reasonable to the officials, and they sent him back to his cell. A few days later all eight were taken to the railroad station and transported to the Westerbork reception camp.

Mr. Frank relates:

We rode in a regular passenger train. The fact that the door was bolted did not matter very much to us. We were together again, and had been given a little food for the journey. We knew where we were bound, but in spite of that it was almost as if we were once more going traveling, or having an outing, and we were actually cheerful. Cheerful, at least, when I compare this journey with our next. In our hearts, of course, we were already anticipating the possibility that we might not remain in Westerbork to the end. We knew about deportation to Poland, after all. And we also knew what was happening in Auschwitz, Treblinka, and Maidenek. But then, were not the Russians already deep in Poland? The war was so far advanced that we could begin to place a little hope in luck. As we rode toward Westerbork we were hoping our luck would hold. Anne would not move from the window. Outside, it was summer. Meadows, stubble fields, and villages flew by. The telephone wires along the right of way curvetted up and down along the windows. It was like freedom. Can you understand that?

They do not know what led to their arrest. Mr. Frank does not think anyone betrayed them. He is rather inclined to believe that someone who shared the secret may have dropped an incautious remark in the presence of someone he did not know too well.

Mr. [Kleiman] shrugs when he is asked the question. Miep and [Jan], too, have no explanation. When asked whether they thought it possible that [W. G. van Maaren], the warehouse clerk, denounced them, they replied shortly:

"He was brought to trial after the war. He disclaimed every accusation, and nothing could be proved against him. We have no idea where he is today."

[Bep] alone is firmly convinced the [van Maaren] was the one, despite the fact that she, also, has no proof. But little things have lived on in her memory more vividly than in the minds of the others. Nothing she says has been filtered, nothing censored by caution or scruples. She retains everything just as it happened, and careless slips occurred at the time—tiny ones, certainly, but enough for anyone who was on the lookout. For example, [Bep] says, a good many mornings the pencils would be slightly displaced on the desks, and [van Maaren] used to hustle about the office a good deal more than he had to. Once in a while the feeding bowls for the two warehouse cats would be full in the morning, although they had been left empty in the evening. And it also happened that Mr. [Van Pels] once left his briefcase lying on [Kugler's] desk, and the following morning, when [Kugler] came to work, [van Maaren] was already there, waiting in the office for him, for they were going to go over some warehouse inventories that day. As they were comparing listings and checking them off, [van Maaren] suddenly asked:

"Is that your briefcase, Mr. [Kugler]?"

[Kugler] looked up briefly, and replied: "No."

He bent over the list again. But a moment later he looked up once more, and said:

"Why, of course, it is my briefcase. I guess I must have left it here last night."

Twenty-five months are a long time, [Bep] says, and eight persons are eight individuals. If each one of them committed a single slip each year, that would be sixteen telltale signs. How many would [van Maaren] have needed?

But Mr. Frank and his friends do not like to talk about this, and [Bep], too, felt easier when I dropped the question. Our fate was as it was, they say, and if someone betrayed us, then it was our fate to be betrayed.

5

Her Last Days

Hannah Elisabeth Pick-Goslar

There's nothing we can do but wait as calmly as we can till the misery comes to an end. Jews and Christians wait, the whole world waits, and there are many who wait for death.
—*January 13, 1943*

Mr. Frank's factory, Opekta, produced a substance for making jam. My mother always got the old packages as a gift. Soon after school let out, my mother sent me to the Franks' house to get the scale because she wanted to make jam. It was a beautiful day.

I went as usual to the Franks' house and rang and rang and rang, but no one opened the door. I didn't know why no one answered. I rang again, and finally, Mr. [Goldschmith], a tenant, opened the door.

"What do you want? What have you come for?" he asked in astonishment.

"I've come to borrow the scale."

"Don't you know that the entire Frank family has gone to Switzerland?"

I didn't know anything about it. "Why?" I asked.

He didn't know either.

This was a bolt out of the blue. Why had they gone to Switzerland? The only connection the Frank family had with Switzerland was that Otto Frank's mother lived there.

But later it appeared that, in fact, the family had always reckoned that it would get worse for Jews. They had been preparing for a whole year to go into hiding. We didn't know anything about this. You can't talk about something like that. Because if anyone talked, then the whole affair would go amiss.

We couldn't go into hiding because my mother was expecting another baby, and my little sister was only two years old. So we never thought of doing anything like that. Mr. Frank visited us often when my father was depressed about the war and the Germans and how it would all turn out and how terrible everything was. And Mr. Frank would always say, "Everything is fine; the war is almost over."

I have often been asked why Mr. Frank chose that other family, the [Van Pelses], to join them in hiding and not us, because we were such close friends. But you mustn't forget: in the first place, I had a little two-year-old sister, and with a little girl, you can't go into hiding. In the diary, it tells how they couldn't flush the toilet and could only move a bit freely during the evening. Such measures are naturally impossible with a two-year-old. In the second, my mother was pregnant again, and a woman expecting a baby is also not much good in hiding. For those reasons we never resented it. I never considered it to be a problem.

And so I went home and said to my mother, "No Frank family; here's the scale."

My parents got very upset; they couldn't understand what had happened. But on the way home, I'd met a friend who said, "You know what? I received a letter from the Germans. Next week, I have to go to an *Arbeitslager* (work camp)." He was sixteen years old. Then we put two and two together and figured that perhaps Margot was also supposed to go to that *Lager*. Later, that appeared to have been the case. Margot had been sent a summons, saying that she had to go to such an *Arbeitslager*. It was at that moment that Mr. Frank said, "You aren't going to the *Arbeitslager;* we're going into hiding."

We had no idea that the family had been making preparations for a year. I learned that only after the war, from Mr. Frank. And of course we didn't know that they had actually stayed in Amsterdam. We knew that his mother lived in Switzerland, so we believed that the Frank family had fled to Switzerland. By spreading this rumor, they hoped that there would be no further search for them. At that time, a lot of Jews tried to escape across the border to Switzerland, so that wasn't anything unusual. Most of them were not successful.

I believe that Anne was the first girlfriend that I lost. It was, of course, very frightening, but we began to get used to the idea. When I went back to school after the summer, fewer children came to class every day.

We stayed in Amsterdam almost a full year longer, until June 20, 1943, and all this time things were getting worse and worse. [. . .]

So we continued to live, with little to eat and with a great deal of fear, but at least we were at home. In October, my mother died during childbirth. The baby was born dead. That was in Anne's diary. Someone told Anne that our baby had died, but not that my mother had died too. They probably didn't have the heart to tell her. [. . .]

Everything went along fine until June 20, 1943, when there was the big roundup in Amsterdam-South. On that day, the Germans started something new. At five o'clock in the morning while everyone was asleep they blocked off all the southern part of Amsterdam. They went from door to door, rang, and asked:

"Do Jews live here?"

"Yes."

"You have fifteen minutes; take a backpack, put a few things in it, and get outside quickly."

That was our neighborhood, so we had to pack too. A passport no longer helped. We had a quarter of an hour, and we had to go with them. [. . .]

On February 15, 1944, neither our Palestine papers nor our passports could help any more. But the big difference for us was that we weren't sent to Auschwitz. If we had been sent to Auschwitz in 1943, I wouldn't be able to tell about it now. Because those people who were taken away in the beginning were almost all killed.

But then I didn't know what Auschwitz was. People talked about an *Arbeitslager* (a work camp) in the east. We were going to an *Austauschlager* (exchange camp). I said at the time: "The Germans want to keep us alive so that they can exchange us for German soldiers."

On February 15, 1944, we were transported to Bergen-Belsen. That was a somewhat better camp. What was better about it? In the first place, we were transported in passenger cars and not in cattle cars. And then, when we arrived, our clothes weren't taken away and families weren't separated. My father and my sister stayed with me. We slept in different places, but we could see each other every evening. The trip took—I don't remember precisely—two or three days to get to Bergen-Belsen. [. . .]

One day, we looked in the direction where there hadn't been any barracks and saw that tents had suddenly appeared there. It was already quite cold, and we didn't know who was in those tents. Two or three months later, there were very strong wind storms and they were all blown down. On that same day, we received an order: our beds, which were stacked in two levels, one above the other, were taken away, and we got stacks of three beds. Two of us had to sleep in one bed, and half the camp had to be emptied. Then a barbed-wire fence was built through the middle of the camp and filled with straw so that we couldn't see the other side. But we were, of course, very close to each other, because the camp wasn't large. All those people from the tents were taken to the barracks on the other side. In spite of the German guards on the high watchtowers, we tried to make contact. It was, of course, strictly forbidden to talk with those people, and if the Germans saw or heard someone doing that, that person would have been shot at once. Because of that some of us went to the fence after dark to try to pick up something. I never went there, but we learned that they were all people who had come from Poland—Jews and non-Jews.

About a month later, in early February when there was snow on the ground, one of my acquaintances, an older woman, came up to me one day. "Do you know, there are some Dutch people there. I spoke to Mrs. [Van Pels]." The woman had known her from before, and she told me that Anne was there. She knew that I knew Anne.

"Go over to the barbed-wire fence and try to talk to her." And, of course, I did. In the evening, I stood by the barbed-wire fence and began to call out. And quite by chance Mrs. [Van Pels] was there again. I asked her, "Could you call Anne?"

She said, "Yes, yes, wait a minute, I'll go to get Anne. I can't get Margot; she is very, very ill and is in bed."

But naturally I was much more interested in Anne, and I waited there a few minutes in the dark.

Anne came to the barbed-wire fence—I couldn't see her. The fence and the straw were between us. There wasn't much light. Maybe I saw her shadow. It wasn't the same Anne. She was a broken girl. I probably was, too, but it was so terrible. She immediately began to cry, and she told me, "I don't have any parents anymore."

I remember that with absolute certainty. That was terribly sad, because she couldn't have known anything else. She thought that her father had been gassed right away. But Mr. Frank looked very young and healthy, and of course the Germans didn't know how old everybody was who they wanted to gas, but selected them on the basis of their appearance. Someone who looked healthy had to work, but another who might even be younger, but who was sick or looked bad, went directly to the gas chamber.

I always think, if Anne had known that her father was still alive, she might have had more strength to survive, because she died very shortly before the end—only a few days before [liberation]. But maybe it was all predestined.

So we stood there, two young girls, and we cried. I told her about my mother. She hadn't known that; she only knew that the baby had died. And I told her about my little sister. I told her that my father was in the hospital. He died two weeks later; he was already very sick. She told me that Margot was seriously ill and she told me about going into hiding because I was, of course, extremely curious.

"But what are you doing here? You were supposed to be in Switzerland, weren't you?" And then she told me what had happened. That they didn't go to Switzerland at all and why they had said that; so that everyone should think that they had gone to her grandmother's.

Then she said, "We don't have anything at all to eat here, almost nothing, and we are cold; we don't have any clothes and I've gotten very thin and they shaved my hair." That was terrible for her. She had always been very proud of her hair. It may have grown back a bit in the meantime, but it certainly wasn't the long hair she'd had before, which she playfully curled around her fingers. It was much worse for them than for us. I said, "They didn't take away our clothes." That was our first meeting.

Then for the first time—we had already been in the camp for more than a year; we arrived in February 1944, and this was February 1945—we received a very small Red Cross package: my sister, my father, and I. A very small package, the size of a book, with *knäckebrot* (Scandinavian crackers), and a few cookies. You can't imagine how little that was. My son always says, "But Mama, that was something really very special." But in those days we really collected everything, half a cookie, a sock, a glove—anything that gave a little warmth or something to eat. My friends also gave me something for Anne. I certainly couldn't have thrown a large package over the barbed-wire fence; not that I had one, but that wouldn't have been possible at all.

We agreed to try to meet the next evening at eight o'clock—I believe I still had a watch. And, in fact, I succeeded in throwing the package over.

But I heard her screaming, and I called out, "What happened?"

And Anne answered, "Oh, the woman standing next to me caught it, and she won't give it back to me."

Then she began to scream.

I calmed her down a bit and said, "I'll try again but I don't know if I'll be able to." We arranged to meet again, two or three days later, and I was actually able to throw over another package. She caught it; that was the main thing.

After these three or four meetings at the barbed-wire fence in Bergen-Belsen, I didn't see her again, because the people in Anne's camp were transferred to another section in Bergen-Belsen. That happened around the end of February.

That was the last time I saw Anne alive and spoke to her.

During that time, my father died, on February 25, 1945, and I didn't go out for a few days. When I went to look for her again, I found that the section was empty.

Translated from the Dutch by Alison Meersschaert.

6

Bergen-Belsen

Lin Jaldati

I don't think I shall easily bow down before the blows that inevitably come
to everyone.
—*July 15, 1944*

So it's happening soon, quicker. Move, move, screams the SS man. We were
pushed out of the boxcar. Many perished along the way; we had to pull the corpses
out and leave them there. I was so dazed from the stench and from the fatigue
that I could not respond any longer. [My sister] Jannie and I held our hands
together tightly; we were fearful we'd lose each other. There we were standing on
a wide roadway; to the right and left were woods, pines, and firs. But there was
no time left to look at the scenery. We were pushed and hit until we were in rows
of ten, a long line of emaciated, tattered figures.

We couldn't see the beginning of the line, nor its end. The guards screamed
throughout, dogs barked. Escape was impossible, the dogs would have torn us
apart. The assemblage set off in motion, feet shuffled over the ground. But it
smelled of the woods, the air was fresh. No stench line [as] in Auschwitz and in
the train. Along the way we came across a lot of men on bicycles, horsecarts, and
also pedestrians; all had seen us. But since the war no one's come forward who
knew anything. [. . .]

Then we had to walk further over a sandpit, now in rows of five. The woods,
the heath, and the air all reminded us of Holland. We went through a fence
opening and then yet through a barbed-wire fence that wasn't electrified, and then
to an enormous parade ground. We were in Bergen-Belsen. Each of us got a metal
plate, a spoon, and a blanket. Jannie and I were still in luck, as at the end of the
line there were many that got nothing. We froze, wrapped in our blankets, and
collapsed from fatigue. And we exhaled. Here there were no gas chambers, no
crematoria, it was all so green. Finally we got something to eat, soup with a few
pieces of carrot in it. Carrots, something really rare. Then we could walk about

a bit. Someone told us that if you went to the top of a hill there was a place to get washed. We went up there, and there was a long water draw with a lot of taps. To wash with fresh, cold water, we couldn't do that since Auschwitz. We threw on our blankets again, as two scrawny threadbare figures emerged. They looked like little frozen birds. We lay down in the bunkhouse and wept. They were Margot and Anne Frank. We asked about their mother. Anne said only, "selected."

We went back to the parade ground, past the barracks. Then we came to several big tents that looked as if the circus had left them behind. In one of those tents we took a break. We lay down on some straw and cringed together under our blankets. In the first days it was warm, we slept a lot. It started to rain. Also, our blankets didn't warm us up. There were lice here, too.

Then we were called to work. In one barracks we had to pull apart soles from old shoes. That was tiring. But we did get soup and bread for it. Soon hands began to bleed and fester. Anne and I had to stop first with the day work; the others held out a little longer. A few days later harsh November storms raged. The circus tents collapsed together, destroyed. We were hustled off to a barn where old shoes and other things were piled up. Anne asked, "Why do they want us to live like animals?" Jannie answered, "Because they themselves are predatory animals."

Then we were back in the barracks. It was death again, from starvation. New transports came in. Where would everyone go? We were displaced from our bunks. Now we had no roof over our heads. Every day there was roll call. But at dusk we had to be back in the bunks, or we would have been shot. We had to find our own billet. We were subject to the whim of the guards, that we could only curse. Every night an armed sentry came out, quite drunk. With a plank that he swung he made quite a racket. "You dirty pigs, I'll show you!" [. . .]

One day in December we all got a few pieces of hard cheese and some marmalade. The SS and the matrons went off afternoons and celebrated. It was Christmas. With Margot and Anne Frank and the Daniels sisters we were three pairs of sisters. We wanted that night to celebrate St. Nicholas, Hanukkah, and Christmas in our own way. Jannie had gotten to know a group of Hungarians, a few of whom worked in the SS kitchen. With their help she succeeded in getting two handfuls of potato peelings to "organize." Anne gathered up a clove of garlic, the Daniels sisters found a beet and a carrot. I sang a few songs for the matrons in another bunk and danced a Chopin waltz, singing the melody myself, for which I got a handful of sauerkraut. We saved a bit of bread from the rations, and each of us prepared a little surprise for the others. [. . .]

So, that's how we celebrated. Luise sang Dutch and Yiddish songs, funny ones like "Constant Had a Walking-Stick." We told stories and said aloud what we'd do when we'd get home. "Then we'd be at Dikker and Thijs, one of the expensive restaurants of Amsterdam, having a holiday dinner," said Anne. And we'd imagine ordering together from the menu, nothing but delicious things. We dreamed and were even for the moment lucky. We saw each other's eyes, round eyes, with a greenish pallor; we were getting thinner.

We asked Margot and Anne Frank whether they wanted to come with us. But Margot had diarrhea and couldn't go on. Due to the communicability of intestinal typhus she was confined to the bunk. Anne cared for her, so it went well. In the following weeks we went across to visit and brought things up for them to eat. It had to have been in March, as the snow was already melting as we went to look for them, but they weren't in the bunk any longer. In the quarantine [sick bunk] is where we found them. We begged them not to stay there, as people in there deteriorated so quickly and couldn't bring themselves to resist, that they'd be soon at the end. Anne simply said, "Here we can both lie on the plankbed; we'll be together and at peace." Margot only whispered; she had a high fever.

The following day we went to them again. Margot had fallen from the bed, just barely conscious. Anne also was feverish, yet she was friendly and sweet. "Margot's going to sleep well, and when she sleeps, I won't have to stay up." A few days later, the plankbed was empty. We knew what that meant. Behind the barracks we found her. We placed her thin body in a blanket and carried her to the mass grave. That was all that we could do.

What played out in these last weeks in the camp, I can't describe it in words. Unimaginable, horrible. It was just death, death slight and faint. The bodies remained outside where they lay about. Those that survived didn't have the strength to take them away.

Translated from the German by Ethan Izak Enzer.

7

The Darkest Days

Miep Gies and Alison Leslie Gold

Miep has so much to carry she looks like a pack mule. She goes forth every day
to scrounge up vegetables, and then bicycles back with her purchases in large
shopping bags. She's also the one who brings five library books with her every
Saturday.
—*July 11, 1944*

I just sat there, frozen. I'd lost track of time. At some point the two workers from
downstairs in the workplace came up to me and said that they were so sorry, that
they hadn't known. Then [van Maaren] came and said something, and I saw that
the Austrian had given him the keys that he had taken from me. I can't imagine
where the time had gone. First, it had been eleven or twelve o'clock when the
Dutch Nazi had come. Then it must have been about one-thirty when I'd heard
the footsteps on the inner stairway. Then, suddenly, [Bep] was back, and [Jan]
had arrived, and I realized that it was five o'clock and the day had passed.

[Jan] said right away to [W. G. van Maaren], "As soon as your assistants have
left, lock the door and come back to us." When [van Maaren] returned, [Jan]
said to [Bep, van Maaren,] and me, "Now we'll go upstairs and see what the situation is."

[Van Maaren] was carrying the keys that he'd been given. We all went to the
bookcase and turned it away from the door leading to the hiding place. The door
was locked but otherwise undisturbed. Fortunately, I'd kept a duplicate key, which
I went and got. We opened the door and went into the hiding place.

Right away, from the door, I saw that the place had been ransacked. Drawers
were open, things strewn all over the floor. Everywhere objects were overturned.
My eyes took in a scene of terrible pillage.

Then I walked into Mr. and Mrs. Frank's bedroom. On the floor, amidst the
chaos of papers and books, my eye lit on the little red-orange checkered, cloth-
bound diary that Anne had received from her father on her thirteenth birthday.

I pointed it out to [Bep]. Obeying my gesture, she leaned down and picked it up for me, putting it into my hands. I remembered how happy Anne had been to receive this little book to write her private thoughts in. I knew how precious her diary was to Anne. My eyes scanned the rubble for more of Anne's writings, and I saw the old accounting books and many more writing papers that [Bep] and I had given to her when she had run out of pages in the checkered diary. [Bep] was still very scared, and looked to me for direction. I told [Bep], "Help me pick up all Anne's writings."

Quickly, we gathered up handfuls of pages in Anne's scrawling handwriting. My heart beat in fear that the Austrian would return and catch us among the now-captured "Jewish possessions." [Jan] had gathered up books in his arms, including the library books and [Fritz Pfeffer's] Spanish books. He was giving me a look to hurry. [Van Maaren] was standing uncomfortably by the doorway. My arms and [Bep's] arms were filled with papers. [Jan] started down the stairs. Quickly, [van Maaren] hurried after him. [Bep] followed too, looking very young and very scared. I was the last, with the key in my hand.

As I was about to leave, I passed through the bathroom. My eye caught sight of Anne's soft beige combing shawl, with the colored roses and other small figures, hanging on the clothes rack. Even though my arms were filled with papers, I reached out and grabbed the shawl with my fingers. I still don't know why.

Trying not to drop anything, I bent to lock the door to the hiding place and returned to the office.

There [Bep] and I stood facing each other, both loaded down with papers. [Bep] said to me, "You're older; you must decide what to do."

I opened the bottom drawer of my desk and began to pile in the diary, the old accounting books, and the papers. "Yes," I told [Bep], "I will keep everything." I took the papers she was holding and continued filling the drawer. "I'll keep everything safe for Anne until she comes back."

I shut the desk drawer, but I did not lock it.

At home, [Jan] and I were like people who'd been beaten up. We sat across from each other at the dinner table, with Karel chattering as usual. We said nothing about what happened until we were alone. Then [Jan] told me what he'd done after he'd come to the door and I'd given him the warning and sent him off with the money and illegal ration coupons.

[Jan] told me: "I went straight to my office with the money and ration coupons and my lunch. It's a seven-minute walk from the hiding place at normal times, but I got there in four minutes, even though I had refrained from running. I didn't want to do anything that would cast suspicion on me, in case they'd come after me.

"At the office, I took the incriminating materials out of my pocket and hid them in between some other papers in the middle of my file cabinet. My mind was racing. I knew I should do nothing but wait, but with every nerve in my body I wanted to do something. I found it impossible to stay there, and decided to go to see [Kleiman's] brother, who is the supervisor in a watch factory right around the corner from my office.

"I found him and told him of the situation. He was stunned too. We stared at each other, neither of us knowing what to say or do. At last, I suggested that perhaps we should go back to the Prinsengracht and stand across the canal, at the corner, and see if we could see what was going on. We agreed this might be the best thing.

"We quickly walked over to the Prinsengracht and stood on the opposite side of the canal, diagonally across from the hiding place. Almost as soon as we got there, a dark green German police truck pulled up in front of 263. No one was about, and the truck did not have its siren on.

"The truck had pulled up almost against the building, way up on the sidewalk. In our diagonal view, we could still see the doors to the building. Suddenly the door opened, and I saw our friends in a bunch, each carrying a little something, going right from the door into the truck. Because I was across the canal I could hardly see their faces. I could see that [Kleiman] and [Kugler] were with them. There were two men not in uniform escorting the group. They put the prisoners into the back of the truck and went around to the front and got in. I did not know for sure if you were with them.

"When the prisoners were all inside, a Green Policeman slammed the door shut, and right away drove up the Prinsengracht in the opposite direction from where we were standing. Then the truck crossed the bridge, turned completely around, and came right down the Prinsengracht on our side of the canal. Before we could make a move to be less conspicuous, the truck drove right toward us, and passed not two feet from us. Because the door was shut I could not see inside. I turned my face away.

"Then, because we didn't know who was still inside the office, nor what was going on, and how dangerous it was, we went back to our respective offices and stayed until the end of the day, when it would appear normal to return to Prinsengracht."

[Jan] and I looked at each other. We both knew what was next, and neither of us had the heart to mention it. Finally, [Jan] slowly let his breath out. "I'll go tomorrow morning." The next day [Jan] went to tell Mrs. [Pfeffer] about the arrest.

"She took it very well," he told me later. "She was very surprised that all this time he was right in the center of Amsterdam. She said that she'd always imagined him way out in the country and that he wasn't the sort of man who much liked the country." [. . .]

Day after day, [Jan] went to the Centraal Station and gave vouchers to returning Dutchmen, most of whom had lost everything and had either lost or been separated from their families. Day after day, he would ask, "Do you know Otto Frank? Have you seen the Frank family—Otto, Frank, Margot, and Anne?" And day after day, head after head, would shake, "No." Or, "No, I have not seen or heard of these people."

Undaunted by this, [Jan] would ask the next person, and the next, "Do you know the Franks?" Always expecting one more ravaged head to shake, he finally heard a voice reply to his question, "Mister, I have seen Otto Frank, and he is coming back!"

[Jan] flew home that day to tell me. It was June 3, 1945. He ran into the living room and grabbed me. "Miep, Otto Frank is coming back!"

My heart took flight. Deep down I'd always known that he would, that the others would, too.

Just then, my eye caught sight of a figure passing outside our window. My throat closed. I ran outside.

There was Mr. Frank himself, walking toward our door.

We looked at each other. There were no words. He was thin, but he'd always been thin. He carried a little bundle. My eyes swam. My heart melted. Suddenly, I was afraid to know more. I didn't want to know what had happened. I knew I would not ask.

We stood facing each other, speechless. Finally, Frank spoke.

"Miep," he said quietly. "Miep, Edith is not coming back."

My throat was pierced. I tried to hide my reaction to his thunderbolt. "Come inside," I insisted.

He went on. "But I have great hope for Margot and Anne."

"Yes. Great hope," I echoed encouragingly. "Come inside."

He still stood there. "Miep, I came here because you and [Jan] are the ones closest to me who are still here."

I grabbed his bundle from his hand. "Come, you stay right here with us. Now, some food. You have a room here with us for as long as you want."

He came inside. I made up a bedroom for him and put everything we had into a fine meal for him. We ate. Mr. Frank told us he had ended up in Auschwitz. That was the last time he'd seen Edith, Margot, and Anne. The men had been separated from the women immediately. When the Russians liberated the camp in January, he had been taken on a very long trip to Odessa. Then from there to Marseille by ship, and at last, by train and truck to Holland.

He told us these few things in his soft voice. He spoke very little, but between us there was no need for words.

Mr. Frank settled in with [Jan] and me. Right away, he came back to the office and took his place again as the head of the business. I know he was relieved to have something to do each day. Meanwhile, he began exploring the network of information on Jews in the camps—the refugee agencies, the daily lists, the most crucial word-of-mouth information—trying everything to get news about Margot and Anne.

When Auschwitz was liberated, Otto Frank had gone right away to the women's camp to find out about his wife and children. In the chaos and desolation of the camps, he had learned that Edith had died shortly before the liberation.

He had also learned that in all likelihood, Margot and Anne had been transferred to another camp, along with Mrs. [Van Pels]. The camp was called Bergen-Belsen and was quite a distance from Auschwitz. That was as far as his trail had gone so far, though. Now he was trying to pick up the search.

As to the other men, Mr. Frank had lost track of [Fritz Pfeffer]. He had no idea what had happened to him after he was transferred from Auschwitz. He had seen with his own eyes Mr. [Van Pels] on his way to be gassed. And Peter [Van Pels] had come to visit Frank in the Auschwitz infirmary. Mr. Frank knew that right before the liberation of the camp, the Germans had taken groups of prisoners with them in their retreat. Peter had been in one of these groups.

Otto Frank had begged Peter to try to get into the infirmary himself, but Peter couldn't or wouldn't. He had last been seen going off with the retreating Germans into the snow-covered countryside. There was no further news about him.

Mr. Frank held high hopes for the girls, because Bergen-Belsen was not a death camp. There were no gassings there. It was a work camp—filled with hunger and disease, but with no apparatus for liquidation. Because Margot and Anne had been sent to the camp later than most other inmates they were relatively healthy. I too lived on hope for Margot and Anne. In some deep part of me, like a rock, I counted on their survival and their safe return to Amsterdam.

Mr. Frank had written for news to several Dutch people who he had learned had been in Bergen-Belsen. Through word of mouth people were being reunited every day. Daily, he waited for answers to his letters and for the new lists of survivors to be released and posted. Every time there was a knock at the door or footfalls on the steps, all our hearts would stand still. Perhaps Margot and Anne had found their way back home, and we would see them with our own eyes at last. Anne's sixteenth birthday was coming on June 12. Perhaps, we hoped, . . . but then the birthday came and went, and still no news. [. . .]

One morning, Mr. Frank and I were alone in the office, opening mail. He was standing beside me, and I was sitting at my desk. I was vaguely aware of the sound of a letter being slit open. Then, a moment of silence. Something made me look away from my mail. Then, Otto Frank's voice, tonelessly, totally crushed: "Miep."

My eyes looked up at him, seeking out his eyes.

"Miep." He gripped a sheet of paper in both his hands. "I've gotten a letter from the nurse in Rotterdam. Miep, Margot and Anne are not coming back."

We stayed there like that, both struck by lightning, burnt thoroughly through our hearts, our eyes fixed on each other's. Then Mr. Frank walked toward his office and said in that defeated voice, "I'll be in my office."

I heard him walk across the room and down the hall, and the door closed.

I sat at my desk utterly crushed. Everything that had happened before, I could somehow accept. Like it or not, I had to accept this. But this, I could not accept. It was the one thing I'd been sure would not happen.

I heard the others coming into the office. I heard a door opening and a voice chattering. Then, good-morning greetings and coffee cups. I reached into the drawer on the side of my desk and took out the papers that had been waiting there for Anne for nearly a year now. No one, including me, had touched them. Now Anne was not coming back for her diary.

I took out all the papers, placing the little red-orange checkered diary on top, and carried everything into Mr. Frank's office.

Mr. Frank was sitting at his desk, his eyes murky with shock. I held out the diary and the papers to him. I said, "Here is your daughter Anne's legacy to you."

I could tell that he recognized the diary. He had given it to her just over three years before, on her thirteenth birthday, right before going into hiding. He touched it with the tips of his fingers. I pressed everything into his hands; then I left his office, closing the door quietly.

Shortly afterward, the phone on my desk rang. It was Mr. Frank's voice. "Miep, please see to it that I'm not disturbed," he said.

"I've already done that," I replied.

8

Epilogue to the Diary of Anne Frank

Simon Wiesenthal

Who has inflicted this on us? Who has set us apart from the rest? Who has
put us through such suffering?
—*April 11, 1944*

At half past nine one night in October 1958, a friend called me in great excitement in my apartment in Linz. Could I come at once to the Landestheater?

A performance of *The Diary of Anne Frank* had just been interrupted by anti-
Semitic demonstrations. Groups of young people, most of them between fifteen
and seventeen, had shouted "Traitors! Toadies! Swindle!" Others booed and hissed.
The lights went on. From the gallery the youthful demonstrators showered leaflets
upon the people in the orchestra. People who picked them up read: "This play
is a fraud. Anne Frank never existed. The Jews have invented the whole story
because they want to extort more restitution money. Don't believe a word of it!
It's a fake!"

The police were summoned and took down the names of several demonstrators, students at local high schools. Then the performance continued. When I
arrived at the Landestheater the play had just ended, but there was still much
excitement. Two police cars were parked in front of the theater, and groups of
young people stood around discussing the incident. I listened to them. The consensus seemed to be that the demonstrators had been right. This whole Anne
Frank business was a fraud. Just as well that somebody had the guts to show those
Jews what they thought of them.

Many of these young people had not yet been born when Anne Frank went to
her death. And now, here in Linz, where Hitler had gone to school and Eichmann
had grown up, they were told to believe in lies and hatred, prejudice and nihilism.

The next morning I went to the police and looked at the names of the arrested
youths. It wasn't easy—they had powerful friends, and their parents wanted to

quash the whole thing. After all, it wasn't really serious, they said; just a few young people raising hell and having fun. I was told that the names of the students would be given to their schools for disciplinary action. No one was punished. The boys in Linz didn't matter, I thought, but something else did. A few weeks earlier, a Lübeck high-school teacher, *Studienrat* Lothar Stielau, had publicly declared that Anne Frank's diary was a forgery. He had been sued by the girl's father, and three experts had confirmed the authenticity of the diary. [. . .]

A few days after the demonstrations in Linz, I gave a lecture on neo-nazism at the headquarters of the Vienna archdiocese. The discussion that followed lasted until two in the morning. A professor reported an incident that had happened to a friend, a priest who taught religion at the *Gymnasium* in Wels, not far from Linz. The priest had been talking about Nazi atrocities at Mauthausen. One of the students stood up.

"Father, it's no use talking about those things. We know that the gas chambers of Mauthausen served only for the disinfection of clothes." The priest was shocked. "But you've seen the newsreels, the photographs. You saw the bodies."

"Made of papier-mâché," said the boy. "Nothing but clever propaganda to make the Nazis look guilty."

"Who said that?"

"Everybody knows it. My father could tell you a lot about these things."

The priest had reported the incident to the boy's school principal. An investigation was started, and a survey made in the region. More than 50 percent of the students in that class had parents who had been active in the Nazi movement. Their fathers loved to tell their sons about the heroism and glory of their past— how they had joined the Nazi party in Austria in the early 1930s (when it was illegal), had helped blow up trains and bridges, had printed and distributed illegal literature against the Dollfuss government. Later the fathers had become proud SS men. It is not easy for young people to grow up in such an environment and remain unaffected by it. Their fathers had been afraid, and quiet, during the early postwar years, but in the late 1950s they were once more talking nostalgically about the great past. The boys would listen excitedly. Their schoolteachers, many of them former Nazis, did nothing to challenge the glorious stories told by the students' fathers. [. . .]

Two days after the incident at the Landestheater, I was with a friend in a coffee house in Linz. Everybody was talking about the incident. Could the boys be blamed for the sins of their elders? Certainly they were not responsible.

A group of *Gymnasium* students sat down at the next table. My friend called over a boy whose parents he knew well.

"Fritz, were you at the theater during the demonstrations?"

"Unfortunately not, but some boys in my class were there. Two were even arrested," Fritz said proudly.

"What do you think about it?" my friend asked.

"Well—it's easy. There is no evidence that Anne Frank lived."

"But the diary?" I said.

"The diary may be a clever forgery. Certainly it doesn't prove that Anne Frank existed."

"She's buried in a mass grave in Bergen-Belsen."

He gave a shrug. "There is no proof."

Proof. One would have to produce proof—irrefutable proof that would convince these young skeptics. One would have to tear one single brick out of the edifice of lies that had been constructed, then the whole structure would collapse. But to find that one brick . . .

Something occurred to me. I said: "Young man, if we could prove to you that Anne Frank existed, would you accept the diary as genuine?"

He looked at me. "How can you prove it?"

"Her father is alive."

"That proves nothing."

"Wait. Her father reported to the authorities that they were arrested by the Gestapo."

"Yes," the boy said impatiently. "We've heard all that."

"Suppose the Gestapo officer who actually arrested Anne Frank were found. Would *that* be accepted as proof?"

He seemed startled. The idea had never occurred to him.

"Yes," he said at last, reluctantly. "*If* the man himself admitted it."

It was simple: I had to find the man who had arrested Anne Frank fourteen years before. Tens of thousands of people had been taken away all over Europe by nameless little men, the anonymous handymen of death. Even in the concentration camps we didn't always know the names of our torturers. They were aware of the possible consequences and tried to camouflage their identity. [. . .]

[The name of the Viennese SS man was initially reported as "Silvernagel," which] caused ironic comment among the Austrian Nazis because it was naturally well known that the name Silvernagel did not exist in Austria—further proof that the Anne Frank story was a fake.

I had very little to start out with. I knew that the SS man was Viennese or at least Austrian—many Austrians abroad call themselves Viennese. He must have been an SS man of low rank, since his job was to arrest people—SS *Schütze,* SS *Rottenführer,* or at the most, SS *Unterscharführer.*

That narrowed it down. The *v* in Silvernagel was probably [an] error; it could have been Silbernagel, a common name in Austria. Seven people named Silbernagel were listed in the Vienna telephone directory; almost a hundred more were in various city registers. The name was also well known in the provinces of Carinthia and Burgenland. If at least I knew the man's first name!

I continued to search. Among all the Silbernagels there must have been one who had held a low SS rank during the war and had served in Holland with the Gestapo. Names were investigated and eliminated. Rumors were sifted, facts checked. It was a long, tedious process, and I had to be extremely careful. If I implicated an innocent man, I might be sued for libel.

When the police want to find a motorist who has committed a crime, they can stop all cars and ask all the drivers for their licenses and no one can protest. I couldn't do that. I found eight men named Silbernagel who had been Nazi party members or SS men and were of the right age. One of them, a former *Obersturmführer* (a high rank, which automatically excluded him from my list), is now a prominent functionary in Burgenland. In any event, he had never been in Holland. [. . .]

In 1963 I was invited to appear on the Dutch television network. In Amsterdam, I went to the Anne Frank House, now a memorial, and I touched the walls the girl had touched. I talked to the custodian of the house. He said he'd often wondered about the man who had taken the girl and her family away. No one had any idea who it had been. He'd asked people and they had just shrugged.

"Nineteen years is a long time," he said. "It seems hopeless."

"Nothing is ever hopeless," I said. "Just suppose that I found the SS man who arrested her, and that he confessed that he had done it?"

The man gave me a long glance. "Then you would have written the missing epilogue to Anne Frank's diary."

For a while I thought I should go and see Otto Frank, Anne's father. He *might* remember the man who had come for them on the morning of August 4, 1944. He *might* be able to describe him to me. Any lead would help. The SS man must have changed in all these years—but there might be *something* to recognize him by.

I did not contact Mr. Frank. I admit it was not only my reluctance at upsetting this man who had suffered so much, at forcing him to search his memory once again. Something else bothered me. Suppose Mr. Frank asked me *not* to do anything about it? Could I comply with his request? I'd met other people who had not wanted me to search for the people who had killed their fathers and mothers and children. They said they couldn't bear it. "What's the use?" they asked. "You cannot bring back the dead. You can only make the survivors suffer."

I was still wondering what to do when I read in the papers that Mr. Frank, at a meeting in Germany, had spoken out in favor of forgiveness and reconciliation.

The German papers praised his magnanimity and tolerance. I respect Otto Frank's point of view. He has revealed the ethics of a man who doesn't just preach forgiveness but also practices it. But I am above all concerned with the practical and legal aspects of the case. Time and again I saw how tolerance and forgiveness were misunderstood by the Nazis. The fact that the father of Anne Frank had pardoned the murderers of his child was cited as an important argument in favor of ending the prosecution of all Nazi crimes. "What is good enough for Otto Frank should be good enough for anyone," it was said. "If he forgives, then all ought to forgive." Mr. Frank's conscience permits him to forgive. My conscience forces me to bring the guilty ones to trial. Obviously we operate on different ethical levels; we follow different paths. Somewhere our paths meet, and we complete each other. [. . .]

Presently friends in Holland told me that the SS man I was looking for might not be named Silbernagel but Silbertaler. Several people called Silbertaler had lived in Vienna before the war, but they were Jews and had disappeared. I found three non-Jewish Silbertalers in Vienna and elsewhere in Austria, but none had been active Nazis. I began to realize that it was highly improbable that I would ever find the one historical witness I needed. I began to wonder whether this witness was still alive.

On my next visit to Amsterdam I happened to talk to two friends, both familiar with the case of Anne Frank. They were Ben A. Sijes of the Dutch Institute for War Documentation and a Mr. Taconis, a high-ranking Dutch police official. Many names were mentioned in the course of our conversation—SS leaders Wilhelm Harster, Alfons Werner, Willy Zoepf, Gertrud Slottke, and others who had worked for Eichmann. In our line of work, one criminal leads to another. There were new leads, new names I'd never heard of. As I got ready to leave, Taconis said he had some "travel literature" for me, and he smiled. He brought me a photostatic copy of the 1943 telephone directory of the Gestapo in Holland. There were about three hundred names in it.

"Read it on the plane," he said. "That will keep you awake."

"On the contrary. Looking through a telephone directory has a soporific effect on me. When I'm in a hotel room in a strange place, I usually look through the local directory. Always makes me sleepy."

The flight to Vienna lasted about two hours. I settled back in my seat and looked through the Gestapo directory. I was almost asleep when I turned to the page headed "IV, *Sonderkommando*." Under "IV B 4, *Joden* [Jews]" I read:

Kempin
Buschmann
Scherf
Silberbauer

I was wide awake. Section IV B 4 had handled the roundup and transport of Jews to death camps. If anyone had tipped off the Gestapo about Jews hiding out somewhere in Holland, the report would inevitably reach Section IV B 4 in Amsterdam. All of a sudden the plane seemed to be very slow. I could hardly wait to get to Vienna. I knew that most officials of Section IV B 4 had been recruited from police forces in Germany and Austria, mostly among the *Kriminalpolizei* (detectives).

Back home, before I could take off my coat I opened the Vienna telephone directory. My heart sank. There were almost a dozen people called Silberbauer. Probably there were many more in other Austrian city directories. If I had to investigate each of them, as I had the Silbernagels and Silbertalers before, years might go by. I had reached the stage where some deductive thinking was needed. I couldn't investigate everyone named Silberbauer. I decided I would look for a man of that name who had worked (or was still working) for the Vienna police. It was like solving an equation with many unknown factors with the help of one known factor. I had to start from a definite premise if I wanted to build a structure.

I called up Polizeirat Dr. Josef Wiesinger, head of Section IIc at the Ministry of the Interior, which deals with Nazi crimes. Wiesinger has often helped me with my investigations. I told him—rather boastfully, I'm afraid—that I had found the Gestapo man who arrested Anne Frank.

"He's a Viennese policeman named Silberbauer," I said.

Wiesinger didn't call my bluff. "What's his first name?"

"I don't know his first name."

"There must be at least six men called Silberbauer on the Vienna police force," he said. "What one do you want?"

"That should be easy to find. All you have to do is go through their service records. I want the man who was with Section IV B 4 in Amsterdam in August 1944."

"That was nineteen years ago," Wiesinger said skeptically.

"Your records go back that far, don't they?"

"All right," he said. "Submit a written request to my office."

On June 2, 1963, I mailed a detailed report. Several weeks went by. When I went to see Wiesinger in July about something else, I asked again about Silberbauer. He said the files of all policemen called Silberbauer were "still being examined." In September, when I was back from my vacation, I called him again. I was told that "So far nothing concrete had become known. [. . .]"

On the morning of November 11, *Volksstimme,* the official organ of Austria's Communist party, came out with a sensational story. *Inspektor* Karl Silberbauer of the Vienna police force had been suspended "pending investigation and possible prosecution" for his role in the Anne Frank case. The communists made the most of their scoop. Radio Moscow broadcast that the captor of Anne Frank had been unmasked "through the vigilance of Austria's resistance fighters and progressive elements." *Izvestia* later praised the detective work of the Austrian comrades.

I telephoned Dr. Wiesinger. He was embarrassed. "Naturally we would have preferred to have the story disclosed by you, and not by the Communists. How could we know that Silberbauer was going to talk? He was supposed to keep his mouth shut."

I decided not to keep mine shut either. I called a Dutch newspaper editor in Amsterdam and gave him the story. It made front-page news all over the world. I received more cables and letters than I had after Eichmann's capture. There were radio and TV interviews. [Victor Kugler], now in Canada, told the world about how the Franks had lived up there in the attic. And in Switzerland, Mr. Frank said that he had always known that their Gestapo captor had been an SS man named Silberbauer.

Everybody was excited except the Austrian authorities, who said they didn't comprehend "what all the fuss was about," as one high-ranking official said to me. The journalists wanted to talk to Silberbauer, but the minister of the interior refused to release pictures of Silberbauer and tried to keep him incommunicado. I didn't go along with this. I gave Silberbauer's private address to a Dutch newspaperman. I thought the Dutch were entitled to at least one exclusive interview. When the Dutchman came to see Silberbauer, he found the police inspector (the second-lowest rank in the Austrian police) in a very angry mood. He said he'd been railroaded.

"Why pick on me after all these years? I only did my duty. We've just bought some new furniture, on installment, and now they suspend me. How am I going to pay for the furniture?"

"Don't you feel sorry about what you did?" the reporter asked.

"Sure I feel sorry. Sometimes I feel downright humiliated. Now each time I take a streetcar I have to buy a ticket, just like everyone else. I can no longer show my service pass."

"And what about Anne Frank? Have you read her diary?"

Silberbauer shrugged. "Bought the little book last week to see whether I'm in it. But I am not."

The reporter said: "Millions of people have read the diary before you. And you could have been the first who read it."

Silberbauer looked at him in surprise.

"Say, that's true. I never thought of it. Maybe I should have picked it up from the floor."

If he had, no one would ever have heard of him—or of Anne Frank.

When Dr. Wiesinger had told me, on October 15, "We are not yet ready with this matter," he already knew that *Inspektor* Karl Silberbauer, attached to First District Police Headquarters, had admitted that he had been in charge of the Gestapo posse, that he had personally arrested Anne Frank and the other people in the attic in Amsterdam, on the morning of August 4, 1944. I asked Dr. Wiesinger why he had kept this information from me. He said he'd had "orders from above" to keep the matter a secret.

After the capitulation of Germany, Silberbauer had fled from the Netherlands and returned to Vienna. Since he had left the Vienna police force in 1943 to join the SS, he had to submit to "de-Nazification" proceedings in 1952. He was cleared and returned to duty with the rank of inspector.

For a month after Silberbauer's confession his superiors had done nothing. On October 4 he was suspended from service and was ordered not to mention a word about the whole matter, pending investigation. [. . .]

The Austrian authorities found no evidence that Silberbauer was guilty of the deportation of the Franks. A spokesman for the Interior Ministry said that the arrest of Anne Frank "did not warrant Silberbauer's arrest or persecution as a war criminal." He had only obeyed orders. Disciplinary proceedings followed, because Silberbauer had concealed from the de-Nazification board the fact that he had worked for the Jewish Affairs Section of the Gestapo in Holland.

Mr. Frank, asked to testify, said his captor had "only done his duty and acted correctly."

"The only thing I ask is not to have to see the man again," said Anne Frank's father.

A police review board exonerated Silberbauer of any official guilt. He is back on the Vienna police force, assigned to the *Erkennungsamt* (Identification Office).

Incidentally, Silberbauer had been working at police headquarters during all those years I'd been looking for him. It's a ten-minute walk from my office to headquarters. Probably we'd met in the street. And also, across from our Documentation Center there is a big textile store with a sign reading SILBERBAUER. A second such store, also called SILBERBAUER, is next to the entrance to our building. Of course, Silberbauer doesn't matter at all. Compared to other names in my files, he is a nobody, a zero. But the figure before the zero was Anne Frank.

Part 2

Writer and Rewriter

9

The Legend and Art of Anne Frank

Henry F. Pommer

I want to go on living even after my death! And that's why I'm so grateful to God for having given me this gift, which I can use to develop myself and to express all that's inside me!
—*April 5, 1944*

On an unrecorded [day in] March 1945, Anne Frank succumbed to the malnutrition, exposure, typhus, and despair of the Bergen-Belsen concentration camp. She was back in her native Germany because her family had not fled far enough in 1933, going only to Amsterdam. And she was back because the Allies had not advanced fast enough in the summer of 1944, the long train of freight cars which on September 3 took Anne to [Auschwitz] was the last shipment of Jews to leave Holland. It moved on the day that Brussels was freed by the Allies.

The quality of both her death and her life have given Anne Frank an extraordinary status in our culture. Antigone represents a willingness to die for principles; Juliet's is the tragedy of ironic confusion; Marguerite was the victim of her own and Faust's sensuality; St. Joan was martyred by jealous institutions. Anne was destroyed by a pattern of evil perhaps not unique to our century, but at least unique within Western culture of the past two thousand years.

But her fame rests on knowledge of her life as much as of her death. She is not a fictional character like Juliet or Tolstoy's Natasha, nor a girl with widespread and immediate effects like St. Joan or the young Cleopatra. Yet she shares with Cleopatra and St. Joan the fact of being historical; and her life is already, like theirs, the source of a legend. As a historical figure relatively unimportant to her immediate contemporaries but affecting a larger and larger circle after her death, she is most like St. Thérèse of Lisieux. But over all these girls from Antigone to St. Thérèse, Anne has the great advantage that she left a diary. Therefore, we need not know her through the documents of her contemporaries or the professional imagination of middle-aged authors. Her legend lacks the support of patriotic and ecclesiastical power, but it has the strength of her authentic, self-drawn portrait.

The legend she founded is the kind her destroyers had tried to wipe out. She is a Jewess spoken of by Germans as a saint; she was an object of hatred, and has become a vehicle of love. In Frankfurt-am-Main, a memorial plaque now marks the house where she lived from 1930 to 1933, and in 1957 her birthday was celebrated in St. Paul's Church. In Amsterdam, the Montessori school she attended has been given her name, and the house where she wrote the diary has been turned into a museum by a group of Christians. In Vienna and Tel Aviv, money has been raised to plant an Anne Frank forest near Jerusalem. In West Berlin, a center for social work with young people has been named for her "to symbolize racial and social tolerance." In the United States, Anne's twenty-five months of hiding became the object of an extremely popular Pulitzer Prize play and a costly, top-notch film. The play, in its turn, produced a wave of philo-Semitism in Germany. [. . .]

Some writers have considered the diary as primarily "one of the most moving stories that anyone, anywhere, has managed to tell about World War II." At Oradour-sur-Glane, where Nazis wantonly destroyed the entire population, is printed "Remember," and in the ruins of bomb-destroyed Coventry have been carved "Father Forgive." Anne's diary helps us remember what there is to forgive. [. . .]

If the Nazis' deeds are to be remembered as well as forgiven, the deeds of many non-Jewish Dutch are to be remembered as well as admired. During the seventeenth century René Descartes had lived in a house which Anne could see from her secret annex. [. . .] Anne told her diary, "It is not the Dutch people's fault that we are having such a miserable time." Some Dutch did, of course, cooperate with the Nazis; the hiders recognized two alternatives if they were discovered by Dutch police: "they would either be good Dutch people, then we'd be saved," or members of the Dutch National Socialist Movement, and then the hiders would have to try bribery. And probably it was a Dutch citizen who finally betrayed the Franks. Yet against the small number of these collaborators stand the loyal friends and strangers who helped the hiders at the cost of money, time, and comfort, and at the risk of death. For example, in the play Anne very briefly mentions a vegetable man. He lives in the diary as an unnamed grocer who came to suspect the presence of hiders in the warehouse, delivered potatoes to the Dutch staff at the least conspicuous times, and was alert enough once to scare burglars from the warehouse without calling the police. He was later arrested for harboring two Jews in his own home. His tact and willingness to expose himself are symptomatic of a great many Dutchmen's deeds—deeds which were some of the most heroic of the war.

All these deeds deserve to be remembered because the truths of Anne's history, the bitter as well as the sweet, are not about Germans alone or Dutchmen or Jews, but humanity. And these truths must be recalled whenever we try to measure human nature, to estimate its heights and depths, its capacities for good and evil. The extremes of cruelty temper all our hopes. [. . .]

A second group of critics has praised the diary as primarily an intimate account of adolescence. For these it is of only secondary importance that Anne hid with her family in an attic of old Amsterdam; of primary importance is her frankness in telling what it is like to grow up. [. . .]

Anne was thirteen when she started her diary. Six months later she regretted not having had her first menstruation. "I'm so longing to have it too," she wrote, "it seems so important." She tried to bleach her black moustache hairs with hydrogen peroxide; she collected pictures of film stars and hung them around her room. She betrayed further immaturity by remarking about Margot, "She lacks the nonchalance for conducting deep discussions."

Often she was difficult to live with. Tensions were almost inevitable for eight people living with so many restrictions in such cramped quarters, but Anne seems to have done more than her share to stir up ill will. She had a temper and was not always either anxious or able to control it. At times she must have been obnoxiously precocious in telling the other hiders what they were like; she may have appeared very patronizing at times, particularly in dealing with Margot and Peter. She was very critical of her mother, very fond of her father, and from time to time hurt both of them deeply. Her sense of justice, her loathing of whatever was pompous or artificial, and her desire to be treated as an adult led to frequent quarrels with Mr. and Mrs. [Van Pels], and with [Fritz Pfeffer].

Bit by bit, however, these evidences of immaturity and of being difficult decreased. Mixed with them, yet gradually replacing them, came the actions and reactions of a more mature young woman. Probably the most striking measure of these changes is her love affair with Peter [Van Pels]. Before she went into hiding she had delighted in the company of many boys—and had developed a considerable self-conscious skill in handling them. As she settled down in the secret annex, she decided that Peter was completely uninteresting—"a rather soft, shy, gawky youth; can't expect much from his company." But during the next eighteen months Anne's need for a confidant of her own age greatly increased, and she had her first periods. Finally, on January 6, 1944, "My longing to talk to someone became so intense that somehow or other I took it into my head to choose Peter. [. . .]"

Whatever their relationship was for Peter, for Anne it was a flood of new feelings, new problems, new insights concerning herself and other people; it helped her on the road to maturity. But other traits and experiences also helped—particularly her intellectualism and humor, her religious sense and courage, her capacity for self-analysis. [. . .]

Her humor, like her love for Peter, helped make her situation much better than merely bearable. So did her religious sentiment, which appears to have deepened during the months of hiding. The Franks were not Orthodox Jews. In their home they had not observed the ritual of the sabbath; Anne and her father had attended synagogue only on high holidays, although Mrs. Frank and Margot attended regularly. During the period of hiding, Anne prayed each night. She prayed for miracles to save at least some of the Jews not fortunate enough to be in hiding; after scares which caused the hiders to think they had been discovered, she thanked God for having protected them. At times her religious sentiment contained clear marks of the Old Testament, as when she asked:

> Who has inflicted this upon us? Who has made us Jews different from all other people? Who has allowed us to suffer so terribly up till now? It is God that has made us as we are, but it will be God, too, who will raise us up again. If we bear all this suffering and if there are still Jews left, when it is over, then Jews, instead of being doomed, will be held up as an example. Who knows, it might even be our religion from which the world and all peoples learn good, and for that reason, and that reason only, do we have to suffer now. [April 11, 1944]

Other expressions of religion suggest a Wordsworthian reliance on nature: "The best remedy for those who are afraid, lonely, or unhappy is to go outside, somewhere where they can be quite alone with the heavens, nature, and God. Because only then does one feel that all is as it should be and that God wishes to see people happy, amidst the simple beauty of nature. As long as this exists, and it certainly always will, I know that then there will always be comfort for every sorrow, whatever the circumstances may be. And I firmly believe that nature brings solace in all troubles" [February 23, 1944].

It is hardly surprising that Anne with her sense of humor and religious sentiment had an abundance of courage. She wrote that "he who has courage and faith will never perish in misery" [March 7, 1944], and we can only hope that the statement was true of her to the end. She also wrote, "I have often been downcast, but never in despair; I regard our hiding as a dangerous adventure, romantic and interesting at the same time [. . .]" [May 2, 1944].

Anne could write well. Her self-consciousness and skill as an author receive only implicit acknowledgments if we regard her diary as no more than an educative historical document or an intimate disclosure of adolescence. W. A. Darlington is probably correct in predicting that "in time to come, when the horrors of Nazi occupation in Europe are no longer quite so fresh in quite so many minds and 'The Diary of Anne Frank' comes to be judged purely on its merits as a play, the piece will . . . lose its place on the stage."[1] But Anne's diary may have a longer life. It is, to be sure, a mixture of good and bad writing—but so, too, are the diaries of Pepys, Samuel Sewall, and William Byrd. [. . .]

The chief literary merit of the diary is its permitting us to know intimately Anne's young, eager, difficult, lovable self. We follow the quick alternations of her great gaiety and sometimes equally great depression, and we benefit from the introspections generated by her sharply contrasting moods. Some pages read as though they had been written in the security of a Long Island suburbia; on the next page we are plunged into Nazi terror; and both passages use vivid details. Sometimes our delight is simply in her charm, as in "Daddy always says I'm prudish and vain but that's not true. I'm just simply vain" [March 24, 1944]. At other times her wisdom surprises us, as in her distinction that "laziness may *appear* attractive, but work *gives* satisfaction" [July 6, 1944]. She sensed the need for variety in reporting and used effective techniques for achieving it. Life in the secret annex was terribly repetitious, but there is little repetition in the diary itself.

Even if the last entry told of Jews liberated by the arrival of Allied armies in Amsterdam, the book would still have real interest and value. And it would still have its chief moral significance.

Note

1. W. A. Darlington, "London Letter," *New York Times,* Jan. 20, 1957, sect. 2, p. 3.

10

The Development of Anne Frank

John Berryman

We learn in time of pestilence that there are more things to admire than to despise.
—*Albert Camus,* The Plague

When the first installment of the translated text of *The Diary of Anne Frank* appeared in the spring of 1952, in *Commentary,* I read it with amazement. The next day, when I went into town to see my analyst, I stopped in the magazine's offices—I often did, to argue with Clem Greenberg, who was a sort of senior adviser to what was at that time the best general magazine in the country in spite of, maybe because of, its special Jewish concerns—to see if proofs of the diary's continuation were available, and they were. Like millions of people later, I was bowled over with pity and horror and admiration for the astounding doomed little girl. But what I *thought* was: a sane person. A sane person, in the twentieth century. It was as long ago as 1889 when Tolstoy wound up his terrible story "The Devil" with this sentence: "And, indeed, if Evgeni Irrenev was mentally deranged, then all people are mentally deranged, but undoubtedly those are most surely mentally deranged who see in others symptoms of insanity which they fail to see in themselves." Some years later (1955), setting up a course called Humanities in the Modern World at the University of Minnesota, I assigned the diary and re-read it with feelings even more powerful than before but now highly structured. I decided that it was the most remarkable account of *normal* human adolescent maturation I had ever read, and that it was universally valued for reasons comparatively insignificant. I waited for someone to agree with me. An article by Bettelheim was announced in *Politics,* appeared, and was irrelevant. The astute Alfred Kazin and his wife, the novelist Ann Birstein, edited Anne Frank's short fiction—ah! I thought—and missed the boat.

Here we have a book only fifteen years old, the sole considerable surviving production of a young girl who died after writing it. While decisively rejecting the proposal—which acts as a blight in some areas of modern criticism—that a critic should address himself only to masterworks, still I would agree that some preliminary justification seems desirable.

It is true that the book is world famous. I am not much impressed by this fact, which I take to be due in large part to circumstances that have nothing to do with art. The author has been made into a spokesman against one of the grand crimes of our age, and for her race, and for all its victims, and for the victims (especially children) of all the tyrannies of this horrifying century—and we could extend this list of circumstances irrelevant to the *critical* question. Some proportion of the book's fame, moreover, is even more irrelevant, as arising from the widespread success of a play adapted from it, and a film. That the book *is* by a young girl—an attractive one, as photographs show—must count heavily in its sentimental popularity. And, finally, the work has decided literary merit; it is vivid, witty, candid, astute, dramatic, pathetic, terrible—one falls in love with the girl, one finds her formidable, and she breaks one's heart. All right. It is a work infinitely superior to a similar production that has been compared to it, *The Diary of "Helena Morley,"* beautifully translated by Elizabeth Bishop in 1957. Here is a favorable specimen of the Brazilian narrative: "When I get married I wonder if I'll love my husband as much as mama loves my father? God willing. Mama lives only for him and thinks of nothing else. When he's at home the two spend the whole day in endless conversation. When papa's in Boa Vista during the week, mama gets up singing wistful love songs and we can see she misses him, and she passes the time going over his clothes, collecting the eggs, and fattening the chickens for dinner on Saturday and Sunday. We eat best on those days."[1] Clearly the temperature here is nothing very unusual, and no serious reader of Anne Frank, with her extraordinary range and tension, will entertain any comparison between the two writers. But I am obliged to wonder whether Anne Frank has *had* any serious readers, for I find no indication in anything written about her that anyone has taken her with real seriousness. A moment ago we passed, after all, the critical question. *One finds her formidable:* why, and how, ought to engage us. And first it is necessary to discover what she is writing about. Perhaps, to be sure, she is not truly writing about anything—you know, "thoughts of a young girl," "Jews in hiding from the Nazis," "a poignant love affair"; but such is not my opinion.

Suppose one became interested in the phenomenon called religious conversion. There are books one can read. There is one by Sante de Sanctis entitled *Religious Conversion,* there are narratives admirably collected in William James's lectures, *The Varieties of Religious Experience,* there is an acute account of the most momentous Christian conversion, Paul's, by Maurice Goguel in the second volume (*The Birth of Christianity*) of his great history of Christian origins. If one wants, however, to experience the phenomenon, so far as one can do so at second hand—

a phenomenon as gradual and intensely reluctant as it is also drastic—there is so far as I know one book and one only to be read, written by an African fifteen hundred years ago. Now in Augustine's *Confessions* we are reckoning with just one of a vast number of works by an architect of Western history, and it may appear grotesque to compare to even that one, tumultuous and gigantic, the isolated recent production of a girl who can give us nothing else. A comparison of the *authors* would be grotesque. But I am thinking of the originality and ambition and indispensability of the two books *in the heart of their substances*—leaving out of account therefore book 10 of the *Confessions,* which happens to award man his deepest account of his own memory. I would call the subject of Anne Frank's diary even more mysterious and fundamental than St. Augustine's, and describe it as: the conversion of a child into a person.

At once it may be exclaimed that we have thousands of books on this subject. I agree: autobiographies, diaries, biographies, novels. They seem to me—those that in various literatures I have come on—to bear the same sort of relation to the diary that the works *on* religious conversion bear to the first seven books of the *Confessions.* Anne Frank has made the process itself available.

Why—I asked myself with astonishment when I first encountered the diary, or the extracts that *Commentary* published—has this process not been described before? universal as it is, and universally interesting? And answers came. It is *not* universal, for most people do not grow up, in any degree that will correspond to Anne Frank's growing up; and it is *not* universally interesting, for nobody cares to recall his own, or can. It took, I believe, a special pressure forcing the child-adult conversion, and exceptional self-awareness and exceptional candor and exceptional powers of expression, to bring that strange or normal change into view. This, if I am right, is what she has done, and what we are to study.

The process of her development, then, is our subject. But it is not possible to examine this without some prior sense of two unusual sets of conditions in which it took place: its physical and psychological context, first, and second, the qualities that she took into it. Both, I hope to show, were *necessary* conditions.

For the context: it was both strange, sinister, even an "extreme situation" in Bettelheim's sense,[2] and pseudo-ordinary; and it is hard to say which aspect of the environment was more crippling and crushing. We take a quicksilver-active girl thirteen years old, pretty, popular, voluble, brilliant, and hide her, as it were, in prison; in a concealed annex upstairs at the rear of the business premises her father had commanded; in darkness, behind blackout curtains; in slowness—any movement might be heard—such that after a time when she peeks out to see cyclists going by they seem to be flying; in closeness—not only were she and her parents and sister hopelessly on top of each other, but so were another family with them, and another stranger—savagely bickering, in whispers, of course; in fear—

of Nazis, of air raids, of betrayal by any of the Dutch who knew (this, it seems, is what finally happened, but the marvelous goodness of the responsible Dutch is one of the themes of the *Diary*), of thieves (who came)—the building, even, was once sold out from under them, and the new owner simply missed the entrance to their hiding place. All this calls for heroism and it's clear that the personalities of the others except Mr. Frank withered and deteriorated under conditions barely tolerable. It took Anne Frank herself more than a year to make the sort of "adjustment" (detestable word) that would let her free for the development that is to be our subject.

But I said, "as it were, in prison." To prison one can become accustomed; it is *different,* and one has no responsibilities. Here there was a simulacrum of ordinary life: she studied, her family was about her, she was near—very near—the real world. The distortion and anxiety are best recorded in the dreadful letter of April 1, 1943. Her father was still (sort of) running the company and had briefed his Dutch assistant for an important conference; the assistant fell ill and there wasn't time to explain "fully" to his replacement; the responsible executive, in hiding, "was trembling with anxiety as to how the talks would go." Someone suggested that if he lay with his face on the floor he might hear. So he did, at 10:30 a.m., with the other daughter, Margot, until 2:30, when half-paralyzed he gave up. The daughters took over, understanding scarcely a word. I have seldom, even in modern literature, read a more painful scene. It takes Anne Frank, a concise writer, thirteen sentences to describe.

Let's distinguish, without resorting to the psychologists, temperament from character. The former would be the disposition with which one arrives in the world, the latter what has happened to that disposition in terms of environment, challenge, failure, and success, by the time of maturity—a period individually fixed between, somewhere between, fifteen and seventy-five, say. Dictionaries will not help us; try *Webster's Dictionary of Synonyms* if you doubt it. Americans like dictionaries, and they are also hopeless environmentalists (although they do not let it trouble their science, as Communists do). I ought therefore perhaps to make it plain that children do differ. The small son of another friend was taking a walk, hand in hand, with his father, when they came to an uneven piece of sidewalk and his father heard him say to himself, "Now, Peter, take it easy, Peter, that's all right, Peter," and they went down the other end of the slightly tilted block. My own son, a friend of both, is in between, Dionysiac with the first, Apollonian with Peter. I think we ought to form some opinion of the *temperament* of Anne Frank before entering on her ordeal and thereafter trying to construct a picture of her character.

The materials are abundant, the diary lies open. She was vivacious but intensely serious, devoted but playful. It may later on be a question for us as to whether this conjunction *but* is the right conjunction, in her thought. She was imaginative but practical, passionate but ironic and cold-eyed. Most of the qualities that I am naming need no illustration for a reader of the diary; perhaps "cold-eyed" may have an exemplar: "Pim, who was sitting on a chair in a beam of sunlight that shone through the window, kept being pushed from one side to the other. In addition, I think his rheumatism was bothering him, because he sat rather hunched up with a miserable look on his face. . . . He looked exactly like some shriveled-up old man from an old people's home" [December 10, 1942]. So much for an image of the man—her adored father—whom she loves best in the world. She was self-absorbed but unselfpitying, charitable but sarcastic, industrious but dreamy, brave but sensitive. Garrulous but secretive; skeptical but eloquent. This last *but* may engage us, too. My little word *industrious,* like a refugee from a recommendation for a graduate student, finds its best instance in the letter, daunting to an American student, of April 27, 1944, where in various languages she is studying in one day matters that—if they ever came up for an American student— would take him months.

The reason this matters is that the process we are to follow displays itself in a more complicated fashion than one might have expected: in the will, in emotion, in the intellect, in libido. It is surprising what it takes to make an adult human being.

Notes

1. Helena Morley, *The Diary of Helena Morley,* trans. Elizabeth Bishop (New York: Ecco Press, 1977), 82.

2. Bruno Bettelheim's well-known article, "[Individual and Mass Behavior in] Extreme Situations," [*Journal of Abnormal and Social Psychology* 38 (1943): 417–52, reprinted] in *Politics.* I am unable to make anything of his recent article in *Harper's,* weirdly titled "The [Ignored] Lesson of Anne Frank," which charges that the Franks should not have gone into hiding as a family but should have dispersed for greater safety; I really do not know what to say to this, except that a man at his desk in Chicago, many years later, ought not to make such decisions perhaps; he also complains that they were not armed. Some social scientist will next inform the Buddha of *his* mistake—in leaving court at all, in austerity, in illumination, and in teaching.

11

Introduction to
The Tales from the House Behind
G. B. Stern

I also need to finish "Cady's Life." I've thought up the rest of the plot. . . .
It's not sentimental nonsense: it's based on the story of Father's life.
—*May 11, 1944*

Let us for the moment remember Anne Frank as just a delightful child, a chatterbox, a flirt, and even with the characteristic childish need to invent an imaginary friend called Kitty to whom she addressed the now world-famous diary found after she and her family had been taken away by the Nazis to die in concentration camps at Auschwitz and Belsen; and be glad that she lives again in this collection of fables, personal reminiscences, and short stories found in a notebook and on odd sheets of paper—the Nazis thought that neither these nor the diary were of the least importance, and left them lying in a heap on the floor. Which is where the Nazis were wrong. [. . .]

One thing is certain, that Anne was a writer in embryo. Her title for the book she was planning to write after the war was *Het Achterhuis,* meaning the "House Behind," referring of course to the house in Amsterdam where they all lived cooped up and in hiding for over two years, but it could also have stood for an unconsciously symbolic title to indicate that behind her passionate zest for life, we should find wisdom and a deeply religious sense of values. For instance, in one of her fables, the elf who takes Eve on a tour of a big park dismisses the rose as too obviously the queen of flowers, lovely, elegant, and fragrant—"and if she wouldn't always push herself into the foreground, she might be lovable as well," and then completes the lesson by analogy between two of Eve's friends, Lena symbolizing the rose, and little Marie, plain and poor, as a bluebell: "This flower is much happier than the rose. It doesn't care about the praise of others."[1] Though the language of this fable may be immature, it reveals nevertheless that amazing sense of values which we have already noticed.

And according to Anne Frank, the overworked little flowergirl, Krista, is never dissatisfied so long as the end of every day she might have a brief rest "in the field, amid the flowers, beneath the darkening sky. . . . Gone is fatigue . . . the little girl thinks only of the bliss of having this short while alone with God and nature"— as Anne herself found endless compensation in looking up at the sky or at the chestnut tree, from the attic window of *Het Achterhuis*.[2]

And indeed, the more we read of her or by her, the more strange and incongruous it seems that she could combine in one human being the contradictory qualities of extrovert and introvert. In spite of her overflowing exuberance, her reputation as a chatterbox, unable to refrain from pouring out to her companions whatever might have danced into her head, in these fables we are allowed to penetrate into the House Behind—and aware of the end of Anne Frank, we can hardly bear to read the vivid fable called "Fear," written, according to its date, only a few days before she was taken away[:] she dreamed that bombs were falling and she ran outside the city and fell asleep in the grass under the sky—"Fear is a sickness for which there is only one remedy. Anyone who is afraid, as I was then, should look at nature and see that God is much closer than most people think."[3] Like all the best fabulists, she applies her own experience to a universal need.

And that brings us to her last fable, of the "Wise Old Dwarf" who keeps captive two elves of widely different temperaments, Dora and Peldron, and would not let them go home until four months later: he explains his motive—"I took you here and left you together to teach you there are other things in this world beside *your* fun and *your* gloom. [. . .] Dora has become somewhat more serious, and Peldron has cheered up a bit, because you were obliged to make the best of having to live together."[4]

We have already seen that Anne Frank was by no means lacking in a subtle vein of humor; she concluded her story of Blurry, the little bear who set off to "discover the world," [thus:] when after all his crowded experiences he had to admit that he had failed to discover it because—"You see, I couldn't find it!"[5]

And so we pass on to the section of personal reminiscences, her school days in retrospect, gay and entirely youthful, with no heartbreak for the reader until her fervent wish at the end that those happy days could come again. Among these reminiscences is a study of a certain Miss Riegel, a clever woman who gives them lectures in biology "starting with fish and ending with reindeer. Her favourite topic is propagation, which surely must be so because she is an old maid"—satire, pungent and mature, co-dweller in the House Behind with Anne's merry description of her six reprimands for talking incessantly in class, when she pleads that little can be done because her case is hereditary: "My mother, too, is fond of chatting and has handed this weakness down to me"; thus our young extrovert finds a plausible excuse for her fault.[6] In "Dreams of Movie Stardom" she lapses again into the child daydreaming of herself as a movie star—well, she had the looks, the exuberance, and animation, but the world would have lost an author revealing already those infallible signs of genius, including the necessary flair for conveying personality; as where in "My First Article" she brings her friend Peter vividly before us with every touch.

The essay called "Give" strikes a note startlingly up to date and prophetic; since the date of its conception we have all read a hundred essays and leaders, heard a thousand sermons and speeches, on the theme of the true communal spirit of sharing—"Oh, if only the whole world would realise that people were really kindly disposed toward one another, that they are all equal and everything else is just transitory! . . . No one has ever become poor from giving! . . . There is plenty of room for everyone in the world, enough money, riches, and beauty for all to share! God has made enough for everyone. Let us all begin by sharing it fairly."[7]

But more than all the rest of this collection, Anne Frank's fragment of a novel, which she called "Cady's Life," corroborates all one has said about her potential powers. In it she combines a wisdom beyond her years, a sense of character and a feeling for religion, until at the very end a lapse from fiction into the grim reality of the danger to all Jews under Hitler's regime that autumn of 1942, though she still continues to call her heroine "Cady" and Cady's friend "Mary," foreshadows what was shortly to prove the fate of her own family and herself.

"Cady's Life" starts straight into the story without unnecessary preliminaries: Cady had been knocked down and injured by a car, and opened her eyes in hospital—"The first thing she saw was that everything around her was white," and the first thing she felt was a panic that she would be a cripple for life.[8] When she woke again, her parents had come to visit her, and immediately we get an impression that her father means far more to her than her mother, who—the nurse looking after her noticed—"tired the child out with her incessant nervous prattle."[9] After a fortnight, Cady confided in the nursing sister, who was calm and always talked softly, her reactions toward her mother, and here Anne Frank's talent for drawing character emerges clearly: she longs for a mother who, as well as loving her, would truly and sensitively understand how to handle her. She also wonders how her own attitude could be improved, and wishes she could feel true warmth toward her mother so that there could be fullest trust and understanding between them; but instead: "She discusses even the most tender subjects in an ordinary way. She does not understand what is happening inside me, and yet she always says she is interested in youth. She has no idea of patience and softness."[10]

All this is psychologically perceptive to a marked degree; as far as can be surmised, Anne Frank would have developed into a subjective novelist, never objective.

After several weeks Cady's health slowly improves, and for a moment Anne

Frank herself intrudes on fiction: "Her father bought her a diary. Now she often sat up and wrote down her feelings and thoughts."[11]

In three months they sent her to a sanatorium in the country, where she began to learn to walk without support and then to go out alone into the gardens and grounds or into the wood, where she loved to sit and meditate "about the world and its meaning" and "suddenly realised that here in the wood and in the quiet hours in hospital she had discovered something new about herself, she had discovered that she was a human being with her own feelings, thoughts, and views, apart from anyone else. . . . What does a child know of the lives of others, of her girl friends, her family, her teachers, what else did she know of them but the outer side? Had she ever had serious talks with any of them?"[12]

Enter romance and a panacea for loneliness both in one—Hans Donkert, a boy of seventeen on holiday from school, who passed by her in the wood every morning on his way to visit his friends in the neighborhood. For some time they knew each other only by sight, until one day he stopped and introduced himself; after that, he came along earlier and sat and talked with her, though not profoundly [. . .] until on one occasion they looked at each other longer than they really wanted to and he asked her what she was thinking about. She could not at first bring herself to tell him, and then she suddenly said: "Do you also often feel lonely, even if you have friends, lonely inside, I mean?"[13] Hans owned up to it and added that boys confide even less in their friends than do girls and were even more afraid of being laughed at.

Again neither of them spoke for a long time, until: "Do you believe in God, Hans?" "Yes, I do firmly believe in God."[14] And the discussion between them which followed this, although simply phrased, contained the essence of so much that one has read in profound theological works of the true nature of God and how he expresses himself, that one is staggered at its maturity.

Yes, perhaps Cady and Hans were destined by their author, could she have completed the volume, to be en route for a happy marriage in a few years . . . when suddenly, as we noted earlier, Anne Frank was swept away from fiction into stark unbearable reality.

Notes

1. Anne Frank, "Eve's Dream," in *Tales from the House Behind: Fables, Personal Reminiscences, and Short Stories,* trans. Michel Mok and H. H. B. Mosberg (Kingswood, Great Britain: World's Work [1913], 1962), 27, 28.

2. "The Flower Girl," 42.

3. "Fear," 49.

4. "The Wise Old Dwarf," 55.

5. "Blurry the Explorer," 70.

6. "A Lecture in Biology," 91; "A Geometry Lesson," 95.

7. "Give," 130.

8. "Cady's Life," 135.

9. Ibid., 138.

10. Ibid., 140.

11. Ibid., 142.

12. Ibid., 146.

13. Ibid., 150.

14. Ibid., 151.

12

Writing Herself against History: Anne Frank's Self-Portrait as a Young Artist

Rachel Feldhay Brenner

It is necessary . . . to believe that new narrative forms, which we do not yet know how to name, are already being born.
—*Paul Ricoueur,* Time and Narrative

Strictly speaking, the diary of Anne Frank is not a testimony of the Holocaust atrocity. In contrast with ghetto diaries and concentration camp memoirs, Frank's text depicts the anticipation of the Holocaust persecution. It is a story of the victim coping with the inexorable awareness of the Final Solution.

The eventual encounter with the persecutors and the physical destruction itself are not part of Frank's narrative. However, I suggest that Frank's death constitutes a crucially important addendum to her story. The consciousness of her death in Bergen-Belsen confronts us with the reality of the decreed catastrophe and thus highlights the heroic quality of her artistic struggle with the "indescribable" life narrative.

As a rule, autobiographers write their lives in order to understand their motivations and attain an extent of self-understanding. They draw upon their past experiences to illuminate their present situation and to gain a measure of foresight. Frank, whose young age could hardly offer a sustaining perspective of the past, drew support and strength from her aspiration to become an artist. Despite the imminence of death, writing seemed to afford her a sense of future.

Frank treated her desire to become a writer with utmost seriousness. In preparation for the possible publication of *Het Achterhuis* after the war, she started to recopy and to edit her diary. The seriousness about her future vocation is also evident in the frequency of the entries, the range of topics, and the insistence on an accurate portrayal of life in the secret annex. Methodically and meticulously, Frank created a record of a world in the throes of terror, a world which, as she knew very well, was on the brink of collapse.

To persist at creating such a record meant a constant struggle against despair. The fear that dominated the annex was so overwhelming that it often put the diarist in a state of utter desperation. In a moving entry of October 29, 1943, Frank portrays herself as "a songbird whose wings have been clipped and who is hurling himself in utter darkness against the bars of his cage." Depressed, she lies down to sleep, "to make the time pass more quickly, and the *stillness* and the terrible fear, because there is no way of killing time" (my emphasis).

The sense of the end is so palpable that soon after it transforms into a truly apocalyptic vision of destruction. On November 8, 1943, Frank wrote:

> I see the eight of us with our "Secret Annexe" as if we were a little piece of blue heaven, surrounded by heavy black rain clouds. The round, clearly defined spot where we stand is still safe, but the clouds gather more closely about us and the circle which separates us from the approaching danger closes more and more tightly. Now we are so surrounded by danger and darkness that we bump against each other, as we search desperately for a means of escape. We look down below, where people are fighting each other, we look above, where it is quiet and beautiful, and meanwhile we are cut off by the great dark mass, which will not let us go upwards, but which stands before us as an impenetrable wall; it tries to crush us, but cannot do so yet. I can only cry and implore: "Oh, if only the black circle could recede and open the way for us!"

This poetic visualization presents a surprisingly lucid picture of reality. The apocalyptic tenor of the vision calls attention to Frank's lack of self-delusion. The act of writing, therefore, was by no means a panacea. Despite her youth, Frank was capable of articulating a poignant and unsparing assessment of the circumstances.

Frank's imagination and intelligence enabled her to assume a detached "bird's eye view" which she articulated in a striking, poetic language. A remarkable confluence of sensitivity, integrity, and artistic inspiration precluded escape into self-deception and false optimism. Insistence on a faithful and systematic representation of the experience compelled the diarist to relive her fear in the act of writing.

Frank's determination to confront reality in writing raises the question of the rationale for this reimmersion in the terrifying situation. Why would the young victim feel the need to tell about her world coming to its end? What would make her write about a reality in which both recounting and foretelling became meaningless?

To understand the *telos* of Frank's writing we need to remember that the time span that she sets out to describe is the present of immediate, direct menace and dread. It is therefore important, first of all, to comprehend the artistic significance of such a foreshortened perspective.

The mimetic representation of the world at the edge of the apocalypse sub-verts the Aristotelian notion of the mimetic plot as a carefully selected sequence of events. Mimesis, "the medium of imitation," as Aristotle defines it, foregrounds the "unity of plot" and is, therefore, predicated upon the selection of the "prob-able or the necessary" events which center around "one action."[1] The unity of action results from the process of artistic selection out of the "infinitely various . . . incidents in one man's life."[2] The narrative is directed at the audience and, if ef-fective, the cathartic impact of its mimetic construct, especially in the case of a tragic tale, "will thrill with horror and melt to pity" all those who hear the story.[3]

When applied to the life in the annex, the Aristotelian precepts of mimesis highlight the fact that the range of events subject to selection was extremely lim-ited. Needless to say, the expectation to elicit a cathartic sense of horror and pity under the circumstances presented a totally incongruous proposition.

We should mention in passing that the diary's theatrical production did fol-low the Aristotelian precepts of the tragic plot. The staging of the text as a trag-edy ended with a cathartic relief. The dramatic adaptation complied with Aristotle's injunction that "the tragic plot must not be composed of irrational parts," since "the poet should prefer probable impossibilities to improbable pos-sibilities."[4] The dramatized version of the diary defused the "irrationality" of the Holocaust horror. It suggested the probability of a cathartic response to the Holo-caust.

In contrast to its dramatic production, the narrative of the diary focuses on the irrational. The story deals with the unprecedented problematic of the "im-probable possibility" of the Holocaust.

The possibility of the Holocaust signifies that history improbably turned life itself into an artifact. Life became an arbitrarily controlled and extremely lim-ited existence in the shadow of the apocalypse. In the Aristotelian *ars poetica,* the function of art is to reshape and refigure life through conscious selection and compression of [an] infinite number of events. In contrast, the terrible confines of the *univers concentrationnaire* of the Holocaust ineluctably reduced life in the annex to the lifelessness of an absolute lack of choice.

The courage that we detect in Frank's poetic rendition of the fear of death highlights the energizing power of art in the presence of death. The humanistic message in the diary should not be sought in its subject matter but, rather, in its artistic form. In other words, the act of literary representation of the annex pre-sents literary creativity as a life sustaining system.

Indeed, time and again, Frank affirms her writing as a life line which saves her from despair. On March 16, 1944, she confides in Kitty that writing enables her to endure the unbearable situation: "Yes, Kitty, Anne is a crazy child, but I do live in crazy times and under still crazier circumstances. But, still, the brightest spot of all is that at least I can write down my thoughts and feelings, otherwise I would be absolutely stifled!"

Frank shows a full awareness of the role that the diary plays in her life. In the entry of April 4, she reports she has overcome a spell of incapacitating misery and depression. She reasserts herself as a writer who defeats fear through writing: "I can shake off everything if I write; my sorrows disappear, my courage is reborn . . . for I can recapture everything when I write, my thoughts, my ideals and my fantasies."

The entry on April 11, 1944, which describes the terror of a close call that the people in hiding experienced illustrates Frank's perception of art as sustenance and endurance: there was a burglary in the offices below and the investigating police came up the stairs to the camouflaged door leading to the secret annex. The terrified people inside discussed what needed to be destroyed in case they should be discovered. Somebody suggested burning the diary to which Frank responded with an emotional outburst: "This (suggestion) and when the police rattled the cupboard door, were my worst moments. 'Not my diary; if my diary goes, I go with it!'"

The connection she makes between the destruction of the diary and physical destruction reiterates dramatically Frank's view of writing as a life-giving activity. Her behavior illustrates how the ability to abstract, to interpret, and to transform through language signals the vitality of being. To be able to *give voice* to her helplessness liberates her from the stillness and the terrible fear that this very helplessness incurs.

It is therefore important to examine the voice of art in Frank's writing. How does the artist's creative act redeem vitality in the apocalyptic void of paralyzing fear and deepening depression?

To an extent, the answer seems to lie in understanding the time factor implicit in diaristic writing. The diary represents two kinds of time: the period that it records and the actual duration of the recording. I would argue that in the annex situation the time of the diaristic recording counteracts the timelessness of the apocalyptic ending.

Frank's constant preoccupation with her diary infuses the duration of hiding with an ongoing artistic invention. Looking at reality as material for diaristic recording elicits a sense of meaningful continuity. The purpose of recording contravenes the episodic disconnectedness of the reality of destruction.

In her diaristic recording, Frank creates an illusion of a "normal" existence. Further, the mode of her writing *becomes* the signifier of a normally continuing life. By virtue of its calendric recording, the diary reflects a "microscopic" historical continuity which extends into the future and therefore offsets the ahistoricity of the apocalyptic ending.

As an evolving record, Frank's diary becomes the annex's chronicle. It enables the diarist to read "backward" and write "forward," to draw analogies to formerly described events, and to incorporate the past into the present. In the entry of January 2, 1944, for instance, Frank comments disapprovingly on past events which she recalled when '[she] turned over some of the pages of [her] diary." By rereading past entries, Frank can reevaluate her past experiences. The sense of the past enters and affects her present, as she observes: "This diary is of great value to me, because it has become a book of memoirs in many places, but on a good many pages I could certainly put 'past and done with.'"

The accumulation of memories and events enhances the importance of the diary as a life story. The possibility of maintaining a historical record even in the limited time span allows Frank to infuse the stagnant existence in the annex with a meaningful theme worthy of an artistic representation. The rereading and also, let us recall, the rewriting of the diary in preparation for future publication, defer, even if for a short while, the diarist's listless anticipation of the end.

At the point when "the sense of an ending" threatens to invade and when despair is about to take over, the consciousness of life as narrative intervenes, allowing the author to feel, even if only temporarily, in charge of her art and life:

> I have often been downcast but never in despair. I regard our hiding as a dangerous adventure, romantic and interesting at the same time. In my diary I treat all the privations as amusing. . . . My start has been so very full of interest, and that is the sole reason why I have to laugh at the humorous side of the most dangerous moments. . . . I am young and strong and am living a great adventure; I am still in the midst of it and can't grumble the whole day long. . . . I have been given a lot, a happy nature, a great deal of cheerfulness and strength. Why, then, should I be in despair? (May 3, 1944)

The process of gaining control over life through art points to the reflective function of the diary. Frank's autobiographical story is also the story of her growth as an artist. As the entries follow each other, Frank crystallizes and defines the autobiographical purpose of her writing. In the above quote, she sees her writing as an act of self-assertion. Life writing reverts an existence of incapacitating helplessness and despair into a humorous adventure.

Like the foremost Yiddish storyteller Sholom Aleichem, who proscribed tears and prescribed laughter to heal suffering and pain, Frank exercises her authorial prerogative to review the world that surrounds her. She neutralizes her fear by establishing an alternate point of view. In her ongoing struggle with despair, she enlists humor to cope with the desperate situation.

The choice of the humorous perspective is concomitant with the qualities of "cheerfulness and strength" that she constantly strives to develop. The hopeful passages do not support, therefore, the popular notion of Frank's naive faith in the goodness of man. Rather, they disclose the subtext of an immense effort to affirm meaning in the meaningless, hopeless ordeal.

Frank refers to her struggle when she says on April 14, 1944: "everyone must try to be the master of his own moods . . . . My work, my hope, my love, my courage, all these things *keep my head above water* and keep me from complaining" (my emphasis). Significantly, the list of things that sustains her starts with "work," that is, her writing. However tenuous and temporary, the victory over despair signals the vitality of creative imagination.

The ability to ascribe the meaning of a "romantic adventure" to Jewish existence at the time of the Holocaust engenders a sense of control. And the capability of experiencing her "adventure" through the act of writing reinforces the hope to develop the inner discipline to become "the master" of her moods.

The diary as a testimonial directed to a distant reader defines Frank as a witness-victim. In this respect, therefore, "Kitty," the reader-outsider, represents all of us, the postwar readers of Frank's diary. In this respect, the diarist's intention to inform and teach does not differ from the intention of other witnesses-victims of the Holocaust who wished to bequeath their testimony to posterity.

However, the placement of the addressee *in* the text calls attention to the uniqueness of the diary as a Holocaust testimony. As the marker of the epistolary form of the diary, "Kitty" communicates Frank's need for an audience. Writing to a particular, singled-out reader highlights the therapeutic function of the imagined addressee.

In this respect, it is, perhaps, not so much the need to inform posterity, as the urgency to alleviate the specter of despair that motivates Frank's constant dialogue with her imaginary friend. The special friend, a confessant ready to hear, but not to condemn, indicates Frank's ingenuous search for support in art.

The addressee as a *naive* listener highlights further the complexity of this artistic effort. In Kitty, the author creates a mind unaffected by the horror. This intentional creation of a *tabula rasa* receiving consciousness ineluctably affects the manner and the voice in which the narrative unfolds.

The construct of an ignorant addressee incurs the need to devise adequate narrative strategies. The complete unawareness of the addressee regarding the reality of the Holocaust deintensifies the teller's emotional involvement with her tale. The naivete of the addressee compels the writer to innovate, diversify, infuse comic relief—in brief, to seek literary devices to ensure the accessibility of the story.

Let us recall Sholom Aleichem who, as a rule, defuses the tragic tenor of his narrator's tale of woe by invariably incorporating into his story the character of an unimplicated narratee. In a similar way, Frank achieves respite from feelings of despondency and hopelessness by focusing on communication with her remote addressee. To communicate, she must distance herself from misery and despair. She must gain control over her subject matter and see it, even if only for a moment, as "a romantic adventure." The role of the teller that she constructed for herself by devising a naive "Kitty" allows Frank the freedom to exercise her creativity and imagination as a writer.

As a continuing, daily activity, Frank's diaristic writing becomes a source of vitality. In this sense, Frank's testimonial defies the Final Solution. Her creative energy, persistence, and artistic ability to record this world carve an enclave of normalcy in the midst of uncontrollable madness of destruction. As a coherent narrative as well as a dialogue, the diary records and, at the same time, contravenes the terror. The rhetorical strategies in the work indicate an effort to maintain meaningfulness even in the situation of the apocalypse. Thus, against all odds, Frank attempts to create the time span characteristic of an autobiographical self-representation.

Considered as a pledge for the future, the diary offers more than a chronologically unfolding testimonial. It is also a remarkably insightful self-representation of the growing artist.

Beside the factual observations and reports, Frank expresses her expectations, thoughts, and desires. As she sets her goals, she deplores her weaknesses and laments over her disappointments. Above all, she articulates the desire for a spiritual change. Let us keep in mind that Frank's preoccupation with moral self-improvement takes place in the context of increasing certainty of deportation and death.

In the limited time that she has, Frank tries to actualize her artistic and moral potential despite the reality of imminent ending. Tragically, she is aware that under the circumstances neither her ethical nor her artistic actualization can be deferred. Conscious of impending death, she knows that it is in the present that she must actualize herself both as a human being and as an artist. She writes on March 25, 1944: "I want to go on living even after my death! And therefore I am grateful to God for giving me this *gift*, this possibility of *developing myself* and of *writing*, of expressing all that is in me" (my emphasis).

Indeed, the diary presents Frank as a growing and *developing person*. I am using the term *developing person* advisedly. Let us recall that most critics read the diary as a text of a precocious young girl. I, however, concur with John Berryman's notion that Frank's inner struggle to establish a moral *Weltanschauung* transcends the typically adolescent development.

It is true that Anne experiences physical changes and emotional vicissitudes related to her growth into adolescence (menstruation, the discovery of sexuality, defiance of the adult world, mood fluctuations, etc.). Yet, it seems impossible to explain the seriousness and the integrity of her ethical self-examination as characteristic of a thirteen- or fourteen-year-old. Despite her young age, both Frank's self-perception and her perception of others reveal remarkable maturity. As Berryman asserts, "most people do not grow up, in any degree that will correspond to Anne Frank's growing up."

Ironically, the intention to dehumanize Jews by stripping them of their identity, reducing them to nonpersons, and in Frank's particular case, forcing her into hiding, had a countereffect on Frank's process of individuation. As a written and rewritten text, the diary defiantly affirms Frank's dignified self-perception as an individual whose story deserves to be recorded. Even further, her understanding of self-writing as a vehicle of ethical self-development demonstrates Frank's self-assertion against the tyranny of depersonalization.

The need to defy the hatred that enforced the self-image of a hunted, terrified Jew "in chains" (April 11, 1944) engages Frank in a rigorously sustained process of shaping her moral values. In view of Frank's complete awareness of her situation, her uncompromising and unsparing quest for self-knowledge and for moral self-improvement assumes heroic dimensions.

Against the reality of imminent annihilation, Frank proclaims her uniqueness and assumes responsibility to become a whole human being. Her desire to fulfill herself reminds us of the famous Hasidic rabbi Zusya who said: "In the world to come they will not ask me, 'Why were you not Moses?' They will ask me, 'Why were you not Zusya?'" The complex message of the diary lies precisely in Anne's desire to assert herself as an artist in the reality of the Holocaust. The unrealized desire for self-fulfillment haunts the reader as a particularly poignant act of resistance against the tyrannic decree of dehumanization.

Notes

1. Aristotle, "Poetics," in *Criticism: The Major Texts,* ed. Walter Jackson Bate (New York: Harcourt Brace Jovanovich, 1952), 20, 24–25.

2. Ibid., 24.

3. Ibid., 27.

4. Ibid., 36.

13

Death and the Maiden

Harry Mulisch

The recreation of the daily, ordinary texture of an individual life—full of the
mundane, trivial, funny and humdrum goings-on . . . is almost the hardest thing
in biography; and, when achieved, the most triumphant.
—*Richard Holmes,* Footsteps

I must begin by making a confession. In 1957, the American couple Frances
Goodrich and Albert Hackett, who adapted *The Diary of Anne Frank* into a successful play, established the Anne Frank Prize, intended for young writers in the
Netherlands. The prize no longer exists, but I was the first to receive it. And yet
I had not yet read her book at the time. Even more shameful is the admission
that when almost thirty years later I was invited to open an exhibition dedicated
to Anne Frank, at the Akademie der Künste in Berlin, I still had not read the
book. This is partly owing to a professional idiosyncrasy on my part. I only read
what is more or less directly related to what I am writing at the time and is therefore of use to me. Reading is, for me, a part of writing and not an end in itself, as
it is for legitimate readers. But there may be yet another cause for this omission
of mine, namely Anne Frank's place in Dutch literature, which is, actually, non-
existent. Her book has been translated into [more than fifty] languages and . . .
million[s of] copies of it have been sold. If one asks anyone in the world at large
if he knows the name of a Dutch writer the answer will be "Anne Frank." But in
our own literary annuals, any second- or third-rate novelist, wholly unknown
abroad and hardly known at home, receives more notice than Anne Frank.

I am not going to insist that this is a scandal that should be corrected, but I
would like to understand the reason for it. The number of her readers and translations is not significant in itself, of course. There are literary, and especially poetic, masterpieces that are admired by only a few thousand people in the world,
while books that one reads sitting by the swimming pool also sell in the millions

but are not, and rightly so, remembered at all. But Anne Frank's book is not one of these; on the contrary, I would say. It is read throughout the world; it is not trivial, but is nevertheless not considered to be literature. Why is this? Could it be that a third category exists?

It has, first of all, something to do with reality, and with death. We know that everything we read in her book is true, and at the same time we are continuously aware of the fact that the writer will seal the written word with her death. The total isolation of the secret annex of which the windows and curtains are never allowed to be opened is reminiscent of a stage on which the relationships between the eight characters keep growing with increasing intensity, the girl being both one of the actors and the author. In this high-pressure atmosphere, her own development too accelerates; she grows from girl into woman and one witnesses her increasing astuteness in her analysis of self as well as others; her voice becomes purer, her forebodings of the approaching end become more ominously defined. In Sartre's *No Exit* the action goes on indefinitely because everyone is already dead, but here we know that the murderers will be arriving three days after her last sentence. This last sentence is probably the longest in the book, as if she were unable to part from it:

> Oh, I would like to listen, but it doesn't work; if I'm quiet and serious, everyone thinks it's a new comedy and then I have to get out of it by turning it into a joke, not to mention my own family, who are sure to think I'm ill, make me swallow pills for headaches and nerves, feel my neck and my head to see whether I'm running a temperature, ask if I'm constipated and criticize me for being in a bad mood. I can't keep that up: if I'm watched to that extent that I start by getting snappy, then unhappy, and finally I twist my heart around again, so that the bad is on the outside and the good is on the inside and keep on trying to find a way of becoming what I would so like to be, and what I could be, if . . . there weren't any other people living in the world.

From a purely technical point of view the theatrical finality is, of course, ideal for a writer of diaries: the classical unities of place and action are here dictated by circumstance. And yet this too is still in the realm of truth and reality, as is the final catastrophe, which is never shown but always pending. But the aim of literature is not truth about the world. The truth always implies a lack of freedom: things are as they are. Yet in literature things also are what they are not.

Take one of the greatest masterpieces of all time: *Don Quixote.* There is not a word of truth in the whole book. The man didn't even exist. This fictional character has, furthermore, been created by his own reading of chivalrous novels, and he wants to make what he has read come true in his own life. But the outcome of this triple fiction is a new kind of truth: not the truth of the world, but the truth of the reader. This is what makes it literature. Literature does not teach us about life in general, but about ourselves. Don Quixote is not out there, in the world, but here: I am Don Quixote. I am Hamlet. I am Anna Karenina.

Am I also Anne Frank? No, I am not. Her book, which I have since read, affected me for several days with a devastating emotion that even made me sob at times, mixed with a strong dose of murderous hate. But this has to do with reality, not with art. She has remained precisely one murdered girl who longed so much to live and become a writer. That is what makes her book so effective. If she were still alive she would now be my colleague and two years my junior. She would then undoubtedly have written a novel about her years in hiding and used her diary as raw material but these diaries would then have remained unpublished whereas the novel would have had only a tiny fraction of their power. In short, we would then not have gathered in Berlin where the murders were once planned.

Has she left us then no more than a human document? Was she then no more than a kind of intelligent journalist, recording her own experience and thoughts? This too is not quite the case either. A journalist gives a truthful account of something that has happened, whereas in literature the actual happening takes place during the act of writing, and for the reader during the act of reading. As it is not for the journalist, writing is a *necessity* to the writer. And this literary aspect of the diary (the actual experience of writing and reading) derives from the circumstance that it is not simply a diary. She abandons the vague, fragmentary, suspended character intrinsic to diary writing after the first week and changes it into imaginary letters to "Kitty." This friend Kitty, she says, is first of all her own diary. But of course this person she addresses has, inversely, an influence on the writing, which would have been quite different if the person addressed had been called Magdalena or Frederik. We too describe events of some complexity differently if addressing a girlfriend or a boyfriend. The event in itself, *an sich* as I might say in German, does not exist at all; yet what comes closest to it is the journalistic impersonality of the diary.

Just as Anne Frank immediately came to personify millions of others, so the Kitty she addresses too has taken on the identity of millions. The artistic device of the letter, the Aristotelian unities inherent in the situation, and the very real catastrophe that occurs after the writing of the final sentence, all contribute to the devastating effect of the book. The work by this child is not simply *not* a work of art, but in a certain sense it is a work of art made by life itself: it is a found object. It was after all literally found among the debris on the floor after the eight characters departed. Her father had put the notebooks in his briefcase to take them along on their final voyage, but an employee of the *Grüne Polizei* held the briefcase upside down to steal the money and jewels it contained. If his daughter noticed this, she might have left the notebooks there on purpose.

Would it be embarrassing if I too came to the conclusion that the diary does not really belong in a literary category? I think the opposite is true, for who would profit the most from classifying this book as belles-lettres, so situating it in a world of free choice? The neo-Nazis. For that is, after all, what they have been claiming all along: that Anne Frank is a literary creation, just like Anna Karenina or Emma Bovary, but a literary creation that falsely passes for the truth. According to them, Anne Frank is just as fictitious as her Kitty; just another Jewish contribution to the "Auschwitz Lie."

The first time that the authenticity of the diary was disputed was in 1957, in Norway; in 1959 the first lawsuit took place in Frankfurt, the city of Anne Frank's birth, and this sort of thing is still going on in a great many countries. The anti-fascist effect of this book is being disputed with the most ridiculous arguments and circumlocutions in all manner of ways by rightist radicals. All those accusations and lawsuits . . . just imagine their effect on the father who *saw* his murdered daughter writing night after night in her notebooks. In 1980, when the Federal Bureau of Criminal Investigation in Wiesbaden discovered that corrections had been made with a ball point pen—an instrument that was not available in Europe until after the war—the government Institute for War Documentation in Holland decided to commission a thoroughly scientific analysis of the manuscripts. [. . .]

I was of course very interested in the results of all this before coming to Berlin. I hadn't forgotten Hitler's diaries, or our own Van Meegeren.* Imagine if we had indeed had a case of fraud here, no matter how slim the chance; it would have been a political disaster. It was therefore imperative that I know the results. I tried to get access to the report, but it was kept secret from me, which of course made me suspicious. One learns to tread carefully in life. I had illegal access to a secret document once before. It was in 1961 in Jerusalem; ironically it was the memoirs of Adolf Eichmann, written at the request of the Israeli police—Adolf Eichmann, the very man who in 1944 organized the last transport of Dutch Jews to Auschwitz, Anne Frank being one of them.

I regret to have to assure the Nazis that the book is authentic. The notorious ball point pen was not used in the text itself but only on two separate pieces of paper concerning the editing of the book. In the text there are only some corrections of mistakes in grammar and spelling all in Otto Frank's handwriting. (He also omitted some brief passages having to do with sexual matters and with Anne Frank's dislike of her mother, and [most of] these appear in the [critical] edition.) One mustn't forget that Anneliese Frank came to Holland when she was four and that her first language was, therefore, German, and that all around her in the secret

*Editors' note: Hans van Meegeren (1898–1947) was a notoriously skillful forger.

annex a kind of Germanic Dutch language was being spoken. This was why, instead of the Dutch sentence structure, "I have him learned to know," she wrote, "I have him to know learned," which comes from the German, *Ich habe ihn kennengelernt.*" This was corrected by her father after the war. Otto Frank, himself of German origin, did not catch several of these Germanisms. The report might have mentioned that the very fact of these Germanic expressions was a proof of authenticity.

And so a powerful weapon against fascism has, fortunately, been preserved. I try to envision Kitty, those notebooks, scribbled at a rickety table by a girl about to become a woman and looking forward to life, but forced to hide because she is doomed to be murdered and will be—in that hopeless, menacing stillness of the war. Then suddenly those same notebooks are in a laboratory where police experts in white lab coats test samples of ink and paper, because those who admire the murderers insist that none of this was authentic. And why shouldn't it be? It is not just because of the murders they committed that the murderers are admired by them? No neo-Nazi really questions whether it all happened. But as a neo-Nazi, or perhaps I should say antiquo-Nazi, one must act in bad faith; if any one of that group should really doubt the mass murders, he would immediately be expelled from their midst for desecration of their idols.

The fact that it happened is the most persuasive deterrent for its ever happening again, just as the atom bombs that fell on Hiroshima and Nagasaki have probably prevented World War III until now. We must continue to speak of the deaths of those millions of innocents till the end of time, not only to commemorate them but to prevent the death of any further innocents. There is no better instrument for this than Auschwitz. And how about all those who keep complaining that it is time to stop talking about that war, because it happened forty years ago? *They* are the ones to keep an eye on. For first of all, that war did not happen all of forty years ago but *only* forty years ago. And besides, there was hardly any connection between the liquidation of the Jews and the war. World War II could have managed perfectly well without the Jewish Holocaust. The Holocaust was not an act of war, but something of a much darker nature—a slaughter that was made possible by the chaotic circumstances of war but was not necessarily a part of it. Except in Russia, people in western Europe have mostly stopped talking about the war. Who here still mentions the invasion or the Battle of the Bulge? No, we speak about Auschwitz and Treblinka and Maidanek, not battlefields but places for which there are no other names than Auschwitz, Treblinka, and Maidanek. We can learn nothing about Auschwitz by calling it hell, but should one want to find out about hell, then Auschwitz is the place to study.

So, having finally read *The Diary of a Young Girl,* I also went to visit the house on the Prinsengracht where she was in hiding. Though I live in Amsterdam I had never been there before. It was a chilly Thursday afternoon out of season, but already from a distance I could tell the address because dozens of young people from all over the world, the United States, Japan, and also Germany were, with almost tangible youthful solidarity, photographing the gable of this spot where it had actually happened, not in literature but in reality. And yet, in a third sense the diary is literature—at least in the same sense as the work of someone like Solzhenitsyn is. Inside, on the steep staircase, in the narrow rooms where everything took place, it was as crowded as in a warehouse. Through a window I could see the back of the house where, at a mere fifty feet away, Descartes for several years found a safe refuge. No one else was aware of this and there were no tourists visiting that spot.

In the girl's room hung pictures of film stars, but also reproductions of Leonardo da Vinci, as well as one of Heinz Rühmann—a star of the German UFA, a protégé of Goebbels. Anne was after all of German origin. But my own Jewish mother's family also came from Frankfurt, and they too died in the gas chambers—not my mother herself, but her mother and her mother's mother, aged eighty-five.

The most unbearable detail in that hiding place is a series of horizontal pencil marks on the wallpaper, in a corner, covered with glass, showing how much Anne Frank and her sister grew during those two years. My own great-grandmother in the meantime kept shrinking.

What, after all, was the meaning of all this? The more I find out, the less I understand it.

Translated from the Dutch by Claire Nicholas White.

14

Anne Frank's Reading:
A Retrospective

Sylvia P. Iskander

I'm crazy about reading and books.
—*April 6, 1944*

On July 11, 1943, almost a year to the day after the family entered their hiding place in the unused laboratory and storehouse of Mr. Frank's office, Anne writes to Kitty, her fictional diary correspondent: "Ordinary people don't know how much books can mean to someone who's cooped up. Our only diversions are reading, studying, and listening to the radio." Reading relieved the long hours of silence imposed on the Franks, the [Van Pelses], and [Fritz Pfeffer] for fear of being overheard by employees carrying on their daily business in the front of the house on the Prinsengracht Canal. Since the group frequently read the same books, they could discuss them in the evenings and late afternoons when, according to Anne on November 28, 1942, they "while away the time with all kinds of crazy activities: telling riddles, doing calisthenics in the dark, speaking English or French, reviewing books." Anne often discusses books with sixteen-year-old Peter [Van Pels] in their solitary talks in the attic room, and Otto Frank frequently reads aloud to the children from Dickens (August 5, 1943, August 23, 1943, March 4, 1944) and from plays by Goethe and Schiller, such as *Don Carlos* (October 29, 1942). Mr. Frank's emphasis on books is attested to by his request that Anne and her sister, Margot, keep a card file of titles and authors of books which they read (February 27, 1943). Anne even gives a daily schedule including times for reading: 8:30–9:30 A.M., 2:30–3:45 P.M., and 7:30–8:30 P.M. (March 20, 1944, in the *a* version only).

Anne compares on July 11, 1943, the residents of the secret annex to little children receiving a present when new books arrive on Saturdays, brought by friends and employees of Mr. Frank's firm—Mr. Kleiman, Mr. Kugler, Bep Voskuijl, and Miep and Jan Gies for whom Anne invented the pseudonyms of Mr. Koophuis,

Mr. Kraler, Elli Vossen, and Miep and Henk Van Santen. Some books are gifts; others are loaned from the library or from friends. Occasionally, a library due date challenges Anne to complete a book (May 11, 1944). Once, August 10, 1943, a forbidden book incites Anne's criticism of [Pfeffer] for "put[ting] us in danger for the umpteenth time" because an SS vehicle knocked Miep down while carrying a book for him, "an anti-Mussolini tirade." Under Mr. Frank's editing (in the *c* version [. . .]), however, the book is referred to as one that "abuses Mussolini and Hitler." In the *b* version [. . .] only Mussolini is mentioned. One can hardly fault Mr. Frank for adding Hitler's name after the war.

Annuals, magazines, and newspapers are welcome gifts. On July 11, 1942, Mr. Kleiman presents Anne with the *Young People's Annual,* containing fairy tales, stories, and poems by such writers as Hans Christian Andersen, the Brothers Grimm, Jack London, Jules Verne, and H. G. Wells (see the appendix for the complete reference to the *Young People's Annual,* as well as to all other works mentioned in the diary). Anne loves to read *Cinema and Theater,* a movie magazine which Mr. Kugler delivers on Mondays, enabling her to keep current with the latest films and stars (January 28, 1944). The collection of cutout photographs hanging on the walls of her small room, measuring approximately seven feet by sixteen feet, reflects her interest in such famous people as Deanna Durbin, Robert Stack, Rudy Vallee, Norma Shearer, Greta Garbo, Ray Milland, Ginger Rogers, and even skating great Sonja Henie. Other visitors to the hiding place, such as Mr. Kleiman and Jan, bring newspapers and books which they discuss with the young people (e.g., January 28, 1944). Anne even dreams about a book, one of drawings by Mary Bos (January 6, 1944), one of Anne's eight friends pictured with her in the oft-published photograph taken on her birthday.

One article Anne discusses just with Kitty, not visitors, however, is about blushing by Sis Heyster, who authored several books on child and adolescent psychology. Anne believes the article might have been addressed to her personally, for its discussion of pubescent girls' feelings coincides with her experiences (January 5, 1944). Her strong emotions about certain books elicit the comment of November 8, 1943, "If I'm engrossed in a book, I have to rearrange my thoughts before I can mingle with other people, because otherwise they might think I was strange." Her frequent identification with books she reads can have negative results as well. For example, her dislike of math makes her algebra her most loathed book; when a vase breaks, spilling water over her books and papers on May 20, 1944, she is disappointed that the algebra book is not ruined and threatens its destruction: "The next time I'm in a wicked mood, I'm going to tear the darned thing to pieces!"

In addition to algebra, Anne studies under Otto Frank's tutelage languages, history, science, religion, art, and geography. She frequently refers to Koenen, author of many Dutch dictionaries, whose name became synonymous with the dictionary. Relating her studies for one day, April 27, 1944, she states:

First, I translated a passage on Nelson's last battle from Dutch into English. Then, I read more about the Northern War (1700–21) involving Peter the Great, Charles XII, Augustus the Strong, Stanislaus Leczinsky, Mazeppa, Von Görz, Brandenburg, Western Pomerania, Eastern Pomerania, and Denmark, plus the usual dates. Next I wound up in Brazil, where I read about Bahia tobacco, the abundance of coffee, the one and a half million inhabitants of Rio de Janeiro, Pernambuco and São Paulo and, last but not least, the Amazon River. Then about Negroes, mulattos, mestizos, whites, the illiteracy rate—over 50 percent—and malaria. Since I had some time left, I glanced through a genealogical chart: John the Old, William Louis, Ernest Casimir I, Henry Casimir I, right up to little Margriet Franciska (born in 1943 in Ottawa).

Twelve o'clock: I resumed my studies in the attic, reading about deans, priests, ministers, popes and . . . whew, it was one o'clock.

At two, the poor child (ho hum) was back at work. Old World and New World monkeys were next. Kitty, tell me quickly how many how many toes does a hippopotamus have?

Then came the Bible, Noah's Ark, Shem, Ham and Japheth. After that, Charles V. Then with Peter, Thackeray's book about the colonel, in English. A French test, and then a comparison between the Mississippi and the Missouri!

Under this program of study, Anne advanced rapidly, yet the Franks maintain that Margot is the real student of the family.

In conjunction with her study of French and English, Anne keeps a notebook for foreign words and reads in French Alphonse Daudet's delightful *La Belle Nivernaise: Histoire d'un view bateau et son équipage* (October 3 and 16, 1942) and in English Oscar Wilde's four-act comedy *An Ideal Husband* (June 30, 1944), as well as the book by Thackeray mentioned above, which perhaps may be *The History of Henry Esmond, Esq.: A Colonel in the Service of Her Majesty Queen Anne.*

Clearly Anne learns much history, music, and science from reading biographies, such as *Emperor Charles V,* which took Professor Karl Brandi forty years to write (April 27, 1944); *Maria Theresa* by Karl Tschuppik (June 13, 1944), who also wrote biographies on Franz Joseph and Elizabeth of Austria; *Hungarian Rhapsody,* the life of Franz Liszt (June 9, 1944) by Zsolt Harsányi, who authored as well a biography of Galileo Galilei (May 11, 1944); and perhaps Knut Hagberg's *Carl Linnaeus,* a book Mr. Frank received for his birthday on May 12, 1944, from Mr. Kleiman, which Anne may not have read. She does read contemporary history, however, such as *Palestine on the Eve* (May 11, 1944), and her strong interest in the genealogy of many royal families evokes the reference to genealogy on April 6, 1944, as her number two hobby (number one being writing); this interest, furthered by her reading in biography and history, is attested to by her copying the long genealogical tables found in *Emperor Charles V* (May 11, 1944) and by her posting on her bedroom wall pictures of the youthful Princesses Elizabeth and Margaret Rose. She even states her wish that Margaret might marry Prince Baudouin of Belgium (April 21, 1944).

Another of Anne's interests, religion, apparently increases with time. On October 29, 1942, Mrs. Frank gives her prayer book in German to Anne to read, but the prayers do not have much meaning for Anne. A year later on November 3, 1943, her father requests a copy of a children's Bible from Mr. Kleiman so that she can learn about the New Testament. When Margot asks if Anne will receive the book for Hanukkah, Mr. Frank suggests St. Nicholas's Day as more appropriate. Although Anne clearly recognizes her Jewish heritage and daily confronts the problems of being Jewish in Hitler's reign of terror, she also posts on her wall a picture of Jesus from Michelangelo's famous *Pietà*.

Her fondness for art, perhaps accounting for the *Pietà* picture and a copy of Rembrandt's *Portrait of an Old Man* on her wall, is strengthened by the gift of Anton Springer's five-volume *History of Art* for Anne's fifteenth birthday (June 13, 1944). In fact, books are some of her favorite birthday gifts.

Although Anne receives Hildebrand's *Camera Obscura* for her thirteenth birthday, she trades it and another book for the first volume of Joseph Cohen's vividly illustrated *Tales and Legends of the Netherlands;* she has also just received volume two. She trades *Camera Obscura* because Margot already has a copy, but Anne never says if she read it. She intends to use her own money to purchase *The Myths of Greece and Rome* by H. A. Guerber, who collected myths about the Norsemen and the Middle Ages as well. Anne's interest in mythology, hobby number four and not a part of her regular program of study, is confirmed by a picture of an unidentified Greek god in her room and sparked by Guerber's book, which she never purchases, but ultimately receives on her fourteenth birthday (June 13, 1943).

The Franks obviously oversee their children's reading, occasionally restricting it. On September 2, 1942, Anne says, "Margot and Peter are allowed to read nearly all the books Mr. Kleiman lends us," but they are forbidden to read a certain book (unnamed) about women. Peter's quite normal curiosity urges him to disobey and continue reading the book until he is caught by his parents and punished. Margot is allowed to read one book, forbidden to Anne because of her younger age (September 21, 1942): *Heeren, knechten en vrouwen,* or *Gentlemen, Servants, and Women,* but about a month later on October 18, 1942, Anne says, "I am allowed to read that as well now, great!" In this first book of a trilogy about a *burgemeester,* or mayor of Amsterdam, and his family, the mayor considers betraying his country's alliance with England by assisting the French in sending arms to the American colonies in their fight for independence. Whether the issues of patriotism, betrayal, or sex, or all of them made the Franks temporarily censor the book for their thirteen year old is impossible to say. To the Franks' credit, however, is the fact that a year and a half later on March 17, 1944, Anne reveals that although all books she reads have to be approved, her parents are "not at all strict about that and let me read nearly everything."

Three other books mentioned in the diary (May 13, 1944) not expressly forbidden to Anne, but which she may not have read, are Arend Tael's *Little Martin,* a birthday gift to [Pfeffer] from Kugler; a nature book (title and author not stated), a gift to Otto Frank from Kugler; and Gerhard Werkman's *Amsterdam by the Water,* a book containing numerous photographs of the waterways of Amsterdam, some depicting such sports activities as swimming, boating, and fishing.

Other adult fiction which Anne reads are John Galsworthy's *The Forsyte Saga* (March 15, 1944), Jo van Ammers-Küller's *The Rebels,* a "first-class" book about a family with fourteen children (October 20, 1942), and Paul de Kruif's *The Fight for Life,* which discusses such topics as women's roles and struggles, including those in giving birth (June 15, 1944). Eric Lowe's *Cloudless Morn,* the first in a trilogy entitled *The History of Robin Stuart,* is a book everyone in the annex enjoys (January 12, 1944) and Mrs. Frank particularly likes because of its presentation of the problems of youth; Ina Boudier-Bakker's *The Knock at the Door,* a story of four generations from 1860 to 1920, includes philosophical ideas prevalent at the time. Anne's mixed emotions about the latter are reflected in her comments of March 12, 1943, when she first says, "I can't tear myself away from the book," and then reveals that "this family saga is extremely well-written, but the parts dealing with war, writers and the emancipation of women aren't very good. To be honest, these subjects don't interest me much."

Contrasting with the textbooks and adult works are those which might be classified as young-adult fiction: Niklaus Bolt's *Daisy's Mountain Holiday,* described by Anne as "terrific" when she received it for her thirteenth birthday; Theo Thijssen's *Kees de Jongen* [Kees the Boy], which she requests from Mr. Kleiman on September 22, 1942, but never records if she received or read it; Nico van Suchtelen's *Eva's Youth,* a romantic story about the youth of a small girl Eva, whose monthly period is discussed and which is perhaps the source of Anne's forthright discussion of hers (October 3 and 29, 1942); Helene Haluschka's *What Do You Think of the Modern Young Girl?* a library book criticizing the youth of the time and evoking one of Anne's most insightful discussions about herself, her relationship with her parents and with Peter [Van Pels], and finally her belief in the goodness of people and her hope for peace and tranquility (July 15, 1944); and last, Marianne Philips's *Henry from across the Street,* a book [Pfeffer] likes enough to recommend, but then criticizes Anne's dislike of it by complaining (July 29, 1943) that she cannot "understand the psychology of a man." This book and others (e.g., see the November 7, 1942, entry) ostensibly appear to be the source of arguments, but in reality that source is the inevitable tension resulting from such differing personality types in extremely close quarters over an extended period of time.

No one argued, however, with Anne about her favorite author, Cissy van Marxveldt, a prolific writer who composed in Anne's lifetime four of the five books in the Joop ter Heul series, still popular in Holland. The series about a young girl growing to maturity with a most unusual name for a female made Anne "enthusiastic" when she read it in September and October of 1942, and she claims that she enjoyed "very much" all of van Marxveldt's works, having read *Een Zomerzotheid* [The Zaniest Summer] four times. She did not like *De Stormers* [The Storm Family] as well as the Joop series, although she found it "amusing." Anne describes van Marxveldt as "terrific" and also as one whom she will let her own children read one day. The fun-loving Joop, who corresponds with her friend Net until her father limits her letter writing and she turns to keeping a diary, also has a friend named Kitty, perhaps Anne's inspiration for her imaginary correspondent. Anne also refers to another van Marxveldt book, *The Arcadia*, about "a voyage to Spitsbergen" that she receives from Mr. Kleiman on October 18, 1942.

In fact, October 1942 is a busy month for Anne in regard to reading. On the tenth, Mr. Kleiman gives her two of his children's books: *Else's Jobs* and *Riek the Scamp*, and on the eighteenth *The Purge*, all books that she does not comment on. Two days later on October 20, 1942, Anne joins Peter and Margot to read Gulbranssen's *The Woods Are Singing for All Eternity*, which she characterizes as "a beautiful book, but very unusual." Also Mr. Frank encourages Anne to read the works of German writers such as Frederick Hebbel and the plays of Theodor Körner, such as *Hedwig, The Cousin from Bremen, The Governess, The Green Domino,* etc. Anne considers Körner "a fine writer." During the same week, Kugler also brings twelve *Panoramas* for the group to read (October 26, 1942).

Anne reads stories and articles in addition to books. She refers to Brer Rabbit from Uncle Remus (January 24, 1944), the Grimms (March 16, 1944), and even Popeye (May 8, 1944). Besides her beloved *Cinema and Theater* magazine (January 22, 27, and 28, 1944), she names several others: *Libelle,* copies of which the group receives one Christmas (December 22, 1943); *Rijk der Vrouw* [Woman's Realm]; *Haagse Post* [Hauge Post]; *Das Reich;* and *Prinsen* [Princess], the latter one she hopes might publish one of her fairy stories under a pseudonym (April 21, 1944).

These then are most of the books, plays, articles, and magazines specifically named in the diary. The importance of reading cannot be overstated for the role it played in the education as well as the recreation of Anne and the others. Mr. Frank and the helpers should be credited not only with a most appropriate selection of gifts, but Mr. Frank should also be praised for encouraging his daughters to read, discuss, and think critically. Surprisingly, almost all the books they read were at the time quite recent publications. Authored by writers from Germany, England, France, Sweden, Norway, Australia, Hungary, Switzerland, as well as the Netherlands, they represent a wide diversity and a broad spectrum and reflect Anne's reading in Dutch, German, French, and English. Perhaps they contributed to her tolerance for others and her hope for the future in the midst of undeniable fear and horror, for Anne wished to publish her diary to achieve her desire for peace, as well as her longing for fame as a writer.

The untimely death of Anne Frank from typhus at Bergen-Belsen concentration camp just two months prior to the end of the war adds a poignancy to the diary, whose universality is confirmed by the sale of [. . .] million[s of] copies and by its translation into more than fifty languages. Exhibitions, plays, films, even art work attest to the success of this youthful writer, who certainly has achieved her desire for fame, although not yet her desire for peace in the world.

Appendix: Books Mentioned in the Diary

*Ammers-Küller, Jo van. *Heeren, knechten, en vrouwen* [Gentlemen, Servants, and Women]. Amsterdam: J. M. Meulenhoff, 1934–35. (Referred to by Anne as *Heeren, vrouwen, en knechten*. Later *Heeren* becomes vol. 1 of *The Tavelincks: The History of Amsterdam's Governing Families in the Stressful Years 1778 to 1813*. Amsterdam: J. M. Meulenhoff, 1942.)

———. *De opstandigen: Een familie-roman in drie boeken* [The Rebels: A Family Novel in Three Books]. Amsterdam: J. M. Meulenhoff, 1932.

Bible. (Also Mr. Frank requests a children's Bible for Anne to study the New Testament.)

Het boek voor de jeugd [Young People's Annual]. Comp. C. Bruyn, A. Pleysier, A. Scheffer, Th. J. Thijssen, and P. Schuhmacher. Intro. by R. Casimir. Amsterdam: Amsterdam Book and Newspaper, 1938.

Bolt, Niklaus. *Daisy's bergvacantie* [Daisy's Mountain Holiday or Daisy Goes to the Mountains]. Trans. Frida Brinkman based on the Swiss *Daisy auf der Gemmernalp*. Zeist: J. Ploegsma, 1940.

Bosloper-Harting, Heleen [pseud. Elisabeth van Beymerwerdt]. *Else's baantjes* [Else's Jobs]. Zutphen: W. J. Thieme, 1935.

Boudier-Bakker, Ina. *De klop op de deur* [The Knock at the Door]. Amsterdam: P. N. van Kempen and Zoon, 1930.

Brandi, Karl. *Keizer Karel V: Vorming en lot van een persoonlijkheid en van een wereldrijk* [Emperor Charles V: Formation and Destiny of a Personality and of a World Empire]. Trans. from the German *Kaiser Karl V: Werden und Schicksal einer Persönlichkeit und eines Weltreiches* under the supervision of and with a foreword by N. B. Tenahaeff. Amsterdam: H. Meulenhoff, 1943–45.

Cohen, Joseph. *Nederlandsche sagen en legenden* [Tales and Legends of the Netherlands]. With 32 illus. Zutphen: W. J. Thieme, 1922.

Daudet, Alphonse. *La Belle Nivernaise: Histoire d'un vieux bateau et son équipage* [La Belle Nivernaise: The Story of an Old Boat and Its Crew]. Ed. W. Bartels. 16th-18th eds. Groningen: J. B. Wolters, 1936–40.

Faragó, László. *Palestina op de tweesprong* [Palestine at the Crossroads]. Trans. E. Straat from the English *Palestine on the Eve*. Amsterdam: Nederlandsche Keurboekerij, 1937.

Galsworthy, John. *De Forsyte sage* [The Forsyte Saga]. Rev. and ed. for Holland by R. H. G. Nahuys. Utrecht: A. W. Bruna and Zoon, 1934.

Guerber, H[elene] A[deline]. *De mythen van Griekenland en Rome* [The Myths of Greece and Rome]. Ed. B. C. Goudsmit. Zutphen: W. J. Thieme, 1934.

Gulbranssen, Trygve. *En eeuwig zingen de bosschen* [The Woods Are Singing for All Eternity: The Lineage of the Björndal Family]. Trans. Annie Posthumus from the Norwegian *Og bakom synger Skogene*. Illus. by Anton Pieck. 's-Gravenhage: Zuid-Holl. U. M., 1936–39.

**Hagberg, Knut. *Carl Linnaeus, de bloemenkonig* [Carl Linnaeus, the King of Flowers]. Trans. Marie Vos from the Swedish *Carl Linnaeus*. Amsterdam: A. J. G. Strengholt, 1944.

Haluschka, Helene. *Hoe vindt u het moderne jonge meisje?* [What Do You Think of the Modern Young Girl?]. Trans. Annie Salomons from the German *Was sagst du zu unsrem Evchen?* Cover and illus. Rudolf Wirth. Heemstede: De Toorts, 1937.

Harsányi, Zsolt. *Een hemelbestormer: De roman van Galilei's levee* [The Star-Gazer: The Story of Galilei's Life]. Trans. A. M. de Jong from the Hungarian *Mégis mozog a föld*. Amsterdam: A. J. G. Strengholt, 1941. (Anne refers on May 11, 1944, to a two-part edition, the first part having 320 pages; the above edition contains 600 pages.)

———. *Honguarsche rhapsodie* [Hungarian Rhapsody]. Trans. Frans Schneiders from the Hungarian *Magyar Rapszodia*. 3 vols. Leiden: A. W. Sijthoff, 1941.

**Hildebrand [pseud. Nicolaas Beets]. *Camera obscura*. Haarlem: De Erven F. Bohn, 1942. (Several printings including a school edition were available prior to World War II.)

Koenen, [Matthijs Jacobus]. *Verklarend zakwoordenboekje der Nederlandse* [Pocket Dictionary of the Dutch Language]. 9th-10th eds. Groningen: J. B. Wolters, 1942–43. (Anne may have used any of Koenen's many Dutch dictionaries.)

Körner, Theodor. *De Neef uit Bremen* [The Cousin from Bremen]. Trans. M. van Staveren from the German. N.p.: n.p., 1924. (I was unable to locate other plays by Körner.)

Kruif, Paul de. *Strijders voor het leven* [The Fight for Life or Men against Death]. Trans. J. H. Pauls from the English. Amsterdam: Van Holkema and Warendorf, 1938.

Lowe, Eric. *Ochtend zonder wolken* [Cloudless Morn]. Vol. 1 of *De geschiedenis van Robin Stuart* [The History of Robin Stuart]. Trans. S. Vestdijk from the English. Cultuur Serie. The Hague: Zuid-Holl, 1940.

Marxveldt, Cissy van [pseud. Setske van Beek-de Haan]. *De Arcadia*. Amersfoort: Valkhoff, n.d.

———. *Der H. B. S. tijd van Joop ter Heul* [The High School Years of Joop ter Heul]. Amersfoort: Valkhoff, 1919.

————. *Joop van Dil-ter Heul* [Joop of Dil-ter Heul]. Amersfoort: Valkhoff, 1923.

————. *Joop en haar jongen* [Joop and Her Son]. Amersfoort: Valkhoff, 1925.

————. *Joop ter Heuls problemen* [Joop ter Heul's Problems]. Amersfoort: Valkhoff, 1921.

————. *De Stormers* [The Storm Family or The Assault]. Amersfoort: Valkhoff, 1925.

————. *Een Zomerzotheid* [The Zaniest Summer]. Amersfoort: Valkhoff, 1927.

Philips, Marianne. *Henri van den overkant* [Henry from across the Street or Henry from the Other Side]. Bussum: C. A. J. van Dishoeck, 1936.

Springer, Anton Heinric. *Geschiedenis der beeledende kunst* [History of Art]. (Author also cited as Sprenger.) Ed. A. W. Weissman. 4 vols. Leiden: A. W. Sijthoff, 1896–98. (Anne says she received a five-volume version, perhaps the German *Handbuch der Kunstgeschicht.* 5 vols. Leipzig: E. A. Seaman, 1898–1906.)

Suchtelen, Nico[laas Johannes] van. *Eva's Jeugd* [Eva's Youth]. Serie Nieuwe romans. Amsterdam: Maatschappij voor goede en goedkoope lectuur, 1925.

**Tael, Arend. *Martijntje* [Little Martin]. Amsterdam: Amsterdam Boeken Courantmij, 1941.

**Thijssen, Theo J. *Kees de jongen en Het grijze kind* [Kees the Boy and the Gray-Headed Child]. Amsterdam: De Arbeider spers, 1939.

Tschuppik, Karl. *Maria Theresia: Biographie.* Amsterdam: Allert de Lange, 1934.

**Werkman, Gerhard. *Amsterdam Stad te water* [Amsterdam by the Water or The Canals of Amsterdam]. Illus. Jan Reinders. Photographs J. Berkhout. Bussum: F. G. Kroonder, 1944.

Wilde, Oscar. *An Ideal Husband: A Play.* Explanatory notes by D. H. Meyer. 5th ed. Stories and Sketches, no. 13. Zwolle: W. E. J. Tjeenk Willink, 1926. (Later editions, which Anne may have read, 6th-8th, rev. W. van Maanen. Zwolle: W. E. J. Tjeenk Willink, 1932, 1938, 1944.)

*Book expressly forbidden for Anne to read.

*Book Anne may not have read.

Incomplete References to Authors/Works Mentioned in the Diary

Book about women that Peter read when forbidden to do so (September 2, 1942).

Riek de Kwajongen [Riek the Scamp] (October 10, 1942)

De Louteringskuur [The Purge] (October 18, 1942)

Books by Hebbel [Friedrich] (October 18, 1942)

Panoramas (October 26, 1942)

Prayerbook in German belonging to Mrs. Frank (October 29, 1942)

Plays of Goethe and Schiller, including *Don Carlos* (October 29, 1942)

Dickens (August 5, 1942, August 23, 1943, March 4, 1944)

Forbidden book criticizing Mussolini (August 10, 1943)

Margot's Latin book and dictionary (November 3, 1943)

Article on blushing by Sis Heyster, author of several books on child psychology (January 5, 1944)

Unnamed book on sex education (January 5, 1944)

W. M. Thackeray's *De kolonel* [The Colonel] (possibly *The History of Henry Esmond, Esq.: A Colonel in the Services of Her Majesty Queen Anne*) (April 27, 1944)

Nature book given to Anne's father by Kugler (May 13, 1944)

Knaur's Encyclopedia and Lexicon (May 16, 1944)

Anne's algebra book (May 20, 1944)

Anne's botany book (June 13, 1944)

Note

Charles "Dutch" Spekschate translated references to the Joop ter Heul series and Gerjan van Mechelen translated terms from *Brinkman's Catalogue*.

Selected Bibliography

Brinkman's Catalogus van Boeken [Brinkman's Catalogue of Books]. 1850– . Leiden: A. W. Sijthoff, n.d.

Frank, Anne. *Anne Frank: The Diary of a Young Girl.* Trans. B. M. Mooyaart-Doubleday. Garden City: Doubleday, 1952.

———. *De Dagboeken van Anne Frank.* Ed. David Barnouw and Gerrold van der Stroom. Amsterdam: Bert Bakker, 1986.

———. *The Diary of Anne Frank: The Critical Edition.* Ed. David Barnouw and Gerrold van der Stroom. Trans. Arnold J. Pomerans and B. M. Mooyaart-Doubleday. New York: Doubleday, 1989. [English version of *De Dagboeken van Anne Frank.*]

———. *The Diary of a Young Girl: The Definitive Edition.* Ed. Otto H. Frank and Mirjam Pressler. Trans. Susan Massotty. New York: Doubleday, 1995.

———. *Tales from the Secret Annex.* New York: Washington Square, 1984.

Gies, Miep, with Alison Leslie Gold. *Anne Frank Remembered: The Story of the Woman Who Helped to Hide the Frank Family.* New York: Simon and Schuster, 1987.

Luns, Martijn. "The Anne Frank House Amsterdam." [English version]. Amsterdam: Anne Frank Foundation, n.d.

Schnabel, Ernst. *Anne Frank: A Portrait in Courage.* Trans. Richard Winston and Clara Winston. New York: Harcourt, 1958.

van Marxveldt, Cissy [pseud. Setske van Beek-de Haan]. Joop ter Heul series. Amersfoort: Valkhoff, 1919–46.

Western, Richard D. "The Case for *Anne Frank: The Diary of a Young Girl.*" *Celebrating Censored Books.* Ed. Nicholas J. Karolides and Lee Burress. ERIC, 1985. 12–14. ED 264 600.

Wiesenthal, Simon. "Epilogue to Anne Frank's Diary." *The Murderers among Us: The Simon Wiesenthal Memoirs.* Ed. Joseph Wechsberg. New York: McGraw-Hill, 1967. 171–83.

15

Reading Anne Frank as a Woman

Berteke Waaldijk

One of the many questions that have often bothered me is why women have been, and still are, thought to be so inferior to men. . . . I'd really like to know the reason for this great injustice.
—*June 13, 1944*

"Who besides me will ever read these letters? From whom but myself shall I get comfort?" When Anne Frank wrote these words in 1944 she could not foresee that she would one day be one of the best known women authors of the Netherlands. Her diary has been published in [many] countries, and her work has been translated into more languages than that of any other Dutch writer. The house she hid in during the war has been visited by millions, and her diary has been acclaimed as a testimony. [. . .]

Anne Frank's fame has resulted in the juxtaposition of a public symbolic value and a "pure" Anne, whose private writing can be seen as a direct reflection of her inner self and her everyday life during her two years in hiding. In this reading, her diaries are regarded as pure and untainted, and her gendered symbolic value as innocent victim is substituted for the author. The interest in the literary aspects of the act of writing would in some way reduce her value as a symbol of innocence. The question of Anne Frank's literary talent is raised time and again, but somehow her importance is considered to transcend the field of literature. In her preface to the 1947 Dutch edition (viii), Annie Romein stated: "This diary, which is not the work of a great writer—she might have become one, but how pointless and tragic it is to raise this issue!—is so pure and precise" it is "without any disturbing or strained thought of future readers."[1] In 1985, Harry Mulisch, himself famous for a novel based on real events in the Netherlands under German occupation, saw the need to create a new category of writing, which was neither literature nor historical document, calling it "object [*sic*] trouvé." This, he wrote, is where Anne Frank's diary belongs. Admitting that Anne was talented, he suggested that, had she survived the war and made a novel out of this material, she would not have become as influential as she now is. Earlier, other reviewers had described her diary as pure, unspoiled, a moving human document, and they praised its great clarity and honesty [and] its uniquely tragic quality. [. . .]

In this [essay] I will argue that Anne Frank's symbolic value as an innocent victim of fascism should not prevent us from reading her diaries as a literary work. The outrage of her death is in no way diminished by taking her seriously as a writer. As the quotation at the very beginning of this [essay] shows, Anne was well aware of a possible readership and purposefully worked at becoming a writer. I want to read the diary as a *literary* text and to argue that it can be read as a women's text in both its content and in its links with other texts.

Feminist literary criticism has in recent years developed a critical apparatus that enables us to study traditions of female writing and female writing in its own intertextuality. Instead of claiming an abstract literary value that should grant women a place in the literary canon, feminist research has sought traditions of female writing that can be detected in common stylistic and thematic character- istics and intertextual references. In the case of Anne Frank, this approach seems to offer a particularly useful way of rereading her diaries. It makes possible a re- evaluation of the literary qualities of her writing. Reading her diary as a woman's text is by no means the only possibility. One could also read her as a Jewish au- thor or as a Dutch writer whose first language was German, and in a way all these readings would intersect. My interpretation therefore does not claim to be ex- clusive: It is one way of reading Anne Frank, one that has been relatively neglected until recently.[2] [. . .]

In 1986, the Netherlands State Institute for War Documentation published a critical edition of the different versions of the diary. For the first time the com- plete and unabridged versions by Anne Frank herself were made available to the public. The publication originated in the wish to refute once and for all any al- legations of forgery that had been raised by neo-Nazis since the late 1950s. It offers the reader the opportunity to compare Anne's original writing with the version of the diary that made her work famous. The editors of the critical edition rightly conclude that the differences are too small to justify any accusations of forgery, but the importance of publishing the unabridged texts goes well beyond this conclusion. Although the differences may be negligible from the point of view of the political and judicial claims of authenticity, they are extremely significant for readers interested in Anne Frank as a woman writer. The critical edition pro- vides an exciting opportunity to compare the editing done by her father and the publishers with the editing and rewriting Anne Frank did herself.

A prize-winning typographic design enables the reader to compare easily the different descriptions of the same events on the same page. Because my reading relies on the critical edition, I follow the editors in distinguishing version *a* (Anne's original day-to-day entries) from version *b* (Anne's rewritten version covering June 1942-March 1944), and I call the diary as it was first published version *c*.

Comparison of the unabridged diary entries with the diary as it was first published (comparing versions *b* and *c*) shows that a great deal of what was significant to Anne's development as a female author has been omitted by both her father and the publisher. In the following section I discuss the importance of some of those omissions. However, for a full understanding of this aspect of her writing, a study of Anne's own revision and editing of her text (comparing versions *a* and *b*) offers still more possibilities. This comparison shifts the focus from the silencing of a female text by men—and that is only part of the story, because Anne Frank was, in her own words, "her own sharpest critic"—to the intertextual relations that made Anne Frank's diary possible (*Critical Edition* 587). This second comparison precludes the creation of a new symbol of pure innocence: Anne Frank as a woman writer who was censored by male editors.

"The Essential Anne" (Comparing Versions *B* and *C*)

When Otto Frank offered a typescript based on his daughter's diaries to the publisher, he was convinced that he had saved "das Wesentliche," the essentials of the literary bequest (*Critical Edition* 166). After his editing of the text, [those at] the publishing company [. . .] edited and deleted as they saw fit. The result was a text that the editors of the critical edition introduce as a "literary text by Anne Frank" rather than an "autobiographical document sensu strictu." Although I do not agree with this strict separation of literature and autobiography, the differences between version *c* and Anne's own versions are indeed very real.[3] Scholars interested in Anne "as a woman," in her ideas on sex and gender, will find many new and interesting things in the now published version *b*.

The parts Otto Frank omitted mostly concerned Anne's mother. Anne was experiencing conflicts with her mother that seem typical for adolescent girls— conflicts possibly intensified by the stresses of the family's living conditions—and some of her remarks about her mother were harsh. In loving memory of his wife, Otto Frank left out some, but not all, of these remarks. It is pointless to accuse Anne's father of willfully silencing part of Anne's female experiences. From the history [given in] the English edition [of the critical edition] in 1989 it is clear that he was not as worried about the public's response as the Dutch publisher. Nevertheless, in my opinion, it is much more worthwhile to take a closer look at the significance of the deletions.

Most of the passages left out refer to Anne's experiences as a woman. They have to do with her body, menstruation and sexuality, her conversations with Peter about sex, and her relationship with her mother. Other parts were deleted because they were deemed uninteresting for a postwar audience; these include the occasional dirty jokes Anne recounted in her diary and references to books she read. One such deletion concerns a reference to a famous Dutch woman novelist Ina Boudier-Bakker. Anne praises her description of a family, but confesses that she is not interested in the writer's feminism.

A very interesting omission that received no attention from editors or reviewers was an entry dealing with the social position of women. Written [on] June [13,] 1944, it considers an issue "that has been raised more than once and that gives me no inner peace. . . . Why did so many nations in the past, and often still now, treat women as inferior to men?" In this entry, Anne discusses a book on the history of childbirth and condemns men's lack of respect for the "important, arduous, and in the long run, beautiful part women play in society. . . . It is stupid enough of women to have borne it all in silence for such a long time, since the more centuries this arrangement lasts, the more deeply rooted it becomes. Luckily schooling, work and progress have opened women's eyes." It is striking that neither editors nor reviewers have commented on this entry that contains such interesting ideas about women and culture. If published in the *Diary of a Young Girl* (version *c*), this page would have added a very different angle to Anne Frank's diary: an attempt to write in a historical and political mode, explicitly defending a woman's point of view.

In the 1950s, many Dutch, and probably also British and American, girls were given the diary to relieve their parents (mothers) from the obligation of telling them about menstruation. Anne's words were considered a beautiful and pure description of what a growing girl went through. Yet, it was precisely on this subject that deletions were made in the Dutch edition. In this case, one could speak of a double silencing of the female experience. The irony is that Anne, who privately wrote freely and openly about sex, was first silenced herself, and then her work was used as a substitute for the spoken word. However, the irony does not stop here: Anne herself subsequently omitted some of her references to sex. In revising her first diary entries, she left out extensive parts, for example, a one-page description of her own genitals [March 24, 1944]. Because Anne Frank never finished her editing, we cannot be sure that this would not have resurfaced in some other form, but it would clearly be wrong to picture her only as the *object* of silencing. In January 22, 1944, Anne added the following remark to the page dated October 20, 1942, describing that she expects to have her first period: "I shall never be able to write such things again!" And also on January 22, 1944 she writes: "When I look over my diary today, 1 ½ years on, I cannot believe that I was ever such an innocent young thing. . . . I really blush with shame when I read the pages dealing with subjects that I'd much better left to the imagination. I put it all down so bluntly!"*

A novel she was initially forbidden to read led her to write the following passage [on] October [26,] 1942: "In 'Eva's Youth' there are also bits about unknown women selling their bodies in back streets, and they ask a packet of money for it. I'd die of shame if anything like that happened to me." Reading this novel also prompted Anne to write that she longed to have her period, just like the novel's heroine. In version *a,* this remark is followed by "then at last I'd be grown up." In version *c,* the editors substituted this with: "It seems so important," a remarkable change in content. However, it is even more interesting that Anne herself dropped the whole passage in revising her diary. She only kept a reference to being allowed to read the book and inserted a new sentence about the novel in general: "I can't see much difference between this and the schoolgirl love stories." In this case, she apparently preferred publicizing her ideas about books and genres to making a comment about her menstruation. Even though the Dutch edition was on the whole quite prudish, it reintroduced the original remark that showed Anne's innocence regarding menstruation and prostitution.

The English version *c,* the *Diary of a Young Girl,* contained more open discussion of sexuality than the Dutch version. An important deletion in the Dutch version *c* concerns the entry describing Anne's curiosity about the body of her best friend Jacqueline: "I asked Jacque whether as a proof of our friendship we might feel one another's breasts. Jacque refused. I also had a terrible desire to kiss Jacque and that I did. I go into ecstasies every time I see the naked figure of a woman, such as Venus in the Springer History of Art, for example. It strikes me sometimes as so wonderful and exquisite that I have difficulty not letting the tears roll down my cheeks. If only I had a girlfriend!" (January 5, 1944). In the Dutch version, the references to feeling her friend's breasts and the kiss are left out, but both appear in the English version. Anne herself left out the whole passage when rewriting the diary.

There are more parts in version *c* that Anne had chosen not to incorporate in her revised version *b,* but which were taken from version *a* and published anyway. One example of a strategic alteration in the text concerns the implications of Anne's desire for Peter. A passage from a different place in version *a,* about Anne's desire to be alone, is inserted instead of a sentence Anne herself had included in version *a,* about how she went to the attic to meet Peter "by accident." Such a change makes Anne's behavior toward Peter look more "innocent" than she herself meant it to appear (February 13, 14, 1944).

*Editors' note: In the critical edition Anne's rewritten entries are not printed immediately following the original entries. In this case, see pages 287, 304, and 460–62.

Anne's remarks about her mother are a combination of her feelings of rejection as a daughter and of superiority as a woman. [. . .]

[Her] observations (on April 5 and 11, 1944) show that for Anne the rejection of her mother was linked to her ambition to write. Anne's wish to lead the life of a writer coincides with her desire to lead a better life than that of her mother.

Reading a Diary, Writing a Diary

For a closer look at the way Anne Frank wrote, I now turn to a comparison of versions *a* and *b*. Comparing versions *a* and *b* provides a clear insight into the way Anne revised her diaries. The differences also enable me to pinpoint certain literary influences on her writing. I argue that she was heavily influenced by one author in particular—Cissy van Marxveldt. Van Marxveldt's work was not exactly part of the Dutch literary canon, but it is no exaggeration to say that almost all women raised in the Netherlands since the 1920s are familiar with her books for girls.

The direct and important influence Cissy van Marxveldt had on Anne can easily be traced in the striking differences between versions *a* and *b* for the first six months. We can detect how Anne read van Marxveldt and used form and content from the Joop ter Heul series in finding a form for her own diary.[4] The series consists of four books [written during Anne's lifetime] describing the life of a girl, Joop ter Heul, in an upper-middle-class family in Amsterdam, her friends, her marriage and her life as a mother, and later her involvement in charity work. The books are well-written, funny, and touching. Updated reprints (substituting cars for carriages) still sell in huge numbers.[5]

We can easily determine the date of Anne's reading of [the first] Joop ter Heul [book]: An entry in version *a*, dated September 22, reads: "I've finished *Joop ter Heul* so quickly that I am not allowed new books till next Saturday." Like so many girls of her generation, Anne took an immediate liking to Cissy van Marxveldt's style. The day before she had referred to [the] Joop ter Heul [series] for the first time. So Anne Frank must have read [the first] Joop ter Heul [book] sometime in the third week of September 1942. Remarkably, from this point until December, Anne wrote almost all her diary entries in the form of letters to one of the characters from the Joop ter Heul books. The letters are addressed to the heroine's friends, never to Joop herself. In these letters, Anne chronicled life in *het achterhuis* and daily events in her family life. But more often than not she also included references to events in the lives of these fictional friends. For example, she sent greetings to an addressee's fiance. Writing to Pien, a newly wed friend, she asks her whether, after the first days of the honeymoon, there are "signs of fertilization" yet, continuing with a story about real friends expecting a baby (October

14, 1942). Needless to say, Cissy van Marxveldt never discussed pregnancy openly in her book.

The Dutch editors went to great lengths to identify all the names that cropped up in the diaries. They checked whether people objected to having their names published in the diaries. But Pop, Pien, Conney, and Kit could not, of course, be identified. They only existed in the novels that the male editors of the diaries had not read. The German translator (a woman) was the first to recognize the origin of these names. Now a note is included in the German and English editions.

From the third week in September 1942, Anne's diary entries were much more regular than [during] the first two months, which showed large gaps. Anne later covered these gaps when she rewrote the first version. We do not know how long Anne continued to write to these fictional characters because the original diaries of December 1942 to December 1943 are missing. From December 1943 on she wrote all her entries in the form of letters to Kitty. At some point between December 1942 and December 1943 she must have decided that this was going to be the form of her diary.

The name Kitty was at least partly derived from [the] Joop ter Heul [series]. In the [series], a character appears by the name of Kit Franken (sometimes Kitty). The first time Anne addressed a letter to Kitty was on September 22, 1942 (version *a*). This is the same entry that mentions Joop ter Heul for the first time. In a series of one-line letters to all but one of Joop's friends, dated September 28, 1942 (version *a*), the first is addressed to Kitty. In the [series], Kit is not Joop ter Heul's best friend, but she is portrayed as the one most like Joop, the heroine. The resemblance of Kit Franken's last name to Anne's own name may have added to her attraction to this character. Whatever the reason, sometime between December 1942 and December 1943 Anne decided to write all her diary entries as letters to Kitty, the name that also became famous in version *c*.

Van Marxveldt's influence goes further. The form of *The Diary of a Young Girl*, letters to friends that become a diary, is modeled on the Joop ter Heul novels as well. The fictional Joop starts off writing letters to a friend, but her father soon forbids her to correspond with her friends because he believes this interferes with her homework. Joop turns to writing in her diary, which remains the form of the rest of the novel. Anne was also kept from writing to friends, not by her father, but by the precautions her family had to take.

In one of the most moving passages in version *a*, Anne one day switches from writing to a real friend to addressing fictional friends. The entry dated September 25, 1942, contains a letter to Jacqueline with the heading: "*This is the promised fare-well letter.*" I do not know whether Anne believed that this letter would be delivered to her friend (nor whether it was sent), but it asks Jacque to be silent and not say anything about this letter to their friends. Anne promises that after the war she will explain why this was necessary. After signing this letter, Anne turns to Pop (Joop ter Heul's best friend) and writes her first long letter to one of van Marxveldt's characters. From that date on, Anne's entries are more regular than they had been before. The diary form of [the] Joop ter Heul [series] helped her to envisage her own diary. But Joop ter Heul also offered Anne a lonely heroine to identify with as a role model.

One can detect van Marxveldt's direct influences on Anne's writing style. In the Netherlands of this period, it was considered impolite to start letters with the word *I*. Joop ter Heul refers to this in her first letters, after she had started one letter that way. Anne wrote "Dear Kitty: I have to tell you . . ." and after "I" she added: "the same old mistake!" (January 19, 1944).

A reference to [one Joop ter Heul novel] that is more difficult to interpret is found in the letter dated September 21 (version *a*): "this afternoon I wrote a fairly sheepish letter to Jettje, but I had hardly sat down for a minute when I had to peel potatoes for 'her ladyship my mamma,' she says it in such commanding tones, and if I don't hop to it she shouts 'loos,' that's German and I don't know exactly how you spell it. Just as in *Joop ter Heul*" (September 21, 1942). This may be a reference to Joop ter Heul's mother, who is portrayed as equally demanding, or it may refer to an ignorance of foreign spelling, something that turns up regularly in the novel, where it is used to stress the fact that Joop is the youngest and least sophisticated member of her family. It is difficult to determine exactly what Anne was referring to, the content or form of the novel.

There are a number of similarities between Anne's life and the life of Joop ter Heul the heroine. They might explain why Anne identified with Joop ter Heul. To begin with, [the] Joop ter Heul [series] is set in Amsterdam. The neighborhood Joop ter Heul grew up in—a district in south Amsterdam—was known to Anne as well and she might even have recognized the ice-cream shops mentioned in [the novels.] Then, there is Joop's strong affection for her father and problematic relationship with her mother. Both Anne and Joop have an older sister, whom they consider a model girl and daughter. Just like Joop, Anne formed a club with her friends and tried writing poetry. In general, one could argue that Joop's personality resembles Anne's: both are cheerful and fun-loving on the outside, but lonely, insecure, and serious on the inside. All this might explain why the Joop ter Heul novels moved and influenced Anne to the extent they did.

However, it would be wrong to give the impression that there are nothing but similarities between [the] Joop ter Heul [series] and Anne's diary. From our present-day perspective, the differences between the two are just as striking. In her diaries, Anne wrote about herself in relation to the world. She discussed whether she would withdraw her faith in humankind and decided not to. This is a wider and deeper question than van Marxveldt ever explored. Anne expressed her aspirations for the future, her wish to become a writer. In contrast, Joop ter Heul unquestioningly entered into marriage, motherhood, and some welfare work. Anne wrote about desire, her desire for love and a friend, be it man or woman. She thought of herself as a woman. In [the] Joop ter Heul [series], desire and femininity are only hinted at.

Anne Frank thought and wrote delicately, clearly, openly, and passionately about subjects that never seem to figure in the life of van Marxveldt's heroine. Perhaps this is what distinguishes "Literature" from books for girls. In recognizing what Anne learned and took from [the] Joop ter Heul [series], it is also possible to see where she outdid her favorite author and how she developed her own style for describing her sexual and personal development.

Woman Writer between Genres

Comparing Anne's writing with that of other authors brings home how very few examples were available to her as a writer and how well she made use of them. Many references to books she read have not survived the triple editing that her words underwent (first by herself, then by her father, and finally by the publisher). In the beginning, she was forbidden to read some adult books, because they would have been too explicit for a young girl. Later, Anne remarked that, although she was now allowed to read virtually everything, she still resented her parents' power to withhold books from her. The publication of the unabridged edition of her diaries has made it clear that her father and the people helping the family provided her with many books. As Anne herself stated, she read "History, Geography, History of Art, Mythology, Biology, Bible history [and] Dutch Literature" (May 16, 1944).

Like many female authors, Anne had to find a place for her own writing in the impressive and mostly male traditions she was faced with. The books helped her in many ways. Seeing the *Venus de Milo* in an art history book helped her to express her own feelings about her body. Reading historical biographies no doubt helped her to express her own wish to live on after death. In her search for words to describe her experiences of growing up to be a woman, Anne did not just use the canonical texts of Western civilization, she also turned to popular culture. She was an avid reader of film magazines. Her diary offers evidence that a schoolgirl novel [series] like Joop ter Heul was just as important in forming her sense of identity as a writer as were the classical German novels by Schiller and Goethe that her father read with her.

One might ask whether Anne did not, in a sense, profit from her lack of formal education. After all, there were no peers or teachers to influence her, no one who might have taken her writing less seriously than her family. Both her family and her companions in hiding respected her writing and her privacy. Although Anne did not have the means to lock her diary away, no one seems to have read it during the whole time they lived in the secret annex.

Describing the interests of the different members of the *achterhuis* group, Anne wrote ([on May [6,] 1944) that her father liked to read "serious and dry as dust descriptions of people and countries," while "Mr. v.P. [liked] to read detective stories, medical books, exciting and trivial romances" and "Mrs. v.P. [liked] to read fictional biography and some novels." She described herself as someone who "loves reading biographies, dull or exciting, historical books, (novels and light reading sometimes)." Clearly, her own reading was a combination of two extremes: her father's serious reading and the van Pelses' less cultured reading. Anne seems to have been aware of her position between two kinds of reading, and maybe the key to her own writing lies in the combination of different genres. This resulted in remarkably fresh and "innocent" descriptions. However, they were not only a reflection, an innocent description, or a pure testimony of life in hiding and of a girl growing up. Anne's writing was shaped by deliberate attempts to create a publishable text. It was influenced by literary and popular texts she knew.

In conclusion, it is ironic that the critical edition that settled the question of the diaries' authenticity simultaneously provided evidence of fictional elements in her diaries. It is now clear that Anne rewrote her diaries when she was almost fifteen years old. It has also become apparent that she started rewriting her diary with the idea of publishing it after the war, because she wanted to be a writer.

When she rewrote her first version, she carefully left out all references to events in [the] Joop ter Heul [series], retaining only the real events of her life in hiding. Yet, she also rewrote the September 21 entry about Cissy van Marxveldt, adding: "I'm thrilled with the Joop ter Heul series. I've enjoyed the whole of Cissy van Marxveldt very much. And I've read *Zomerzotheid* four times and I still laugh about some of the ludicrous situations that arise" (September 21, 1942). Actually, this entry contains a lie: Anne read *Zomerzotheid* later, but with these words paid tribute to the author who played such an important role in the creation of her diary.

One of the things I can do to honor Anne Frank is to read her as the writer she wanted to be and the writer she was. Modern readers need to acknowledge that Anne Frank's thinking and writing were heavily influenced by the texts available to her. Instead of considering this influence a contamination, we can admire the way Anne gave these texts new meaning and transcended them. Purity and innocence are metaphors of virginity that do not apply to Anne Frank's writing: "Love, what is love? I believe love is something that can't really be put into words. Love is understanding someone, caring for someone, sharing their ups and downs. And in the long run that also means physical love, you have shared something, given something away and received something, no matter whether you are married or unmarried, or whether you are with child or not. It doesn't matter in the least if you've lost your honor as long as you know that someone will stand by you, will understand you for the rest of your life, someone you won't have to share with anyone else" (March 2, 1944).

She created a diary that combined private with public observations and mixed "great literature" with schoolgirl romance. In this way, Anne Frank produced a story about the Nazi persecution of Jews as well as a story relating a young girl's growth into a writer. In their turn, Anne Frank's words will be part of the texts that influenced millions of readers' feelings and writings, not only because of her symbolic value as a victim of racism, but also because of the text's value as a mode of writing for women writers.

Notes

The author is grateful to Monica Soeting and Mary Carlson, and to colleagues and students at Utrecht University for their support and valuable suggestions.

1. Annie Romein-Verschoor, "Inleiding" [Introduction], in Anne Frank, *Het Achterhuis: Dagboekbrieven von 14 juni 1942–1 agustus 1945* [The Secret Annex, Diary Letters June 14, 1942–August 1, 1945]. (Amsterdam: Contact, 1947), viii.

2. In Utrecht, Denise de Costa was the first literary critic to use the concept *écriture feminine* in order to read the diaries of Anne Frank.

3. The study of women's (auto-)biographies is a main research theme in Utrecht.

4. Cissy van Marxveldt, *Der H. B. S. tijd van Joop ter Heul* [The High School Years of Joop ter Heul]. Amersfoort: Valkhoff, 1919; *Joop ter Heuls problemen* [Joop ter Heul's Problems]. Amersfoort: Valkhoff, 1921; *Joop van Dil-ter Heul* [Joop of Dil-ter Heul]. Amersfoort: Valkhoff, 1923; *Joop en haar jongen* [Joop and Her Son]. Amersfoort: Valkhoff, 1925.

5. As far as I know, there are no translations of [the Joop ter Heul series] in English.

Part 3

Anne Frank on Stage and Screen

16

The American History of Anne Frank's Diary

Judith E. Doneson

We can never be just Dutch, or just English, or whatever, we will always be Jews as well. And we'll have to keep on being Jews, but then, we'll want to be.
—*April 14, 1944*

In 1947, a journalist visiting displaced persons' camps could not help but compare the continuing presence and influence of the war and destruction in Europe with the existing atmosphere in the United States: "America has already come out of the war, has almost forgotten it. Even the post-World War II mood is in back of us."[1] Indeed, Americans were "lucky" that they were far away from the fields of battle; for them, the postwar period was a time of unparalleled prosperity. The war was history, though inevitably new problems and concerns appeared.

The major postwar theme in America was the fight against communism: one totalitarian ideology replaced another as the target for American political passions. But whereas fascism was regarded as a right-wing movement, communism was identified with the left wing, resulting in a more conservative mood in America to replace the New Deal liberalism of the war years.[2] The House Un-American Activities Committee (HUAC) hearings, beginning with the "Hollywood Communists" in 1947, soon dominated the political scene, creating an environment of fear, suppression, and mistrust—the age of McCarthyism—which would haunt the "liberal" American image.

At the same time, and somewhat paradoxically, Robin Williams Jr. saw in postwar America a more liberal social attitude, an "institutionalized universalism . . . and . . . the increasing similarity of 'majority' and 'minority' Americans."[3] The Supreme Court decided in 1954 that segregating black schoolchildren from the white school system was unlawful, and anti-Semitism, which had escalated during the war and peaked in 1944, began to decline, making life for the Jews more comfortable than they had perhaps thought possible.

"Un-American" seemed to be an underlying motif for both liberals and conservatives in an odd combination of suppression and liberalism. It was un-American to be associated with the Communist party, but it was also un-American to be anti-Semitic or to prevent blacks from participating in the American dream. The prevailing lifestyle would be "American," "democratic," "universal." Political conformity and social equality were predominant trends of the era.

It was within this environment that *The Diary of Anne Frank* made its appearance, as it became representative of the postwar period and the 1950s. The history of the diary parallels the age in question. First published in Holland in 1947, the diary was published in America in the early 1950s. Later it was dramatized, and finally filmed in 1959. During this time, the diary evolved from a European work written by a young Jew hiding from the Nazis in Holland to a more Americanized, universal symbol; indeed, it became one of the first enduring popular symbols of the Holocaust.

Few American films of the late 1940s and 1950s dealt with the Holocaust. Only *The Diary of Anne Frank,* as a play and film, had a significant impact, as it is rooted in American traditions of the late 1950s, even though it deals with events foreign to both gentile and Jewish Americans. How was the diary transformed into a work of popular culture relevant to an American audience? We can best explain this by tracing the American history of the diary as it evolved into a play and film. Our discussion will focus on three pertinent areas: the universalization of the Holocaust, the image of the Jew, and the question of historical accuracy.

The universalization of the Holocaust through the diary, that is, the adapting and adjusting of images so that a broad consensus of the population can identify with the event, diminishes its Jewish particularity. As the Holocaust becomes a universal symbol of suffering, it also becomes possible for Americans to find significance in an event that they have not experienced. In this context, it is relevant to discuss Meyer Levin's private war against Anne's father, Otto Frank, because Levin believed, among other things, that Anne's message had been bastardized. In addition, the question arises as to whether the Americanization and ultimate universalization of the Holocaust through the diary mirrored America's attitude toward its Jews and other minorities—the growing phenomenon of "sameness"—rather than a blatant desire to alter the Jewish meaning of the Holocaust? Or, was there a communist/Stalinist influence through Lillian Hellman's input, as Meyer Levin argued, which intentionally robbed the diary of its Jewish specificity?

In examining the cinematic image of the Jew we ask: Are the Jews portrayed as weak figures? If so, what does this mean? And how does Israel influence this image? Finally, we will deal with historicity and the film as a reflection of contemporary events. How important is historical accuracy? What role does it play in universalizing the diary's message? And what is the significance of the film's content in relation to then current issues in America? Perhaps in answering these questions, we can see how the Americanization/democratization/universalization of the Holocaust through one of its first popular symbols diminished its particular Jewishness while at the same time imprinted the Holocaust into the American imagination.[4]

A brief glimpse at events which helped shape the postwar environment through the decade of the 1950s can help us gain insight into the diary's course in its adopted American home. In 1947, the Hollywood Motion Picture Project, later known as the Jewish Film Advisory Committee, was founded in Los Angeles as a reaction to anti-Semitism, even though anti-Semitism was then waning in the United States. Funding was provided by the National Jewish Community Relations Advisory Council, the American Jewish Committee, and the Anti-Defamation League. The goal of the project was to work closely with Hollywood filmmakers as advisers in order to prevent negative portrayals of Jews in film and television.[5] That same year also saw the House Un-American Activities Committee (HUAC) begin its hearings. The defendants known as the "Hollywood Ten" were the first of many to be brought before the committee and were subsequently blacklisted by the film industry. Stifling their initial anger, Hollywood executives publicly pledged not to knowingly employ communists or others who might advocate the overthrow of the United States government, "by an illegal or unconstitutional method."[6] This atmosphere resulted in the destruction of many fine careers. The initial hearings did have anti-Semitic overtones attributed mainly to Congressman John Rankin of Mississippi. Anti-Semitism, however, was not at the core of McCarthyism and would play a minor role, if any, at later hearings.

It is interesting to note that during the first hearings, "Holocaust terminology," today commonplace, was a reference point to describe the atmosphere of suppression created by hearings. When Dalton Trumbo, one of the original Ten, testified before the committee, he stated: "For those who remember German history in the autumn of 1932 there is the smell of smoke in this room."[7] At one point, Trumbo shouted at Chairman J. Parnell Thomas: "This is the beginning of an American concentration camp."[8] This would signal a trend in which the Holocaust, along with its symbols, came to be understood as a watershed event, a basis for comparison for all persecution and tragedy. The Holocaust as a verbal symbol for suffering was entering into the popular imagination, becoming part of the vernacular of tragedy.

In any case, the prevalent fears in America were the supposed communist threat and the cold war. By 1948, most of Eastern Europe was under Soviet domination, the Chinese revolution in 1949 established communist rule in that country, and the communist "threat" seemed real. Espionage trials became commonplace in the United States. Whittaker Chambers testified that Alger Hiss had been passing state secrets to the [Soviets,] while Julius and Ethel Rosenberg were tried and executed on charges of espionage for the [Soviets.]

During the time Senator Joseph McCarthy, whose name became synonymous with the period, headed the HUAC hearings, "the thrust was to establish anti-Communism as the religion of America, with communism as the antireligion. It cut across sectarian lines and blended with the secularized faith of America."[9] The goal of the HUAC hearings was to "stigmatize," to publicly destroy the reputation of anyone who had been associated with the Communist party, for most of the "subversives" were already known to intelligence agencies. The idea was to compel "friendly" witnesses to "name names," thereby creating a system of informers. An atmosphere of fear and mistrust prevailed.[10]

Hollywood was totally intimidated by the hearings. It seems as if the McCarthy era was the closest the American film industry ever came to being politically controlled. Films were cleansed of any obvious "subversive" message. As summed up by one of the original Hollywood Ten, producer Adrian Scott: "the blacklisting of other men was in reality the blacklisting of the liberals' own ideas."[11]

The tense atmosphere created by the HUAC hearings instilled in American Jewry a fear of increased anti-Semitism. In addition, there was a fear of an anti-Semitic backlash to the emergence of Israel, but a majority of Americans supported Israel.[12] Another possible target for anti-Semites was the close Jewish ties with emerging black political activism, which had been stimulated by the 1954 Supreme Court ruling against segregation. Though Jews were more committed to integration than other groups, they were not popularly associated with aiding the black struggle.[13] The trend in the United States was toward a decline in both anti-Semitism and traditional anti-Semitic images. All of this combined with congressional legislation against social discrimination to ease the Jews' assimilation into mainstream American society.[14]

Universalist tendencies defined the mood of the 1950s, with "Americanization" as a goal for minorities. This included ideas of equality and freedom as well as conformity and assimilation on both the Left and the Right. The liberals, in calling for equality, sought "sameness" for minority groups, while the anticommunist conservatives' notion of freedom was to protect the "American way," in this case, protection from enemy influence. As Will Herberg has suggested, America "really has a common religion in the 'American way of life.'"[15]

Understandably, the Jews conformed to the existing principles of the day. As Jews became more socially acceptable, they tried not to "stand out." In the arts, this expressed itself in what Henry Popkin called "de-Semitization," the elimination of "Jewish characters, Jewish names, the word 'Jew.'" As Popkin states: "If we pretend that the Jew does not exist, the reasoning goes, then he will not be noticed; the anti-Semite, unable to find his victim, will simply forget about him."

Popkin infers that this was perhaps an unconscious attitude.[16] Politically, the Jews associated themselves with liberal, universal causes. Many Jews working for civil rights movements would never dream of involving themselves with Jewish causes, while Jewish organizations extended their activities to include other minorities. Even the Jewish Film Advisory Committee (JFAC) felt that "the office's interest is not limited to the Jewish community itself. It is aware that a hurt inflicted on one minority group is a hurt inflicted on all minority groups—and in turn, on all humanity."[17] Within this context of the quest for universal meaning in American society, *The Diary of Anne Frank* becomes a universal symbol.

Anne's diary, though a chronicle of her experiences during the war, is not an account of the war. She was isolated from external events, receiving information about the outside world either from the radio or the Dutch Christians who visited the attic daily. While diarists like Emmanuel Ringelblum and Chaim Kaplan kept daily records of the Nazi destruction of the Jews in the Warsaw Ghetto and the Jewish reactions to their persecution, Anne focused mainly on her own inner turmoil and on those with whom she was confined. For a young girl, Anne's writing has unusual depth and insight; war, however, simply provides the backdrop for Anne's inner quest. Otto Frank, Anne's father, expressed a similar view in a letter to Meyer Levin: "As to the Jewish side you are right that I do not feel the same way you do. I always said, that Anne's book is not a warbook. War is the background. It is not a Jewish book either, though Jewish sphere, sentiment and surrounding is the background. . . . It is read and understood more by gentiles than in Jewish circles. So do not make a Jewish play of it."[18] Otto Frank understood the limitations of his daughter's writing. In addition, he wanted to memorialize Anne, which meant stressing the diary's universal aspects over its specific Jewish content for the purpose of providing a means of identification for the general public.

The Levin-Frank connection began when Meyer Levin came across a copy of the diary in Paris. He contacted Otto Frank, and they agreed that Levin would look for an American publisher for the diary.[19] Otto Frank also allowed Levin to attempt a dramatization of the diary. Levin's play was refused production, he was told, because it was not a good dramatic piece. This rejection, which Levin felt was unjustified, caused him much anguish until his death in 1981. He blamed the rejection on politics, accusing playwright Lillian Hellman and other "intellectual pro-Stalinists" of ostracizing him and rejecting his play because both were too Jewish. Over the years, he claimed that the play which became the accepted, legitimized version only served to destroy Anne's message by universalizing its Jewish aspects.[20]

As it happened, producer Kermit Bloomgarden, who had the rights to the diary, contacted Lillian Hellman and asked her for a suggestion as to who could write the play. On Hellman's recommendation, Albert [Hackett] and Frances Goodrich [. . .] a husband-and-wife writing team from Hollywood, were hired.

Frances Goodrich kept a diary of her own while she and her husband worked on the play.[21] The sincerity with which [Goodrich and Hackett] approached the material seems genuine.[22] They read books on Dutch history, Jewish history, and Judaism ([Goodrich and Hackett] are not Jewish—another point which disturbed Levin). [Goodrich] wrote in her diary: "This is not like any other job we have done. Terrible emotional impact. I cry all the time." In a later entry she said: "We are brazen about asking people for help. But feel this play tremendous responsibility. It can mean so very much." Upon completing their fourth draft, [Goodrich and Hackett] flew from Los Angeles to New York to present it to Kermit Bloomgarden and Lillian Hellman; both felt the play was too loyal to the diary at the expense of dramatic structure. According to [Goodrich's] diary, everyone hated it, including Otto Frank.

Otto Frank wrote [Goodrich and Hackett] that though it pained him to have to tell them, there was a great deal wrong with the script. He explained to them:

> Having read thousands of reviews and hundreds of personal letters about Anne's book from different countries in the world, I know what creates the impression of it [sic] on people and their impressions ought to be conveyed by the play to the public. Young people identify themselves very frequently with Anne in their struggle during puberty and the problems of the relations mother-daughter are existing all over the world. These and the love affair with Peter attract young people, whereas parents, teachers and psychologists learn about the inner feelings of the young generation. When I talked to Mrs. Roosevelt about the book, she urged me to give permission for play and film as only then we could reach the masses and influence them by the mission of the book which she saw in Anne's wish to work for mankind, to achieve something valuable still after her death, her horror against war and discrimination.[23]

Clearly, the universal aspects of Anne's diary are what was important to Otto Frank.

So, [Goodrich and Hackett] began to write. They completed a fifth version, and this time mailed copies to Bloomgarden and Hellman. According to [Goodrich's] diary entry of September 5, 1954: "Lilly . . . was amazing. Brilliant advice on construction." Again, [Goodrich and Hackett] reworked the play, until finally, having completed their sixth version, it was accepted by Kermit Bloomgarden.

Meyer Levin's main complaint all along has been the removal of the Jewish content from the play. One section particularly disturbed Levin. Anne wrote in her diary:

Who has inflicted this upon us? Who has made us Jews different from all other people? Who has allowed us to suffer so terribly up till now? It is God that has made us as we are, but it will be God, too, who will raise us up again. If we bear all this suffering and if there are still Jews left, when it is over, then Jews, instead of being doomed, will be held up as an example. Who knows, it might even be our religion from which the world and all people learn good, and for that reason only do we have to suffer now.[24]

Levin's reading of this as a central idea of the diary was accurate, and his anger was justified when in the final version of the play, Anne's words were changed to read: "We're not the only people that've had to suffer. There've always been people that've had to. . . . Sometimes one race . . . Sometimes another . . . and yet . . . "[25] Levin attributed this change to Lillian Hellman's influence.[26] However, according to Frances Goodrich's diary, which clearly delineated Hellman's input, it seems as if Hellman stopped contributing ideas after the fifth version, or perhaps the sixth (accepted) version. At this point, the lines in question still retained their Jewish focus: "We're not the only Jews that've had to suffer. Right down through the ages there have been Jews and they've had to suffer."[27] Not until the seventh version were these lines changed, most likely to secure better audience identification with the subject and the characters. This does cast doubt on Meyer Levin's accusation regarding Lillian Hellman's responsibility for his having lost the play because his version was too Jewish, although, in keeping with her beliefs, Hellman might conceivably have supported universal concepts in the play.

Levin believed, however, that it was Hellman's pro-Stalinist politics that influenced her attitude toward him. Yet, Lillian Hellman was herself a victim of the McCarthy witch-hunt, which, it might be expected, would have precluded her supporting even a hint of blacklisting another writer solely for his political beliefs. Rather, it seems more plausible that the universalization of the diary was in keeping with the times, when conformity was a motif of both the Left and the Right.

However, there is one scene that does indicate a misunderstanding of Nazi anti-Semitic ideology and the goals of the Final Solution. In the Hanukkah scene, one the writers felt was central to the dramatic structure of the play, neither director Garson Kanin nor [Goodrich and Hackett] wanted the Hanukkah song sung in the original Hebrew. In a letter to Otto Frank, [Goodrich and Hackett] explained their reason: "It would set the characters in the play apart from the people watching them . . . for the majority of our audience is not Jewish. And the thing that we have striven for, toiled for, fought for throughout the whole play is to make the audience understand and identify themselves . . . to make them one with them . . . to make them feel 'that, but for the grace of God, might have been I.'"[28]

This approach obscures the fact that it was not by chance that Anne was hiding, but specifically because she was Jewish. In any case, it would be impossible for an American audience to identify with characters who had been victims of Nazi racial hatred and persecution. It was not an American experience. In order to portray historical truth, [Goodrich and Hackett] would have needed to clarify the Nazis' planned genocide against the Jews. The play's insistence that fate chose the Jews only serves to universalize Nazi anti-Semitic ideology at the expense of the particularity of the historical facts. Otto Frank concurred with [Goodrich and Hackett] when he wrote that "it was my point of view to try to bring Anne's message to as many people as possible even if there are some who think it is a sacrilege and does not bring the greatest part of the public to understand."[29]

The play opened on Broadway in October 1955 and was an enormous success, winning a Pulitzer Prize in 1956. It was performed throughout Europe as well. In autumn 1956, Twentieth Century-Fox secured the film rights. Meyer Levin was still hopeful that he might at least be allowed to write the screenplay. Otto Frank, however, preferred [Goodrich and Hackett], though the final choice was not his but the studio's.

Realizing he had no chance to participate in any adaptation of *The Diary of Anne Frank,* Levin began legal proceedings against Otto Frank and Kermit Bloomgarden. Levin accused them of having shown [his] version of the play to [Goodrich and Hackett], who in turn plagiarized the structure of Levin's play. Twentieth Century-Fox, concerned about the outcome of the suit, considered holding up production on the film until the case was settled. Levin, it appears, had traveled to the West Coast in an attempt to influence executives at Fox.[30] In the end, the studio proceeded with the film.

While in preparation, a copy of the script was sent to John Stone, director of the Jewish Film Advisory Committee. In a letter to director George Stevens, Stone assessed the script's importance: "this screenplay is even better than the stage play. You have given the story a more 'universal' meaning and appeal. It could very easily have been an outdated Jewish tragedy by less creative or more emotional handling—even a Jewish 'Wailing Wall', and hence regarded as mere propaganda."[31] John Stone, too, voiced the apparent mood of the period—universalization.

Following the success of the play, and realizing the even larger audience potential for the film, [Goodrich and Hackett] pursued their course of universalizing the diary. This did not mean totally disguising the particular Jewishness of the Holocaust, but it did necessitate minimizing the horrors involved, which, with Anne's diary, was not difficult. In this way, the likeness of all suffering is maintained for the purpose of audience identification: whoever has faced adversity can identify with the suffering of the Franks and Europe's Jews. Even so, the thrust remains ambiguous in that though the film does universalize the Holocaust, it still relates the Jewish specificity of the event in some fashion.

How does the film corroborate the specific Jewish aspects of Anne's diary, and how does it alter, or eliminate, Anne's intent in order to broaden the appeal of the film? The tone of the script, in keeping with the diary, is extremely optimistic. Yet it is clear that Anne and those in hiding with her are Jewish. In the beginning of the film, when Anne explains the anti-Jewish laws, she uses the term *we*—"we had to wear yellow stars"—instead of "Jews had to wear yellow stars," as she writes in her diary. Does the absence of the word *Jew* change the meaning of Anne's statement? No, for who else but Jews would be wearing the yellow star? When Dr. Dussel, the dentist, arrives at the secret annex, as Anne calls it, he is bombarded with questions. Through him, in both the [play] and the film, circumstances are revealed: the deteriorating conditions for the Jews and the daily arrests and deportations. The emphasis here is on the persecution of the Jews.

As in the play, the Hanukkah celebration is a pivotal scene, even though Anne writes in her diary that they do not fuss over Hanukkah. Again, a discussion ensued as to whether the Hanukkah prayers should be recited in Hebrew. [Goodrich and Hackett] preferred English for the sake of audience identification. Their idea was to demystify these "strange people," to Americanize a "foreign" religious rite in order to make it comprehensible. In this way, Hanukkah is like Christmas—just a little different. Religion becomes the only barrier separating one American from another. Rabbi Max Nussbaum of Los Angeles, a survivor of the Holocaust, advised [Goodrich and Hackett]. Though at first he agreed to the English, he later changed his mind because he believed in reality the prayers could only be spoken in Hebrew. [Goodrich and Hackett] felt otherwise: "What we all of us hoped, and prayed for, and what we are devoutly thankful to have achieved, is an identification of the audience with the people in hiding. They see them, not as some strange people, but persons like themselves, thrown into this horrible situation. With them they suffer the deprivations, the terrors, the moments of tenderness, of exaltation and courage beyond belief."[32] This desire for the audience to identify with an event beyond their comprehension again confirms the writers' inability or unwillingness to understand the Holocaust and National Socialist ideology. Perhaps, this was because Holocaust historiography was only in its infancy, but it was also possibly a reflection of the general atmosphere in America, one of combating specific differences among its citizens for the sake of conformity.

There are sections of the diary where Anne is explicit about Jewish persecutions that could have been incorporated into the film. Anne describes, for instance, what she knew of deportations to the Dutch concentration camp of Westerbork. She also writes: "I get frightened when I think of close friends who have now been delivered into the hands of the cruelest brutes that walk the earth. And all because they are Jews."[33] Anti-Semitism in Dutch circles where it had never before existed is also a topic of the diary. None of this is mentioned in the film. Instead, the film seeks an audience identification with the Jewish victims for the purpose of appealing to a universal antipathy toward the persecution of all men. The Jews and the Holocaust become a symbol for the suffering of man in general.

Bruno Bettelheim has posited a connection between universalization and *The Diary of Anne Frank* which is relevant to a discussion of the image of [Jews] in the film. Bettelheim asserts: "The universal success of *The Diary of Anne Frank* suggests how much the tendency to deny the reality of the camps is still with us."[34] In Bettelheim's view, the Frank family, hiding as a family unit and seeking to live a normal daily life, actually contributed to their own destruction by denying the reality of the Holocaust. Bettelheim bases his theory only on the diary, the play, and the film (as opposed to the actual history of the Frank family). His image of the Jew[s] is one of a people aiding their own destruction.

A corollary of this image is an image which perhaps can help explain the universal success of the diary as a play and film, that of the weak Jew. The issue is probably more theological than psychological, as Bettelheim [implies]. Essentially, Jews in Christian countries are at the mercy of Christians and Christian civilization. Christian belief in the universal tenet "love thy neighbor" forms the basis of the relationship between Christians and Jews and assumes the majority Christians will act in good faith on behalf of the minority Jews when they are in trouble. More to the point, then, is the issue of Christian attitudes during the Holocaust as they influenced the fate of the Jews. Perhaps here we can find a reason for the universal acceptance of the diary.

The Jew in the film is weak because he is a victim. His ability to act in any meaningful fashion is subject to the whims of his oppressor or the kind deeds of his potential savior. It is this dependence on the gentile that makes the passivity of the Jew unavoidable. This is the thrust of the film's structure—the tenuous relationship between the Christian protector and the Jew who relies on him. Bettelheim condemns the wrong party. It is unjust to blame the Franks for falling prey to the same civilization that allowed them to become victimized. The film forces the viewer to assume "that the Nazi terror was predicated on the failure of Christianity."[35]

In this context, Anne's optimism is significant. At the end of the film, Anne says: "In spite of it all, I still believe men are good." Bettelheim sees this as a negation of the reality of Auschwitz. If man is good, asserts Bettelheim, then Auschwitz could not exist (Anne, of course, wrote these lines before she was deported to Bergen-Belsen). Instead, we might say that this ending serves to miti-

gate Christian responsibility. It is not a denial of Aushwitz, but rather the for-
giving of a Christian lapse of goodness. For as Anne becomes a symbol of the
Holocaust, her words become the affirmation of post-Holocaust civilization.
Anne's words give man the opportunity to continue living without guilt because
she still believes in him. Her belief becomes a form of forgiveness, and only Anne
(and other victims) can forgive. Universal forgiveness, then, for the failure to live
up to a fundamental Christian belief is a main function of the film.

The film's portrayal of the Jew as a victim, incapable of acting on his own behalf, coincides, paradoxically, with Bettelheim's myth-propagating theory of the
denial and passivity of the victims when contrasted to the emerging image of the
fighting Israeli (an image Israel seeks to perpetuate). Most dramatic films on the
Holocaust focus on the Jew as a passive victim rather than as a resister or parti-
san. By the time *The Diary of Anne Frank* appeared as a film, Israel had fought
and won two major wars, causing a definite change in the Jewish image in favor
of the fighter.[36] Through Israel's image, new criteria have been established for
Jewish behavior; "weakness" is intolerable, and the victim is judged guilty. The
film's depiction of weak Jewish victims could therefore give a dual message. On
the one hand, it seeks to alleviate guilt for the Holocaust by having Anne signify
hope and forgiveness—a continuing belief in humanity—while on the other
hand, a viewer sharing the popular impression of a fighting Israel could also cite
Israel as evidence of possible alternative Jewish behavior and then blame the victim for his inability to prevent his own destruction.

Another element in the film which must be considered is historicity. *The Diary of Anne Frank* is a historical film in that it takes place within a particular historical framework, and it is a document. Agreeing with Pierre Sorlin that to worry
about mistakes in a historical film is to perhaps worry about a meaningless question,[37] we will instead consider the problems involved in dramatizing a historical document. There are several examples in which the truth of the diary is un-
certain, even harmful to the memory of those who perished.

The title tells the audience it will see a film based on a diary. Because the diary
is authentic, there is an implied obligation to follow its intent. This does not
necessitate quoting Anne verbatim, but it does preclude distorting her meaning.
Yet, the structure of the film forces the issue of authenticity. The voiceover of Anne
reading from her diary, fading into dramatic sequences, stresses the fact that these
scenes are based on Anne's writing; that it is always her diary "speaking" throughout the film. Therefore, the viewer is made to feel as though he is "reading" Anne's
diary. If any elements of the diary are falsified, then Anne's history is distorted.
How then is Anne's history reflected in the adaptation of her diary?

Although the play's producer, Kermit Bloomgarden, understood the importance of authenticity, Otto Frank could not convince him to mention the play's

authenticity in the theater program. Frank told of a Dutch Jewish woman he knew who at one performance sat next to an American woman who had seen the play three times. When the Dutch woman mentioned that she had known Anne before the war, the American woman was amazed that the people in the play had lived and that events were real.[38] In another incident, after Otto Frank had seen the film, he wrote to [Goodrich and Hackett]: "there are a great number of the younger generation who just do not understand what it is all about and that it is a true story. I spoke to youngsters who told me their classmates laughed right at the beginning when the truck came and there were people on it in 'pyjamas'. It seems that some sort of explanation should be given at the beginning—before the film starts."[39] In other words, where the historical setting is unclear, the uniqueness of Anne and her diary are veiled by a more universal message.

One particular scene exemplifies how the memory of one man is altered for the sake of dramatic development. Dr. Dussel, the dentist, perished during the war. His wife, Mrs. Charlotte Pfeffer, wrote to [Goodrich and Hackett] that the Hanukkah scene shows her husband as an unbelieving Jew who did not know about Hanukkah. Yet in reality, he was a master of the Hebrew language and "his religion meant everything to him." She mentions that her husband has a son and brothers who survived, and she wants it made clear "that my husband was neither an inveterate bachelor nor a man without relations." She did not want her husband shown as a psychopath. "I think it enough that this had been done already in the play."[40]

[Goodrich and Hackett] wrote to Mrs. Pfeffer saying that a play cannot mirror reality. In order to inform the non-Jewish audience of Hanukkah and its significant to the Jews, they had to make one character unfamiliar with the service so another character could explain it both to him and the audience. Dr. Dussel became this character. Mrs. Pfeffer had requested a copy of the film script. [Goodrich and Hackett] replied that they were not allowed to send it; and in any case, they did not have final say on the film.[41] Dr. Dussel's character remained unchanged. The result is pernicious, even if unintended, to the memory of someone who had died in the Holocaust. It clearly indicates a lack of creative imagination on the part of [Goodrich and Hackett], for a man's biography is also history.

The question of historicity applies also to the changing of Anne's words. The scene in which the writers substitute "all races" for "Jews" when Anne speaks of suffering through the ages disturbed Meyer Levin, as we remember, because it removes the specific Jewish content of this speech. Moreover, viewers who are aware of the diary's authenticity would believe that what is written in the play and film is accurate, if not precisely Anne's words. So that when André Maurois, in praising the play, "quotes" Anne and writes: "'Nous ne sommes pas les seuls á souffrir', dit Anne. 'Il y en a d'autres. Et pas seulement juifs'" [We are not the only ones who have suffered, says Anne. There are also others and not only Jews],[42] he is actually misquoting Anne and universalizing her particular Jewish emphasis. Fiction merges with history in such a way as to distort even the mood of history. When Louis de Jong, director of the Netherlands State Institute for War Documentation and historical adviser for the film, wrote the director George Stevens, "Of course, I as a historian have discovered here and there some slight touches and details which did not correspond with reality, but these will not hinder the general public and I realize that sometimes certain dramatic effects are necessary in a work of art, even if they did not occur in reality,"[43] he correctly assessed the role of historical detail in film. However, changing the words of a document alters the meaning of the document. The film does this—for one reason—because it reflects in so many ways events occurring in the late 1950s.

The Diary of Anne Frank became a symbol and a metaphor for events in the United States in the 1950s. We are not the only ones to suffer, says Anne, sometimes one race sometimes another. The persecution of the Jews and its results show what can happen when racism prevails, a warning to the American public with regard to blacks. The film also functions as a metaphor for the prevailing domestic political theme of the 1950s—the HUAC hearings. When the end came for Anne and the others in the secret annex, it was because someone informed on them. A system which breeds informers can lead to tragic results, especially when the victims are innocent, as was the case with Anne, as well as those who found themselves blacklisted. The element of fear in the film, that one might be discovered, reflected a fear then current in America, that one's innocent past, perhaps a momentary flirtation with communism, might destroy the future. *The Diary of Anne Frank* shows to what extent the informer can inflict damage.

In the sense that *The Diary of Anne Frank* reflected racial discrimination against blacks along with the danger posed by the informer, its message in the 1950s was a liberal one. At the same time, the universalization and Americanization of its content fit into the dominant mood—one that was simultaneously repressive and liberal—a time when being "different" suggested either the wrong political attitude or the wrong social attitude. Within this environment, *The Diary of Anne Frank* became accepted as a symbol of the Holocaust. A European document dealing with events foreign to Americans became, through the play and the film, one of the first popularizations of the Holocaust on an international scale. It is the American imagination that decides how the Holocaust is to be remembered. The memory of the Holocaust becomes, in a sense, an American memory. Through Anne Frank's diary, America becomes the teacher to Europe of the moral implications of the Holocaust, but in a particularly American idiom. For as Pierre Sorlin explains: "Historiography, far from being universal, is subordinated to national traditions. In studying historical films, we must allow for the cultural backdrop against which history is defined."[44] It is against the historical backdrop of America in the 1950s that *The Diary of Anne Frank* evolves from a European piece to an Americanized work and shares the responsibility for what was becoming the universalization of the Holocaust.

Notes

1. David Bernstein, "Europe's Jews: Summer, 1947," *Commentary* 4 (Aug. 1947): 101. For a general overview of postwar America, see William E. Leuchtenburg, *A Troubled Feast: American Society since 1945* (Boston: Little, Brown, 1973).

2. Seymour Martin Lipset and Earl Raab, *The Politics of Unreason* (New York: Harper Torch Book, 1973), 209–14.

3. Robin M. Williams Jr., "Changes in Value Orientation," in *Jews in the Mind of America* by Charles H. Stember and others (New York: Basic Books, 1966), 348.

4. Since the 1950s, the authenticity of Anne's diary has been questioned by neo-Nazis. The Netherlands Institute for War Documentation published, in 1986, a 714-page, three-volume edition of the diary, which includes Anne's first diary, her own corrected version, and the version selected by her father, Otto Frank, which is the one under discussion. Otto Frank did not alter Anne's words, but rather deleted segments he felt were private. It is Mr. Frank's version that has been read throughout the world and adapted by [Frances Goodrich and Albert Hackett] as a play and film (and much later, a television movie). The only changes in Mr. Frank's version, as proved in laboratory tests, were corrections in spelling and grammar in Mr. Frank's handwriting. See Harry Mulisch, "Death and the Maiden," *New York Review of Books,* July 17, 1986, 7–8, and "The Diary of Anne Frank," *Patterns of Prejudice* 20 (July 1986): 36–38.

5. Report of the Jewish Film Advisory Committee, May 1971, Community Relations Committee Files, Jewish Federation Council of Greater Los Angeles, Los Angeles, California.

6. Howard Suber, "Politics and Popular Culture: Hollywood at Bay, 1933–1953," *American Jewish History* 4 (June 1979): 532.

7. Ibid., 530.

8. Victor S. Navasky, *Naming Names* (New York: Viking Press, 1980), 406.

9. Lipset and Raab, *Politics of Unreason,* 222–23.

10. Navasky, *Naming Names,* 118–21.

11. Ibid., 338–39.

12. Charles H. Stember (with Benjamin B. Ringer), "The Impact of Israel on American Attitudes," in *Jews in the Mind of America,* 171–96.

13. Benjamin B. Ringer, "Jews and the Desegregation Crisis," in *Jews in the Mind of America,* 197–201.

14. Ibid., 208–13. See also Leonard Dinnertein, "Anti-Semitism Exposed and Attacked, 1949–1950," *American Jewish History* 1 (Sept. 1981): 134–49.

15. Will Herberg quoted in Thomas F. O'Dea, "The Changing Image of the Jews and

the Contemporary Religious Situation: An Exploration of Ambiguities," in *Jews in the Mind of America,* 308.

16. Henry Popkin, "The Vanishing Jew of Our Popular Culture," *Commentary* 14 (July 1952): 46–55.

17. Report of the Jewish Film Advisory Committee, May 1971.

18. Letter from Otto Frank to Meyer Levin, June 28, 1952, received from Meyer Levin.

19. *The Diary of Anne Frank* was first published in the United States by Doubleday in 1952.

20. Meyer Levin has written two books on the subject, one nonfiction, *The Obsession* (New York: Simon and Schuster, 1973), and the other, a fictionalized account of the Anne Frank litigation, *The Fanatic* (New York: Simon and Schuster, 1964).

21. Portions of this diary appeared in the *New York Times,* and the rest was taken from the Goodrich/Hackett File, Wisconsin Center for Film and Theatre Research.

22. One can see how careful [Goodrich and Hackett] were in approaching the subject of Anne's diary as well as their sensitivity in dealing with Otto Frank, with whom they corresponded during the writing of the play and film. Goodrich and Hackett also gave scholarships to Brandeis and the Hebrew University. Goodrich/Hackett File, Wisconsin Center for Film and Theater Research.

23. English, we must remember, is not Mr. Frank's native language. Letter from Otto Frank to Goodrich and Hackett, June 14, 1954, Goodrich/Hackett File, Wisconsin Center for Film and Theater Research.

24. *Anne Frank: The Diary of a Young Girl* (New York: Pocket Books, 1959), 184.

25. Acting version of the play, Goodrich/Hackett File, Wisconsin Center for Film and Theater Research.

26. Several people have pointed out that in Lillian Hellman's memoir "Julia" (in *Pentimento: A Book of Portraits* [Boston: Little, Brown, 1973]), when Lilly asks Julia who the money is for [that] she has smuggled into Germany, Julia includes Catholics and communists along with Jews. See, for example, Sidra DeKoven Ezrahi, *By Words Alone: The Holocaust in Literature* (Chicago: University of Chicago Press, 1980). However, "Julia" was written much later than the diary, and there is a question as to the authenticity of "Julia." Nonetheless, it is interesting to contemplate.

27. Goodrich/Hackett File, Wisconsin Center for Film and Theater Research.

28. Letter from Goodrich and Hackett to Otto Frank, July 3, 1956, Goodrich/Hackett File, Wisconsin Center for Film and Theater Research.

29. Letter from Otto Frank to Goodrich and Hackett, Nov. 9, 1955, Goodrich/Hackett File, Wisconsin Center for Film and Theater Research.

30. Letter from Leah Salisbury to Goodrich and Hackett, Jan. 10, 1957, Goodrich/Hackett File, Wisconsin Center for Film and Theater Research. The Goodrich/Hackett File includes the record of the litigation proceedings, as well as letters from Levin requesting consideration of his daughter, Dominique, to star as Anne in the film version of the diary. Levin intimated he would be willing to stop his litigation if Dominique were to get the role. Director George Stevens refused his "offer."

31. Letter from John Stone to George Stevens, Dec. 23, 1957, Goodrich/Hackett File, Wisconsin Center for Film and Theater Research.

32. Letter from Goodrich and Hackett to Rabbi Max Nussbaum, Aug. 8, 1959, Goodrich/Hackett File, Wisconsin Center for Film and Theater Research.

33. *Diary,* 48.

34. Bruno Bettelheim, "The Ignored Lesson of Anne Frank," *Haper's Magazine,* Nov. 1960, 45–46. See also Bruno Bettelheim, *The Informed Heart* (London: Paladin, 1970).

35. See Judith E. Doneson, "The Jew as a Female Figure in Holocaust Film," *Shoah: A Review of Holocaust Studies and Commemorations* (1978): 12. This theme is a common one in many films on the Holocaust, American and otherwise, and in light of Jewish history, a logical one.

36. Stember, *Jews in the Mind of America,* 171–95.

37. Pierre Sorlin, *The Film in History* (Totowa, N.J.: Barnes and Noble, 1980), 49

38. Letter from Otto Frank to Mr. Ecker, Feb. 27, 1956, Goodrich/Hackett File, Wisconsin Center for Film and Theater Research.

39. Letter from Otto Frank to Goodrich and Hackett, Oct. 10, 1959, Goodrich/Hackett File, Wisconsin Center for Film and Theater Research.

40. Letter from Charlotte Pfeffer to Goodrich and Hackett, Apr. 8, 1957, Goodrich/Hackett File, Wisconsin Center for Film and Theater Research.

41. Letter from Goodrich and Hackett to Charlotte Pfeffer, Apr. 25, 1957, Goodrich/Hackett File, Wisconsin Center for Film and Theater Research.

42. André Maurois, "*L'Avant-Scéne,*" n.d.

43. Letter from Louis de Jong to George Stevens, Apr. 20, 1959, Goodrich/Hackett File, Wisconsin Center for Film and Theater Research.

44. Sorlin, *The Film in History,* 64.

17

Metamorphosis into American Adolescent

Algene Ballif

No matter how faithful the artistic adaptation might have been to the diary, it would necessarily have betrayed the very nature of the genre—for the numerous diaries written by the victims in hiding or in ghettos or camps . . . constitute a peculiar genre with a beginning, a middle, but no end.
—*Sidra DeKoven Ezrahi,* By Words Alone

Mr. and Mrs. Hackett have had to find concrete devices for explaining traits of character that are only described in the diary. . . . Most of all, they have had to provide a beginning, middle and end.
—*Brooks Atkinson, Foreword to* The Diary of Anne Frank

Those of us who have read and loved *Anne Frank: The Diary of a Young Girl* might well be interested in the production currently enjoying success at the Cort Theater in an adaptation by Frances Goodrich and Albert Hackett called simply *The Diary of Anne Frank.*[1] One knows beforehand that to translate such a work into drama is an impossible task for anyone but a Chekhov, and particularly for the caliber of playwrights who address themselves to the business of "adapting" these days. But at 8:40 P.M. there is a magic of expectation that puts one in a generous frame of mind, and creates the hope that the failure about to be witnessed will at least be an honorable attempt. And when the theater darkens, the hush falls, and the velvet curtain rises slowly on the dimly lit interior we recognize as the secret annex, all is well, because the set, ingeniously compact, is faithful to our impression of the cramped and shabby quarters which the diary describes. Immediately familiar, nostalgic, and poignant, we believe in it.

The play begins rather well. The war is over; Anne's father shuffles up the stairs and enters the disordered hiding place for the first time since he and his family were discovered in it by the *Grüne Polizei* and sent to concentration camps. All have since perished save himself, and he drifts about the old room like a forlorn apparition, picking up wisps of things as if they were memories he cannot remember well enough, can't really touch, yet which prick at his feelings like darning needles at tatters. It has something of the atmosphere of the last scene of *Our Town* about it, when the spirit of Emily returns to the scenes of her youth and is overwhelmed by a sense of never having held life close enough. Here, the living Mr. Frank comes back to a room full of ghosts, the elusive spirits of his beloved family who carry brief whiffs of recent life to his nostrils, and leave him torn between the pain of remembering them too well, and the pain of realizing how utterly alone he is. He peers about, dazedly intent, as if half expecting them to materialize. Perhaps for a moment they do, for suddenly he sinks down in a paroxysm of pathetic little sobs. Not a word has been spoken, but these are the best moments of the play; the kind of experience that Mr. Frank survived has been simply and movingly suggested.

Abruptly the spell is broken. The Dutch friend who had helped hide the family, Miep, invades the scene, pregnant (life goes on), practical (you're not leaving, Mr. Frank, this is your *business*), and speaking in the pedestrian tones of a sensible young American housewife. She produces Anne's diary, gives it to Mr. Frank, and he begins to read it aloud—almost without batting an eyelash, without having properly established a mood for the reading of the diary, or the effect that reading it for the first time would have upon Anne's father.

Then the voice of a girl fades in and takes over the passages of narration which bridge the transitions from scene to scene throughout the play. It is a lovely voice—young and resonant and full of the energy of goodwill and the desire to be loved by her audience. But it is not long before the listener becomes aware of an inadequacy: it is the voice of a girl who has never really listened to the *inner* voice of Anne Frank, which is the true voice of the diary. It is a voice that, like the stock dove of Wordsworth's poem, seems to listen only to itself. It is without the nuance, the quick intelligence, even without the volatility by which we would recognize its prototype. It rises and falls in set cadence, like waves lapping a shore, and toward the end of the play it has taken on a kind of pseudo-caesural pause in the middle of almost every line—intended, I imagine, to convey Anne's having grown up a bit more, having suffered the pangs of falling in love, and having begun to think. The Anne of this play, however, has not actually undergone any of these experiences, at least in the way that the real Anne Frank did, so that these incoherent halts serve only to heighten the effect of superficiality and inarticulateness that renders the script so poor, does pitiful injustice to the diary, and proves too much even for those of the actors who try to make up for it.

For the bulk of the play, this is the Anne Frank who takes over; seldom do we glimpse the Anne Frank of the real diary. There is, for example, an incident in the first act which quite subverts the real Anne's healthy, sturdy nature. When the occupants of the secret annex are seized with panic because of sudden loud noises coming from the landing just beyond their secret door, Anne faints dead away. The Anne of the diary did not faint. There is an entry on October 20, 1942, which speaks of having "nearly fainted," and Anne experienced, throughout her sequestration, many moments of fear, terror, and shock much worse than this one—but she does not ever faint. It is rather important, I think, that seemingly small facts like this should not be violated for the sake of a dramatic situation which would be quite dramatic enough without such extremities of response. Not that Anne was self-sufficient and contained as regards the frightening realities of hiding for two years under the very nose of the Gestapo, but neither was she hysterical about them. That quality of response belongs rather to Mrs. Van Daan, as Anne's diary so thoroughly bears out.

The most seriously dishonest section of the play, however, and the one which I think is the type of its failure, is that which attempts to dramatize Anne's romance with Peter Van Daan. I could not recognize a jot of truth in it. In this scene, Anne is revealed in her small bedroom at stage right wearing a white eyelet-embroidered petticoat and chemise. She is, according to local parlance, "getting all gussied up" to visit Peter, who is waiting restlessly in his small garret on the other side of the stage. As the dialogue proceeds, Anne sweeps her long hair up into a psyche-bun and impulsively tries on her sister's pink lace brassiere, stroking the firmness of her round young breasts as she does so. Then she dons a soft pastel skirt and décolleté blouse of charming simplicity, petit-Louis pumps, and, for the finishing touch, a lengthy knitted stole of soft wool. Before emerging from her room she pauses on the threshold and says to her sister, "Well, here I go . . . to run the gauntlet!" Then out she glides, stately as a debutante, through the room where the parents and Mr. Dussel sit, to Peter's door, conspicuously aloof to the presence of everyone. Peter shows her in and there ensues a conversation between the young lovers that quivers with demure restraint and produces an abundance of the caesural pauses elsewhere described.

The conversation, let alone the manner in which it is carried on, has virtually nothing to do with Anne Frank—or for that matter with Peter Van Daan. The Anne of this scene, for example, hesitatingly asks Peter if he has ever kissed a girl, to which he replies yes, to which she inquires if she was very pretty, and so on in the vein of one of the stock versions of the adolescent; and after a strained little ceremony of saying good night to each other, they suddenly turn back and fall into each other's arms in an ardent, innocent embrace. Then, when the door closes on Peter's room, and Anne stands outside it, presumably with rapidly beating heart, she does a curious and uncharacteristic thing: she lifts her dangling stole and tosses it cavalierly over one shoulder, as if to say, "Ah, now I am a woman of the world!" and as if, too, in secret jest of all that has taken place. It is true that the Anne of the diary once or twice speaks of Peter as her "conquest," but this is never for a moment meant in the sense of a coy spoof or for the purposes of striking a pose or as an innuendo suggesting any fundamental lack of honesty or respect for their relationship. The real Anne Frank would never, at such a moment, have performed this flippant little antic. The audience, I must report, was greatly amused by it.

But if this were not enough, Anne then goes through the extraordinary business of languidly kissing each member of the household good night, hovering over them gently and lovingly as she does so, and imparting to her audience the age-old truth (undiscovered until our century) that a little love is a wonderful thing. With this she floats into her room, and the wholesome little love scene comes to its close. [. . .]

For anyone who has read and understood the diary of Anne Frank I need not point out the utter travesty this scene commits. Anne's relation to Peter was notable for its lack of pretension, its candor and ingenuousness, its freedom from all the ritualized and self-conscious behavior by which American adults identify a "normal" adolescent. Peter is a person whom Anne has found herself able to be and talk with more honestly and easily than with anyone else—even her father—and without the constraint that so oppresses her when she is in the presence of "grownups." In the play it is just the reverse. Anne and Peter cannot really speak to each other, and Anne's preliminary toilet strikes us as a symbol of this state of affairs, for it shows that she cannot even go to Peter as her natural self. As she performed her last rites of the good night kiss for everyone in the room, I could not help remembering the moment in the real Anne's diary when she irritably mentions not feeling like kissing people good night any more, and that it occurs about the same time that she begins to reveal her growing attachment to Peter.

There are numerous other touches of this sort which emphasize the central failure of the play to catch the spirit of the work from which it springs. The plot literally thickens with misrepresentations. Anne's conflicts with her mother are inanely arbitrary and often seem perverse. This is because the character of Mrs. Frank is not created, and what the Anne of the diary reacted to is never here disclosed. Anne's keen and well-articulated insights always told us what it was in other people and herself that caused the friction between them. In her deepest self she never really accepts the explanation that it is "just a stage" she is going through. And when, in the last act, Anne is made to say, "Daddy was right, it was just a phase I was going through," what was left of my sorely tried generosity turned to gall. There was nothing left to hope for, since the very pith and marrow of the diary had with this glib stroke, so wisely spoken, been swept away.

The Broadway Anne Frank had turned out to be not much more than the Jewish Corliss Archer (the adolescent girl in *Kiss and Tell*)—a more human and en-dearing Corliss than we have had for some time perhaps, but still another image of that fixed American idea of the adolescent, the central imperative of which is that this species of creature is not to be taken seriously. (Unless, of course, he becomes a delinquent.)

If the diary of Anne Frank is remarkable for any one thing, it is for the way in which she is able to command our deepest seriousness about everything she is going through—the way she makes us forget she is an adolescent and makes us wish that this way of experiencing life were not so soon lost by some of us, and much sooner found by most of us. Ironically for her, the Anne Frank on Broad-way cannot command our seriousness for all Anne's true seriousness—her honesty, intelligence, and inner strength—has been left out of the script.

It is impossible here to consider why and how this myth of adolescence has taken hold in America, and why Anne Frank's dramatizers seem to have lost touch with her, and have dealt with her story in so false and shallow a fashion. But if we in America cannot present her with the respect and integrity and seriousness she deserves, then I think we should not try to present her at all. Not all adoles-cents, even in America, are the absurd young animals we know from stage and screen. Not all of them are able to spare us the agony of trying to grow up. Not all of them are the desperate young clowns who never do grow up, but only quiet down. Anne Frank was not the American adolescent, as Hackett and Goodrich would have us believe. She was an unaffected young girl, uniquely alive, and self-aware—experiencing more, and in a better way perhaps, than many of us do in the course of a whole lifetime.

Not one of the characters in *The Diary of Anne Frank* is brought to life—not even Anne's father, who is her chiefest source of wisdom, dignity, and strength in the book. It is not the actors' fault; they are all at least competent. They are simply uninspired by the script. Margot barely utters a word, and Dussel is just a laugh man. All are primarily foils for the antics of Anne rather than the people she lived and shared and struggled with for two clandestine years. The wonder-ful patches of their conversation which she wrote down in her diary are never heard. The daily, active dedication to learning of the Frank family, the political discussions that Anne complained about, the wireless that was always tuned to the BBC, and the confirmed Anglophiles who listened to it (Anne's diary seldom mentions the Americans; it is the English who are really fighting the war, and Churchill is their great man)—all these never find their way into the play. They would have been forgivable omissions if the spirit of Anne herself had survived them. That it did not can only turn us back to her real diary for the kind of memorial she requires.

Letters from Readers: The Stage Anne Frank

To the Editor of *Commentary:*

Algene Ballif's complaint that the adaptation of the *Diary of Anne Frank* (in "Anne Frank on Broadway," November 1955) presents Anne Frank as "the image of the American idea of adolescence" and neglects her serious side suggests a major misconception of the original diary and the Broadway play. Miss Ballif calls the stage version of Anne a "Jewish Corliss Archer," a canned adolescent, and objects that she puts her hair up and punctuates her speech with artificial pauses.

Anne Frank revealed herself in her diary as a girl with many of the preoccupations of adolescence. She liked clothes and collected photographs of film stars. She was vain about her appearance and her conquests, and later had a characteristically hesitant love affair. She also had special gifts. She was an unusually precocious reader and . . . an extraordinary writer. She had courage and humor, and was uncommonly aware of herself and others. . . .

But these qualities which resulted in such an achievement as her diary should not make us forget that she was a normal, in many ways still conventional, girl. That the adapters of the diary have managed to present her on the stage as at once typical and extraordinary is much to their credit and to the credit of Anne Frank's remarkable spirit, whose main quality, as she herself so often and so sensibly remarked, was its wholeness. . . . It would have been as much an error for the adapters to overlook this wholeness as for one to assume that Jane Austen never powdered her nose. . . .

But Miss Ballif clearly came prepared to find quite a different young girl from the one who wrote in the diary, and saw on the stage a version of Anne Frank quite unlike the one who appears there. Her claim that the stage Anne reflects a vulgarized (i.e., American) image of adolescence may reflect in turn her own . . . incorrect view of the play.

An example of this is her failure to recognize the adapters' obvious intention in the scene in which Anne dresses herself elegantly, visits Peter, and is kissed. Far from playing the coquette at the end of this scene, as Miss Ballif claims, Anne leaves Peter's room elated, and so obviously full of love and excitement at having reached this long-awaited stage in her development that her reactions are not only dramatically inevitable, but precise reflections of the character we find in the diary. She tosses her scarf over her shoulder, as a great lady should, and eager to share her love, kisses the assembled families as she crosses the stage to her own room.

Miss Ballif went to the theater expecting to find in Anne Frank a woman of "high moral seriousness"—F. R. Leavis in a pinafore. She saw instead a bobby sox Mae West. The complexity of Miss Ballif's visual problem is appalling.

Barbara Epstein
New York City

Miss Ballif writes:

Barbara Epstein's experience both of Anne Frank's diary and the play about her seems too alien to my own to argue about. I hope, however, that my remarks can clarify something.

I do not at all object to Anne's putting up her hair, which she often did, experimentally, in the real secret annex. I object, rather, to the particular use made of this in the play—i.e., to her putting up her hair to go see Peter—a piece of business not in the diary in that connection, and not, I think, relevant to Anne's relation with Peter, which was a notably undecorated one.

The dramatization on Broadway certainly makes Anne "typical," but it does not make her in the least "extraordinary," as Mrs. Epstein seems to feel it does. And to "forget that she was a normal conventional girl" is not a danger—certainly not in these United States where we are never permitted to forget such things, where the normal and conventional are crammed down our throats, and where we constantly seek the normal and conventional to cling to. What is a danger is our not comprehending those "qualities which resulted in such an achievement as her diary." Anne Frank's diary is important not for its caressing little gusts of normality and typicality, but for what is unique and extraordinary about her. A better playwright might have seen this and written a better play.

As it is, it leans heavily upon the crutch of typicality and seems to take for granted that we will supply, from our racial memories, as it were, the uniqueness. The success of the play is in large part due, I think, to this accurate calculation that its audiences would bring to it something that was not actually there. The adapters seemed to feel that they were therefore at liberty to sentimentalize and indulge the "familiar" to the hilt—which is exactly what they did. It is significant that Anne's film collection, and not her elaborate charts of family trees (over which she spent far more time), got into the script. It makes so many of us feel good that she kept a film collection just as we did when we were young girls, and that we shared other fond foolishness with her. In identifying with Anne in these surface similarities we can unconsciously identify with Anne's differences and superiorities—without ever having taken the trouble to learn just what they were. It is one of our usual errors in the search for identity. A fool and a wise man may easily find they have something in common, but it is only the fool who can make the mistake of believing he is a wise man for it.

As for the "love scene," I can only quote from Anne's own entry of Friday, April 28, 1944:

> Every evening, after the last kiss, I would like to dash away, not to look into his eyes any more—away, away, alone in the darkness.
>
> And what do I have to face, when I reach the bottom of the staircase? Bright lights, questions, and laughter; I have to swallow it all and not show a thing. My heart still

feels too much; I can't get over a shock such as I received yesterday [Anne's first kiss on the lips from Peter] all at once. . . . Peter has taken possession of me and turned me inside out; surely it goes without saying that anyone would require a rest and a little while to recover from such an upheaval?

A rereading of the entire section, if not the entire diary, would be helpful.

Algene Ballif
New York City

Note

1. The current [1955] Broadway dramatization of *Anne Frank: The Diary of a Young Girl* recalls the fact that *Commentary* was the first to bring the diary to English-speaking readers, publishing extensive excerpts from it in the issues of May and June 1952.

18

At the Theater: Berlin Postscript

Kenneth Tynan

And now, let's go to the theater!
—*Charlotte Delbo,* Days and Memory

At the Schlosspark, last Monday, I survived the most drastic emotional experience the theater has ever given me. It had little to do with art, for the play was
not a great one, yet its effect, in Berlin, at that moment of history, transcended
anything that art has yet learned to achieve. It invaded the privacy of the whole
audience: I tried hard to stay detached, but the general catharsis engulfed me.

Like all great theatrical occasions, this was not only a theatrical occasion: it
involved the world outside. The first page of the program prepared one: a short,
slight essay on collective guilt. Turn over for the title: "The Diary of Anne Frank,"
directed by Boleslaw Barlog. It is not a vengeful dramatization. Quietly, often
gaily, it recreates the daily life of eight Jews who hid for two years in an Amsterdam
attic before the Gestapo broke in. Otto Frank was the sole survivor; Anne Frank
was killed in Belsen.

When I saw the play in New York it vaguely perturbed me: there seemed no
need to do it: it smacked of exploitation. The Berlin actors (especially Johanna
von Koczian and Walter Prazek) were better on the whole and devouter than the
Americans, but I do not think that was why the play seemed so much more ur-
gent and necessary on Monday night.

After the interval the man in front of me put his head in his hands and did
not afterwards look at the stage. He was not, I believe, Jewish. It was not until
the end that one fully appreciated Barlog's wisdom and valor in using an entirely
non-Jewish cast. Having read the last lines of the diary, which affirm, movingly
and irrationally, Anne Frank's unshattered trust in human goodness, Otto Frank
closes the book and says, very slowly, "She puts me to shame."

Thus the play ended. The house lights went up on an audience that sat drained and ashen, some staring straight ahead, others staring at the ground, for a full half-minute. Then as if awakening from a nightmare they rose and filed out in total silence, not looking at each other, avoiding even the customary blinks of recognition with which friend greets friend. There was no applause, and there were no curtain calls.

All of this, I am well aware, is not drama criticism. In the shadow of an event so desperate and traumatic, criticism would be an irrelevance. I can only record an emotion that I felt, would not have missed, and pray never to feel again.

19

This Time, Another Anne Confronts Life in the Attic

Ben Brantley

I see myself alone in a dungeon. . . . Sometimes I wander by the roadside or our "Secret Annex" is on fire, or they come and take us away at night. . . . I simply can't imagine that the world will ever be normal for us again.
—*November 8, 1943*

To see Natalie Portman on the stage of the Music Box Theater is to understand what Proust meant when he spoke of girls in flower. Ms. Portman, a film actress making her Broadway debut, is only sixteen, and despite her precocious resumé, she gives off a pure rosebud freshness that can't be faked. There is ineffable grace in her awkwardness, and her very skin seems to glow with the promise of miraculous transformations.

That the fate of the character Ms. Portman portrays is known in advance by most of her audience turns that radiance into something that is also infinitely chilling, however, and you may even feel guilty about basking in the warmth of a flame that you realize will be horribly and abruptly extinguished.

Ms. Portman has the title role in the new production of *The Diary of Anne Frank,* the dramatization of the legendary journals of a Jewish girl hiding from the Nazis in Amsterdam. And whatever the shortcomings of Ms. Portman's performance and the production itself, which opened last night, the evening never lets us forget the inhuman darkness waiting to claim its incandescently human heroine.

This version, adapted (which in this instance means almost entirely rewritten) by Wendy Kesselman from Frances Goodrich and Albert Hackett's 1955 script and directed by James Lapine, offers no treacly consolations about the triumph of the spirit. Indeed, the effect is more like watching a vibrant, exquisite fawn seen through the lens of a hunter's rifle.

An uncompromising steadiness of gaze, embedded in a bleak sense of historical context, is the strongest element in a production more notable for its moral conscientiousness than for theatrical inspiration. This version is undeniably moving, with snuffles and sobs from the audience beginning well before the first act is over, and there are beautifully drawn, organic-seeming moments throughout.

Yet in portraying the denizens of the famous secret annex, the actors, who include such top-of-the-line veterans as Linda Lavin and George Hearn, don't always project the sense of a unified ensemble; it is often as if they had set their performances to different metronomes, when the feeling of a natural flow of time is essential.

As a consequence, the production can at times seem little more than serviceable. And yet somehow with this work, particularly as Ms. Kesselman has reshaped it, serviceable can be enough. The horror of its central situation, and the natural dramatic tightness it lends itself to, continue to hold the attention with an iron clamp. It also doesn't hurt that many people who see the play bring their own resonant associations with the diary. Clear, honorable and workmanlike, this *Anne Frank* doesn't achieve greatness in itself. But it doesn't diminish the magnitude of the events behind it.

It should be noted that *Anne Frank* returns to Broadway with an unwieldy load of polemical baggage including furious debates over the diaries' appropriation as a pop commodity. The most resounding salvo was fired two months ago in an essay in the *New Yorker* by the novelist and critic Cynthia Ozick, who argued that Anne Frank's journals had been "infantilized, Americanized, homogenized, sentimentalized," especially in their translation to the stage. "In celebrating Anne Frank's years in the secret annex," Ms. Ozick wrote, "the nature and meaning of her death has been, in effect, forestalled."[1]

Ms. Kesselman's reworking of the original script, which incorporates new material from the complete editions of the diaries made available in the last decade, goes a long way in redressing such objections. The Goodrich-Hackett script, under the director Garson Kanin's supervision, had bleached out much of its source's specific ethnic content for fear of alienating mainstream audiences. Correspondingly, the unspeakable destiny that awaited Anne was eclipsed by a disproportionate emphasis on the girl's idealism.

This new interpretation never relaxes its awareness of the hostile world beyond the attic that was the Franks' sanctuary and prison for two claustrophobic years or of the religious identity that made them a quarry. The earlier version began in a scene of sentimental hindsight, with Anne's father discovering her diaries; this one leaps, with a gripping immediacy, into medias res.

Adrianne Lobel's set, modeled as closely as the Music Box permits on the rooms behind Otto Frank's offices where the family lived, is in full view when we arrive. And for any reader of the diaries, it is hauntingly eloquent before any actor appears.

So is the entrance of the Franks themselves: Otto (Mr. Hearn); his wife, Edith (Sophie Hayden), and their daughters, Margot (Missy Yager) and Ms. Portman's Anne, who arrive on stage wet and disoriented from the rainy trip to their new home. As they turn to us, struggling out of their coats, the large yellow stars sewn onto their clothes are suddenly, glaringly visible.

It's a wonderful piece of staging, unforced yet emphatic; it establishes Judaism, and the ways it is perceived, as the Franks' central defining identity. "Look, it's still there," says Anne of the shadow of the star that remains after she has torn it off.

Indeed. Perplexed, often defiant references to what it means to be a Jew in the occupied Netherlands abound in the diaries, and Ms. Kesselman has incorporated as many as time allows: from Anne's catalogue of the activities forbidden Jews in Amsterdam to her vision of a former classmate in a concentration camp. The evolving sophistication of her writing about the world around her is far more evident now. So is her lyrical consideration of her burgeoning sexuality, and Ms. Kesselman has included a beautiful passage, nicely read by Ms. Portman, in which the girl describes the transporting effects of pictures of female nudes in art books.

As welcome as these additions are, one wishes that the voiceovers in which many of them are delivered had been less clumsily amplified. The effect is bizarre, as if Anne had found a public-address system in that attic. And there is also the sense that in combing through the rich trove of the unedited diaries, Ms. Kesselman was hard put to select just what to use. There is an occasional feeling of material being shoe-horned in and confusingly truncated.

This gives the production a fragmentary quality its predecessor didn't have. Mr. Lapine's staging doesn't always accommodate the lapses from slice-of-life naturalism, though there are moments throughout, particularly among the younger actors, where everything clicks into place. And the climatic scene that finds the characters festively eating strawberries just before they are captured is everything it should be: a wrenching but impeccably rendered fall from what has become ordinary life into perdition.

Presumably, with further time the talented cast—which includes Ms. Lavin, Harris Yulin, Austin Pendleton, and the young Jonathan Kaplan as the other inhabitants of the annex—will grow into a more comfortable ensemble. As it is, all the actors reach isolated, individual heights, most notably in the second act, when the stress of confinement finally brings out the Darwinian animal in everyone.

But in the first act, the performers are still oddly stiff as a team, and there's a sense, in ways that go beyond their characters' discomfort with unfamiliar circumstances, that they have yet to find a shared rhythm.

As the endlessly patient father, Mr. Hearn has an expressly theatrical, heroic voice and carriage that don't provide the troubled, affectionate shading to convey his all-important relationship with Anne. Ms. Lavin brings an impressive technical bravura to the role of the vain, anxious Mrs. Van Daan that achieves some splendid effects, as in a stunning new monologue for the character, and others that seem artificially calculated.

Mr. Pendleton appears slightly at sea as the graceless dentist who is forced to share Anne's room (though the scene in which she introduces him to their sleeping quarters is charming). Mr. Yulin, as the cynical, self-serving Mr. Van Daan, and Ms. Hayden, as Anne's fragile mother, are better in conveying, in very different ways, the aura of the older, more genteel world that shaped their characters.

Ms. Yager and Mr. Kaplan, as the Van Daan son with whom Anne discovers love, provide affectingly restrained portraits of adolescence cramped and frustrated by circumstance. Ms. Portman's comparative lack of stage experience shows, but in a strange way, this works to her advantage.

Even when her line readings are stilted, her delicately expressive face never fails her. It becomes, as it should, the evening's barometer of changing moods in the annex. She has, moreover, an endlessly poignant quality of spontaneity, and of boundless energy in search of an outlet, that is subtly modulated as the evening goes on.

In Philip Roth's short novel *The Ghost Writer,* the narrator speaks of Anne the writer in her diaries. "It's like watching an accelerated film of a fetus sprouting a face," he says.[2] Without ever toning down her innate vitality, Ms. Portman does indeed progress from self-centered girlishness to the cusp of self-aware womanhood. To learn again that she will not be allowed to go further still shatters the heart.

The Diary of Anne Frank

By Frances Goodrich and Albert Hackett; newly adapted by Wendy Kesselman; directed by James Lapine; sets by Adrianne Lobel; costumes by Martin Pakledinaz; lighting by Brian MacDevitt; sound by Dan Moses Schreier; hair and wigs by Paul Huntley; production stage manager, David Hyslop; general management, Stuart Thompson; technical supervisor, Gene O'Donovan. Presented by David Stone, Amy Nederlander-Case, Jon B. Platt, Jujamcyn Theaters, and Hal Luftig, in association with Harriet Newman Leve and James D. Stern. At the Music Box Theater, 239 West 45th Street, Manhattan.
With: Natalie Portman (Anne Frank), George Hearn (Otto Frank), Linda Lavin

(Mrs. Van Daan), Harris Yulin (Mr. Van Daan), Austin Pendleton (Mr. Dussel), Sophie Hayden (Edith Frank), Missy Yager (Margot Frank), Jessica Walling (Miep Gies), Jonathan Kaplan (Peter Van Daan), Philip Goodwin (Mr. Kralcr), Peter Kybart (First Man), James Hallett (Second Man), and Eddie Kaye Thomas (Third Man).

Notes

1. Cynthia Ozick, "A Critic At Large: Who Owns Anne Frank?" *New Yorker,* Oct. 6, 1997, 78–79.

2. Philip Roth, *The Ghost Writer* (New York: Farrar, Straus, Giroux, 1979), 169.

20

Don Quixote and the Star of David

Lawrence Graver

Come with me Anne.
Come . . . .
Come sit with me here.
—*C. K. Williams, "A Day for Anne Frank"*

Although [Meyer] Levin was not, as he thought, the victim of a conspiracy, his career and reputation were certainly impaired by the opposition and mockery of those who did not respect his beliefs about Jewishness and his opposition to Russian communism. He was also thwarted by something less tangible but more pervasive than an overt conspiracy: the coming together of powerful elements in the Zeitgeist—the commercial imperatives of Broadway, the resistance of audiences to disagreeable (not to mention harrowing) subjects, the American craving for universalism and broad consensus, the assimilationist mood among many Jews, the postwar pressure to reconstruct, not to offend Germany, and the reverse McCarthyism in some left-wing intellectual circles that gave anticommunism a bad name.

That the materialism, political fear, conformity, and simplistic pieties of American society in the 1950s, as well as Levin's own hapless, self-defeating behavior, obscured his play and his efforts to deepen public understanding of the significance of what was done to the Jews of Europe is one of the most plangent facts of his thirty-year involvement with Anne Frank's book. Yet in a strange, ironical way, that involvement can also be read as one of Levin's most engrossing, wide-ranging, and resonant stories, a story he in part created, tried to write himself out of, but could never actually write. As he said in his [unpublished] memoir, the affair "was the inevitable expression of all I ever was, all I ever did, as a writer and as a Jew";[1] and the implications of that story continue to have important private and public reverberations.

An American Jewish writer of high talent, ambition, and heightened social consciousness is present at the liberation of the Nazi camps and sets out to convey the significance of the atrocities by writing dispatches, making films about the struggles of survivors, and publishing a blunt autobiographical memoir in which he probes the dilemma of being an "unbelonging" Jew at midcentury. He then proposes adapting for the theater a remarkable diary kept by one of the innocent young victims, hoping that his play will allow him to reach a large audience with its serious message. In his enthusiasm, he writes a draft that faithfully yet awkwardly conveys the book's essence, but the script is summarily rejected as unsuitable for the commercial stage, without his being given a chance to explore and develop its possibilities with the help of experienced theater people. The drama that is chosen achieves enormous success and esteem, quickening the process by which its protagonist becomes one of the best-known, most-loved figures in history and a cultural symbol of lost possibility but of hope as well. Embittered by the loss of the auspicious project he created and by the rejection of his work, the writer undertakes a strenuous campaign to get his version accepted and performed, a campaign motivated by a desire for truth, justice, and freedom of expression, but also by dashed hopes, frustrated ambition, vanity, envy, rage, and unresolved tensions related to his family, heritage, and profession. The campaign eventually brings him into conflict with a cast that includes the respected father of the dead author and eminent people in the worlds of publishing, theater, literature, journalism, politics, religion, and law (many of whom are themselves Jewish). As resistance to his claims intensifies and the stakes get higher, he repudiates agreements, writes abusive letters, distorts past events, develops a conspiracy theory, takes out accusatory newspaper ads, initiates litigation, stirs public scandal, and causes great distress to himself, his adversaries, his family, and his friends. His obsessive battle, which he sees as a fight for truth, justice, and personal redemption as an artist and a Jew, becomes blurred by what many others perceive as an endless, ego-driven, paranoid campaign for self-justification. With so much of his energy and imagination devoted to confronting real and invented enemies, he becomes increasingly isolated. His other writing suffers; much of his later fiction is characterized by tendentiousness and the absence of the imagination, drama, and complexity that mark his best earlier books, except for one novel and a memoir in which the subject is the obsession itself. His family life suffers too; his wife speaks of watching him sink "deeper and deeper into the quicksand" of his Anne Frank obsession as "the most heart-breaking sorrow of my life."[2]

Years later, recalling the effects of the Anne Frank affair on their family life, Levin's adopted daughter remembered his many acts of kindness and generosity, but she also spoke of herself and her brothers as being, in some ways, like battered children who never talked about the traumatic events through which they had lived. In 1991, after reading their mother's book, they were astonished to discover the meaning and consequences of the turbulence that had gone on around them for so long.

Despite the effects, the writer cannot relinquish his cause and free himself of his fixation because over the years they have come to embody, for better and worse, so much of his personality and being. His original cause—to bear witness to the Holocaust—was motivated primarily by shock, outrage, grief, bewilderment, ambivalence about his own heritage, and an idealistic need to now find personal redemption in renewing his connection to the past and the future of the Jewish people. By choosing Anne Frank's diary as the instrument for his own fulfillment, he innocently selects a book that is both well- and ill-suited for the task; and he sets out to enact his redemptive drama in an environment (the American entertainment world) that inevitably turns it into a bruising tragic farce. The wound of the European Jews does become his wound, but in endlessly ironical and diminished ways; and his history testifies to the enormous difficulty, if not the impossibility, of finding an authentic way to bear witness to the Holocaust in a society governed by money, popular taste, media hype, democratic optimism, and a susceptibility to easy consolation. In the process, the writer's wound often seems self-inflicted, a punishment he administered to himself out of guilt and shame about being Jewish, and from disillusionment at being "betrayed" by Otto Frank, the father of "the lost girl" and his surrogate father and rival as well. But, in fact, the wound was caused by unresolvable tensions between his romantic desire for self-fulfillment as a Jew and a writer, his personal limitations as a man and a writer, and the material, political, and cultural conditions of the world in which he lived.

After his death, it becomes clear that he was in vital ways more reliable as a reader of the girl's book than those who helped create the sentimental mystique in America. His drama, while not as theatrical, is a more accurate response to the child and her history than is the acclaimed version. (Indeed, some of his most important insights have been reflected in recent revised versions of the Goodrich and Hackett play, designed to make it more realistic and less uplifting.) But fifteen years after his death, nearly all of his books are out of print; his play is rarely done, even in minor theaters; and he is remembered—if at all—mostly as the writer who fought a strident, interminable, losing battle against Anne Frank's father. In the 1990s, even his valuable early contributions to the success of the diary in America have been unfairly criticized for paying more attention to the specific qualities of the book and its writer than to the particular crime the Nazis committed against the Jews.[3]

Reflecting on this reading of the history, one feels the force of a fine comment by Levin's editor and friend Robert Gottlieb: "I was very fond of him, and admired both his energy and his abilities. But in his quarrelsome and provocative mode he always reminded me of a figure from Molière, about whom one doesn't know whether to laugh or cry."[4] Now, however, from a distance, if we look closely at, and then past, the quarrels and provocations, Levin's accomplishments appear more substantial. Even if recollections of his outrageous behavior can still provoke sadness, laughter, or pain, his cause seems in important ways less lost. He wrote a number of books that deserve to be kept in print: *The Old Bunch, Citizens, In Search, Compulsion,* and *The Obsession.* His prohibited play deserves to be published and performed. He challenged people, often in uncomfortable ways, to think about and act on the meaning and responsibilities of contemporary Jewish identity; and he made essential contributions over a thirty-year period to an understanding of Anne Frank's diary and its connections to the Holocaust.

Notes

1. Meyer Levin, "In Love," unpublished memoir, Meyer Levin Collection, Special Collections, Boston University Libraries.

2. Undated letter, late 1970s, Meyer Levin Collection.

3. See Alvin H. Rosenfeld, "Popularization and Memory: The Case of Anne Frank," in *Lessons and Legacies: The Meaning of the Holocaust in a Changing World,* ed. Peter Hayes (Evanston, Ill.: Northwestern University Press, 1991), 249–51; and Edward Alexander, *The Holocaust and the War of Ideas* (New Brunswick, N.J.: Transaction, 1994), 1–53.

4. Letter to author, Feb. 17, 1994.

21

Germany's New Flagellants
Alfred Werner

Fine specimens of humanity, those Germans, and to think I am actually one of them! No, that's not true, Hitler took away our nationality long ago. And besides, there are no greater enemies on earth than the Germans and the Jews.
—*October 9, 1942*

A not uncommon sight in the Middle Ages was that of half-naked flagellants, strolling the streets in double file, reciting prayers, and scourging themselves with leather thongs until the blood ran. This ferocious manner of doing penance for sins did not originate in Germany, but it was there developed with mystic fervor into a fine art. To quote from the *Catholic Encyclopedia:* "As soon . . . as the Flagellant movement crossed the Alps into Teutonic countries, its whole nature changed. The idea was welcomed with enthusiasm: a ceremonial was rapidly developed, and almost as rapidly a specialized doctrine. . . . The Flagellants became an organized sect, with severe discipline and extravagant claims."

If generalizations are permissible, it might be suggested that no nation is so susceptible to mystic ideas as the German, and that no other can so channelize romantic enthusiasm into a rigid system. The German anti-Semitism of the Hitler period, while influenced by political and economic motives, was predominantly of a hysterical nature, as can best be gathered from Hitler's maniacal foamings. Goebbels, Rosenberg, and other party intellectuals provided this pseudo-religion with a "ceremonial" and a "specialized" doctrine. Like the fifteenth-century Flagellants under the dictatorship of Konrad Schmidt, the German anti-Semites under Hitler became "an organized sect, with severe discipline and extravagant claims," with the slight difference that instead of scourging their own bodies, they beat the Jews, upon whom the sins of the world could conveniently be blamed.

In the Germany of 1956 and 1957, flagellantism has reappeared, although it is now devoid of its abhorrent physical manifestations. To superficial observers it may appear to be an awkward sort of philo-Semitism, but to see it as such and nothing else would amount to neglecting its strong hysterical or, if you prefer, romantic undercurrents. The new flagellantism is not yet a mass movement [. . .] but even at this initial stage certain features—some reassuring, many frightening—can be noted.

It would be oversimplifying to say that the puzzling phenomenon of German philo-Semitism came like a sudden if benevolent cloudburst exactly a dozen years after the closing of the concentration camps. Even the Nazi terror was unable to silence all voices of humanity. Between 1933 and 1945, thousands of Germans came to the aid of persecuted Jews—although there were millions who would not move a finger for them, even when the Gestapo was not looking. There were even a few noble men who performed what they considered their duty as Christians and as human beings, whether or not the Gestapo was watching. For having given active help to "non-Aryans," both the Protestant pastor Maas and the Catholic prelate Lichtenberg were jailed, and the latter did not live to see the day of liberation. After the end of Nazism, quite a few German statesmen, philosophers, journalists, and clergymen felt free to warn their people that they must atone for crimes against the Jews committed, if not by the nation itself, certainly in the name of the German nation.

But it was only in 1956 that thousands rather than scores of Germans (for the most part, in the Western democratic sector) felt an urge for expiation that sometimes was to manifest itself in slightly absurd reactions. One might say that all of it started with a play—not with a literary masterwork like Lessing's *Nathan the Wise,** but the German adaptation of the drama fashioned for the American stage by Frances Goodrich and Albert Hackett from the English translation of Anne Frank's diary. Lessing's theme—that religion was a matter of feeling rather than dogma and that a love of God and good was more important than subscription to any given creed, Christian, Jewish or Mohammedan—was greeted with demonstrative applause in postwar German theaters. But the play's complicated "comedy of confusion" plot and its eighteenth-century blank verse prevented it from reaching the innermost recesses of the spectator's soul. Yet this is exactly what the *Tagebuch der Anne Frank* (The Diary of Anne Frank) did: it broke through the tough shell that the German had grown around his soul. In what may be a natural drive for self-preservation, he had pushed all of the Nazi period into the remote corners of the unconscious mind. The victims who had lived through the Nazi era, or at least part of it, and visited Germany after 1945 knew all the time that this "amnesia" of the Germans was only defense. But they also feared that this repression of a reality too painful to remember might eventually lead to an obliteration, to the myth that nothing had really happened between 1933 and 1945. [. . .]

*Editors' note: Gothold Ephraim Lessing (1729–81) was a noted German dramatist.

The *Tagebuch* was performed in almost all West German cities, running in some theaters for several months, and in a few East German cities as well. But in all places the packed auditoriums were frozen in silence when the curtain came down. Here and there the programs requested "No applause"; but this was not necessary, for the rare outbreaks of applause were hissed down immediately. Silently the crowds filed out, as though leaving a funeral; and the play became a symbol of murder protracted, not only of Anne and her relatives and friends, but of six million Jewish civilians and, indeed, of additional millions of Russians, Poles, French, Dutch, and others.

That television, radio, and the press devoted much time and space to the fate of Anne Frank and her coreligionists, that teachers marched their classes to see the play, that during a few months the *Tagebuch* (the translation of the original Dutch text) topped all other best-sellers—all these were wholesome phenomena. In fact, the spontaneous reception of book and play proved to the world what should have required no proof: Nazism had not succeeded in poisoning the core of the German nation, and there was much hope for the youth.

A note of discord in this sweet harmony was sounded: some German voices were raised to protest that the play, in the last analysis, might have done more harm than good, that it was letting Germans off too lightly and did not even begin to suggest how frightful were the German actions. Other opinions [. . .] minimized the direct moral effect of a play in either the cure of vice or the prevention of crime. And they wondered whether the spectator, having sat through the play, might not consider himself cleansed of any guilt for the price of a ticket—a small sacrifice to obtain freedom from the burden of the sin, without requiring (as does the church) an inward change on the sinner's part.

Skeptics have even criticized what to many observers seemed the most heartening episode in the history of the Bonn Republic: the pilgrimage of more than two thousand young Hamburgers, in March 1957, to the site of the erstwhile concentration camp of Bergen-Belsen. "A ceremonial was rapidly developed," we read in the *Catholic Encyclopedia* concerning the Flagellants. Isn't there a danger in the crass externalization of feelings that should be permitted to grow undisturbed and unseen within, like a well-tended monastery garden? Once the heart is turned into a public park, grass and flowers may be trampled upon, and the holiness of the spot dissipated.

Americans saw on television what occurred March 17 at Bergen-Belsen, that vast cemetery where lie buried, in some unknown spot, the remains of Anne Frank. The youngsters traveled in trains, buses, on bicycles, through the chilling rain to the low hilltop upon which a huge obelisk, a few gravestones and, of course, the burial mounds, serve to remind the visitor of the past tragedy. [. . .]

In postwar Germany, however, it is hard to tell whether the initiative for the new philo-Semitism originated with the young and created pressure upon the older generation or whether the young took their cues from their grandfathers, the old, confirmed liberals, of whom that scholarly man, President [Theodore] Heuss, is a shining example. Their fathers do not count as guides, for it was they who, by voting for Hitler in 1930, made the Nazi party the second largest group in the Weimar Republic's parliament: it was they who contributed to the Nazi party treasury and, in return, reaped profits from Nazi "law" through the wanton confiscation of Jewish-owned shops and plants, the replacement of "non-Aryan" journalists, educators, scientists by "Aryans," and so forth.

Charges like these hurled against their elders obviously are not always and not entirely justifiable. But that this is the prevailing mood can be learned from the writings of the young or from talks with German students. History repeats itself in a curious way: just as in 1930 the college student was the spearhead and carrier of "idealistic" anti-Semitism, trying to make his unwilling elders see the light, so in 1957 youth is the protagonist of the new philo-Semitism. It is significant that German students were among the first to demonstrate publicly against the rehabilitation of movie director Veit Harlan, producer of the notorious propaganda film *Jud Suess,* which was designed to arouse violent anti-Jewish feelings both in Germany and in the Nazi-occupied countries. When Martin Buber came all the way from Israel to Hamburg to receive the Goethe Prize, he was idolized by the youth. His books, despite their difficult subject matter and style, are widely read. Suddenly a demand has developed for volumes on Jewish history, Israel, the pogroms, and what Nietzsche called the "anti-Semitic swindle." Talks by Jewish lecturers, often German Jews who have revisited the places they had been forced to leave, are well attended, and I have frequently heard young Germans express the desire to see Israel. [. . .]

Can't the Jew be just a human being and nothing else? In many countries he can—but not apparently, in Germany, where there is the tendency to romanticize him, to see in him either the horrible *Ewige Jude* (the legend of Ahauserus, the Wandering Jew, originated in central Europe) or a magician of the superior kind, from the fictitious Nathan the Wise to the living Martin Buber the Wise. Around 1800, sophisticated Germans considered it a privilege to be invited to the salons dominated by informed and clever Berlin Jews. In the 1950s, a Berlin hostess is anxious to present to her guests at least one Jewish intellectual. Lessing, son and grandson of pastors, complained in an essay about the shameful oppression of a people that had produced so many prophets and heroes, a people that "no Christian can regard without reverence." In the 1950s, German theologians are revising the common idea of the Jews as Christ-killers by insisting that God commanded the Jews to deny Christ so that, instead of remaining merely a Jewish national messiah, he would become the savior of the world. Contrary to tradition (and in marked contrast, by the way, to Toynbee's "fossil" theory) they maintain that there is a special holy meaning in Jewish existence, that Jews must strengthen their Judaism and retain their characteristics because Judaism, far from being an anachronism, has a very special function in God's plan for the salvation of the world. [. . .]

One suspects in this phenomenon of sudden, exaggerated pro-Jewishness (that manifested itself also in a definite pro-Israel stand during the latest Arab-Jewish war, despite all Arab wooings) a largely unconscious maneuver to avoid the deep soul-searching, the genuine moral stocktaking for which no *Tagebuch der Anne Frank* performances, no pilgrimages to concentration camp sites can be substitutes. The medieval church leaders were against the Flagellants because their way of doing penance failed to probe into the depths of the soul. Modern observers, German or otherwise, fear that the new emotion-charged flagellantism among the Germans may steer them away from a true understanding of the past that can be gained only by a forthright facing of the truth. It is one thing to find "catharsis" in the theater and quite a different thing to admit, "Yes, I am guilty," and to go on living with this feeling of guilt. For at least ten years Germans tried to keep busy and pretend that nothing had happened, and this device did not work. The switch to another method was, of course, not created by the play about Anne Frank. The play simply arrived at the psychological moment and filled the gap when the amnesia policy appeared to be bankrupt.

But it is doubtful whether the new, hysterical approach will yield better results. Guilt feelings, artificially banished from consciousness for years, cannot be resolved by theater parties or torchlight processions. How the tension between ego and superego can be rid of its man-killing dangerousness has been shown by Germany's most famous psychiatrist, Karl Jaspers, a full decade before the staging of the *Tagebuch*. [. . .]

From Kierkegaard, Jaspers has adopted the doctrine that eternity is more important than time, that sin is worse than suffering. Like his spiritual ancestor, Jaspers sought to evoke in his readers a passion for truth, by which alone the human situation can be met. The professor did not expect to convince the diehard Nazis, of whom there must still be millions. He addressed himself, instead, to the much larger number of those inclined to think that the German nation had already been redeemed through the hangings of a few top criminals at Nuremberg. This, he held, was a dangerous delusion.

He knew that quite a few Germans were willing to admit the culpability of those Nazis who actually committed murders and other crimes, but that was as far as their contrition would go. Yet Dr. Jaspers maintained that *all* Germans were tainted with political guilt; that *all* Germans were morally guilty, including those who persuaded themselves that they joined the party for "lofty" reasons, and those countless fellow travelers who might have effectively resisted the Nazi regime had it not been for their sluggishness of heart: that, finally, in a metaphysical sense, *all* Germans, even the anti-Nazi like himself, were guilty because they survived the mass murders of civilians. The Divine Power, Jaspers maintained, may find you guilty because you did not act to prevent a crime, because you continued to live at a time when your neighbor was being murdered.

Jaspers's reasoning was picked up by another septuagenarian, similar to him in staunch liberalism and rejection of all nazism stood for—the venerable Theodore Heuss. But Bonn's president did not entirely agree with the psychiatrist. He rejected the idea of collective guilt, for to accept it would amount to perpetuating the Nazi horror of laying a curse on a whole people. Perhaps the substitute he suggested might be acceptable to all brave and steadfast enough to live with responsibility: If nazism's deeds were not performed by the nation, they were, at least, performed in its name; hence, the German nation cannot but experience collective shame.

To the generation of Jaspers also belongs Max Picard, who, like him, is both physician and philosopher. In *Hitler in Uns Selbst* [The Hitler in Our Selves] he went even further than his colleague. All of us, Dr. Picard declares, gentile and Jew, black and white, European and American, carry some sort of Hitler in ourselves, an inherent sickness of the soul which may grow into a dangerous cancer unless we cure it in time.

Hitler, Picard insists, was far more than just an economic or a political phenomenon: he was an inevitable product of the inner chaos of modern man, of the disordered state of Western civilization. Nazism broke out in Germany because "there had concentrated all the disjointedness, the dissolute, the evil, just as disease concentrated in one bodily organ to form a clear picture there."[1] Nazi Germany forcibly tried to expand in space because she was incapable of expanding into permanence and stillness—or, one might say, because she had lost the garden of her soul.

After being rid of Hitler, the Satan with a nondescript face, the man without reality, the expression of total nothingness, Germany now has to realize that it is her mission to fight, not against the world, but against her own disjointedness. She must remember that although other nations contributed in various degrees to the rise of Hitlerism, it was in the Reich that the counterworld of unreality—that is to say, of a man-made and not God-made reality—first became real.

We do not know how many of the youngsters who visited Bergen-Belsen read these authors. Their teachers certainly should read them to be able to channel sincere feelings and deep-seated desires in the right direction. For it is not enough to identify oneself with Anne Frank. [. . .] There is a danger of equating the sorrows of little Anne, who suffered in an Amsterdam garret, with the anxiety of a

German boy or girl, who heard from an air raid shelter the Allied bombs crash on the city. The difference is that Anne Frank eventually perished in Bergen-Belsen and still did not consider herself a martyr. Young though she was, she was clear in her thinking. And if in Germany this sort of clarity should prevail over romantic emotion, insight over idolatry, there is good hope that German anti-Semitism, as well as all that goes with it, will be swept away by the long-overdue marriage of romance to reason. Germany has never lacked tornadoes of emotion. What she has often lacked is the kind of common sense that has guided many other nations safely through difficult times. Yet this common sense can be noted. [Perhaps . . .] in the letter written by a sixteen-year-old participant in the Bergen-Belsen pilgrimage, a letter published in newspapers in all parts of the Bonn Republic:

> I have sworn that we must do better! All must be made to realize that the highest and the most beautiful being is man—regardless of whether he is a Jew, a Dane, a Russian, an Englishman, a Frenchman, or a German. It does not matter, for they are all men.

> Ann[e], you did not die in vain. We, today's youth, want to believe in what is good in man—like you did. . . . We shall never forget you and all those innocent people who had to die like you. We do not want to forget, and we must never forget.

The feelings are genuine, but the dangerous characteristic of feelings not tempered with reason is that they can be swayed so easily. Wisdom comes with maturity. But Anne Frank would not agree with us: "Oh, those stupid grownups, they'd do better to start learning themselves, before they have so much to say to the younger generation!"

Note

1. Max Picard, *Hitler in Our Selves,* trans. Heinrich Hauser (Hinsdale, Ill.: Henry Regnery, 1947), 250.

22

Anne Frank and Film

David Barnouw

"I suppose that you want to be a film star?"
"Yes, sir, if I have the talent."
— *"Dreams of Movie Stardom"*

Under the catchy heading "War and Turnover," the May 1995 issue of the Dutch *Filmkrant* (Film Magazine) carried a report on a special "War box" issued by Fox video: "Including the 1959 film of the stage production of *The Diary of Anne Frank*. Relive once again the worst moments in the life of Anne Frank." Presumably the reviewer has never seen the film or read the book, because I imagine that "the worst moments" took place in Auschwitz or Bergen-Belsen and not in the annex of the house on the Prinsengracht.

A book which is dramatized and then filmed is almost doomed to oblivion, but this is certainly not true of *The Diary of Anne Frank*. The book is still a bestseller, and although millions of copies have been sold, the market does not yet appear to be saturated. The play is regularly staged in schools and by amateur theater companies. The 1959 film is seldom screened and has been available on video only for a few years.

The film is interesting in two respects. First, it is one of the earliest Hollywood productions in which the Holocaust plays a decisive role[,] according to the American film historian Annette Insdorf.[1] [. . .] While the film was not a box office success, it did make the diary more widely known. It is one of the few films which is less well known than the book on which it is based. Second, the film has been criticized as an example of the trivialization of the Holocaust.

As the film cannot be seen in isolation from the play—in fact, it would be better to speak of [it as] a film of a stage production—attention should also be paid to the American background of the play. The East German (GDR) production *Ein Tagebuch für Anne Frank,* dating from the same year, 1959, clearly shows how the cold war is everywhere. The discussion of the "trivialization" of the Holocaust is a recent phenomenon, and it remains to be seen when films of this mass killing will reach their limits.

Holocaust and Film

The discussion of film and history does not have a long history, but that is just as true of the medium itself. Besides articles in periodicals like *Historical Journal of Film, Radio, and Television,* and *Film and History,* more extensive studies of the theme do appear sporadically, although often in the form of collections of articles. [. . .] The discussions outside the world of the professionals often focus on the degree and accuracy of the reconstruction of the past. The more recent the historical events are, the more vigorous is the discussion. This is even truer when the topic under consideration is virtually taboo. The representation of the largely successful elimination of the European Jews is a topic of this kind, and Spielberg's *Schindler's List* (1994) attracted the usual controversy.

Claude Lanzmann, who directed the nine-hour documentary *Shoah* ten years ago, regarded his documentary as an immutable standard: "With pride and humility, I honestly believed that there was a pre-*Shoah* and a post-*Shoah* period, and after *Shoah* a number of things would no longer be possible."[2] [. . .] Lanzmann is against the feature film as a genre when it comes to [the] Shoah, probably because of the uniqueness of this killing, which is what makes it unfilmable in his eyes. It appears that Lanzmann is opposed to the feature film because he is a documentary filmmaker. [. . .]

By now more than 150 films have been made which are directly or indirectly connected with the Holocaust, but it was very rare for a film of this kind to receive an Oscar before Spielberg. *The Diary of Anne Frank* (1959) and *Sophie's Choice* (1982) come the closest, with an Oscar for the best supporting role for Shelley Winters as Mrs. Van Daan, and one for the best actress for Meryl Streep as Sophie. [. . .] Of course, every period has its own Holocaust films. An interesting early example is Alain Resnais's *Nuit et Brouillard* (Night and Fog), the first European film to deal explicitly with the fate of the victims of the concentration camps. This documentary was commissioned by the official French Committee for the History of the Second World War, but the persecution of the Jews only crops up in passing. [. . .] It has become a genuine classic [though it] is undoubtedly dated, but that is not so strange. Regrettably, the same thing will happen to Lanzmann's *Shoah* in time. [. . .]

The Film

After the success on Broadway (more than one thousand performances) there was nothing (except perhaps Meyer Levin) to stop a screen version of *The Diary of*

Anne Frank. Twentieth Century-Fox had purchased the film rights in the autumn of 1956 and George Stevens was to direct and produce the film. Stevens had been in film since the twenties and had built up a solid reputation. During World War II he had followed in the wake of the U.S. troops in Europe as head of an Army Signal Corps film unit. His pictures of the survivors in the Dachau concentration camp were to be seen all over the world. Besides the official 35 mm black and white footage, he also shot some 16 mm film in color, which only surfaced forty years later.

Suddenly the liberation of western Europe proved to have acquired a different aspect. According to George Stevens Jr., his son, the war had not changed his father, but it gave his work more profundity. This could be seen in *A Place in the Sun,* which won six Oscars, including one for Stevens as director. He also won an Oscar for *Giant* (1956).

Goodrich and Hackett were to write the screenplay. It had already been agreed that not many changes would be made to the dramatized version. Although the conflict with Meyer Levin had not yet been resolved (at a certain point Levin offered to drop all his charges if his daughter Dominique was allowed to play the role of Anne in the film), Stevens started with the preparations in 1957.

A ripple of excitement ran through the Netherlands with the news that an American company was coming to shoot a film in Amsterdam and that there was a possibility that the leading role might be played by a Dutch girl. It would have been natural for Susan Strasberg, who had successfully played the role of Anne on Broadway, to have assumed the role, but according to Shelley Winters, who played Mrs. Van Daan in the film, Susan was involved in her first affair, with Richard Burton. [. . .] But Stevens wanted a new face for Anne as well and preferred an unknown amateur to a famous actress.

Expectations thus were high when Stevens's talent scout Owen McLean came to Amsterdam at the end of 1957 to test seventy Dutch girls aged fifteen or so for their suitability to play the role of Anne. He already had more than twenty-five hundred letters from candidates, most of them from the Netherlands. By now girls had been given screen tests in other countries as well, and it was even rumored that a non-Jewish German girl had set her hopes on the role. [. . .] The Anne Frank Foundation, which had only recently been founded, refused to cooperate with the film in any way if that went ahead.

But to the accompaniment of a loud fanfare, a Dutch candidate was initially chosen: a young dancer with a Dutch ballet company—and, according to a few newspapers, she was luckily half-Jewish. Although the names of Audrey Hepburn and Romy Schneider had been mentioned as possible actresses to play the part of Anne Frank, it came as a blow in the Netherlands when it was later announced that the nineteen-year-old American photo model Millie Perkins had been chosen to play Anne. There was great bitterness at these "Brash American (advertising) methods" and the "trifling" with the memory of Anne Frank. [. . .] The fact that Anne was to be played by a photo model also led to negative comments. Only the Dutch daily *Algemeen Handelsblad* made the liberal remark that photo models could be found in the best families and that it was no reason to turn up one's nose in petit bourgeois self-congratulation. [. . .]

Stevens spent half a year filming in Hollywood, while his son arranged the outdoor shooting in Amsterdam. This naturally attracted the most attention in the Netherlands. It was not often that Hollywood came to Amsterdam, and the transportation of thousands of kilograms of artificial snow to shoot winter scenes in the summer had a strong appeal to the imagination. The plan to dig up a large number of trees, to replace them with artificial trees and later with real trees after the shooting was over, was not put into operation. The Amsterdam Parks department was able to supply only a single big, leafless tree, and even that made the papers. [. . .]

A pilot version of the film was unexpectedly shown in the United States in a sneak preview. The public reaction to seeing Anne in a concentration camp was not convincing enough to retain the scene in the film.

In the Netherlands it was supposed that the world premiere of the film would be held in Amsterdam, and the City and Rialto cinemas had already been mentioned. However, the world premiere was of course in the United States, and it was not for nothing that leading figures in the civil rights movement were conspicuously present. Over there, Anne Frank was no longer the exclusive symbol of the persecution of the Jews.

To judge from the report under the heading "Good Filming of Anne Frank," the important Jewish Dutch weekly *Nieuw Israelitisch Weekblad* (April 17, 1959) did not pay these figures much attention: "The public, understandably consisting mainly of Jews, had dressed up for the evening. The women were dressed in fur cloaks and some of the men were in tuxedos. They amused themselves with great hilarity, as if they were setting out to have a good night out. Fortunately my fears of the worst were not realized on this occasion. [. . .] Finally, it should be stated that this film is certainly one of the few which is worth going to see."

[. . .] When the European premiere took place in the Netherlands in mid-April 1959, it was just as much of a solemn event as the first performance of the play had been two and a half years earlier. The queen and crown prince were there, and most of the visitors had complied with the request to wear subdued clothing. At the end of the film the public stood to sing the Dutch national anthem, the "Wilhelmus." Jaap van der Merwe, who reviewed the film for *Het Vrije Volk,* considered that it had become more the diary of Otto Frank, and that Anne was merely one of the protagonists. Film magazines were clearly even more critical than the papers.

The leading actress came to the Netherlands at the end of May, tired and exhausted from the long publicity tour. "Distressing Hawking of Young Actress" was one of the newspaper headlines. It was as though the events connected with the film were more important than the film itself. [. . .] Her visit, and even the presentation of red Millie Perkins roses, did not do her any good because she disappeared rapidly from the limelight. She went on to play in more than ten films, including the role of one of Elvis Presley's three girlfriends in *Wild in the Country* (1961), but she herself referred to an "Anne Frank hangover."

Although Anne Frank has been played by hundreds, or possibly even thousands, of girls all over the world, Millie Perkins is still Anne Frank; her photograph even graced the cover of the American edition of Anne's diary for a long time. In 1991 she paid a brief visit to the Netherlands on high-gloss paper, when the Spaarnestad Photographic Archive organized a small-scale photographic exhibition of Millie, accompanied by a magnificent catalogue.

The film was not a great success in the United States, and Shelley Winters's Oscar did little to change it. All the same, the film led to a renewal of interest in the book. According to Otto Frank, it was very influential in getting the diary published in other countries.

Ein Tagebuch für Anne Frank

Anne's diary did not escape the cold war either. There was a tradition that the winner of the Pulitzer Prize for drama was performed at the drama festival in Paris in the spring of the following year. This meant that the Goodrich-Hackett stage adaptation was due to be performed in Paris in 1956. However, this did not take place. The U.S. State Department had put on pressure to prevent it so as not to exercise a negative effect on the delicate Franco-German relations. It is natural to make the comparison with Resnais's *Nuit et Brouillard*. The official premiere of Resnais's film was to be at the Cannes Film Festival in May 1956, but the film was withdrawn for "diplomatic reasons." It was then presented outside the festival.

In 1959 a documentary made by the East German DEFA company was released under the title *Ein Tagebuch für Anne Frank*. The film was accompanied by a book of photos. Part of the introductory text ran: "As this tender voice only became audible after the inferno had passed and its bearer had already become [one] of its many victims, it may not be allowed to go unheard in our time. On the contrary, it lays upon us Germans the responsibility of publicly taking action against all those who prepared or facilitated this fate for Anne Frank. Today the diary of Anne Frank demands a *German* standpoint. It is our purpose to provide it."

The twenty-minute documentary showed the raids on the Amsterdam Waterlooplein, the deportation train from Westerbork, and footage from Auschwitz and Bergen-Belsen. It also devoted some attention to the history of the culprits. A number of them from various ranks were mentioned, including their comfortable present [living] conditions in [West Germany]. The documentary names Willy Lages and Hermann Conring, who was the authorized deputy of Seyss-Inquart in the province of Groningen. Now he was a [Christian Democratic Union] representative in the Bundestag. The German companies which were involved in concentration and death camps are indicated, and the film makes clear that not the slightest obstacle has been put in the way of the industrialists responsible. The message could not be clearer: "Those who make money from war have an interest in war," and they are the people who really decided Anne's fate. And they are the same people who now hold high positions in [West Germany].

The film has to be seen within the context of the East German . . . policy of portraying [West Germany] as the direct, guilty descendant of the Hitler regime. According to this ideology, [East Germany] was the genuine successor to the peaceful Weimar Republic and to the resistance against Hitler. Lists of former Nazis who now exercised normal functions in [West Germany] were published, and [West Germany] reacted with volumes of the same kind. Anne Frank hardly featured in the film. [. . .]

In the Netherlands the documentary was screened privately at first. [. . .] The film was scrutinized by the Dutch board of censors. On February 24, 1959, they allowed it to be shown to people above the age of eighteen. On the next day the film was to be shown in the Amsterdam Tropical Institute, but the performance was canceled for political reasons.*

Trivialization

The play made a huge impression everywhere, including Germany, but the performances did not lead to public introspection of how and why the Holocaust had taken place. It was only twenty years later that the television [mini]series *Holocaust,* another Hollywood production, was to have that effect. The [mini]series came in for criticism, as both Europeans and Americans asked themselves whether it was right to treat such a terrible historical episode in this way. Lawrence

---

*Editors' note: The documentary film led to disputes among the board members over whether showing the film meant they were taking sides in the conflict at that time between West and East Germany. The ban has since remained in effect.

Langer referred to "Americanization," and ten years later Alvin Rosenfeld used the term "Popularization."

Anne Frank only became the subject of serious research relatively later on, if we except the often reprinted essay by Bruno Bettelheim, "The Ignored Lesson of Ann Frank." Rosenfeld, for example, shows that the various introductions to the Dutch, French, and other versions of the book each evoke a different picture of Anne Frank. The past, here symbolized by Anne Frank, is reconstructed in a variety of ways and transmitted to a variety of public groups. [. . .] The filming of Anne's diary was also the start of the "Americanization of the Holocaust."

Judith Doneson is the first to set the genesis of the film within the American politico-social context of the fifties. It was largely determined by the cold war against communism, the successor to the real war against fascism. Hollywood was not spared the hot breath of Senator McCarthy, and the film producers censored their own work. Jewish filmmakers and producers were also afraid of a return of American anti-Semitism, though their fears later proved to be unfounded. This resulted in advanced assimilation on the silver screen: if there was no Jew to be seen in the film, anti-Semitism would diminish by itself. The same process took place when the film scripts for *The Diary of Anne Frank* were being written. This was not only because of the fear of anti-Semitism, but also to make the film more accessible to non-Jews. [. . .]

But is it true that the Hollywood dream machine did violence to the Holocaust and in particular to Anne Frank? I do not think so. There is nothing unusual about the fact that the film departs from the original, in this case a book: that happens all the time. Anne Frank wrote a diary. She rewrote parts of this diary in a second version. Her father drew primarily on this second version in putting *The Secret Annex* together. Then a pair of American writers used the English translation to make a stage adaptation, and later a film script. That script was filmed in accordance with the Hollywood conventions of the fifties and the romantic vision of George Stevens. It would be a miracle if the film were to be identical with Anne's diaries.

The main point of concern in the Netherlands was whether the commercial Americans had treated "our" Anne with due respect. On the one hand, there was a certain pride that a Dutch situation had become a subject for Hollywood; on the other hand, there was naturally still a measure of distrust of the medium. The film certainly confirmed the extremely favorable image enjoyed by the Dutch abroad, both then and now, as courageous individuals who risked their lives to protect their Jewish countrymen from the German barbarians. I believe that the idea of the trivialization of the diary of Anne Frank dates from twenty years after the premiere. Neither viewers at the time nor film critics complained about trivialization.

The objections to the film version therefore look more like reconstructions with hindsight. My impression is that [film] critics in the eighties damn *The Diary of Anne Frank* retroactively because it does not present an honest or adequate picture of the Holocaust and is thus a falsification of reality. There is nothing new in this charge, and in the nineties it seems hard to imagine a film about World War II which does not show the Holocaust; but reality—and the reality of the film—is different.

Notes

1. Annette Insdorf, *Indelible Shadows: The Film and the Holocaust* (New York: Random House, 1983), 3, 6–7.

2. Claude Lanzmann, *NRC Handelsblad,* Mar. 26, 1994, 13 (taken from *Le Monde*).

23

Review Essay:
Anne Frank Remembered

G. Jan Colijn

It is very important sometimes to disengage yourself from the mess in which you find yourself, to shut your eyes and turn yourself off. . . . I stood in front of that stinking pit many times and turned around and looked at that magnificent starry sky and said, "Oh God, if you really exist, how could yet let this happen."
—*Janny Brandes-Brilleslijper in Willy Lindwer's* The Last Seven Months of
  Anne Frank

The Misuse of Anne Frank's Legacy

There is little question that the legacy of Anne Frank has created a postwar self-image among the Dutch that differs considerably from reality. Some observers go as far as to argue that Dutch popular culture has fallen victim to a self-deluding public relations campaign that has created an impression that all Jews were in hiding and that the entire Dutch population was in resistance. Dutch culture is seen as self-possessed in its progressiveness and quick to indict racism elsewhere while belittling it at home. Within this context the point is then made that Dutch society has not faced up to its failings in the war in that there has not yet been a national debate on the question why millions of Dutch bystanders allowed nearly the entire Jewish population of their country to be deported. Some scholars argue that the misuse of Anne's diary contributes to this Dutch self-portrait; for example, Dutch historian Nanda van der Zee argues that the legacy of Anne Frank and the use of the diary have directly contributed to the absence of a proper national retrospective because "Anne Frank's Diary fed the myth of the 'heroic' Netherlands in resistance by taking Jews into hiding."[1]

However, recent commemorations surrounding the fiftieth anniversary of V-E day may have led to a growing realization that the destruction of Dutch Jewry, as Ido de Haan puts it (in *Het Parool*) was "a crime against a group of Dutch citizens, committed by Germans, with the knowledge and collaboration of the Dutch" (Apr. 26, 1995).

Such growing realization does not constitute a complete shift in reflections on the Jews and the war. Issues such as the demythologization of the "good" Dutch, and the absence of involvement among the majority, do not constitute a completely new paradigm shift in reflections of the population (the "bystanders"). Notions of passive collaboration, the complicity of Dutch authorities in the deportation of Jews, and the role of the Jewish Council have been aired before. In 1965, prominent Dutch historian Jacob Presser's *De Ondergang* was published in the Netherlands, followed by a British version, *Ashes in the Wind,* in 1968, and by an American version, *The Destruction of the Dutch Jews,* in 1969. The popular success of Presser's *cri de coeur* in the Netherlands mitigates the notion that the legacy of Anne Frank has created a national conspiracy of silence, but some of the myths in the Dutch self-image persist even today.

Presser's focus on Dutch failings is resoundingly braced by the numbers: of approximately 140,000 Jews residing in the Netherlands at the beginning of the Nazi occupation, slightly fewer than 35,000 survived, a survival rate below that of any other western European nation—below that of Belgium, below that of Vichy France, below that of Germany's Axis partner Italy.

One can provide a causal framework for the disproportionate destruction of Dutch Jews. Among Holocaust scholars, as opposed to the public at large, the reasons behind this calamity are fairly well established. Several decades ago Raul Hilberg provided a set of reasons, for example, by noting such realities as the location of the Netherlands that prevented easy escape to Portugal or England; in noting its geography that does not include vast natural hiding places; and by noting the complicity of the civil service bureaucracy. The complacency of the Dutch government-in-exile in London is another factor, yet some components of this element, e.g., the relative silence of Radio Oranje—the official voice of the government-in-exile—still need to be fully explored. These reconstructions of the contributing causes behind the disproportionate destruction of Dutch Jews are subject to rather different interpretations. The role of the Jewish Council can, for instance, be used to shift blame from non-Jews. The topographical realities that Hilberg noted can also be used to make the argument that the majority of approximately 25,000 Jews who went into hiding could not have been saved if it were not for the assistance of tens of thousands of Dutch citizens. As the provision of shelter (and food) entailed risk of the death penalty upon discovery, such assistance was certainly remarkable. One prominent Holocaust survivor, Jack Polak, has described such rescue and resistance efforts at length in an effort to denote what was and what was not possible, not just what was not done. The passion with which Polak attempts to counter the position of Judith Miller—

who is highly critical of Dutch inaction during the Holocaust—is indicative of deep differences in interpretation. One can also reach a conclusion that takes a middle ground, [. . .] i.e., that the history of the Dutch and the Jews of the Netherlands in World War II was simply unexceptional.

The point here is not that there remain deep differences in scholarly interpretations of the destruction of Dutch Jewry. Such differences may be inevitable. The point is also not that popular retrospectives on Dutch history during the war years lag behind scholarly advances on the same subject. Such lag time is not uncommon. For example, French public opinion did not really begin to deal with the Vichy experience until the Klaus Barbie trial in 1982, and again in connection with the Touvier case. These media circuses should not let us forget that the 1972 film by Max Ophuls, *The Sorrow and the Pity,* was not allowed to be shown on French television until 1981.

However, the demythologization of the "good" Dutch *should* be at the center of an honest reckoning of Dutch history during the war years. The point is simply that the diary and Anne Frank's story *can* be used, and *have been* used, to further the myth of the "good" Dutch. To do so is easy enough. One can simply emphasize the role of the "righteous"—Miep Gies and others—while deemphasizing the betrayal of the Franks and the collective Dutch indifference to the fate of the Jews. One must not divorce the diary from the larger context of Anne Frank's fate and the inaction of the majority of Dutch as the tragedy unfolded. Within a didactic context the best solution is then to read the diary *and* to read Presser, but reflections on the issues Presser raises are just the first part of a responsible treatment of the Anne Frank symbol. There are other problems in the treatment of the Anne Frank legacy.

Many treatments of the Anne Frank story succumb to the "cheap sentimentality" against which Hannah Arendt railed in *Eichmann in Jerusalem.* American screen and stage treatments, for example, have been full of misplaced emphasis on naiveté and optimism, and often attempt to use the diary as a metaphor for universalist—read de-Judaized—suffering. There is probably no line in the diary more misused in this regard than "in spite of everything, I still believe people are good at heart." It is this misuse in the "projection of single images of ubiquitous and compelling power" that has created false popular perceptions. When a responsible historical encasement of the diary is subordinated to such sentiments as hope, redemption, or forgiveness, one, in effect, dehistoricizes Anne Frank's legacy. [. . .]

Given the iconography surrounding Anne Frank, the unfinished demythologization of the "good Dutch," and such issues as the aforementioned de-Judaization of Anne's life, the prospects for a current, balanced documentary rendering of the Anne Frank story are daunting, but not impossible. I note in this regard the Anne Frank Foundation's traveling exhibit "Anne Frank in the World 1929–1945," seen by thousands wherever the exhibit is shown. The exhibit does a remarkably effective job in *connecting* Anne's story to the Holocaust in a historically balanced fashion, for example, in describing the rise of the Nazis in Germany, and in sketching circumstances in the Netherlands, including references to considerable support for the Nazis prior to World War II. The exhibit notes some of the factors Hilberg cited in the disproportionate destruction of Dutch Jews. The photographs provide an unsentimental yet moving photographic essay on the Frank family. However, the exhibit does not fully explore Anne's fate after her deportation from Westerbork to Auschwitz in September 1944 but focuses more on the collective fate of Dutch Jewry, on the last stages of the Final Solution, and, in its final panels, on the lessons to be learned from the current resurgence of racism and anti-Semitism.

This lacuna is particularly filled by Willy Lindwer's 1988 television documentary, *The Last Seven Months of Anne Frank,* which follows the Frank family after their arrest and deportation, through interviews with several women who were in Westerbork, Auschwitz, or Bergen-Belsen with members of the family. Lindwer's treatment certainly does not suffer from previously noted shortcomings such as cheap sentimentality or de-Judaization. The film emphasizes that by the time the Franks were deported from Westerbork to Auschwitz in September 1944 (on what turned out to be the last such transport), more than 100,000 Jews had already been deported from the Netherlands. The film also emphasizes that of the 1,019 men, women, and children on the Franks' train, only 45 men and 82 women would return. Parts of the film are extraordinarily poignant. Margot's classmate, Dr. Bloeme Evers-Emden, gives us a sober yet powerful sense of the arrival at the Auschwitz inferno on the night of September 5, including the women's first confrontation with the "selection" process—which they did not yet comprehend. And through the accounts of Janny Brandes-Brilleslijper and Hannah Pick-Goslar—a neighbor of the Franks in the Merwedeplein where the family lived before going into hiding—we are offered eyewitness recollections of the last several terrifying months in the lives of Margot and Anne. We learn of the desperate attempts by Edith Frank to protect and to feed her daughters before they were separated from her and sent from Auschwitz to Bergen-Belsen on October 28, 1944. [. . .]

However, the title of the Lindwer documentary may lead one to presume we are going to "know" if not the Franks, at least Anne, if not fully, at least partially. We come away not "knowing" Anne much more. In a curious way, Lindwer's documentary is an almost forced attempt to graft Anne's tragedy onto the collective experience of women in the concentration camps as they witnessed the destruction around them. Lindwer's treatment documents that collective experience soberly and evocatively, but Anne remains a bit player—not quite marginal but certainly not central to the collective experience either. The marginalization of Anne, the film's central shortcoming, underscores the enormous difficulty of putting Anne—a symbol, if not an icon—center stage. Lindwer does not fall into the aforementioned traps into which other treatments of Anne's life have fallen. The documentary is certainly a very good contribution to our understanding of the fate of Dutch Jews during the Holocaust, but the complete story of *Anne Frank,* even of the last few months, remains unfinished and to a certain degree untold business.

Earlier in this review we outlined some of the criticisms of previous treatments of the Anne Frank story. Semifictionalized screen and stage treatments can also be criticized on purely esthetic grounds and, as noted, a documentary about Anne's entire life is a daunting prospect because the symbolism of that life has turned her into a modern icon. That fact may be one of the reasons that no one had tried to make such a documentary until Jon Blair made *Anne Frank Remembered.* [. . .]

Anne Frank Remembered

Now turning to the actual review of the documentary it is perhaps useful to recall the criticisms of previous screen and stage treatments by pointing out which pitfalls Mr. Blair avoids.

First of all, *Anne Frank Remembered* does not dehistoricize Anne's life story. The script makes an early allusion to the memory of her legacy today: hers is not just a Holocaust story, but the voice of Anne Frank stands as a warning to all those who would discriminate on the basis of color, culture, or creed. This theme is quickly dropped as an explicit one and does not return until the very end of the film when Nelson Mandela recalls the inspiration he derived from Anne Frank's diary while imprisoned. The director's touch here is light. He neither preaches nor attempts to superimpose his interpretation of Anne's legacy on the film. He also does not dehistoricize the story by drawing superficial parallels between the Holocaust and other atrocities as we so often find in today's media, for example when the Bosnian crisis is unanalytically compared with the Holocaust, ignoring the fact that the former is a civil war—a critical difference with the Holocaust. The film relies extensively on archival footage, including footage shot in Westerbork. This dependence anchors the film in its historical context, but Barry Achroyd's cinematography also plays a distinct role in keeping matters firmly anchored in their time. Mr. Achroyd frames such locations as the Franks' residence in Amsterdam in muted tones and "crops" the location by excluding distracting visual imagery, e.g., contemporary cars parked on the street.

Second, *Anne Frank Remembered* does not de-Judaize the story. The film high-lights the German-Jewish origins not only of the Franks, but also of their neighbors and friends, such as Hanneli Goslar. The film notes Hitler's victory at the ballot box and depicts vitriolic anti-Semitic propaganda (*Der Ewige Jude* [The Eternal Jew]), Dutch Nazi sympathizers, the Nazi infiltration of the Dutch police civil service, even Prime Minister Colijn's cabinet office. The film is particularly effective in depicting the gradual, never-ending series of anti-Jewish decrees issued during the early years of the Nazi occupation of the Netherlands. Mr. Blair notes that by 1942 no area of Jewish life was excluded from German control. The film leaves no doubt that a *war against Jews* was under way and that the destruction of Dutch *Jewry* was made possible by ever tightening isolation from *non-Jews*. Yet nowhere are we left with the pretense that the Franks were "ghetto Jews." Their prosperity and cultivation are emphasized, the fact that Otto Frank had considerable means to facilitate the move to the annex when it came is not forgotten. Highlighting the Frank's exceptional position renders their eventual, unexceptional fate even more poignant.

The greatest achievement of *Anne Frank Remembered* is the *normalization* of Anne as a child, a normalization that does not diminish her accomplishment in the diary. Isa Baschwitz, whose parents were friends of the Franks, remembers Anne as "naughty" and "impertinent." Henk van Beusekom, an employee of Mr. Frank's Opekta company, remembers Anne as a great, fun-loving girl. Anne's very good friend Hanneli ("Lies") Goslar (mentioned extensively in the diary) remembers Anne's very lively disposition, particularly her prank of removing her shoulder from its socket. Lies recalls that her mother used to say, "God knows everything [but] Anne knows everything better." Another contemporary of Margot and Anne, Laureen Nussbaum, notes that children generally acculturated to their Dutch environment with greater ease than their parents. She recalls how she found the experience "immensely democratizing." The first twenty minutes of *Anne Frank Remembered* leave us with an indelible sense that we are beginning to *know* Anne.

The second part of the film covers the period July 1942–August 1944 when the Franks were in hiding. The family's dilemma whether or not to go, once Margot had been called up for deportation to a "labor camp," or the psychological impact on the family of the subsequent confinement, the claustrophobia, the fear of betrayal or making an error that would give them away, the beginnings of the diary while roundups continue outside—all are carefully rendered with quiet voiceovers by Glenn Close, who reads excerpts from the diary. Particularly evocative also are the readings and comments by Bernd Elias, Anne's first cousin and last living relative. In the diary, Anne fantasizes about living with him in Switzerland and designing a skating dress. Mr. Elias's rueful closing: "I would have loved to go skating with her."

The authenticity of the hiding place is augmented by the reconstruction of the annex with furniture, bedding, and clothing of the early 1940s. We are led around the annex by Miep Gies, the sole survivor of the five helpers of the family in hiding. Helping the family survive entailed the purchase of food on the black market or with forged ration books, and Miep's sober remembrances do not ultimately belie the considerable courage of the helpers, the risks they took, and the ringing undertone of the lessons to be derived from this saga of exemplary personal responsibility.

Here, again, the film does not surrender to sentimentality or to notions of universalist suffering for which others have applied the diary. The *normalization* of Anne continues by vivid excerpts of Anne's feelings toward the others in the annex, such as Margot and her mother, who were "subject to the fury of her pen."

Of particular interest is the juxtaposition of Miep's memories of Fritz Pfeffer, the dentist who became Anne's "roommate" in hiding. Miep's memories and a conversation with Peter Pepper (Fritz's son who would pass away two months after the interview), in essence rehabilitate the view of Fritz Pfeffer in the diary. When Mr. Pepper finally gets to meet Miep Gies during the filming of *Anne Frank Remembered* she tells him: "He was a lovely, lovely man." Mr. Pepper can say only two words: "Many thanks." It is an extraordinary moment. [. . .]

The final chapter, the Franks' imprisonment and the death of all but Otto, first highlights the odd circumstances in transit camp Westerbork. In the eyes of some survivors, such as Frieda Menco, this was the "best time" of the war, as there was "no hunger" and there were "nice boys." As the Allies advanced in Europe, creating hope among the Jews in Westerbork, the inmates also lived with the terrifying fear of the weekly transports. The surreal "normalcy" of Westerbork is shown through footage of daily life in Westerbork, e.g., of calisthenics and the weekly cabaret organized under orders of the camp commander. The visual "normalcy" of this footage is juxtaposed by the concurrent narration of Kenneth Branagh, who, in a virtually reverent monotonous tone, recites the facts as we now know them: 104,000 Jews were transported to various concentration camps, approximately 60,000 to Auschwitz, of whom 673 would return; 34,313 to Sobibor of whom a mere 19 came back.

All those who had been in hiding in the annex were put onto the very last transport to Auschwitz on September 3, 1944. When the train arrived at Auschwitz approximately half of the 1,019 Jews were immediately gassed. [. . .]

The rendering of death factory Auschwitz, the desperate circumstances, and overcrowding at Bergen-Belsen, whereto Margot and Anne were sent without their mother on October 28, 1944, inevitably parallel *The Last Seven Months of Anne Frank.* Blair, too, notes the attempts of the women to support one another, but even more so than in *The Last Seven Months* we become aware of the utter vulnerability of the girls. The deliberate pacing of Karen Steininger's editing gives an interminable aura to a period which, in time alone, was as brief as it was immeasurably horrible. The extraordinary horror of the last months in Bergen-Belsen reaches its climax in the testimony of Janny Brandes-Brilleslijper, who begins to recall, for one brief moment, incidents of cannibalism in the camp. Then her voice trails off to silence.

Lies Goslar remembers that while Margot was already desperately ill, Anne, who was confined to another section of the camp, told her across a barbed wire fence she had nobody anymore. Anne presumed her mother dead and thought that her father had been selected for the gas chamber on the basis of age, whereas his relatively healthy appearance had saved him from the selections. Lies Goslar's reflections that Anne had given up hope and simply had nothing more to live for are among the most evocative in the film.

Unlike *The Last Seven Months, Anne Frank Remembered* also follows the fate of the others who had been in the annex, particularly the fate of Otto, through the testimony of fellow prisoners and Otto's own recollections in a 1979 interview. Hence, *Anne Frank Remembered* is simply more complete.

The postwar phase of the film covers familiar terrain: Otto's desperate attempts to get information about the fate of his daughters, the eventual publication of the diary, the reopening of the Anne Frank House and the purpose of the Anne Frank Stichting. Even here, *Anne Frank Remembered* keeps its viewers firmly in its grasp with new material and insights. Otto's nephew, Bernd Elias, for example, reads letters written by Otto to his mother, letters only recently rediscovered (in May 1994). Mr. Blair reads a letter to Miep Gies wherein Otto recalls the "dangers and unprecedented sacrifices," a letter Miep had never seen. Miep Gies recalls the reunification with Otto and giving him the diary: "This is the testament of your daughter Anne." Janny Brandes-Brilleslijper remembers the moment when she informed Otto that his daughters were dead. The sadness of her testimony, without any hint of sentimentality, is almost overwhelming.

Mr. Blair also includes a film clip, never seen before, of a 1941 wedding on the Merwedeplein, which includes the only known moving footage of Anne, then twelve years old. Carefully restored by technicians who had previously restored Walt Disney's *Fantasia,* the painstaking effort to bring this footage to usable life is a metaphor of Mr. Blair's determination to bring Anne Frank to us as completely and as honestly as possible.

Most Holocaust scholars are familiar with the arguments made by Saul Friedländer and by George Steiner to the effect that literature and language are often inadequate to describe the horrors of the Holocaust, that only visual imagery can do so. The views of Claude Lanzmann on what *kinds* of imagery are appropriate (i.e., his opposition to archival footage) are well known. The great strength of

Mr. Blair's film is that he liberally uses a wide variety of visual sources, yet underpins the visual *imagery* of *Anne Frank Remembered* with extraordinary language—an extremely carefully constructed script that gives the film its beautiful cadences, its cohesion, and its power. He has managed to normalize Anne's life without belittling her legacy in the slightest way, and his treatment of the Anne Frank story—unlike any before it—succeeds by *description,* not *ascription.* In being so true to Anne's life, this documentary on Hitler's best-known victim is an account of such authoritative definition that the only fitting accolade is simply: a masterpiece.

Note

1. Nanda van der Zee, "The Recurrent Myth of 'Dutch Heroism' and Anne Frank as a Symbol," in *The Netherlands and Nazi Genocide,* ed. G. Jan Colijn and Marcia Sachs Littell (Lewiston, N.Y.: Edwin Mellen Press, 1992), 12.

Part 4

Memorializing the Holocaust

24

The Ignored Lesson of Anne Frank

Bruno Bettelheim

I've asked myself again and again whether it wouldn't have been better if we
hadn't gone into hiding, if we were dead now and didn't have to go through this
misery.
—*May 26, 1944*

When the world first learned about the Nazi concentration and death camps,
most civilized people felt the horrors committed in them to be so uncanny as to
be unbelievable. It came as a severe shock that supposedly civilized nations could
stoop to such inhumane acts. The implication that modern man has such inadequate control over his cruel and destructive proclivities was felt as a threat to
our views of ourselves and our humanity. Three different psychological mechanisms were most frequently used for dealing with the appalling revelation of what
had gone on in the camps.

(1) its applicability to man in general was denied by asserting—contrary to
evidence—that the acts of torture and mass murder were committed by a small
group of insane or perverted persons;

(2) the truth of the reports was denied by declaring them vastly exaggerated
and ascribing them to propaganda (this originated with the German government,
which called all reports on terror in the camps "horror propaganda"—
Greuelpropaganda);

(3) the reports were believed, but the knowledge of the horror repressed as soon
as possible.

All three mechanisms could be seen at work after liberation of those prisoners
remaining. At first, after the discovery of the camps and their death-dealing, a
wave of extreme outrage swept the Allied nations. It was soon followed by a general repression of the discovery in people's minds. Possibly this reaction was due
to something more than the blow dealt to modern man's narcissism by the realization that cruelty is still rampant among men. Also present may have been the

dim but extremely threatening realization that the modern state now has available the means for changing personality and for destroying millions it deems undesirable. The ideas that in our day a people's personalities might be changed against their will by the state, and that other populations might be wholly or partially exterminated, are so fearful that one tries to free oneself of them and their impact by defensive denial or by repression.

The extraordinary worldwide success of the book, play, and movie *The Diary of Anne Frank* suggests the power of the desire to counteract the realization of the personality-destroying and murderous nature of the camps by concentrating all attention on what is experienced as a demonstration that private and intimate life can continue to flourish even under the direct persecution by the most ruthless totalitarian system. And this, although Anne Frank's fate demonstrates how efforts at disregarding in private life what goes on around one in society can hasten one's own destruction.

What concerns me here is not what actually happened to the Frank family, how they tried—and failed—to survive their terrible ordeal. It would be very wrong to take apart so humane and moving a story, which aroused so much well-merited compassion for gentle Anne Frank and her tragic fate. What is at issue is the universal and uncritical response to her diary and to the play and movie based on it and what this reaction tells us about our attempts to cope with the feelings her fate—used by us to serve as a symbol of a most human reaction to Nazi terror—arouses in us. I believe that the worldwide acclaim given her story cannot be explained unless we recognize in it our wish to forget the gas chambers and our effort to do so by glorifying the ability to react into an extremely private, gentle, sensitive world, and there to cling as much as possible to what have been one's usual daily attitudes and activities, although surrounded by a maelstrom apt to engulf one at any moment.

The Frank family's attitude that life could be carried on as before may well have been what led to their destruction. By eulogizing how they lived in their hiding place while neglecting to examine first whether it was a reasonable or an effective choice, we are able to ignore the crucial lesson of their story—that such an attitude can be fatal in extreme circumstances.

While the Franks were making their preparations for going passively into hiding, thousands of other Jews in Holland (as elsewhere in Europe) were trying to escape to the free world, in order to survive and/or fight. Others who could not escape went underground—into hiding—each family member with, for example, a different gentile family. We gather from the diary, however, that the chief desire of the Frank family was to continue living as nearly as possible in the same fashion to which they had been accustomed in happier times.

Little Anne, too, wanted only to go on with life as usual, and what else could she have done but fall in with the pattern her parents created for her existence? But hers was not a necessary fate, much less a heroic one; it was a terrible but also a senseless fate. Anne had a good chance to survive, as did many Jewish children in Holland. But she would have had to leave her parents and go to live with a gentile Dutch family, posing as their own child, something her parents would have had to arrange for her.

Everyone who recognized the obvious knew that the hardest way to go underground was to do it as a family; to hide out together made detection by the SS most likely; and when detected, everybody was doomed. By hiding singly, even when one got caught, the others had a chance to survive. The Franks, with their excellent connections among gentile Dutch families, might well have been able to hide out singly, each with a different family. But instead, the main principle of their planning was continuing their beloved family—an understandable desire, but highly unrealistic in those times. Choosing any other course would have meant not merely giving up living together, but also realizing the full measure of the danger to their lives.

The Franks were unable to accept that going on living as a family as they had done before the Nazi invasion of Holland was no longer a desirable way of life, much as they loved each other; in fact, for them and others like them, it was most dangerous behavior. But even given their wish not to separate, they failed to make appropriate preparations for what was likely to happen.

There is little doubt that the Franks, who were able to provide themselves with so much while arranging for going into hiding, and even while hiding, could have provided themselves with some weapons had they wished. Had they had a gun, Mr. Frank could have shot down at least one or two of the Green Police who came for them. There was no surplus of such police, and the loss of an SS with every Jew arrested would have noticeably hindered the functioning of the police state. Even a butcher knife, which they certainly could have taken with them into hiding, could have been used by them in self-defense. The fate of the Franks wouldn't have been very different, because they all died anyway except for Anne's father. But they could have sold their lives for a high price, instead of walking into their death. Still, although one must assume that Mr. Frank would have fought courageously, as we know he did when a soldier in World War I, it is not everybody who can plan to kill those who are bent on killing him, although many who would not be ready to contemplate doing so would be willing to kill those who are bent on murdering not only them but also their wives and little daughters.

An entirely different matter would have been planning for escape in case of discovery. The Franks' hiding place had only one entrance; it did not have any other exit. Despite this fact, during their many months of hiding, they did not try to devise one. Nor did they make other plans for escape, such as that one of the family members—as likely as not Mr. Frank—would try to detain the police in the narrow entrance way—maybe even fight them, as suggested above—thus giving other members of the family a chance to escape, either by reaching the roofs of adjacent houses or down a ladder into the alley behind the house in which they were living.

Any of this would have required recognizing and accepting the desperate straits in which they found themselves and concentrating on how best to cope with them. This was quite possible to do, even under the terrible conditions in which the Jews found themselves after the Nazi occupation of Holland. It can be seen from many other accounts, for example from the story of Marga Minco, a girl of about Anne Frank's age who lived to tell about it. Her parents had planned that when the police should come for them, the father would try to detain them by arguing and fighting with them, to give the wife and daughter a chance to escape through a rear door. Unfortunately it did not quite work out this way, and both parents got killed. But their short-lived resistance permitted their daughter to make her escape as planned and to reach a Dutch family who saved her.[1]

This is not mentioned as a criticism that the Frank family did not plan or behave along similar lines. A family has every right to arrange their life as they wish or think best and to take the risks they want to take. My point is not to criticize what the Franks did, but only the universal admiration of their way of coping, or rather of not coping. The story of little Marga who survived, every bit as touching, remains totally neglected by comparison.

Many Jews—unlike the Franks, who through listening to British radio news were better informed than most—had no detailed knowledge of the extermination camps. Thus it was easier for them to make themselves believe that complete compliance with even the most outrageously debilitating and degrading Nazi orders might offer a chance for survival. But neither tremendous anxiety that inhibits clear thinking and with it well-planned and determined action, nor ignorance about what happened to those who responded with passive waiting for being rounded up for their extermination, can explain the reaction of audiences to the play and movie retelling Anne's story, which are all about such waiting that results finally in destruction.

I think it is the fictitious ending that explains the enormous success of this play and movie. At the conclusion we hear Anne's voice from the beyond, saying, "In spite of everything, I still believe that people are really good at heart." This improbable sentiment is supposedly from a girl who had been starved to death, had watched her sister meet the same fate before she did, knew that her mother had been murdered, and had watched untold thousands of adults and children being killed. This statement is not justified by anything Anne actually told her diary.

Going on with intimate family living, no matter how dangerous it might be to survival, was fatal to all too many during the Nazi regime. And if all men are good, then indeed we can all go on with living our lives as we have been accustomed to in times of undisturbed safety and can afford to forget about Auschwitz. But Anne, her sister, her mother, may well have died because her parents could not get themselves to believe in Auschwitz.

While play and movie are ostensibly about Nazi persecution and destruction, in actuality what we watch is the way that, despite this terror, lovable people manage to continue living their satisfying intimate lives with each other. The heroine grows from a child into a young adult as normally as any other girl would, despite the most abnormal conditions of all other aspects of her existence and that of her family. Thus the play reassures us that despite the destructiveness of Nazi racism and tyranny in general, it is possible to disregard it in one's private life much of the time, even if one is Jewish.

True, the ending happens just as the Franks and their friends had feared all along: their hiding place is discovered, and they are carried away to their doom. But the fictitious declaration of faith in the goodness of all men which concludes the play falsely reassures us since it impresses on us that in the combat between Nazi terror and continuance of intimate family living the latter wins out, since Anne has the last word. This is simply contrary to fact, because it was she who got killed. Her seeming survival through her moving statement about the goodness of men releases us effectively of the need to cope with the problems Auschwitz presents. That is why we are so relieved by her statement. It explains why millions loved play and movie, because while it confronts us with the fact that Auschwitz existed, it encourages us at the same time to ignore any of its implications. If all men are good at heart, there never really was an Auschwitz; nor is there any possibility that it may recur.

The desire of Anne Frank's parents not to interrupt their intimate family living, and their inability to plan more effectively for their survival, reflect the failure of all too many others faced with the threat of Nazi terror. It is a failure that deserves close examination because of the inherent warnings it contains for us, the living.

Submission to the threatening power of the Nazi state often led both to the disintegration of what had once seemed well-integrated personalities and to a return to an immature disregard for the dangers of reality. Those Jews who submitted passively to Nazi persecution came to depend on primitive and infantile thought processes: wishful thinking and disregard for the possibility of death. Many persuaded themselves that they, out of all others, would be spared. Many more simply disbelieved in the possibility of their own death. Not believing in it, they did not take what seemed to them desperate precautions, such as giving up everything to hide out singly; or trying to escape even if it meant risking their lives in doing so; or preparing to fight for their lives when no escape was possible and death had become an immediate possibility. It is true that defending their lives in active combat before they were rounded up to be transported into the camps might have hastened their deaths, and so, up to a point, they were protecting themselves by "rolling with the punches" of the enemy.

But the longer one rolls with the punches dealt not only by the normal vagaries of life, but by one's eventual executioner, the more likely it becomes that one will no longer have the strength to resist when death becomes imminent. This is particularly true if yielding to the enemy is accompanied not by a commensurate strengthening of the personality, but by an inner disintegration. We can observe such a process among the Franks, who bickered with each other over trifles, instead of supporting each other's ability to resist the demoralizing impact of their living conditions.

Those who faced up to the announced intentions of the Nazis prepared for the worst as a real and imminent possibility. It meant risking one's life for a self-chosen purpose, but in doing so, creating at least a small chance for saving one's own life or those of others, or both. When Jews in Germany were restricted to their homes, those who did not succumb to inertia took the new restrictions as a warning that it was high time to go underground, join the resistance movement, provide themselves with forged papers, and so on, if they had not done so long ago. Many of them survived.

Some distant relatives of mine may furnish an example. Early in the war, a young man living in a small Hungarian town banded together with a number of other Jews to prepare against a German invasion. As soon as the Nazis imposed curfews on the Jews, his group left for Budapest—because the bigger capital city with its greater anonymity offered chances for escaping detection. Similar groups from other towns converged in Budapest and joined forces. From among themselves they selected typically "Aryan"-looking men who equipped themselves with false papers and immediately joined the Hungarian SS. These spies were then able to warn of impending persecution and raids.

Many of these groups survived intact. Furthermore, they had also equipped themselves with small arms, so that if they were detected they could put up enough of a fight for the majority to escape while a few would die fighting to make the escape possible. A few of the Jews who had joined the SS were discovered and immediately shot, probably a death preferable to one in the gas chambers. But most of even these Jews survived, hiding within the SS until liberation.

Compare these arrangements not just to the Frank's selection of a hiding place that was basically a trap without an outlet but with Mr. Frank's teaching typically academic high school subjects to his children rather than how to make a getaway: a token of his inability to face the seriousness of the threat of death.

Teaching high school subjects had, of course, its constructive aspects. It relieved the ever-present anxiety about their fate to some degree by concentrating on different matters, and by implication it encouraged hope for a future in which such knowledge would be useful. In this sense such teaching was purposeful, but it was erroneous in that it took the place of much pertinent teaching and planning: how best to try escape when detected.

Unfortunately the Franks were by no means the only ones who, out of anxiety, became unable to contemplate their true situation and with it to plan accordingly. Anxiety, and the wish to counteract it by clinging to each other, and to reduce its sting by continuing as much as possible with their usual way of life incapacitated many, particularly when survival plans required changing radically old ways of living that they cherished, and which had become their only source of satisfaction.

Note

1. Marga Minco, *Bitter Herbs* (New York: Oxford University Press, 1960).

25

Twisting the Truth:
The Diary of Anne Frank

Deborah E. Lipstadt

Writing in a diary is a really strange experience for someone like me. Not only because I've never written anything before, but also because it seems to me that later on neither I nor anyone else will be interested in the musings of a thirteen-year-old school girl.
—*June 20, 1942*

Anne Frank's diary has become one of the deniers' of the Holocaust's most popular targets. For more than thirty years they have tried to prove that it was written after the war. It would seem to be a dubious allocation of the deniers' energies that they try to prove that a small book by a young girl full of musings about her life, relationships with her parents, emerging sexuality, and movie stars was not written by her. But they have chosen their target purposefully.

Since its publication shortly after the war, the diary has sold [millions of] copies in [many] countries. For many readers it is their introduction to the Holocaust. Countless grade school and high school classes use it as a required text. The diary's popularity and impact, particularly on the young, make discrediting it as important a goal for the deniers as their attack on the gas chambers. By instilling doubts in the minds of young people about this powerful book, they hope also to instill doubts about the Holocaust itself.

On what do these deniers and neo-Nazis build their case? The deniers cite the different versions [of the diary] and different copies of the typescript to buttress their claim that it is all a fabrication and that there was no original diary. They also point to the fact that two different types of handwriting—printing and cursive—were used in the diary. They claim that the paper and ink were not produced until the 1950s and would have been unavailable to a girl hiding in an attic in Amsterdam in 1942.

But it is the Meyer Levin affair on which the deniers have most often relied to make their spurious charges. Levin, who had first read the diary while he was living in France, wrote a laudatory review of it when Doubleday published it. Levin's review, which appeared in the *New York Times Book Review*, was followed by other articles by him on the diary in which he urged that it be made into a play and film.[1] In 1952 Otto Frank appointed Levin his literary agent in the United States to explore the possibility of producing a play. Levin wrote a script that was turned down by a series of producers. Frustrated by Levin's failures and convinced that this script would not be accepted, Frank awarded the production rights to Kermit Bloomgarden, who turned, at the suggestion of American author Lillian Hellman, to two accomplished MGM screenwriters. Their version of the play was a success and won the 1955 Pulitzer Prize.

Levin, deeply embittered, sued, charging that the playwrights had plagiarized his material and ideas. In January 1958 a jury ruled that Levin should be awarded fifty thousand dollars in damages. However, the New York State Supreme Court set aside the jury's verdict, explaining that since Levin and the MGM playwrights had both relied on the same original source—Anne's diary—there were bound to be similarities between the two.[2]

Since it appeared that another lawsuit would be filed, the court refused to lift the freeze that Levin had placed on the royalties. After two years of an impasse, Frank and Levin reached an out-of-court settlement. Frank agreed to pay fifteen thousand dollars to Levin, who dropped all his claims to royalties and rights to the dramatization of the play. Levin remained obsessed by his desire to dramatize the diary. In 1966 he attempted to stage a production in Israel, though he did not have the right to do so, and Frank's lawyers insisted that it be terminated.[3]

It is against this background that the deniers built their assault on the diary. The first documented attack appeared in Sweden in 1957. A Danish literary critic claimed that the diary had actually been produced by Levin, citing as one of his "proofs" that names such as Peter and Anne were not Jewish names.[4] His charges were repeated in Norway, Austria, and West Germany. In 1958 a German high school teacher who had been a member of the SA and a Hitler Youth leader charged that Anne Frank's diary was a forgery that had earned "millions for the profiteers from Germany's defeat."[5] His allegations were reiterated by the chairman of a right-wing German political party. Otto Frank and the diary's publishers sued them for libel, slander, defamation of the memory of a dead person, and anti-Semitic utterances. The case was settled out of court when the defendants declared that they were convinced the diary was not a forgery and apologized for unverified statements they had made.[6]

In 1967 *American Mercury* published an article by Teressa Hendry, entitled "Was Anne Frank's Diary a Hoax?" in which she suggested that the diary might be the work of Meyer Levin and that if it was, a massive fraud had been perpetrated.[7]

In a fashion that will by now have become familiar [. . .] Hendry's allegations were repeated by other deniers as established fact. This is their typical pattern of cross-fertilization as they create a merry-go-round of allegations. In *Did Six Million Really Die? The Truth at Last,* [Richard] Harwood repeated these charges, unequivocally declaring the diary to be a hoax.[8] In one short paragraph in his book, Arthur Butz likewise stated that he had "looked it over" and determined that the diary was a hoax.[9]

In his 1975 attack on the diary, David Irving replied on the familiar charge that an American court had "proved" that a New York scriptwriter had written it "in collaboration with the girl's father." In 1978 Ditlieb Felderer, publisher of the sexually explicit cartoons of Holocaust survivors, produced a book devoted to certifying the diary as a hoax. He repeated the Levin charge but then went on to label Anne a sex fiend and the book "the first child porno."[10] (Some of his chapter titles are indicative of his approach: "Sexual Extravaganza" and "Anne's Character—Not Even a Nice Girl." Felderer's charges are designed to build on what is often part of the inventory of anti-Semitic stereotypes: Jews, unnaturally concerned about sex, are also producers of pornography designed to corrupt young children.)

In 1975 Heinz Roth, a West German publisher of neo-Nazi brochures, began to circulate pamphlets calling the diary a forgery actually written by a New York playwright. He cited Irving's and Harwood's findings as "proof" of his charges. When asked to desist by Otto Frank, he refused, claiming, in the familiar defense used by deniers, that he was only interested in "pure historical truth." At this point Frank took him to court in West Germany. Roth defended himself by citing statements by Harwood and Butz declaring the diary to be fraudulent. In addition, Roth's lawyers produced an "expert opinion" by Robert Faurisson, among whose charges to prove the diary fictitious was that the annex's inhabitants had made too much noise. Anne wrote of vacuum cleaners being used, "resounding" laughter, and noise that was "enough to wake the dead" (Dec. 6, 1943). How, Faurisson asked, could people in hiding, knowing that the slightest noise would be their undoing, have behaved in this fashion and not been discovered?[11] But Faurisson quoted the diary selectively, distorting its contents to build his case. When Anne wrote of the use of the vacuum cleaner, she preceded it by noting that the "warehouse men have gone home now" (Aug. 5, 1943). The scene in which she described resounding laughter among the inhabitants of the annex took place the preceding evening—a Sunday night—when the warehouse would have been empty (Dec. 6, 1943). When she wrote that a sack of beans broke open and the noise was enough to "wake the dead," Faurisson neglected to quote the next sentence in the diary: "Thank God there were no strangers in the house" (Nov. 9, 1943).

In his description of his visit to Otto Frank, Faurisson engaged in the same tactics he used in relation to his encounter with the official from the Auschwitz museum. He tried to make it appear as if he had caught Frank in a monstrous lie: "The interview turned out to be grueling for Anne Frank's father."[12] Not surprisingly Frank's description of the interchange differs markedly, and he challenged the veracity of much of what Faurisson claimed he said. Faurisson also claimed to have found a witness who was "well informed and of good faith" but who refused to allow his name to be made public. Faurisson assured readers that the name and address of this secret witness had been placed in a "sealed envelope." As proof of this evidence he included a photograph of the sealed envelope as an appendix to his "investigation."[13] In 1980 the court, unconvinced by Faurisson's claims, found that Roth had not proved the diary false.

In 1977 charges were again brought against two men in the West German courts for distributing pamphlets charging that the diary was a hoax. The Bundeskriminalamt (the BKA, or Federal Criminal Investigation Bureau) was asked to prepare a report as to whether the paper and writing material used in the diary were available between 1941 and 1944. The BKA report, which ran just four pages in length, did not deal with the authenticity of the diary itself. It found that the materials had all been manufactured prior to 1950–51 and consequently could have been used by Anne. It also observed, almost parenthetically, that emendations had been made in ballpoint pen on loose pages found with the diary. The ink used to make them had only been on the market since 1951.[14] (The BKA did not address itself to the substance of the emendations, nor did it publish any data explaining how it had reached this conclusion. When the editors of the critical edition of the diary asked for the data they were told by the BKA that they had none.[15])

Given the history of the editing of the diary it is not surprising that these kinds of corrections were made. This did not prevent *Der Spiegel* from publishing a sensationalist article on the diary which began with the following boldface paragraph: "'The Diary of Anne Frank' was edited at a later date. Further doubt is therefore cast on the authenticity of that document." The author of the article did not question whether these corrections had been substantive or grammatical, whether they had been incorporated into the printed text, or when they had been made. Nor did he refer to them as corrections as the BKA had. He referred to the possibility of an impostor at work and charged that the diary had been subjected to countless "manipulations."

These sensationalist observations notwithstanding, *Der Spiegel* dismissed the charge made by David Irving and other deniers that Levin wrote the diary as an "oft-repeated legend." It also stressed that those who wished to shed doubt on the diary were the same types who wished to end "gas chamber fraud."[16]

On Otto Frank's death in 1980, the diary was given to the Netherlands State Institute for War Documentation. By that time the attacks on it had become so frequent and vehement—though the charges that were made were all essentially the same—that the institute felt obliged to subject the diary, as well as the paper on which it was written, glue that bound it together, and ink to a myriad of scientific tests in order to determine whether they were authentic. They also tested postage stamps, postmarks, and censorship stamps on postcards, letters, and greeting cards sent by Anne and her family during this period (in addition to the diary the institute examined twenty-two different documents containing writings by Anne and her family). Forensic science experts analyzed Anne's handwriting, paying particular attention to the two different scripts, and produced a 250-page highly technical report of their findings.

The reports found that the paper, glue, fibers in the binding, and ink were all in use in the 1940s. The ink contained iron, which was standard for inks used prior to 1950 (after that date ink with no, or a much lower, iron content was used). The conclusions of the forensic experts were unequivocal: the diaries were written by one person during the period in question. The emendations were of a limited nature and varied from a single letter to three words. They did not in any way alter the meaning of the text when compared to the earlier version.[17] The institute determined that the different handwriting styles were indicative of normal development in a child and left no doubt that it was convinced that it had all been written in the same hand that wrote the letters and cards Anne had sent to classmates in previous years.

The final result of the institute's investigation was a 712-page critical edition of the diary containing the original version, Anne's edited copy, and the published version as well as the experts' findings. While some may argue that the Netherlands State Institute for War Documentation used an elephant to swat a fly, once again it becomes clear that the deniers' claims have no relationship to the most basic rules of truth and evidence.

Notes

This essay is based on David Barnouw's "Attacks on the Authenticity of the Diary," in *The Diary of Anne Frank: The Critical Edition,* prepared by the Netherlands State Institute for War Documentation, ed. David Barnouw and Gerrold van der Stroom, trans. Arnold J. Pomerans and B. M. Mooyaart-Doubleday (New York: Doubleday, 1989), 84–101.

1. *New York Times Book Review,* June 15, 1952; *Congress Weekly,* Nov. 13, 1950; and *National Jewish Post,* June 30, 1952, all cited in David Barnouw, "The Play," *The Diary of Anne Frank: The Critical Edition,* prepared by the Netherlands State Institute for War

Documentation, ed. David Barnouw and Gerrold van der Stroom, trans. Arnold J. Pomerans and B. M. Mooyaart-Doubleday (New York: Doubleday, 1989), 78.

2. *New York Law Journal,* Feb. 27, 1959, cited in Barnouw, "The Play," 80.

3. *New York Times,* Nov. 27, 1966; Meyer Levin, *The Obsession* (New York: Simon and Schuster, 1973), 262.

4. David Barnouw, "Attacks on the Authenticity of the Diary," *Critical Edition,* 84.

5. Ibid., 84.

6. Ibid., 84–89.

7. Teressa Hendry, "Was Anne Frank's Diary a Hoax?" *American Mercury* (Summer 1967), 26–28.

8. Richard Harwood, *Did Six Million Really Die? The Truth at Last* (Richmond, England: Historical Review Press, 1974), 19.

9. Arthur R. Butz, *The Hoax of the Twentieth Century* (Richmond, England: Historical Review Press, 1975), 37.

10. Ditlieb Felderer, *Anne Frank's Diary—a Hoax?* (Taby, Sweden: Bible Researcher, 1978). When the book was reprinted by the IHR [Institute for Historical Review] the question mark was omitted from the title.

11. Robert Faurisson, *Le Journal d'Anne Frank est-il authentique?* in Serge Thion, *Vérité historique ou vérité politique?* (Paris: La Veille Taupe, 1980), cited in Barnouw, "Attacks on the Authenticity," 94–95.

12. Robert Faurisson, *Het Dagboek van Anne Frank—een Vervalsing* (The Diary of Anne Frank—a Forgery) (Antwerp: Vrij Historisch Onderzoek, 1985), 18, cited in Barnouw, "Attacks on the Authenticity," 95.

13. Barnouw, "Attacks on the Authenticity," 96.

14. Opinion of Federal Criminal Investigation Bureau, May 28, 1980; Hamburg, Landgericht, Romer/Geiss dossier, cited in Barnouw, "Attacks on the Authenticity," 97–98.

15. Barnouw, "Attacks on the Authenticity," 99.

16. *Der Spiegel,* Oct. 6, 1980, cited in ibid., 98.

17. H. J. J. Hardy, "Document Examination and Handwriting Identification of the Text Known as the Diary of Anne Frank: Summary of Findings," *Critical Edition,* 164.

26

The Americanization of the Holocaust on Stage and Screen

Lawrence L. Langer

Yesterday evening, before I fell asleep, who should suddenly appear before my eyes but Lies! I saw her in front of me, clothed in rags. . . . Her eyes were very big and she looked so sadly and reproachfully at me that I could read in her eyes: Oh, Anne, why have you deserted me? Help, oh help me, rescue me from this hell!"
—*November 27, 1943*

We bring to the imaginative experience of the Holocaust a foreknowledge of man's doom. Not his fate, but his doom. The Greeks sat spellbound in their arenas in Athens and witnessed the unfolding of what they already knew; proud and defiant men and women submitting to an insurrection in their spirit that rebelled against limitations. Oedipus and Phaedra, Orestes and Antigone hurl their own natures against laws human or divine, suffer the intrusions of chance and coincidence, but *make their fate* by pursuing or being driven by weaknesses or strengths that are expressions of the human will. Whether they survive or die, they affirm the painful, exultant feeling of being human; they declare that man, in the moral world at least, is an agent in the fate we call his death.

But the doom we call extermination is another matter. The Athenians could identify the death of their heroes on the stage with a ritual for renewal, ally tragedy with comedy, and make both a cause for celebration. The human drama allowed it. But the Holocaust presents us with the spectacle of an inhuman drama: we sit in the audience and witness the unfolding of what we will never "know," even though the tales are already history. The tradition of fate encourages identification: we may not achieve the stature of an Oedipus or a Phaedra, but their problems of identity, of passion, of moral courage, or retribution are human— are ours. The tradition of doom—a fate, one might say, imposed on man by other men against his will, without his agency—forbids identification: for who can share the last gasp of the victim of annihilation, whose innocence so totally dissevers him from his end? We lack the psychological, emotional, and even intellectual powers to participate in a ritual that celebrates *such* a demise. We feel alien, not akin. The drama of fate reminds us that man, should he so choose, can die for something; the drama of doom, the history of the Holocaust, reveals whether they chose or not, men died for nothing.

This is not a comfortable theme for the artist to develop or for an audience to absorb. Traditions of heroic enterprise, in literature or in life; conceptions of the human spirit, secular or divine; patterns for imagining reality whether written or oral—all have prepared us to view individual men and women in a familiar way. Hence it should not be surprising that some of the best-known attempts to bring the Holocaust theme to the American stage—Frances Goodrich and Albert Hackett's *The Diary of Anne Frank,* Millard Lampell's *The Wall,* and Arthur Miller's *Incident at Vichy*—as well as films like *Judgment at Nuremberg* and the TV "epic" *Holocaust,* should draw on old forms to reassert man's fate instead of new ones to help us appreciate his doom. To be sure, visually we have progressed in thirty years from the moderate misery of a little room in Amsterdam to execution pits and peepholes into the gas chambers of Auschwitz in *Holocaust;* but imaginatively, most of these works still cling valiantly to the illusion that the Nazi genocide of nearly six million human beings has not substantially altered our vision of human dignity. When Conrad's Marlow in *Heart of Darkness* returns from the Congo to speak with Kurtz's Intended, he brings a message about Kurtz's inhuman doom to a woman who wishes only to hear about his human fate. And Marlow submits: the truth "would have been too dark—too dark altogether."

How much darkness must we acknowledge before we will be able to confess that the Holocaust story cannot be told in terms of heroic dignity, moral courage, and the triumph of the human spirit in adversity? Those words adhere like burrs to the back of a patient beast, who lacks the energy or desire to flick them away lest in doing so he disturb his tranquility. Kurtz's Intended pleads with Marlow for "something—something—to—live with." The Holocaust—alas!—provides us with only something to die with, something from those who died with nothing left to give. There is no final solace, no redeeming truth, no hope that so many millions may not have died in vain. They have. But the American vision of the Holocaust, in the works under consideration here, continues to insist that they have not, trying to parlay hope, sacrifice, justice, and the future into a victory that will mitigate despair. Perhaps it is characteristically American, perhaps merely human, but these works share a deafness (in varying degrees) to those other words that Conrad's Marlow brings back only to find that he has no audience prepared to listen: "'Don't you hear them?' The dusk was repeating them in a persistent whisper all around us, in a whisper that seemed to swell menacingly like the first whisper of a rising wind. 'The horror! The horror!'"

There is little horror in the stage version of *The Diary of Anne Frank:* there is very little in the original diary itself. Perhaps this is one source of their appeal: they permit the imagination to cope with the idea of the Holocaust without forcing a confrontation with its grim details. Like the diary, the play (though even more so) gives us only the bearable part of the story of Anne and the other occupants of the secret annex; the unbearable part begins after the final curtain falls and ends in Auschwitz and Bergen-Belsen. An audience coming to this play in 1955, only a decade after the event, would find little to threaten their psychological or emotional security. No one dies, and the inhabitants of the annex endure minimal suffering. The play really celebrates the struggle for harmony in the midst of impending disruption, thus supporting those values which the viewer instinctively hopes to find affirmed on the stage. To be sure, in the diary, Anne is not oblivious to the doom of the Jews, despite her limited access to information; but there is no hint in the play of this entry from October 9, 1942: "if it is as bad as this in Holland whatever will it be like in the distant and barbarous regions [the Jews] are sent to? We assume that most of them are murdered. The English radio speaks of their being gassed." In the diary, however, Anne does not brood on the prospects of annihilation; she devotes most of her reflections to her aspirations as a writer and her passage through adolescence and puberty to young womanhood. Nevertheless, a certain amount of ambiguity lingers in her young mind (absent from her character in the play) that at least adds some complexity to her youthful vision. "I see the world being turned into a wilderness," she writes (July 15, 1944), "I hear the ever approaching thunder, which will destroy us too, I can feel the sufferings of millions and yet, if I look up into the heavens, I think that it will all come right, that this cruelty too will end, and that peace and tranquillity will return again." But for all but one of the inhabitants of the annex, nothing came right, cruelty grew worse, and neither peace nor tranquility ever returned.

Yet this is not the feeling we are left with in the play, which accents Anne's mercurial optimism at the expense of the encroaching doom that finally engulfed them all. Upbeat endings seem to be de rigueur for the American imagination, which traditionally buries its tragedies and lets them fester in the shadow of forgetfulness. The drama begins with Otto Frank, a "bitter old man," returning to the secret annex after the war and finding that Anne's diary has been preserved. His "reading" of excerpts becomes the substance of the play, which after the discovery and arrest fades back into the present, revealing a calm Otto Frank, his bitterness gone. Considering the numerous "last glimpses" of Anne we might have received from this epilogue—one eyewitness in Bergen-Belsen, where she died, described her like this: "She was in rags. I saw her emaciated, sunken face in the darkness. Her eyes were very large"[1]—one wonders at the stubborn, almost perverse insistence in the play on an affirmative epigraph, almost a denial of Anne's doom. Why should the authors think it important that we hear from Otto Frank, in almost the last words of the play, the following tribute, *even if those words were quoted verbatim from Anne's real father:* "It seems strange to say this," muses Frank, "that anyone could be happy in a concentration camp. But Anne was happy in Holland where they first took us [Westerbork detention camp]."[2]

The authors of the dramatic version of Anne Frank's diary lacked the artistic will—or courage—to leave their audiences overwhelmed by the feeling that Anne's bright spirit was extinguished, that Anne, together with millions of others, was killed simply because she was Jewish, and for no other reason. This theme lurks on the play's periphery, but never emerges into the foreground, though one gets a vague hint during the Hanukkah celebration that ends act 1. That Anne herself, had she survived, would have been equal to this challenge is suggested by her brief description of a roundup of Amsterdam Jews witnessed from her attic window: "In the evenings when it's dark, I often see rows of good, innocent people accompanied by crying children, walking on and on, in charge of a couple of Germans, bullied and knocked about until they almost drop. No one is spared— old people, babies, expectant mothers, the sick—each and all join in the march of death" (November 19, 1942).

But the audience in the theater is sheltered from this somber vision, lest it disrupt the mood of carefully orchestrated faith in human nature that swells into a crescendo just before the play's climax, when the Gestapo and Green Police arrive to arrest the inhabitants of the annex. One is forced to contemplate Anne's restive intelligence at its most simple-minded, as Goodrich and Hackett have her reply to Peter Van Daan's irritable impatience at their dilemma with the pitiful cliché: "We're not the only people that've had to suffer. There've always been people that've had to."[3] Ann's mind was more capacious, if still undeveloped, but a probe into the darker realms that Conrad and Marlow knew of, an entry like the following from Anne's diary, would have introduced a discordant note into the crescendo I have mentioned: "There's in people simply an urge to destroy, an urge to kill, to murder and rage, and until all mankind, without exception, undergoes a great change, wars will be waged, everything that has been built up, cultivated, and grown will be destroyed and disfigured, after which mankind will have to begin all over again" (May 3, 1944).

This view of the apocalypse before any fresh resurrection appears nowhere in the stage version of Anne's diary. Indeed, its presence in the other works I will examine will be one test of their authenticity as Holocaust literature. If in the end even Anne Frank retreated to a safer cheerfulness, we need to remember that she was not yet fifteen when she wrote that passage. The line that concludes her play, floating over the audience like a benediction assuring grace after momentary gloom, is the least appropriate epitaph conceivable for the millions of victims and thousands of survivors of Nazi genocide: "in spite of everything, I still believe that people are really good at heart." Those who permit such heartwarming terms to insulate them against the blood-chilling events they belie need to recall that they were written by a teenager who could also say of her situation: "I have often been downcast, but never in despair; I regard our hiding as a dangerous adventure, romantic and interesting at the same time." Her strong sentimental strain, which was only part of her nature, dominates the drama and ultimately diverts the audience's attention from the sanguinary to the sanguine, causing them to forget that the roots are identical, and that during the Holocaust man's hope was stained by a blood more indelible than the imaginary spot so distressing to Lady Macbeth. By sparing us the imaginative ordeal of such consanguinity, the drama of *The Diary of Anne Frank* cannot begin to evoke the doom that eventually denied the annex's victims the dignity of human choice.

The play presents instead a drama of domestic pathos; it begins and ends with the figure of Otto Frank, a paterfamilias without a family who nevertheless is inspired, like the rest of us, by his dead daughter's steadfast devotion to hope. Bruno Bettelheim's needlessly harsh criticism of the Frank family for failing to recognize the crisis for Jews in Europe and to increase the prospect of survival by seeking separate hiding places nevertheless implies an important truth for anyone seeking to portray the Holocaust experience with insight. The family unit, that traditional bulwark in moments of familiar stress, was worthless and occasionally injurious to individual survival in the unpredictable atmosphere of the death camp. The tensions that sundered such ancient loyalties are absent from *Anne Frank:* they begin to appear in Millard Lampell's play *The Wall* (1960), based on John Hersey's novel, but even here, under the pressures of life in the Warsaw ghetto, family unity finally asserts itself and triumphs over the strains that threaten to crack it.

Notes

1. Ernst Schnabel, *Anne Frank: A Portrait in Courage* (New York: Harcourt, Brace, and World, 1958), 177.

2. Frances Goodrich and Albert Hackett, *The Diary of Anne Frank* (New York: Random House, 1956), 72.

3. Ibid., 168.

27

The Uses—and Misuses—of a Young Girl's Diary: "If Anne Frank Could Return from among the Murdered, She Would Be Appalled"

Lawrence L. Langer

If I just think of how we live here, I usually come to the conclusion that it is a
paradise compared with how other Jews who are not in hiding must be living.
—*May 1, 1943*

In a recent review in the *New York Times* of the newly translated definitive edition of Anne Frank's *Diary of a Young Girl,* the reviewer calls the work "the single
most compelling account of the Holocaust." Nothing could be further from the
truth. Anyone familiar with the detailed memoirs of this grim event by Elie
Wiesel, Alexander Donat, Filip Müller, Charlotte Delbo, and dozens of others
must wonder at the spirit of naivete, not to say covert denial, that continues to
classify Anne's innocent diary as a major Holocaust text.

Prudish Publisher

The Diary of a Young Girl: The Definitive Edition, just published by Doubleday,
contains 30 percent more material than the original version, first published in
1947. Readers familiar with the scholarly critical edition of 1989 will find nothing new. Those unfamiliar with that edition will encounter several explicit allu-
sions to Anne's sexual awakening, expunged by a prudish Dutch publisher, and
numerous disparaging remarks about her mother and other inhabitants of the
hiding place, which her father decided to censor. These additions do little to alter our image of a gifted young girl who has been inflated into a figure of mythic
proportions by an adoring public who never knew her as she really was.

Sentimental Line

I am convinced that if Anne Frank could return from among the murdered, she would be appalled at the misuse to which her journal entries had been put. Above all, her journey via Westerbork and Auschwitz to Bergen-Belsen, where she died miserably of typhus and malnutrition, would have led her to regret writing the single sentimental line by which she is most remembered, even by admirers who have never read the diary: "I still believe, in spite of everything, that people are truly good at heart." What, she might have asked, of my other views? For example: "There's a destructive urge in people, the urge to rage, murder and kill."

Like many other adolescents, Anne Frank was a creature of moods, shifting attitudes as befit her mercurial temperament. A few lines following the above gloomy commentary, she could write: "I look upon our life in hiding as an interesting adventure, full of danger and romance." How can any mature mind accept this as a serious reflection of the Holocaust experience? Thousands of Jews who spent the war hiding in chilly attics and barns, or in pits which they shared with ground water and rats, cold, hungry, and alone, would be stunned to learn that such an ordeal might be labeled an "interesting adventure."

Filled with Foreboding

Anne Frank's experience was distinct, not representative, and those who canonize her as an archetypal victim and use her story to reflect the anguish of an entire people are guilty of a double injustice—to her and to the millions of other victims. Of the two Annes who exist in the diary, one filled with foreboding and the other unable to suppress her love of life, neither could imagine the atrocities she would be exposed to once she left her attic sanctuary. One appeal of the diary is that it shelters both students and teachers from the worst, to say nothing of the unthinkable, making them feel that they have encountered the Holocaust without being threatened by intolerable images.

Anne Frank herself is to blame for none of this. She knew that the Dutch Jews were being deported somewhere, and that BBC news broadcasts mentioned their being gassed, but she never intended her diary to be concerned primarily with the plight of the Jews. Less than 20 percent of its text is involved with this subject. Anne was proud of her Jewishness, but she did not practice its rituals. She and the other inhabitants of the secret annex celebrated St. Nicholas Day with much greater enthusiasm than they lit Hanukkah candles, and in more than two years of entries, she never mentioned the celebration of Passover at all. As for the fate that lay before her and the others should they be discovered, aside from the rumors about "gassing" she had no idea what shape it might take. Indeed, in the diary itself she is far more frightened by the periodic air raids over Amsterdam than by the prospect of being caught.

Rite of Passage

It is certainly time to recognize Anne Frank's literary achievement for what it was—not as a source of important information about the Holocaust, but the unfolding of a particular feminine self. The additional material in the new translation, already familiar to readers of the critical edition, confirms this view. Moving through puberty into adolescence, Anne captured with a remarkable precocity and sharpness of observation the physical and psychological tensions that are natural to that rite of passage. As the months pass, her entries surge to higher and keener plateaus of understanding, and had she lived, I have no doubt that she would have become a renowned journalist and perhaps novelist too. Her literary style was mature beyond her years, but this has led some of her most enthusiastic admirers to expect more than she was capable of.

Wisdom and spiritual insight rarely fall from the lips of a thirteen- or fourteen-year-old girl. Indeed, as many of the new entries in the diary will show, Anne Frank was essentially a physical being, a lover of nature, intrigued with her own sexuality. Students and teachers should continue to read this unusual diary, but for the right reasons. A wrong one is to consider it a vital text about the doom of European Jewry.

28

Anne Frank—and Us: Finding the Right Words

Alvin H. Rosenfeld

The legend she founded is the kind her destroyers had tried to wipe out. She is a Jewess spoken of by Germans as a saint; she was an object of hatred, and has become a vehicle of love.
—*Henry F. Pommer, "The Legend and Art of Anne Frank"*

Almost fifty years after the end of World War II, the crime that we have come to call the Holocaust haunts our consciousness like almost no other event in this century. It is a crime that both compels and eludes us. We know that it happened, but inasmuch as it resists understanding within the received categories of historical explanation, it remains in its essence somehow unfathomable. That is not owing to any serious lack of documentation, for in an effort to describe and explain the Nazi assault against the Jews an enormous body of literature has developed. What we lack is not an adequate written record but the means to assimilate it to the conceptual norms of interpretation. It is for this reason that the historian Saul Friedländer has called the Holocaust "an event at the limit."

The numbers alone tend to make the Nazi campaign of genocide an event that the mind cannot readily digest. And what cannot be satisfactorily represented can be neither fully comprehended in the present nor securely retained in memory for the future. In *One, by One, by One: Facing the Holocaust,* Judith Miller spoke to this dilemma, stating in the concluding sentences of her study: "Abstraction is memory's most ardent enemy. It kills because it encourages distance, and often indifference. We must remind ourselves that the Holocaust was not six million. It was one, plus one, plus one. . . . Only in understanding that civilized people must defend the one, by one, by one . . . can the Holocaust, the incomprehensible, be given meaning."[1]

Just what kind of "meaning" the systematic persecution and slaughter of millions of innocent people can have is a question that Miller does not answer, but nevertheless the point she makes is well taken. Otherwise, as she correctly puts it, memory of the Nazi crimes can fade into a meaningless abstraction of mass, anonymous death.

In fact, memory has already taken such a turn. The photographs and films of the corpse mounds that we have all seen inevitably project anonymity—a heart-stopping image of inert, intertwined limbs that defines and compounds the specter of a grossly dehumanized horror. One is simultaneously drawn to and repelled by such images. In encountering them, it is easy to lose sight of the fact that these pictures of faceless, frozen agony are truly composed of individual men and women, who, before being put to slaughter, were often diminished to the point of nonrecognition by their Nazi murderers. [. . .]

The question of memory's attenuation, which in one form or another haunts all Holocaust survivors, was posed in particularly sharp ways in Primo Levi's last book, *The Drowned and the Saved.* Among other things, Levi was troubled by what he recognized as a "gap that exists and grows wider every year between things as they were 'down there' and things as they are represented by the current imagination fed by approximative books, films, and myths. It slides fatally toward simplification and stereotype."[2]

One way to keep this slide from accelerating is to focus on individual stories, to see precisely how the Holocaust claimed its victims "one, by one, by one." Levi noted as much when he wrote that "a single Anne Frank excites more emotion than the myriads who suffered as she did but whose image has remained in the shadows. Perhaps it is necessary that it can be so. If we had to and were able to suffer the sufferings of everyone, we could not live."[3] Levi's own writings are as forceful and lucid an evocation of the sufferings of the victims as any we have been given. Yet it is not he who stands today as the most widely known writer of the Holocaust but the figure he names. It is Anne Frank to whom we must look if we wish to understand how the public at large has come to regard "the myriads who suffered" at the hands of the Nazis two generations ago. [. . .]

Seen within the context of its time and place, the story of Anne Frank is, sadly, unremarkable. At least a million and possibly as many as a million and a half Jewish children were murdered by the Nazis and their allies during World War II. What distinguishes Annes Frank's story from that of these other children, therefore, is not her early death but the diary entries she kept during the last years of her life and the nature of the public response to her writings. As we know from the literature that has come down to us from that time, other children likewise kept diaries. But none has been embraced with anything like the interest and affection that Anne Frank's posthumously published diary has received. [. . .]

It is no exaggeration to say that Anne Frank is probably the best known child of the twentieth century and, as an especially cherished figure, has taken on a symbolic stature almost without rival in the postwar period.

What, though, is the symbolic character of Anne Frank's story? And what explains its continuing popularity? Why is it that she, and almost she alone, stands out among the million or more Jewish children murdered by the Nazis? Does she—indeed, can she—fairly represent the fate of these others? The answer to this last question, unsurprisingly, is no. Her tale, set as it is in Amsterdam, unfolded far away from the places in eastern Europe where most Jews were murdered. During the time when she was hidden in her secret annex, Anne Frank was shielded from the worst aspects of the Nazi terror and knew about them only distantly. It's true that ultimately she came to share the fate of millions of other Jews in the Nazi camp system, but inasmuch as her diary stops before this final, grim chapter of her story, most readers are unaware of the actual circumstances of her end. [. . .]

[The] image of the emaciated, disease-ridden girl lying dead amidst the human waste of the camp latrine, then dumped into a huge hole that serves as a mass grave, forms no part of the cherished "legacy" of Anne Frank. And yet precisely this was Anne Frank's fate, as it was the fate of innumerable other Jewish victims of Nazi Germany. Following prescribed norms, however, the image of Anne Frank that has evolved over the years has been largely sanitized of any realistic sense of her life and death. Her life has been idealized to the point where it can be summed up by a single, often quoted sentence from the diary—"In spite of everything I still believe that people are really good at heart"—and her death is either glossed over or given a hopeful, even beatific character. [. . .]

Indeed, it may well be the case that Anne Frank's popularity is owing to the fact that her story remains only imperfectly known and, by and large, has also been "de-Judaized." What remains, although certainly moving, is relatively mild, given what one finds elsewhere in Holocaust literature. No doubt it is for this reason that Anne Frank's story attracts the attention of the young especially and evokes in them a pathos that is vaguely linked to a sense of their own lives, in particular those aspects of their lives that they understand in terms of youthful aspirations and sorrows. Understood in these terms, Anne Frank reflects the familiar personal fears, frustrations, and yearnings of the average teenager. She is bright, eager, energetic, idealistic, romantic—a young girl on the verge of womanhood and a future life of new sensations and satisfactions. [. . .] She lives in hope, but also in real danger. In all of these respects, she reflects in dramatic form the common teenage fantasies of desire and dread, both of which commingle intimately in her story. They help to account for its immense popularity, not only among the young but, in fact, among all those who retain in adulthood the longings and apprehensions of their youth.

Anne Frank's tale draws a vast audience to the private life of an admirable young girl but at the same time shields it from a closer knowledge of the brutal fate she shared with millions of other European Jews. By learning the little one comes to learn about the Nazi crimes through the story of Anne Frank, one can "know about" the Holocaust in some distant, preliminary way, yet keep from confronting the Nazi horrors at their worst. Furthermore—and this point is crucial—one can embrace Anne Frank as an attractive symbol of youthful idealism and even of martyrdom without recognizing her story as a specifically *Jewish story.* She certainly knew herself as a Jew and was not hesitant to record in her diary some unusually thoughtful reflections on Judaism and Jewish historical fate. But her image has been reconstructed over the past four decades in more neutral terms, and much of her appeal today lies in the vague, universalistic qualities that now surround her story.

Thanks to Broadway and Hollywood, which have projected to millions an Anne Frank who has come to resemble the sweet and lovable girl next door, hers is a story that renders the worst aspects of the Holocaust in grossly understated terms. It is, therefore, a story easy to take. The interpretive stress typically falls on the romantic Anne Frank, the writer Anne Frank, the witty, appealing, and adorable Anne Frank, but rarely on the Anne Frank who would end up as one more anonymous Jewish corpse in the mass graves of Bergen-Belsen. Hounded by her former countrymen as a Jew and placed under a death sentence for the same reason, she has been largely stripped of that part of her identity in her posthumous career as a cultural icon. In this respect she has gone the way of other Jews who have been taken up as culture heroes. The following, from the German writer Sabine Reichel, is a telling response, unusual only for its candor:

> It seems almost impossible to imagine now that I spent most of my teenage years in intense adulation of Kafka and Heine without knowing that they were Jewish. Even stranger, I didn't know about Anne Frank's existence at all, because neither my teachers nor my parents encouraged me to read her moving diary. It was Hollywood that introduced me to that inspiring Dutch teenager, and all I remember is that it was an incredibly sad story—and that Millie Perkins was such a pretty Anne.[4]

Reichel here speaks for a whole generation of Germans in the postwar period, who were raised without much knowledge of the Jewish victims of their parents and grandparents. Anne Frank was either unknown to them altogether or was presented in the hollow terms described above—as a pretty but otherwise nondescript Dutch girl, whose story was moving for its sadness. But the thinking of young Germans in the years following the end of World War II was typically not encouraged to go beyond that point.

The slide toward simplification and stereotype is hardly attributable, however, only to the Germans. One finds plenty of others thinking along lines that likewise tend to reduce a complex history to the simple and the stereotypical. A number of the essays collected in David Rosenberg's *Testimony: Contemporary Writers Make the Holocaust Personal* (1989) refer to Anne Frank, for instance, but do so in ways that demonstrate just how weakened a figure she has become.

Rosenberg asked his contributors, most of them American Jewish writers born during or after the war years, to describe "the shadow of the Holocaust" on their lives. Furthermore, he wanted them to state how and when they first learned of the Holocaust and how it has shaped or been absent from their careers as writers. These are challenging questions, but many of the responses are disappointingly shallow.

Francine Prose, one of Rosenberg's contributors, cites *The Diary of a Young Girl* as an early formative influence on her and remarks that, as a young girl, she read the book again and again. What did it tell her? "For me," she writes, "the book was the story of a girl who had a love affair and a girl who died, and in retrospect I am not sure I knew the difference. . . . I think that I would have been willing to suffer the death if I could have had the romance." Prose writes about the links she felt between herself as a young girl and Anne Frank ("Anne Frank, our sister, our double") and remembers the Holocaust as a focal point for the voluptuous commingling of sex and death. "And so," she notes, "the Holocaust for me became invested with an air of the romantic. It was terrible and glamorous, dark-toned and nostalgic."[5] Whatever else these words may say, they register almost no sense of the extreme character of the events that unfolded in Europe two generations ago. [. . .]

Following [such] examples, one realizes that the conceptual problem with which we began remains, for to look at the Holocaust "one, by one, by one" is not necessarily to see it clearly. In the case of the popularization of Anne Frank, in fact, a far greater part of this history may be kept from view than revealed. To be sure, there are others who regard the crimes of the Third Reich in more sober and responsible ways, but tendencies to "personalize" or politicize the Holocaust are prominent today and represent a cultural trend that is troubling. It is a trend that has the effect of either denying the realities of Auschwitz or transmuting them into something else—erotic indulgences of various sorts or political action programs that dramatize their appeals through emotionally linked references to the Nazi campaign of genocide. The citations from *Testimony* given above illustrate the former. As an illustration of the latter, one need only look at the rhetoric routinely employed in the debates about abortion and AIDS to realize that "genocide" and "Holocaust" are terms that are being applied to social realities that, for all their gravity, do not resemble the Nazi crimes against the Jews.

Those crimes had genocide as their aim and the organized force of a powerful state to implement them in a determined, systematic way. With respect to both intentionality and means, therefore, the Nazi Holocaust was something uniquely evil. An event without identifiable historical precedent, it does not lend itself very readily to comparison or analogy. To say as much is obviously not to say that there are no people today who are suffering, for every day's news shows us that the opposite is true. Nor is it to suggest that we have succeeded in eliminating from our society the various forms of prejudice, intolerance, and injustice that are at the root of so much personal and collective pain, for clearly we have not. However, it is to say that we are likely to obscure rather than to clarify the nature and causes of present-day suffering when we see it as a new form of "genocide" or as the precursor of a second "Holocaust." At the same time, when every instance of human suffering is transfigured as another "Holocaust," the Holocaust itself tends to lose its reality and becomes little more than a figure of speech—its moral claims upon us diminished rather than enlarged by metaphorical extension.

Anne Frank has been appropriated as a symbol in these ways almost from the start. In addition, there have been repeated attempts to deny her story of any value whatsoever. For decades, right-wing groups have attacked the authenticity of the diary through the publication of polemical tracts meant to "expose" Anne Frank's writings as a forgery. The intention is to nullify the historicity of the Holocaust by calling into question the legitimacy of one of its central texts. If Anne Frank's diary can be shown to be a "hoax"—a literary fabrication rather than an authentic historical document—then the reality of Jewish suffering under the Nazis can likewise be "proven" to be bogus. What is truly bogus in all of these cases, of course, is the "scholarship" that is used to advance this kind of radical, right-wing revisionism. But for all of its sinister methods and pernicious effects, the literature of Holocaust denial is widespread today and has given us such meretricious books and pamphlets as *Anne Frank's Diary—a Forgery, Anne Frank's Diary—a Hoax, Anne Frank's Diary—the Big Fraud,* and related tawdry works. Unfortunately the fact that such literature is driven by a palpable bad faith does not mean it lacks for readers. The opposite seems to be true, as the reception for revisionist claims that the Holocaust never happened appears larger and more sympathetic today than it has been in the past.

On the other end of the political spectrum, one finds troubling tendencies of another sort. Those of the Left typically do not seek to attack or suppress the historical memory of the Holocaust, but they are disposed to instrumentalize it for their own political ends. In the 1960s, for instance, it was common practice for the figure of Anne Frank to be pressed into service in the struggle against "fascism."

There was a time during the Vietnam war when the Anne Frank House in Amsterdam itself became a prominent focal point for the "anti-fascist" campaign, which, among other things, sought to expose visitors on the Prinsengracht to vivid denunciations of the United States as a successor to Nazi Germany. [. . .]

Given such practices, one worries that the future memory of the Holocaust may become increasingly tenuous. Indeed, since it has entered the domain of public speech, *Holocaust* has become a highly elastic and highly charged figure of speech and is commonly invoked in the debates that are currently raging about abortion, AIDS, civil rights, gay rights, pornography, etc. These are serious debates, but they spring from a history that does not resemble the history that produced Auschwitz and Bergen-Belsen. They have nothing intrinsically to do with Anne Frank or the other victims of Nazi genocide, and we do no honor to Anne Frank's memory or the memories of so many others like her when we see ourselves as "victims" in their image. In fact, it is our good fortune that we are not Anne Frank's "sister" or "double," and we shouldn't pretend to be.

Julius Lester recognized as much in his own reflections on Anne Frank, which stand in welcome contrast to the other contributions in *Testimony* cited above. Lester first came to learn about the diary as a senior in college, when he attended a lecture about Anne Frank given by a visiting Dutch scholar. The lecture obviously had an impact on the way he looked at the world and his own place in it. "I don't know how to live with the knowledge of such evil and such suffering," he realized. He continued to think about the nature of the new knowledge he had acquired and found some important clarifications in a revealing conversation he had with the poet Robert Hayden:

> "We think we know something about suffering," he [Hayden] says, referring to black people. "We don't know what suffering means. . . . Well, that's not entirely true. Maybe it's a problem of language. . . . Maybe I'm not comfortable using the same word 'suffering' to describe what we have gone through and what the Jews went through. Do you know what I mean?"
>
> I did. I had ridden at the backs of buses all of my life, had read signs telling me where I could and could not eat, what doors I could and could not go through, what water fountains I could and could not drink from. I had been trained by my parents not to look at white women. Then I thought about living in an attic and gas chambers and furnaces into which human beings were shoveled like waste paper.
>
> I'm not saying that Jews have suffered more. How can you measure what a human being suffers? But there is a difference . . . and we need a word to make the difference clear. . . . That's what writing is, you know. Finding the right word.
>
> I would like to be the one to find the right word. . . . But is there a word strong enough to hold naked bodies stacked in hills beneath a sunny sky? Being forced to ride at the back of a bus is not in the same realm of experience.

But Jews had to wear yellow Stars of David on their clothes to be identified as Jews. My star is my skin color. Yet I am alive. Anne Frank is not.[6]

With the simple acknowledgment of difference recorded in those last two sentences, Lester restores some much-needed balance to the issues under review here. One suspects, however, that his point of view may not be widely shared. We are living at a time when there are strong encouragements to flatten history into the shapes we would wish to have, a revisionary process advanced by many people of all kinds to express a personal and collective sense of "oppression" and "victimization." Following this sense of things, there is a temptation to readily proclaim, "We are all Anne Frank." But, in fact, we are nothing of the sort, as Julius Lester is wise enough to know. Knowing enables him to recognize clearly what is distinctive about Anne Frank's story as well as his own. The two are both important, and each deserves to be widely known. It makes little sense to view them as competing stories, or as stories of "comparative suffering," as Robert Hayden cautions, for each has a significant historical and moral claim upon us. In a cultural climate where historical memory is either reduced to popular entertainment or made subservient to strong assertions of personal and political will, it is not at all clear that any story will be remembered in the future with the integrity it deserves.

Notes

1. Judith Miller, *One, by One, by One: Facing the Holocaust* (New York: Simon and Schuster, 1990), 287.

2. Primo Levi, *The Drowned and the Saved,* trans. Raymond Rosenthal (New York: Simon and Schuster, 1986), 157.

3. Ibid., 56.

4. Sabine Reichel, *What Did You Do in the War, Daddy?* (New York: Hill and Wang, 1989), 40–41.

5. Francine Prose, "Protecting the Dead," in *Testimony: Contemporary Writers Make the Holocaust Personal,* ed. David Rosenberg (New York: Random House, 1989), 102, 101.

6. Julius Lester, "The Stone that Weeps," in *Testimony,* 195–96.

29

Anne Frank and Etty Hillesum: Diarists

Denise de Costa

We're Jews in chains, chained to one spot, without any rights, but with a thousand obligations.
—*April 11, 1944*

I must admit a new insight into my life. . . . What is at stake is our impending destruction. . . . They are out to destroy us completely; we must accept that and go from there.
—*Etty Hillesum, July 3, 1944*

Anne Frank was a young girl and Etty Hillesum a young woman. They both came from a well-to-do environment. Both lived in Amsterdam and perished in concentration camps: Anne Frank in Bergen-Belsen and Etty Hillesum in Auschwitz-Birkenau.

They left behind diaries, letters, and stories that have inspired novels, documentaries, music, plays, and various forms of art. My work seeks to change the interpretation of these writings and to change the direction of their canonization. By analyzing the texts of Anne Frank and Etty Hillesum from the point of view of their persecution and their being female, I hope to add to recent developments within and around women's studies, focusing on gender and ethnic identity.

Each woman represents "the other" in the sense of being a woman and a Jew. Being females, their place in the symbolic order is not a matter of course. They both have to exercise strong willpower to enter the realms of language and culture. Both rebel against the normal patterns that society expects of a woman's behavior and tasks. As Jews they find their life paths blocked. They move between fear and hope, acceptance and denial, will to survive and acceptance of death. With death surrounding them, they try to lead a meaningful life through the written word and their faith in God.

Anne Frank: As Exile

The position of exile was one of the most dominant aspects of life and work of Anne Frank. Like many other German Jews the Franks fled to Amsterdam after Hitler came to power in 1933. Anne adapted quickly to her new surroundings and acquired many friends. [. . . However,] after the family had moved to the secret annex, she wrote, on December 24, 1943, "We're stuck here like outcasts."

Anne Frank became fully aware of her position as an exile when the secret annex was broken into. The occupants were terrified and their helpers urged them to be careful. "We have been pointedly reminded that we are in hiding, and that we are Jews in chains, chained to one spot," Anne wrote on April 11, 1944. She began to wonder where she belonged. She was German by birth, but due to her Jewish identity the Germans had become her greatest enemies. Anne's hope to become a Dutch citizen after the war was rudely destroyed when she heard that anti-Semitic feelings were alive also among the Dutch. "We, too, shall have to move on again with our little bundles," she wrote on May 22, 1944, "and leave this beautiful country which offered us such a warm welcome and which now turns its back on us." Her words reflect the theme of the eternally hunted Jew, the eternal fugitive.

Multiple Otherness: As Adolescent, Girl, and Jew

When Anne started rewriting her diaries she was almost fifteen years old. By then she had learned what was expected of a woman and she felt embarrassed when she reread her notes from 1942 and 1943 in which she had expressed sexual curiosity or negative feelings about her mother. In the *a* version, for instance, Anne is quite outspoken about her first menstrual period. Eighteen months later (January 22, 1944) she reread the fragments in question and added, "I shall never be able to write such things again. . . . I can't believe that I was ever such an innocent thing. I cannot help but realize that no matter how much I should like to, I can never be like that again."

Such effusions of feeling are lacking in the *b* version: Anne did not consider them fit for publication. Although she was fearlessly honest in the original diaries, she wanted to comply with the feminine ideal of modesty and chastity in the public version. She used the original diaries most of all to express and deal with the emotions that accompanied her developing sexuality, the collisions she had with her mother, her fears and despair. On March 16, 1944, she wrote: "The brightest spot of all is that I can write down my thoughts and feelings, otherwise I would be absolutely stifled." The revised *b* version had a different purpose. Anne censored her own text to give prominence to an "adapted" Anne so that the "real" Anne would be more difficult to discern.

The diaries of Anne Frank not only describe the physical and mental experiences of a girl growing into a young woman. They also provide an insight into the persecution of the Jews during World War II. I would like to argue in favor of an analysis that includes both dimensions. I will clarify this position by responding to S[em] Dresden, professor emeritus of general literature at Leiden University and author of [. . .] a poignant book about war literature relating to the persecution and extermination of the Jews. Although I attach great importance to his research and to the way in which he analyzes his material, I object to the way in which Dresden tries to banish the diaries of Anne Frank from the canon of important literature about the Shoah.[1]

First of all, Dresden claims that Anne's texts are not authentic enough to be referred to as diaries because they do not have the spontaneity of such genres. To substantiate his claim Dresden points to Anne's literary ambitions which made her change the texts to express herself more clearly and correctly. Since his criticism applies only to the revised version, version *b,* Dresden apparently denies the existence of the original version of the diaries. Dresden also holds the view that Anne Frank's texts do not belong to the genre of the war diary. War diaries, Dresden states, focus on the outside world rather than on inner experiences. In my opinion this is an extremely restricted view. Dresden appears to be thinking in terms of mutually exclusive opposites, as if war takes place only in the outside world and in politics and does not affect the minds and emotions of individual human beings.

Anne's diaries demonstrate that her personal thoughts and feelings cannot be interpreted outside the context of World War II:

> Is it true then that grownups have a more difficult time here then we do? No. I know it isn't. Older people have formed their opinions about everything and don't waver before they act. It's twice as hard for us young ones to hold our ground, and maintain our opinions, in a time when all ideals are being shattered and destroyed, when people are showing their worst side, and do not know whether to believe in truth and right and in God. [. . .] I simply can't build up my hopes on a foundation consisting of confusion, misery, and death. I see the world gradually being turned into a wilderness, I hear the ever approaching thunder, which will destroy us too, I can feel the sufferings of millions and yet, if I look up into the heavens I think that it will all come right, that this cruelty too will end, and that peace and tranquility will return again. In the meantime, I must uphold my ideals, for perhaps the time will come when I shall be able to carry them out. (July 15, 1944)

Political Developments

Dresden blames Anne Frank for not writing about the war. She does not often comment on the political development of the war, but this can be attributed to her situation. The occupants of the secret annex frequently listened to the radio and their helpers also provided them with information about the outside world. This information led to heated discussions about the war and the political situation, which in Anne's eyes caused a lot of tension, irritation, disagreement, and commotion. To her mind these conversations were a waste of energy. Besides, Anne was convinced that she should not burden the other occupants of the secret annex with her own worries and fears. She tried to remain as cheerful as possible and not to lose courage. In the meantime, peace did not come closer. Because the war reports depressed her, Anne tried to let them occupy her mind as little as possible. This paradox has not been noted by Dresden. Although he acknowledges that Anne was writing under difficult and painful circumstances that would obviously have been unthinkable without a war, he does not pay sufficient attention to the consequences of this situation. It was not until after the Allied invasion of Normandy (D day, June 6, 1944) that Anne too could no longer suppress her curiosity about political developments. For the first time she started to believe that the war would soon be over.

Dresden refers to the diaries of Anne Frank once more toward the end of his book. He discusses Anne's hiding situation and goes more deeply into the Jewish aspects of her texts. Only then does it become clear that Dresden's rejection of Anne's diaries is related to his skepticism about her worldwide success. His attack appears to be directed not so much to Anne Frank as to her reading public. According to Dresden the diaries are generally considered to be characteristic of the persecution of the Jews, whereas most of its manifestations were much worse. He does not blame Anne Frank for this. He blames the readers who can or are willing to absorb only a small dose of suffering. He claims that the diaries of Anne Frank are so widely read because her suffering can in a sense still be comprehended, unlike a major part of the literature about the ghettos and the concentration camps.

I agree with Dresden on this point. The images that are evoked in his book, for instance, are unbearable. I also found it virtually impossible to read and listen to the eyewitness reports of women who had met Anne Frank in Bergen-Belsen. Putting Anne's suffering in perspective does however not alter the fact that going into hiding was an important aspect of the persecution of the Jews. Dresden seems to want to establish different degrees of suffering, which in my opinion is pointless, especially if it leads to exclusion. If it comes to literature about the Shoah the diaries of Anne Frank should also be read.

Finally, Dresden discusses the in his view insubstantial Jewish character of the diaries. According to him, Anne's texts are of a generally human character rather than specifically Jewish, but he does not blame her for this either since much more could not be expected of a child. Disparaging comments such as these seriously misrepresent Anne Frank, whose diaries express a strong religious awareness and a deeply rooted notion of God, disregarded by Dresden. He concludes that the diaries would have become less popular if they had contained more Jewish elements. This thought has been expressed before, also in connection with Etty Hillesum.

Yet, there is no reason to suggest that general humanness and specific Jewishness cannot go together. Besides, who decides what is and what is not Jewish? The Franks were not Orthodox Jews but liberal Jews. Anne, however, often reflected upon her Jewish identity: she criticized the aversion Peter, her boyfriend and housemate, had against religion, and chose a different path herself. She addressed her anxious questions about the Jewish fate to God who she believed would never abandon her. "We Jews [. . .] must do what is within our power and trust in God. Sometime this terrible war will be over. Surely the time will come when we are people again, and not just Jews" (April 11, 1944).

Etty Hillesum: A Hand That Wrote

Between March 1941 and September 1943, Etty Hillesum was engaged in a "paper war." She began her diary in an attempt to understand herself, to overcome her physical and psychological depressions. The course of her diary reflects the process of her inner growth, in which she created possibilities for involvement with other people.

In more than one sense, her writing is an act of resistance: in a period of unprecedented anti-Semitism, in which the Nazis aimed at the death of every single Jew, Etty Hillesum concentrated on her own and other people's morality and spiritual development. Whereas Nazi ideology was aimed at the annihilation of what was different and marginal, she found a style of life and philosophy that highlights the Other. In a double sense Anne Frank and Etty Hillesum were "the other": as Jews in the era of extreme anti-Semitism and as women in a patriarchal, phallocentric culture.

Both women fought against a Zeitgeist of death and destruction; they sought an attitude in which, against all odds, the affirmation of life is primary. The genre of the diary was their way of giving meaning to life in a time when all meaning seems to be lost. [. . .] Writing became an act of resistance and survival [. . .] a way of self-development.

Ten of Etty Hillesum's diaries have remained. Some are lost, such as the ones she wrote in Westerbork. Moreover, she wrote many letters to friends and acquaintances. In the context of the Shoah, the genre of writing letters is significant. [. . .] It can reach places that are closed to the sender. While the Nazis exercised their policy of exclusion by isolating Jewish people in ghettos and concentration camps, Etty Hillesum's letters mediate between two worlds: from Westerbork, for example, she wrote letters to her beloved ones in Amsterdam, and from Amsterdam she wrote to friends in Westerbork.

The complete edition of her diaries and letters contains almost six hundred clustered pages of the diaries, plus more than one hundred pages of her letters. [. . .] Her oeuvre shows seemingly opposite dynamics. On the one hand, the chronology of her diaries and letters have a "false trap" effect: the impending and far away war closes in on her. Eventually, the war is not something seen from "behind a window" but actually happening before her eyes in Westerbork. On the other hand, Etty Hillesum writes her diary to cope with herself and by so doing she manages to find inner peace and harmony, something she had hardly known before. In spite of the violence of the war, this dynamic in her texts is apparent. While there is destruction all around, Etty Hillesum's affirmation of life grows immensely against all odds.

It is probably this inner growth in times of extreme destruction that made her writings, like Anne Frank's, serve as a great inspiration to many people. It is a process of liberation so profound that her attitude to life, in which love and gratitude are so essential, transcends the circumstances of persecution in which she had to live and eventually to die.

Transforming Loss into Blessing

Etty Hillesum's letters and diaries testify to her apprenticeship to bereavement. For example: "Every pretty blouse I put on is a kind of celebration. And so is every occasion I have to wash with scented soap in a bathroom all to myself for half-an-hour. It's as if I were revelling in these civilized luxuries for the last time. But even if I have to forego them one day, I shall always know that they exist and they can make life pleasant. [. . .]"[2] Etty Hillesum is in mourning for all the blessings of Western civilization which are still around her, but she knows she is going to lose them. She makes ceremonies of the little things of everyday life: ceremonies of enjoyment and of farewell to the enjoyment. She makes a sort of inventory of all the losses, but this inventory is also an enumeration of all the riches.

In the summer of 1942 it becomes difficult for her to continue writing her diary. The deportation of the Jews is beginning to take its definite form. She finds a job as a sort of social worker in the transit camp of Westerbork. Because of this job she has more freedom than other Jews: she travels between Westerbork, in the north of the Netherlands, and Amsterdam. In this period she writes many letters to friends in both places. In June 1943 her relative freedom comes to an end. She too has to stay in Westerbork, awaiting deportation to Auschwitz, which occurs in September 1943. On November 30 the Red Cross reports her death.

The diaries of Etty Hillesum reflect a process of inner growth. Her aim was to become a better person, opposite to the aim of the Nazis, that in effect was a deed of resistance. The Nazis wanted the annihilation of the Jewish people; she stresses the importance of changing oneself. In a discussion with a friend, she said: "I no longer believe we can change anything in the world until we have first changed ourselves. And that seems to me the only lesson to be learned from this war. We must look into ourselves and nowhere else."[3] Etty Hillesum turns the world upside down. While the rulers plot a mass murder, from which she too shall not escape, she accentuates the individual. While most people worry about violence and terror, she pleads for repentance.

In an article by the social critic Hélène Cixous [. . .] Etty Hillesum's lifestyle has been aptly described as one of "feminine libidinal economy," rooted in an economy of positive lack. Unlike the "male libidinal economy" which strives for the accumulation of wealth as resistance to death, women with nothing to lose have learned to transform lack into wealth: "Culturally, women have been taught how to lose; they've been sent to the school of losing."[4] Etty Hillesum went to this school. Confronted with bereavement, she learns to give it a positive meaning. She learns about goodness, wealth, and happiness in that particular period of her short life in which she has to say farewell to everything and everybody.

In the past she was a depressive person, feeling the emptiness behind everything. Under the influence of her good friend Julius Spier she gets fulfilled every minute of her existence. Uncertainty and fear for the future disappear. She realizes very well how paradoxical this state of mind is in the context of destruction and death: "For after all it is quite an achievement: actually being happy inside, accepting God's world and enjoying it and still not facing away from all sorrow."[5] Even when she and her friends are required to wear the yellow Star of David, the symbol of the stigmatization of the Jews, she derives a special feeling that this too is part of the world she enjoys: "In years to come, children will be taught about ghettos and yellow stars and terror at school and it will make their hair stand on end. But parallel with that textbook history, there also runs another . . . a cup of coffee, a few good friends, a happy atmosphere, and a little philosophizing. . . . We were contented, the three of us together that night—the very night on which the 'yellow star' was issued."[6]

Etty Hillesum does not exclude certain dimensions of life. She accepts every part of it: the good things and the bad things. Living in one of the darkest times of Western history, she keeps in contact with the bright spots. She wants to live life in all its complexities and paradoxes. Sometimes her friends could hardly follow her, and the later reception of her diaries and letters show that people have difficulties with her philosophy. She often is received as a semi-saint, but though she did become a very spiritual woman in the end, I want to emphasize that she was very human too. In her first diary she notes: "You'd better be either a definite street-walker or a real saint. Then you have rest and know who you are. The ambivalence in me is quite awful."[7] Maybe in the end she became almost a saint, but she wasn't born one. Her power, which emerges from her text, lies exactly in her capacity to accept the paradoxes and complexities of life itself. Her diaries do not describe a static personality, but a work in process. She underwent a development in which she became more and more spiritual.

Unfortunately, only selections from the diaries and letters have been translated in English, and these often present a very distorted image by removing her complexities. For example, where Etty calls for an acceptance of the contradictions of life, the translation reads "try to simplify your inner conflicts, then your life will become simpler as well."

In language very reminiscent of Anne Frank's last several entries, Etty Hillesum speaks of gaining "new insight" into her life:

> [. . .] For what life is at stake is our impending destruction and annihilation. We can have no more illusions about that. They are out to destroy us completely, we must accept that and go on from there. Today I was filled with terrible despair, and I shall have to come to terms with that as well. Even if we are consigned to hell, let us go there as gracefully as we can. I did not really want to put it so blandly. [. . .] I wish I could live for a long time so that one day I may know how to explain it.[8]

In Westerbork many women around her tell her that they don't want to feel anymore, to think anymore, afraid of becoming crazy otherwise. Etty Hillesum resolves to do it. Even in the concentration camp she wants to remain sensitive to everything: "I want to keep living fully. I want to become the Chronicler of many things that are happening now."[9] She doesn't want to become a traditional chronicler of war history. She wants to show future generations that every minute of our existence is filled with everything.

Translated from the Dutch by Corinne Assink, Frits Smeets, and Marianne de Rooy.

Notes

1. Sem Dresden, *Persecution, Extermination, Literature,* trans. Hewy S. Schlogt (Toronto: University of Toronto Press, 1995).

2. Etty Hillesum, *An Interrupted Life: The Diaries of Etty Hillesum,* trans. Arnold J. Pomerans (New York: Pantheon Books, 1983), 135–36.

3. Ibid., 71.

4. Cited in Susan Sellers, ed. *Writing Differences: Readings from the Seminar of Hélène Cixous* (Milton Keynes: Open University Press, 1988), 150.

5. Hillesum, *Interrupted Life,* 47.

6. Ibid., 109.

7. Etty Hillesum, *Etty. De nagelaten geschriften van Etty Hillesum, 1941–43* [The Neglected Writings of Etty Hillesum, 1942–43] (Amsterdam: Uitgeverij Balans, 1986), 51.

8. Hillesum, *Interrupted Life,* 130–31.

9. Hillesum, *Etty,* 91.

30

The Anne Frank House:
Holland's Memorial Shrine of the Book

James E. Young

Father, Mother and Margot still can't get used to the chiming of the Westertoren clock, which tells the time every quarter of an hour. Not me. I liked it from the start; it sounds so reassuring, especially at night. . . . The Annex is an ideal place to hide in. It may be damp and lopsided, but there's probably not a more comfortable hiding place in all of Amsterdam. No, in all of Holland.
—*July 11, 1942*

Given the innumerable Anne Frank streets, squares, and schools spread throughout Dutch land- and cityscapes, many have suggested that the young diarist may well be the patron saint of Holland. But this is not the mere appropriation of a Jewish life by a country in search of a national martyr or the simple self-aggrandizement of Anne Frank's adopted motherland. Rather, the memorial canonization of Anne Frank in Holland has much more to do with the deeply mixed Dutch self-perception as traditional refuge, on the one hand, and as a nation of passive bystanders, on the other.

As a young girl, Anne Frank exemplifies the blamelessness of Jews killed for no reason other than for being Jews. By extension, she represents for the Dutch their own, uninvited violation by the Nazis; at the same time, she reminds the Dutch that even though they harbored her, they also betrayed her in the end, as well as 100,000 Dutch Jews. By reflecting back to the Dutch their own mixed record of resistance and neutrality, victimization and passive complicity, Anne Frank has effectively become an archetypal figure for all of Holland's war memory. [. . .]

According to the Museum of Dutch Resistance, over 300,000 Dutch were in hiding by 1944, including about 25,000 Jews. Thus, depending on how one looks at these numbers, either the Jews in Holland could be regarded as a mainstay of Dutch resistance or vast numbers of non-Jews in Holland can be seen as having shared part of their Jewish neighbors' experiences under the Nazis. In both cases, Holland's national memory of resistance is linked specifically to the memory of the Dutch Jews' fate during the war, the memory a distillation of pride, shame, and ambivalence.

That the Anne Frank House at 263 Prinsengracht has become the preeminent Dutch war shrine cannot be surprising in this context. After the Rijksmuseum and Van Gogh Museum, it is the most popular tourist site in Amsterdam for foreign tourists, practically a place of pilgrimage for student backpackers in Europe. In fact, the Anne Frank House tends to perform on at least two different, if parallel, memorial tracks, one each for foreign and domestic tourists. Before Eastern Europe opened up, the Anne Frank House was the most likely introduction to the Holocaust for young Americans traveling abroad. By the early 1960s, most American tourists were at least nominally familiar with the diary and play, which constituted much of their knowledge of the Jews' plight during World War II. It was an easy, accessible window to this period, for like the version of the diary they found in the play, the Anne Frank House represented an open, universal, even optimistic understanding of events.

Domestic tourists from Holland, however, especially from the city of Amsterdam itself, find a subtly different memorial on the canal at 263 Prinsengracht. As surely as its place on the canal links the building to the rest of Amsterdam, this house is also part of a neighborhood that was already legendary in Dutch tradition for its hospitality to political refugees, the Dutch equivalent of a "freedom trail." For the Dutch know, if no one else does, that a year after finding refuge in Amsterdam at 6 Westermarkt in 1634, exiled French philosopher René Descartes probably watched construction of the house and annex at 263 Prinsengracht, which were visible from his back window. Though the original annex was torn down and replaced by a larger one in 1739, the front part of the house stood intact over the years, remodeled on occasion to accommodate stables, offices, a merchant warehouse, and, for ten years, until 1939, a factory for player-piano roll music. To the Dutch mind, it seems only fitting that the radically enlightened Descartes, a refugee from seventeenth-century France, should have gazed at what would become the national shrine to persecution and refuge of the twentieth century. Both sites are now linked spatially and metaphysically, reinforcing each other as shrines to Dutch enlightenment and tolerance. [. . .]

For the first five years after the war, the houses between the corner at Westermarkt and 263 Prinsengracht stood empty and dilapidated. Between 1950 and 1953, a large textile firm, Berghaus, bought up the entire block with a plan to demolish the old buildings and erect modern offices. Published in America in 1952, the diary had already become an international best-seller; it was adapted for the stage and became a prize-winning Broadway play in 1955. Thus, when

Berghaus announced plans to raze the block and begin building new offices, a great hue and cry rose up across the country. The house had already become a tourist attraction, open, by appointment only, to visitors who could wend their way through the maze of abandoned rooms to the creaking hinged bookcase and annex behind. Concerned citizens throughout the city joined with the historical society Amstelodamum to block demolition. At one point, an Amsterdam artist, Anton Witsel, and several of his friends posted a day and night vigil in front of the house to protect it from demolition teams. As protests grew, Berghaus ran into further difficulties securing approval from the city architectural commission, which declared their planned buildings "out of harmony" with their surroundings. Finally, in January 1956, Berghaus announced that other property was being sought for the office buildings. A citywide campaign led by Mayor Gijs van Hall and Otto Frank was then launched to save the Anne Frank House.

Fundraising was unexpectedly, extraordinarily successful, presaging the power of the Holocaust to raise money for all kinds of causes. Major contributions poured in from West Germany, Otto Frank, and hundreds of private donors. On May 3, 1957, the eve of Dutch National Memorial Day, the Anne Frank Foundation was established. A further outpouring of support followed, including donations from Berghaus itself, which gave the house and annex to the foundation on the condition that they be used as a cultural center. Otto Frank put up funds to buy the house next door and stipulated that it be used as a center for education. Exactly three years later, May 3, 1960, again on the eve of Dutch National Memorial Day, the doors opened to the Anne Frank House and Museum.

Between 1957 and 1960, the Anne Frank House was open two hours a day, and about ten thousand visitors a year were guided through the annex by student volunteers. When it opened officially as a museum in 1960, Otto Frank convened the first public meeting of the International Youth Center next door. In Frank's words, it would "create a dynamic meeting-place for young people from all over the world, . . . propagate and help realize the ideals bequeathed by Anne Frank in her diary. . . . At the same time, an attempt [would] be made through international youth congresses and conferences to stimulate young people to discuss international cooperation, mutual understanding, tolerance, a confrontation of life-philosophies, world peace, modern upbringing, youth problems, modern art, the questions of race and the fight against illiteracy."[1]

Such an ambitious agenda could not be completely realized of course, but it reflected all those issues Otto believed Anne would have honored and pursued. For both Otto Frank and the foundation had set out to fulfill the ideals that Anne had entrusted to her diary. Given Anne's famous July 15, 1944, entry that begins, "It's really a wonder I haven't dropped all my ideals" and ends, "In the meantime, I must uphold my ideals, for perhaps the time will come when I shall be able to carry them out," the foundation clearly sees itself as carrying out Anne's ideals as if they were a kind of last will and testament. The Anne Frank House is thus very much a Dutch "shrine of the book," a place where the nearly holy testament of her diary is to be taught and studied. But if the aim is to impart the lessons of Anne's diary, these lessons depend wholly on who draws them. Since the foundation is in Holland, Anne's experiences have been regarded as part of the Dutch experience as a whole.

The mixing of national and Jewish ideals at the Anne Frank House may be due as much to the redactor of Anne's diary, her father, as they are to the Dutch caretakers of the foundation. While Otto Frank would never have denied his daughter's Jewishness, he felt from the outset that her diary, her story, and now the house would serve humanity best through their universal implications. Accordingly, he wrote that "the Jewish origins of the diary will not be specifically emphasized, but nevertheless, the insights it provides as a Jewish testament may not be forgotten. The diary is a human document of the foundation, whose aim is to keep the annex in its original state as a symbol of the past and as a warning for the future. . . . In this place, one can see the diary in its authentic perspective . . . , the best place to discuss the possibilities of a great future."[2] Whether it was because of the universal success of the diary and the play it spawned or Otto's own universalist reading of the diary itself, Anne's father set a clear precedent for the widest possible application of Anne's beliefs against discrimination and racism of all kinds.

The universalist message of the Anne Frank House has been tapped often and widely. In 1961, for example, John F. Kennedy had his secretary of labor, Arthur Goldberg, lay a wreath at the Anne Frank House, a gesture which he described as "an expression of the American people's enduring sympathy and support for all those who seek freedom. . . . [Anne's] words, written as they were in the face of a monstrous tyranny, have significant meaning today as millions who read them live in the shadow of fear of another such tyranny."[3] Nearing the height of the cold war, and just after the Berlin blockade, Kennedy's implied reference to the Soviet Union was unmistakable. Since then, dozens of other visiting statesmen and women have cast their messages in Anne Frank's memorial form. In its universal raison d'être, the house invites all the oppressed into its memorial sanctuary.

On any given day, the area in front of the museum and the steps leading into the museum are swarming with teenagers waiting to enter or meditating about what they have just seen. Their bicycles chained to rails on the canal, Dutch families mingle with Americans, Germans, Italians, and tourists from other European countries; to each, it seems Anne Frank is one of their own. Every year nearly six hundred thousand people wend their way up the creaking staircase to the annex, where Anne's family lived and where Anne recorded their refuge. Today we are among them: on the third floor, we watch a brief film of Anne Frank's life and her diary, a short history of World War II through Anne's eyes, ending with brutal images of bulldozed bodies at Bergen-Belsen, where Anne died. We then crowd through the false wall behind the bookshelf into the annex proper: the expectation here is slightly magical, as if through this invisible door we were able to go back to both the place and the time of the events. Instead, we find an empty room, where Otto and Edith Frank once slept with Anne's sister, Margot. The next room is Anne's, which she shared with Mr. Dussel, a Jewish dentist who sought refuge with the family later on. As we enter, we note that the wall to the left is covered with Anne's childhood photograph and picture collection, carefully clipped from magazines, which she taped and pasted above her bed. Photographs of Greta Garbo; Deanna Durbin in the film *First Love;* Rudy Vallee; the Dutch royal family; Queen Elizabeth, then a young princess of twelve; and romantic drawings of the outside world, of farms and hills, are now sealed behind a pane of glass. Pictures of the Dutch royal family suggest Anne's strong feelings for her Dutch refuge—and no doubt endear her further to Dutch visitors, in whose eyes every celebration of the royal family was an act of resistance during the war. As we are compelled by the intimacy of her diary, we are similarly drawn to her decorative handiwork: touched by that which Anne has touched, traces of her being, the images she may have fallen asleep with at night, the same sense of intimacy she has unknowingly shared with us in her diary.

Next to her room, we see the family's sink and floral-patterned, porcelain toilet. For a moment, visitors are apt to submit to the reverie created by these remnants of Anne's daily life, forgetting that this setting is not exactly as it was. The contact paper that covered the windows, first to protect Opekta's spices from light and then to protect the refugees from prying eyes, is gone. Light floods into the annex now, children lean out of the great windows, and the scent of trees and sounds of birds wash over us. Anne's only exposure to the outside world during her years in hiding was through a small square window in the attic, from which she and her companion Peter would follow the seasons by the quality of light on the Westerkerk bell tower or catch a glimpse of a blue, black, or cloudy sky. The attic, Anne's inner sanctum, where she wrote most of her diary, is now completely closed to visitors; it remains a space unknown to the masses, unreachable.

As we descend to the exhibition hall, we carry with us such imagined memory, an emotional sense of having "been there," without a corresponding notion of what it means. The permanent exhibition offers the images and information to frame all significance here. First, the diary as holy text is displayed in both facsimile (the original is in the Dutch War Documentation Center) and in over fifty languages. The diary functions as the heart around which the rest of the installation is given meaning: images depicting the rise of nazism and massacre of European Jewry. A temporary exhibition called "2,000 Years of Anti-Semitism," inaugurated by Elie Wiesel, was one of dozens of revolving exhibitions documenting current examples of racism and other forms of discrimination in Europe, Africa, and America: the resurgence of neo-Nazis, the oppression of foreign immigrants in Europe, Africa, and America, the Palestinians' plight in the West Bank.[4] The thrust here is as universal as Anne seems to have been. Though persecuted and put to death because she was a Jew, she perceived her suffering in terms of both Jew and adopted daughter of the Dutch.

The Anne Frank House functions on at least two planes: for adults, it remains a shrine to innocence, a museum representing what they already know. Anne Frank epitomizes the blameless victim, a child whose life, but not hope, was extinguished by the Nazis. Teenagers and children visit the house under slightly different circumstances. For them, Anne's experiences and observations provide perhaps the only somewhat direct access they can have to this period: the keenly observed minutiae of daily life in hiding. The child's view of the war, however precocious and sophisticated, is to some extent also the adolescent visitor's view of the war: changes in daily habits; squabbles with friends and family; young love; limited food, space, and room for playing. Unlike adults, children do not come with a memory of the time to be sparked, but come, instead, to learn what it is the space would have them remember. As such, it is the only truly youthful memorial to the Shoah period, not a children's memorial so much as a memorial for children to visit, conceived and executed with the child's view in mind. Anne and her youthfulness remain forever alive in this way. Her devotion to reading and writing, her curiosity about love, and her insights into a family's suffering are all motifs through which another, younger generation comes to know—and then to remember—war and Holocaust.

Notes

1. Anne Frank Foundation, *Concerning the Diary of Anne Frank, the House, and the Foundation from the Beginning up to the Present* (Amsterdam: Anne Frank House, 1978), 48.

2. From an internal bulletin of the Anne Frank Center, courtesy of the Anne Frank House.

3. "Kennedy, Praising Anne Frank, Warns of New Nazi-Like Peril," *New York Times,* Sept. 20, 1961, 5.

4. For an unsympathetic response to the content of these exhibitions, see Mark Segal, "The Second Agony of Anne Frank," *Jerusalem Post,* June 17, 1977, magazine section.

31

Femme Fatale

Philip Roth

I adore the history of the arts, especially when it concerns writers, poets
and painters.
—*April 6, 1944*

Editors' synopsis: A young novelist, Nathan Zuckerman, is invited for a week-
end to the New England home of his literary idol, Emanuel Isadore Lonoff, and
his wife, Hope. There he meets and is intrigued by Lonoff's graduate assistant,
Amy Bellette, a lovely woman who looks startlingly like Anne Frank. Estranged
from his family because of his shocking stories about Jews, Zuckerman fancies
he could fall in love with Amy/Anne. In his desire to be reconciled with his parents, he thinks he might come back to New Jersey and say to them:

"I met a marvelous young woman while I was up in New England. I love her
and she loves me. We are going to be married."

"Married? But so fast? Nathan, is she Jewish?"

"Yes, she is."

"But who is she?"

"Anne Frank."

Then he fantasizes introducing his bride to Aunt Tessie, Frieda, Dave, Birdie—
his entire *mishpocheh*: "This is my wife, everyone. She is all I have ever wanted.
[. . .] Well, this is she." [. . .] "Anne, says my father—THE Anne? Oh, how I
have misunderstood my son. How mistaken we have been!"

His dream goes further: the new couple have been with her father, Otto—and
Nathan writes his folks: "Anne is pregnant, and happier [. . .] than she ever
thought possible. [. . .]"

Unfortunately for Zuckerman, his Femme Fatale has a passionate attraction
for Lonoff. The history of this intriguing "reincarnation" of Anne Frank begins
shortly after she had attended a performance of the famous stage play of the di-

ary in 1955 when Anne Frank would have been twenty six years old—if she had not died in Bergen-Belsen.]

✦ ✦ ✦

This is the tale that Amy told the morning after she had gone alone to the Cort Theatre to sit amid the weeping and inconsolable audience at the famous New York production of *The Diary of Anne Frank*. This is the story that the twenty-six-year-old young woman with the striking face and the fetching accent and the felicitous prose style and the patience, according to Lonoff, of a Lonoff, expected him to believe was true.

After the war she had become Amy Bellette. She had not taken the new name to disguise her identity—as yet there was no need—but, as she imagined at the time, to forget her life. She had been in a coma for weeks, first in the filthy barracks with the other ailing and starving inmates, and then in the squalid makeshift "infirmary." A dozen dying children had been rounded up by the SS and placed beneath blankets in a room with twelve beds in order to impress the Allied armies advancing upon Belsen with the amenities of concentration-camp living. Those of the twelve still alive when the British got there had been moved to an army field hospital. It was here that she finally came around. She understood sometimes less and sometimes more than the nurses explained to her, but she would not speak. Instead, without howling or hallucinating, she tried to find a way to believe that she was somewhere in Germany, that she was not yet sixteen, and that her family was dead. Those were the facts; now to grasp them.

"Little Beauty" the nurses called her—a silent, dark, emaciated girl—and so, one morning, ready to talk, she told them that the surname was Bellette. Amy she got from an American book she had sobbed over as a child, *Little Women*. She had decided, during her long silence, to finish growing up in America now that there was nobody left to live with in Amsterdam. After Belsen she figured it might be best to put an ocean the size of the Atlantic between herself and what she needed to forget.

She learned of her father's survival while waiting to get her teeth examined by the Lonoffs' family dentist in Stockbridge. She had been three years with foster families in England, and almost a year as a freshman at Athene College, when she picked an old copy of *Time* out of the pile in the waiting room and, just turning pages, saw a photograph of a Jewish businessman named Otto Frank. In July of 1942, some two years after the beginning of the Nazi occupation, he had taken his wife and his two young daughters into hiding. Along with another Jewish family, the Franks lived safely for twenty-five months in a rear upper story of the Amsterdam building where he used to have his business offices. Then, in August 1944, their whereabouts were apparently betrayed by one of the workers in the warehouse below, and the hideout was uncovered by the police. Of the eight who'd been together in the sealed-off attic rooms, only Otto Frank survived the concentration camps. When he came back to Amsterdam after the war, the Dutch family who had been their protectors gave him the notebooks that had been kept in hiding by his younger daughter, a girl of fifteen when she died in Belsen: a diary, some ledgers she wrote in, and a sheaf of papers emptied out of her briefcase when the Nazis were ransacking the place for valuables. Frank printed and circulated the diary only privately at first, as a memorial to his family, but in 1947 it was published in a regular edition under the title *Het Achterhuis*—"The House Behind." Dutch readers, *Time* said, were greatly affected by the young teenager's record of how the hunted Jews tried to carry on a civilized life despite their deprivations and the terror of discovery.

Alongside the article—"A Survivor's Sorrows"—was the photograph of the diarist's father, "now sixty." He stood alone in his coat and hat in front of the building on the Prinsengracht Canal where his late family had improvised a last home.

Next came the part of her story that Lonoff was bound to think improbable. She herself, however, could not consider it all that strange that she should be thought dead when in fact she was alive; nobody who knew the chaos of those final months—the Allies bombing everywhere, the SS in flight—would call that improbable. Whoever claimed to have seen her dead of typhus in Belsen had either confused her with her older sister, Margot, or had figured that she was dead after seeing her so long in a coma or had watched her being carted away, as good as dead, by the Kapos.

"Belsen was the third camp," Amy told him. "We were sent first to Westerbork, north of Amsterdam. There were other children around to talk to, we were back in the open air—aside from being frightened it really wasn't that awful. Daddy lived in the men's barracks, but when I got sick he managed somehow to get into the women's camp at night and to come to my bed and hold my hand. We were there a month, then we were shipped to Auschwitz. Three days and three nights in the freight cars. Then they opened the doors and that was the last I saw of him. The men were pushed in one direction, we were pushed in the other. That was early September. I saw my mother last at the end of October. She could hardly speak by then. When Margot and I were shipped from Auschwitz, I don't even know if she understood."

She told him about Belsen. Those who had survived the cattle cars lived at first in tents on the heath. They slept on the bare ground in rags. Days went by without food or fresh water, and after the autumn storms tore the tents from their moorings, they slept exposed to the wind and rain. When at last they were being moved into barracks, they saw ditches beyond the camp enclosure piled high with bodies—the people who had died on the heath from typhus and starvation. By the time winter came, it seemed as if everyone still alive was either sick or half mad. And then, while watching her sister slowly dying, she grew sick herself. After Margot's death, she could hardly remember the women in the barracks who had helped her and knew nothing of what happened to them.

It was not so improbable either that after her long hospital convalescence she had not made her way to the address in Switzerland where the family had agreed to meet if they should ever lose touch with one another. Would a weak sixteen-year-old girl undertake a journey requiring money, visas—requiring hope—only to learn at the other end that she was as lost and alone as she feared?

No, no, the improbable part was this: that instead of telephoning *Time* and saying, "I'm the one who wrote the diary—find Otto Frank!" she jotted down in her notebook the date on the magazine's cover and, after a tooth had been filled, went off with her school books to the library. What was improbable—inexplicable, indefensible, a torment still to her conscience—was that, calm and studious as ever, she checked *The New York Times Index* and the *Readers' Guide to Periodical Literature* for "Frank, Anne" and "Frank, Otto" and "*Het Achterhuis*," and, when she found nothing, went down to the library's lowest stacks, where the periodicals were shelved. There she spent the remaining hour before dinner re-reading the article in *Time*. She read it until she knew it by heart. She studied her father's photograph. Now sixty. And those were the words that did it—made of her once again the daughter who cut his hair for him in the attic, the daughter who did her lessons there with him as her tutor, the daughter who would run to his bed and cling to him under the covers when she heard the Allied bombers flying over Amsterdam: suddenly she was the daughter for whom he had taken the place of everything she could no longer have. She cried for a very long time. But when she went to dinner in the dormitory, she pretended that nothing catastrophic had once again happened to Otto Frank's Anne.

But then right from the beginning she had resolved not to speak about what she had been through. Resolutions were her strong point as a young girl on her own. How else could she have lasted on her own? One of the thousand reasons she could not bear Uncle Daniel, the first of her foster fathers in England, was that sooner or later he wound up telling whoever walked into the house about all that had happened to Amy during the war. And then there was Miss Giddings, the young teacher in the school north of London who was always giving the orphaned little Jewess tender glances during history class. One day after school Miss Giddings took her for a lemon-curd tart at the local tearoom and asked her questions about the concentration camps. Her eyes filled with tears as Amy, who felt obliged to answer, confirmed the stories she had heard but could never quite believe. "Terrible," Miss Giddings said, "so terrible." Amy silently drank her tea and ate her lovely tart, while Miss Giddings, like one of her own history students, tried in vain to understand the past. "Why is it," the unhappy teacher finally asked, "that for centuries people have hated you Jews?" Amy rose to her feet. She was stunned. "Don't ask me that!" the girl said—"ask the madmen who hate us!" And she had nothing further to do with Miss Giddings as a friend—or with anyone else who asked her anything about what they couldn't possibly understand.

One Saturday only a few months after her arrival in England, vowing that if she heard another plaintive "Belsen" out of Uncle Daniel's mouth she would run off to Southampton and stow away on an American ship—and having had about enough of the snooty brand of sympathy the pure-bred English teachers offered at school—she burned her arm while ironing a blouse. The neighbors came running at the sound of her screams and rushed her to the hospital emergency room. When the bandage was removed, there was a patch of purple scar tissue about half the size of an egg instead of her camp number.

After the accident, as her foster parents called it, Uncle Daniel informed the Jewish Welfare Board that his wife's ill health made it impossible for them to continue to have Amy in their home. The foster child moved on to another family—and then another. She told whoever asked that she had been evacuated from Holland with a group of Jewish schoolchildren the week before the Nazis invaded. Sometimes she did not even say that the schoolchildren were Jewish, an omission for which she was mildly rebuked by the Jewish families who had accepted responsibility for her and were troubled by her lying. But she could not bear them all laying their helpful hands upon her shoulders because of Auschwitz and Belsen. If she was going to be thought exceptional, it would not be because of Auschwitz and Belsen but because of what she had made of herself since.

They were kind and thoughtful people, and they tried to get her to understand that she was not in danger in England. "You needn't feel frightened or threatened in any way," they assured her. "Or ashamed of anything." "I'm not ashamed. That's the point." "Well, that isn't always the point when young people try to hide their Jewish origins." "Maybe it isn't with others," she told them, "but it is with me."

On the Saturday after discovering her father's photograph in *Time,* she took the morning bus to Boston, and in every foreign bookstore looked in vain for a copy of *Het Achterhuis.* Two weeks later she traveled the three hours to Boston again, this time to the main post office to rent a box. She paid for it in cash, then mailed the letter she was carrying in her handbag, along with a money order for fifteen dollars, to Contact Publishers in Amsterdam, requesting them to send, postage paid, to Pilgrim International Bookshop, P.O. Box 152, Boston, Mass., U.S.A., as many copies as fifteen dollars would buy of *Het Achterhuis* by Anne Frank.

She had been dead for him some four years; believing her dead for another month or two would not really hurt much more. Curiously she did not hurt more either, except in bed at night when she cried and begged forgiveness for the cruelty she was practicing on her perfect father, now sixty.

Nearly three months after she had sent the order off to her Amsterdam publisher, on a warm, sunny day at the beginning of August, there was a package too large for the Pilgrim Bookshop post-office box waiting to be picked up in Boston. She was wearing a beige linen skirt and a fresh white cotton blouse, both ironed the night before. Her hair, cut in pageboy style that spring, had been washed and set the previous night, and her skin was evenly tanned. She was swimming a mile every morning and playing tennis every afternoon and, all in all, was as fit and energetic as a twenty-year-old could be. Maybe that was why, when the postal clerk handed her the parcel, she did not tear at the string with her teeth or faint straightaway onto the marble floor. Instead, she walked over to the Common—the package mailed from Holland swinging idly from one hand—and wandered along until she found an unoccupied bench. She sat first on a bench in the shade, but then got up and walked on until she found a perfect spot in the sunshine.

After thoroughly studying the Dutch stamps—postwar issues new to her—and contemplating the postmark, she set about to see how carefully she could undo the package. It was a preposterous display of unruffled patience and she meant it to be. She was feeling at once triumphant and giddy. Forbearance, she thought. Patience. Without patience there is no life. When she had finally untied the string and unfolded, without tearing, the layers of thick brown paper, it seemed to her that what she had so meticulously removed from the wrappings and placed onto the lap of her clean and pretty American girl's beige linen skirt was her survival itself.

Van Anne Frank. Her book. Hers.

✦ ✦ ✦

She had begun keeping a diary less than three weeks before Pim told her that they were going into hiding. Until she ran out of pages and had to carry over onto office ledgers, she made the entries in a cardboard-covered notebook that he'd given her for her thirteenth birthday. She still remembered most of what happened to her in the *achterhuis,* some of it down to the most minute detail, but of the fifty thousand words recording it all, she couldn't remember writing one. Nor could she remember anything much of what she'd confided there about her personal problems to the phantom confidante she'd named Kitty—whole pages of her tribulations as new and strange to her as her native tongue.

Perhaps because *Het Achterhuis* was the first Dutch book she'd read since she'd written it, her first thought when she finished was of her childhood friends in Amsterdam, the boys and girls from the Montessori school where she'd learned to read and write. She tried to remember the names of the Christian children, who would have survived the war. She tried to recall the names of her teachers, going all the way back to kindergarten. She pictured the faces of the shopkeepers, the postman, the milk deliveryman who had known her as a child. She imagined their neighbors in the houses on Merwedeplein. And when she had, she saw each of them closing her book and thinking, Who realized she was so gifted? Who realized we had such a writer in our midst?

The first passage she reread was dated over a year before the birth of Amy Bellette. The first time round she'd bent back the corner of the page; the second time, with a pen from her purse, she drew a dark meaningful line in the margin and beside it wrote—in English, of course—"uncanny." (Everything she marked she was marking for him, or made the mark actually pretending to be him.) *I have an odd way of sometimes, as it were, being able to see myself through someone else's eyes. Then I view the affairs of a certain "Anne" at my ease, and browse through the pages of her life as if she were a stranger. Before we came here, when I didn't think about things as much as I do now, I used at times to have the feeling that I didn't belong to Mansa, Pim, and Margot, and that I would always be a bit of an outsider. Sometimes I used to pretend I was an orphan . . .*

Then she read the whole thing from the start again, making a small marginal notation—and a small grimace—whenever she came upon anything she was sure he would consider "decorative" or "imprecise" or "unclear." But mostly she marked passages she couldn't believe that she had written as little more than a child. Why, what eloquence, Anne—it gave her gooseflesh, whispering her own name in Boston—what deftness, what wit! How nice, she thought, if I could write like this for Mr. Lonoff's English 12. "It's good," she heard him saying, "it's the best thing you've ever done, Miss Bellette."

But of course it was—she'd had a "great subject," as the girls said in English class. Her family's affinity with what families were suffering everywhere had been clear to her right from the beginning. *There is nothing we can do but wait as calmly as we can till the misery comes to an end, Jews and Christians wait, the whole earth waits; and there are many who wait for death.* But while writing these lines ("Quiet, emphatic feeling—that's the idea. E.I.L.") she had had no grandiose delusions about her little *achterhuis* diary's ever standing as part of the record of the misery. It wasn't to educate anybody other than herself—out of her great expectations—that she kept track of how trying it all was. Recording it was enduring it; the diary kept her company and it kept her sane, and whenever being her parents' child seemed to her as harrowing as the war itself, it was where she went to confess. Only to Kitty was she able to speak freely about the hopelessness of trying to satisfy her mother the way Margot did; only to Kitty could she openly bewail her inability even to pronounce the word "Mumsie" to her aloud—and to concede the depth of her feeling for Pim, a father she wanted to want her to the exclusion of all others, *not only as his child, but for me—Anne, myself.*

Of course it had eventually to occur to any child so *mad on books and reading* that for all she knew she was writing a book of her own. But most of the time it was her morale that she was sustaining not, at fourteen, literary ambition. As for developing into a writer—she owed that not to any decision to sit down each day and try to be one but to their stifling life. That, of all things, seemed to have nurtured her talent! Truly, without the terror and the claustrophobia of the *achterhuis,* as a *chatterbox* surrounded by friends and *rollicking with laughter,* free to come and go, free to clown around, free to pursue her every last expectation, would she ever have written sentences so deft and so eloquent and so witty? She thought, Now maybe that's the problem in English 12—not the absence of the great subject but the presence of the lake and the tennis courts and Tanglewood. The perfect tan, the linen skirts, my emerging reputation as the Pallas Athene of Athene College—maybe that's what's doing me in. Maybe if I were locked up again in a room somewhere and fed on rotten potatoes and clothed in rags and terrified out of my wits, maybe then I could write a decent story for Mr. Lonoff!

It was only with the euphoria of *invasion fever,* with the prospect of the Allied landings and the German collapse and the coming of that golden age known around the *achterhuis* as *after the war,* that she was able to announce to Kitty that the diary had perhaps done more than just assuage her adolescent loneliness. After two years of honing her prose, she felt herself ready for the great undertaking: *my greatest wish is to become a journalist someday and later on a famous writer.* But that was in May of 1944, when to be famous someday seemed to her no more or less extraordinary than to be going back to school in September. Oh, that May of marvelous expectations! Never again another winter in the *achterhuis.* Another winter and she would have gone crazy.

The first year there it hadn't been that bad; they'd all been so busy settling in that she didn't have time to feel desperate. In fact, so diligently had they all worked to transform the attic into a *superpractical* home that her father had gotten everybody to agree to subdivide the space still further and take in another Jew. But once the Allied bombing started, the superpractical home became her torture chamber. During the day the two families squabbled over everything, and then at night she couldn't sleep, sure that the Gestapo was going to come in the dark to take them away. In bed she began to have horrifying visions of Lies, her school friend, reproaching her for being safe in bed in Amsterdam and not in a concentration camp, like all her Jewish friends: "*Oh, Anne, why have you deserted me? Help, oh, help me, rescue me from this hell!*" She would see herself *in a dungeon, without Mummy and Daddy*—and worse. Right down to the final hours of 1943 she was dreaming and thinking *the most terrible things*. But then all at once it was over. Miraculously. "And what did it, Professor Lonoff? See *Anna Karenina*. See *Madame Bovary*. See half the literature of the Western world." The miracle: desire. She would be back to school in September, but she would not be returning to class the same girl. She was no longer a girl. Tears would roll down her cheeks at the thought of a naked woman. Her unpleasant menstrual periods became a source of the strangest pleasure. At night in bed she was excited by her breasts. Just these sensations—but all at once forebodings of her miserable death were replaced with a craze for life. One day she was completely recovered, and the next she was, of course, in love. Their troubles had made her her own woman, at fourteen. She began going off on private visits to the secluded corner of the topmost floor, which was occupied exclusively by Peter, the Van Daans' seventeen-year-old son. That she might be stealing him away from Margot didn't stop her, and neither did her scandalized parents: first just teatime visits, then evening assignations—then the defiant letter to the disappointed father. On May 3 of that marvelous May: *I am young and I possess many buried qualities; I am young and strong and am living a great adventure.* And two days later, to the father who had saved her from the hell that had swallowed up Lies, to the Pim whose favorite living creature she had always longed to be, a declaration of her independence, *in mind and body,* as she bluntly put it: *I have now reached the stage that I can live entirely on my own, without Mummy's support or anyone else's for that matter . . . I don't feel in the least bit responsible to any of you . . . I don't have to give an account of my deeds to anyone but myself . . .*

Well, the strength of a woman on her own wasn't all she'd imagined it to be. Neither was the strength of a loving father. He told her it was the most unpleasant letter he'd ever received, and when she began to cry with shame for having been *too low for words,* he wept along with her. He burned the letter in the fire, the weeks passed, and she found herself growing disenchanted with Peter. In fact, by July she was wondering how it would be possible, in their circumstances, to *shake him off,* a problem resolved for her on a sunny August Friday, when in the middle of the morning, as Pim was helping Peter with his English lessons and she was off studying by herself, the Dutch Green Police arrived and dissolved forever the secret household still heedful of propriety, obedience, discretion, self-improvement, and mutual respect. The Franks, as a family, came to an end, and, fittingly enough, thought the diarist, so did her chronicle of their effort to go sensibly on as themselves, in spite of everything.

The third time she read the book through was on the way back to Stockbridge that evening. Would she ever read another book again? How, if she couldn't put this one down? On the bus she began to speculate in the most immodest way about what she had written—had "wrought." Perhaps what got her going was the rumbling, boundless, electrified, indigo sky that had been stalking the bus down the highway since Boston: outside the window the most outlandish El Greco stage effects, outside a biblical thunderstorm complete with baroque trimmings, and inside Amy curled up with her book—and with the lingering sense of tragic grandeur she'd soaked up from the real El Grecos that afternoon in the Boston Museum of Fine Arts. And she was exhausted, which probably doesn't hurt fantastical thinking, either. Still spellbound by her first two readings of *Het Achterhuis,* she had rushed on to the Gardner and the Fogg, where, to top off the day, the self-intoxicated girl with the deep tan and the animated walk had been followed by easily a dozen Harvard summer school students eager to learn her name. Three museums because back at Athene she preferred to tell everyone the truth, more or less, about the big day in Boston. To Mr. Lonoff she planned to speak at length about all the new exhibitions she'd gone to see at his wife's suggestion.

The storm, the paintings, her exhaustion—none of it was really necessary, however, to inspire the sort of expectations that resulted from reading her published diary three times through in the same day. Towering egotism would probably have been sufficient. Perhaps she was only a very young writer on a bus dreaming a very young writer's dreams.

All her reasoning, all her fantastical thinking about the ordained mission of her book followed from this: neither she nor her parents came through in the diary as anything like representative of religious or observant Jews. Her mother lit candles on Friday night and that was about the extent of it. As for celebrations, she had found St. Nicholas's Day, once she'd been introduced to it in hiding, much more fun than Hannukah, and along with Pim made all kinds of clever gifts and even written a Santa Claus poem to enliven the festivities. When Pim settled upon a children's Bible as her present for the holiday—so she might learn something about the New Testament—Margot hadn't approved. Margot's ambition was to be a midwife in Palestine. She was the only one of them who seemed to have given serious thought to religion. The diary that Margot kept, had it ever been found, would not have been quite so sparing as hers in curiosity about Judaism or plans for leading a Jewish life. Certainly it was impossible for her to imagine Margot thinking, let alone writing with longing in her diary, *the time will come when we are people again, and not just Jews.*

She had written these words, to be sure, still suffering the aftereffects of a nighttime burglary in the downstairs warehouse. The burglary had seemed certain to precipitate their discovery by the police, and for days afterward everyone was weak with terror. And for her, along with the residue of fear and the dubious sense of relief, there was, of course, the guilt-tinged bafflement when she realized that, unlike Lies, she had again been spared. In the aftermath of that gruesome night, she went around and around trying to understand the meaning of their persecution, one moment writing about the misery of being Jews and only Jews to their enemies, and then in the next airily wondering if *it might even be our religion from which the world and all peoples learn good . . . We can never become just Netherlanders,* she reminded Kitty, *we will always remain Jews, but we want to, too*—only to close out the argument with an announcement one most assuredly would not have come upon in "The Diary of Margot Frank": *I've been saved again, now my first wish after the war is that I may become Dutch! I love the Dutch, I love this country, I love the language and want to work here. And even if I have to write to the Queen myself, I will not give up until I have reached my goal.*

No, that wasn't mother's Margot talking, that was father's Anne. To London to learn English, to Paris to look at clothes and study art, to Hollywood, California, to interview the stars as someone named "Anne Franklin"—while self-sacrificing Margot delivered babies in the desert. To be truthful, while Margot was thinking about God and the homeland, the only deities she ever seemed to contemplate at any length were to be found in the mythology of Greece and Rome, which she studied all the time in hiding, and adored. To be truthful, the young girl of her diary was, compared to Margot, only dimly Jewish, though in that entirely the daughter of the father who calmed her fears by reading aloud to her at night not the Bible but Goethe in German and Dickens in English.

But that was the point—that was what gave her diary the power to make the nightmare real. To expect the great callous and indifferent world to care about the child of a pious, bearded father living under the sway of the rabbis and the rituals—that was pure folly. To the ordinary person with no great gift for tolerating even the smallest of differences the plight of that family wouldn't mean a thing. To ordinary people it probably would seem that they had invited disaster by stubbornly repudiating everything modern and European—not to say Christian. But the family of Otto Frank, that would be another matter! How could even the most obtuse of the ordinary ignore what had been done to the Jews *just for being Jews,* how could even the most benighted of the gentiles fail to get the idea when they read in *Het Achterhuis* that once a year the Franks sang a harmless Hannukah song, said some Hebrew words, lighted some candles, exchanged some presents—a ceremony lasting about ten minutes—and that was all it took to make them the enemy. It did not even take that much. It took nothing—that was the horror. And that was the truth. And that was the power of her book. The Franks could gather together by the radio to listen to concerts of Mozart, Brahms, and Beethoven; they could entertain themselves with Goethe and Dickens and Schiller; she could look night after night through the genealogical tables of all of Europe's royal families for suitable mates for Princess Elizabeth and Princess

Margaret Rose; she could write passionately in her diary of her love for Queen Wilhelmina and her desire for Holland to be her fatherland—and none of it made any difference. Europe was not theirs nor were they Europe's, not even her Europeanized family. Instead, three flights up from a pretty Amsterdam canal, they lived crammed into a hundred square feet with the Van Daans, as isolated and despised as any ghetto Jews. First expulsion, next confinement, and then, in cattle cars and camps and ovens, obliteration. And why? Because the Jewish problem to be solved, the degenerates whose contamination civilized people could no longer abide, were they themselves, Otto and Edith Frank, and their daughters, Margot and Anne.

This was the lesson that on the journey home she came to believe she had the power to teach. But only if she were believed to be dead. Were *Het Achterhuis* known to be the work of a living writer, it would never be more than it was: a young teenager's diary of her trying years in hiding during the German occupation of Holland, something boys and girls could read in bed at night along with the adventures of the Swiss Family Robinson. But dead she had something more to offer than amusement for ages ten-fifteen; dead she had written, without meaning to or trying to, a book with the force of a masterpiece to make people finally see.

And when people had finally seen? When they had learned what she had the power to teach them, what then? Would suffering come to mean something new to them? Could she actually make them humane creatures for any longer than the few hours it would take to read her diary through? In her room at Athene— after hiding in her dresser the three copies of *Het Achterhuis*—she thought more calmly about her readers-to-be than she had while pretending to be one of them on the stirring bus ride through the lightning storm. She was not, after all, the fifteen-year-old who could, while hiding from a holocaust, tell Kitty, *I still believe that people are really good at heart.* Her youthful ideals had suffered no less than she had in the windowless freight car from Westerbork and in the barracks at Auschwitz and on the Belsen heath. She had not come to hate the human race for what it was—what could it be but what it was?—but she did not feel seemly any more singing its praises.

What would happen when people had finally seen? The only realistic answer was Nothing. To believe anything else was only to yield to longings which even she, the great longer, had a right to question by now. To keep her existence a secret from her father so as to help improve mankind . . . no, not at this late date. The improvement of the living was their business, not hers; they could improve themselves, if they should ever be so disposed; and if not, not. Her responsibility was to the dead, if to anyone—to her sister, to her mother, to all the slaughtered schoolchildren who had been her friends. There was her diary's purpose, there

was her ordained mission: to restore in print their status as flesh and blood . . .
for all the good that would do them. An ax was what she really wanted, not print.
On the stairwell at the end of her corridor in the dormitory there was a large ax
with an enormous red handle, to be used in case of fire. But what about in case
of hatred—what about murderous rage? She stared at it often enough, but never
found the nerve to take it down from the wall. Besides, once she had it in her
hands, whose head would she split open? Whom could she kill in Stockbridge
to avenge the ashes and the skulls? If she even could wield it. No, what she had
been given to wield was *Het Achterhuis, van Anne Frank.* And to draw blood with
it she would have to vanish again into another *achterhuis,* this time fatherless and
all on her own.

So she renewed her belief in the power of her less than three hundred pages,
and with it the resolve to keep from her father, sixty, the secret of her survival.
"For them," she cried, "for them," meaning all who had met the fate that she
had been spared and was now pretending to. "For Margot, for my mother, for
Lies."

Now every day she went to the library to read the *New York Times.* Each week
she read carefully through the newsmagazines. On Sundays she read about all the
new books being published in America: novels said to be "notable" and
"significant," none of which could possibly be more notable and more significant
than her posthumously published diary; insipid best-sellers from which real people
learned about fake people who could not exist and would not matter if they did.
She read praise for historians and biographers whose books, whatever their merit,
couldn't possibly be as worthy of recognition as hers. And in every column in
every periodical she found in the library—American, French, German, English—
she looked for her own real name. It could not end with just a few thousand Dutch
readers shaking their heads and going about their business—it was too important for that! "For them, for them"—over and over, week after week, "for them"—
until at last she began to wonder if having survived in the *achterhuis,* if having
outlived the death camps, if masquerading here in New England as somebody
other than herself did not make something very suspect—and a little mad—of
this seething passion to "come back" as the avenging ghost. She began to fear that
she was succumbing to having not succumbed.

And why should she! Who was she pretending to be but who she would have
been anyway if no *achterhuis* and no death camps had intervened? Amy was not
somebody else. The Amy who had rescued her from her memories and restored
her to life—beguiling, commonsensical, brave, and realistic Amy—was herself.
Who she had every right to be! Responsibility to the dead? Rhetoric for the pious! There was nothing to give the dead—they were dead. "Exactly. The importance, so-called, of this book is a morbid illusion. And playing dead is melodra-

matic and disgusting. And hiding from Daddy is worse. No atonement is required," said Amy to Anne. "Just get on the phone and tell Pim you're alive. He is sixty."

Her longing for him now exceeded even what it had been in childhood, when she wanted more than anything to be his only love. But she was young and strong and she was living a great adventure, and she did nothing to inform him or anyone that she was still alive; and then one day it was just too late. No one would have believed her; no one other than her father would have wanted to. Now people came every day to visit their secret hideaway and to look at the photographs of the movie stars that she'd pinned to the wall beside her bed. They came to see the tub she had bathed in and the table where she'd studied. They looked out of the loft window where Peter and she had cuddled together watching the stars. They stared at the cupboard camouflaging the door the police had come through to take them away. They looked at the open pages of her secret diary. That was her handwriting, they whispered, those are her words. They stayed to look at everything in the *achterhuis* that she had ever touched. The plain passageways and serviceable little rooms that she had, like a good composition student, dutifully laid out for Kitty in orderly, accurate, workaday Dutch—the superpractical *achterhuis* was now a holy shrine, a Wailing Wall. They went away from it in silence, as bereft as though she had been their own.

But it was they who were hers. "They wept for me," said Amy; "they pitied me; they prayed for me; they begged my forgiveness. I was the incarnation of the millions of unlived years robbed from the murdered Jews. It was too late to be alive now. I was a saint."

That was her story. And what did Lonoff think of it when she was finished? That she meant every word and that not a word was true.

After Amy had showered and dressed, she checked out of the hotel and he took her to eat some lunch. He phoned Hope from the restaurant and explained that he was bringing Amy home. She could walk in the woods, look at the foliage, sleep safely in Becky's bed; over a few days' time she would be able to collect herself, and then she could return to Cambridge. All he explained about her collapse was that she appeared to him to be suffering from exhaustion. He had promised Amy that he would say no more.

On the ride back to the Berkshires, while Amy told him what it had been like for her during the years when she was being read in twenty different languages by twenty million people, he made plans to consult Dr. Boyce. Boyce was at Riggs, the Stockridge psychiatric hospital. Whenever a new book appeared, Dr. Boyce would send a charming note asking the author if he would kindly sign the doctor's copy, and once a year the Lonoffs were invited to the Boyce's big barbecue. At Dr. Boyce's request, Lonoff once reluctantly consented to meet with a staff study group from the hospital to discuss "the creative personality." He didn't want to offend the psychiatrist, and it might for a while pacify his wife, who liked to believe that if he got out and mixed more with people things would be better at home. [. . .]

But an hour wasted some five years ago was hardly to the point. He trusted Boyce and knew that the psychiatrist would not betray his confidence when he went the next day to talk with him about his former student and quasi-daughter, a young woman of twenty-six, who had disclosed to him that of all the Jewish writers, from Franz Kafka to E. I. Lonoff, she was the most famous. As for his own betrayal of the quasi-daughter's confidence, it did not count for much as Amy elaborated further upon her consuming delusion.

"Do you know why I took this sweet name? It wasn't to protect me from my memories. I wasn't hiding the past from myself or myself from the past. I was hiding from hatred, from hating people the way people hate spiders and rats. Manny, I felt flayed. I felt as though the skin had been peeled away from half my body. Half my face had been peeled away, and everybody would stare in horror for the rest of my life. Or they would stare at the other half, at the half still intact; I could see them smiling, pretending that the flayed half wasn't there, and talking to the half that was. And I could hear myself screaming at them, I could see myself thrusting my hideous side right up into their unmarred faces to make them properly horrified. 'I was pretty! I was whole! I was a sunny, lively little girl! Look, look at what they did to me!' But whatever side they looked at, I would always be screaming, 'Look at the other! Why don't you look at the other!' That's what I thought about in the hospital at night. However they look at me, however they talk to me, however they try to comfort me, I will always be this half-flayed thing. I will never be young, I will never be kind or at peace or in love, and I will hate them all my life.

"So I took the sweet name—to impersonate everything that I wasn't. And a very good pretender I was, too. After a while I could imagine that I wasn't pretending at all, that I had become what I would have been anyway. Until the book. The package came from Amsterdam, I opened it, and there it was: my past, myself, my name, *my face intact*—and all I wanted was revenge. It wasn't for the dead— it had nothing to do with bringing back the dead or scourging the living. It wasn't corpses I was avenging—it was the motherless, fatherless, sisterless, venge-filled, hate-filled, shame-filled, half-flayed, seething thing. It was myself. I wanted tears, I wanted their Christian tears to run like Jewish blood, for me. I wanted their pity—and in the most pitiless way. And I wanted love, to be loved mercilessly and endlessly, just the way I'd been debased. I wanted my fresh life and my fresh body, cleansed and unpolluted. And it needed twenty million people for that. Twenty million ten times over.["]

Appendix 1
Anne Frank's Writings

1. Unpublished Diary Typescripts

Title	Date	Language	Description
The First Copy	Fall 1945	Dutch and German	Otto Frank's version of Anne's diary that included the "essentials" for family and friends, which he translated into German for his mother. This copy was lost.
Typescript 1	1945–46	Dutch	Otto Frank's edited version of Anne's diary based on her original and rewritten versions and events from her tales.
Typescript 2	1945–46	Dutch	Anne's diary edited by Otto's friend Albert Cauvern, among others, then retyped by his wife, Isa Cauvern, Otto's former secretary; circulated among friends and reviewed by Jan Romein in *Het Parool,* Apr. 3, 1946; five fragments of the typescript were published in the journal *De Nieuwe Stem.*
Typescript 3	1945–46	German	Typescript 2, with material omitted, translated by Otto's friend, Anneliese Schütz, for his mother in Basel.

2. Major Versions of the Published Diary

Title	Date	Language	Description
Het Achterhuis	1947	Dutch	Preface by Annie Romein-Verschoor; published by Uitgeverij Contact in Amsterdam
Das Tagebuch der Ann Frank	1950	German	Translated by Anneliese Schütz; preface by Albrecht Goes; published by Lambert Schneider GmbH in Heidelberg
Journal de Anne Frank	1950	French	Translated Tylia Caren and Suzanne Lombard; foreword by Daniel Rops; published by Calmann-Levy in Paris
The Diary of a Young Girl (version *c*)	1952	English	Translated by Barbara M. Mooyaart-Doubleday; introduction by Storm Jameson; published by Vallentine Mitchell in London;
The Diary of a Young Girl (version *c*)	1952	English	Translated by Barbara M. Mooyaart-Doubleday; introduction by Eleanor Roosevelt; published by Doubleday in New York
The Diary of Anne Frank	1956	English	The play by Frances Goodrich and Albert Hackett, based on the translation by B. M. Mooyaart-Doubleday; introduction by Brooks Atkinson; published by Random House in New York
The Diaries of Anne Frank: The Critical Edition	1986	Dutch	Prepared by the Netherlands State Institute for War Documentation; edited by David Barnouw and Gerrold van der Stroom; published by Bert Bakker in Amsterdam
The Diary of Anne Frank: The Critical Edition	1989	English	Prepared by the Netherlands State Institute for War Documentation; edited by David Barnouw and Gerrold van der Stroom; translated by Arnold J. Pomerans and B. M. Mooyaart-Doubleday; published by Doubleday in New York
The Diary of Anne Frank: The Definitive Edition	1995	English	Edited by Otto H. Frank and Mirjam Pressler; translated by Susan Massotty; published by Doubleday in New York
The Diary of Anne Frank: The Definitive Edition	1997	English	Edited by Otto H. Frank and Mirjam Pressler; translated by Susan Massotty; introduction by Elie Wiesel, translated by Euan Cameron; published by Penguin Books in London

3. Tales and Other Writings

In addition to her diary, Anne also composed tales, fables, and essays. She included six vignettes within both versions of her diary and wrote down others in an account book or on loose sheets. These tales and other writings were composed between December 1942 and May 1944. In total, Anne wrote at least thirteen fables and short stories and one unfinished novel, "Cady's Life," about which Anne reported: "I've thought up the rest of the plot" (May 11, 1944). She also wrote twenty-one personal reminiscences and essays. Anne prepared her own table of contents for her books of tales that included the page numbers, titles, the "type" of story or the place where the story was written, and the date each was written.

Otto Frank included several of the tales in the published version of the diary, but eventually many of these writings were published separately In 1949 In Dutch as *Weet je nog? Verhalen en Fables sprookjes* by Uitgeverij Contact. Eventually all of these works were published in various forms and in various editions, including *The Works of Anne Frank* (with the diary) (New York: Doubleday, 1959); *Tales from the Secret Annex* (London: Penguin, 1960); *Tales from the House Behind* (Kingswood, England: World's Work [1913], 1962); *Anne Frank's Tales from the House Behind* (London: Pan, 1963); *Tales from the House Behind* (New York: Bantam, 1966); *Het korte leven van Anne Frank* (Amsterdam: Contact, 1970); *Verhaaltjes, en gebeurtenissen uit het achterhuis* (Amsterdam: Bert Bakker, 1982); and *Anne Frank's Tales from the Secret Annex* (New York: Doubleday, 1983).

4. Anne's Handwritten Table of Contents for Her Tales

Title	Type	Date
Front Page of Table of Contents		
Was There a Break-in?	Annex	24 Mar. 1943
The Dentist	"	8 Dec. 1942
Sausage Day	"	10 Dec. 1942
The Flea	"	7 July 1943
Do You Remember?	Jewish Lyceum	—
The Best Little Table	Annex	13 July 1943
Anne in Theory	"	2 Aug. 1943
The Battle of the Potatoes	"	4 Aug. 1943
Evenings and Nights in the Annex	"	4 Aug. 1943
Lunch Break	"	5 Aug. 1943
The Eight Annex Residents at the Dinner Table	"	5 Aug. 1943
When the Clock Strikes Half Past Eight . . .	"	6 Aug. 1943
Villains!	"	6 Aug. 1943
A Daily Chore in Our Community Peeling Potatoes	"	6 Aug. 1943
Freedom in the Annex	"	6 Aug. 1943

Title	Type	Date
Kitty (Katje)	Seen from the Annex	7 Aug. 1943
The Janitor's Family	"	7 Aug. 1943
My First Day at the Lyceum	Lyceum	11 Aug. 1943
A Biology Class	"	11 Aug. 1943
A Math Class	"	12 Aug. 1943
Eve's Dream (Parts 1 and 2)	Made Up	6 Oct. 1943
Paying Guests	Based on Tales of Merwedeplein	15 Oct. 1943
Paula's Flight	Based on P.'s Tale	22 Dec. 1943
Delusions of Stardom	Made Up	24 Dec. 1943
Kathy	"	11 Feb. 1944
Sunday	Annex	20 Feb. 1944
The Flower Girl	Made Up	20 Feb. 1944
My First Interview	Annex	22 Feb. 1944
A Den of Iniquity	Answer to a review	22 Feb. 1944
The Guardian Angel	Made Up	22 Feb. 1944

Back Page of Table of Contents

Happiness
Fear
Give
The Wise Old Dwarf
Blurry, the Explorer

Short Stories on the Loose Sheets

The Fairy
Rita
Jackie
Cady's Life

Note: "Was There a Break-in?" "The Dentist," "Sausage Day," "The Best Little Table," "Anne in Theory," "Evenings and Nights in the Annex," "Lunch Break," "The Eight Annex Residents at the Dinner Table," "When the Clock Strikes Half Past Eight . . . ," "A Daily Chore in Our Community: Peeling Potatoes," and "Freedom in the Annex" were not included with Anne's separate account book of tales but were incorporated into the diary.

Sources: Gerrold van der Stroom, a principal editor of the critical edition, is the primary source for this compilation. His detailed essays and diagrams in that edition (59–72, 168–72) are supplemented with the summary of the document examination by H. J. J. Hardy (102–65). Laureen Nussbaum, Susan Massotty, Yt Stoker, and David Barnouw also reviewed this material and made helpful suggestions. Anne's handwritten works are in the possession of the Netherlands State Institute for War Documentation. Anne's handwritten table of contents for her tales was translated by Susan Massotty.

Appendix 2
Anne Frank Organizations and Resources

The major stimulus for Anne Frank educational and commemorative activities comes from the international foundations established in the mid-1950s by Otto Frank. The Anne Frank House in Amsterdam has produced two large traveling exhibitions, "Anne Frank in the World" (1985) and "Anne Frank: A History for Today" (1996). Information about these programs and related resources may be obtained from the following organizations:

Anne Frank-Fonds
Steinengraben 18
CH-4051, Basel
Switzerland
Phone: 41-61-274-11-74
Fax: 41-61-274-11-75

Anne Frank Center USA
548 Broadway, Suite 408
New York, NY 10012
Phone: 212-431-7993
Fax: 212-431-8375

Anne Frank Educational Trust (AFETUK)
P.O. Box 11880
London, N6 4LN
England
Phone: 44-181-3409077
Fax: 44-181-3409088

Anne Frank House (Stichting)
P.O. Box 730, 1000 AS
Amsterdam
The Netherlands
Phone: 31-20-5567-100
Fax: 31-20-6207-999

Anne Frank Zentrum Berlin
Oranienburger Strasse 26
D-1017 Berlin
Germany
Phone: 49-30-308-72988
Fax: 49-30-308-72989

Association of Holocaust Organizations
Holocaust Resources Center and Archives
Queensborough Community College
City University of New York
Bayside, NY 11364-1497
Phone: 718-225-0378
Fax: 718-631-6306

Bibliography

Works by Anne Frank

No single work includes all of Anne Frank's writings. The following editions contain different portions and versions of her work in English.

Anne Frank's Tales from the Secret Annex: Fables, Short Stories, Essays, and an Unfinished Novel by the Author of "The Diary of a Young Girl." Trans. Michel Mok and Ralph Manheim. 1949. New York: Washington Square Press, 1983.

The Diary of Anne Frank: The Critical Edition. Prepared by the Netherlands State Institute for War Documentation. Introduced by Harry Paape, Gerrold van der Stroom, and David Barnouw, with a summary report by the State Forensic Scientific Laboratory of the Ministry of Justice compiled by J. J. Hardy. Ed. David Barnouw and Gerrold van der Stroom. Trans. Arnold J. Pomerans and B. M. Mooyaart-Doubleday. 1986. New York: Doubleday, 1989.

The Diary of a Young Girl. Trans. B. M. Mooyaart-Doubleday. London: Vallentine, Mitchell, 1952.

The Diary of a Young Girl. Trans. B. M. Mooyaart-Doubleday. Introduction by Eleanor Roosevelt. Garden City: Doubleday, 1952.

The Diary of a Young Girl: The Definitive Edition. Ed. Otto H. Frank and Mirjam Pressler. Trans. Susan Massotty. New York: Doubleday, 1995.

The Diary of a Young Girl: The Definitive Edition. Ed. Otto Frank and Mirjam Pressler. Trans. Susan Massotty. Intro. by Elie Wiesel, trans. Euan Cameron. London: Penguin, 1997.

Tales from the House Behind. Trans. Michel Mok and H. H. B. Mosberg. Introduction by Ann Birstein and Alfred Kazin. Drawings by Peter Spier. 1952. New York: Bantam, 1960.

Tales from the House Behind: Fables, Personal Reminiscences, and Short Stories by Anne Frank.
Trans. Michel Mok and H. H. B. Mosberg. Introduction by G. B. Stern. 1952.
Kingswood, England: World's Work (1913), 1962.

The Works of Anne Frank. Trans. Michel Mok and Ralph Manheim. Introduction by Ann
Birstein and Alfred Kazin. 1959. Westport, Conn.: Greenwood Press, 1974.

Further Reading

Study manuals, picture books, and juvenile versions are starred.

*Adler, David A. *A Picture Book of Anne Frank.* Illus. Karen Ritz. New York: Holiday
House, 1993.

Aercke, Kristian, ed. *Women Writing in Dutch.* New York: Garland Press, 1994.

Agosin, Marjorie. *Dear Anne Frank.* Trans. Richard Schaaf. Washington, D.C.: Azul
Editions, 1994. Bilingual Spanish-English edition of poetry.

*Amdur, Richard. *Anne Frank.* New York: Chelsea House, 1993.

Arendt, Hannah. "Comment." *Midstream* 8 (Sept. 1962): 85–87.

Atkinson, Brooks. Foreword to *The Diary of Anne Frank.* New York: Random House, 1956.
vii–xii.

Barnes, Ian R., and R. P. Vivienne. "A Revisionist Historian Manipulates Anne Frank's
Diary." *Patterns of Culture* 15 (Jan. 1981): 27–32.

Barnouw, David. *Anne Frank voor Beginners en Gevorderden* [Anne Frank for Students and
Scholars]. The Hague: Stu Uitgevers, 1998.

Baruch, Miri. "Anne Frank's 'The Diary of a Young Girl': A New Reading." *Melton Journal* 23 (Spring 1990): 17–18.

*Bennett, Cherie, with Jeff Gottesfeld. *Anne Frank and Me.* Nashville: Shalom Aleichem
Playwriting Commission, 1997. Acting script manuscript.

Bettelheim, Bruno. "Did Anne Frank Die Needlessly? Were Concentration Camp Victims Too Passive?" *Jewish Digest* 6 (Aug. 1960): 1–7.

———. "Hope for Humanity." In *Freud's Vienna and Other Essays.* New York: Alfred A.
Knopf, 1990. 207–13.

Birstein, Ann, and Alfred Kazin, eds. Introduction to *The Works of Anne Frank.* New York:
Doubleday, 1959. 9–24.

Bloom, Harold, ed. *A Scholarly Look at "The Diary of Anne Frank."* Philadelphia: Chelsea
House, 1999.

Blumenthal, Ralph. "Five Precious Pages Renew Wrangling over Anne Frank." *New York
Times,* Sept. 10, 1998, A1, A6.

Boas, Jacob. *We Are Witnesses: Five Diaries of Teenagers Who Died in the Holocaust.* New
York: Henry Holt, 1995.

*Boonstra, Janrense, and Marie-Jose Rijnders, eds. *Anne Frank House: A Museum with a
Story.* Trans. Nancy Forest-Flier. Amsterdam: Anne Frank Stichting, 1992.

Braham, Randolph L., ed. *Reflections of the Holocaust in Art and Literature.* Boulder, Colo.:
Social Science Monographs, 1990.

———, ed. *The Treatment of the Holocaust in Textbooks: The Federal Government of Ger-*

many, Israel, the United States of America. New York: Social Science Monographs and Institute for Holocaust Studies of the City University of New York, 1987.

Brenner, Rachel Feldhay. *Writing as Resistance: Four Women Confronting the Holocaust.* University Park: Pennsylvania State University Press, 1997.

*Brown, Gene. *Anne Frank: Child of the Holocaust.* New York: Blackbirch Press, 1993.

*Bull, Angela. *Anne Frank.* North Pomfret, Vt.: David Charles, 1984.

Buruma, Ian. "The Afterlife of Anne Frank." *New York Review of Books,* Feb. 19, 1998, 4–8.

Carr, Robert K. *The Secret Annex.* Performance script with score by William Charles Barton. New York, 1995.

Dalsimer, Katherine. *Female Adolescence: Psychoanalytic Reflections on Works of Literature.* New Haven: Yale University Press, 1986.

De Costa, M. Denise. *Anne Frank and Etty Hillesum: Inscribing Spirituality and Sexuality.* Trans. Mischa F. C. Hoynick and Robert E. Chesal. New Brunswick, N.J.: Rutgers University Press, 1998.

Doneson, Judith. "Feminine Stereotypes of Jews in Holocaust Films: Focus on *The Diary of Anne Frank.*" In *The Netherlands and Nazi Genocide.* Ed. G. Jan Colijn and Marcia Sachs Littell. Lewiston, N.Y.: Edwin Mellen Press, 1992. 139–53.

Dresden, Sem. *Persecution, Extermination, Literature.* Trans. Hewy S. Schlogt. Toronto: University of Toronto Press, 1995.

Dwork, Deborah. *Children with a Star: Jewish Youth in Nazi Europe.* New Haven: Yale University Press, 1991.

Dworkin, Martin S. "The Vanishing Diary of Anne Frank." *Jewish Frontier* 27 (Apr. 1960): 7–10.

Ehrenburg, Ilya. "About Anne Frank: Introducing Her Diary to Russians and the Unfinished Business of Nazism." *Jewish Currents* 15 (Jan. 1961): 18–21.

Eichengreen, Lucille, with Harriet Heyman Chamberlain. *From Ashes to Life: My Memories of the Holocaust.* San Francisco: Mercury House, 1994.

Enzer, Hyman A. "Review of *The Diary of Anne Frank: The Critical Edition.*" *Contemporary Sociology* 20 (Mar. 1991): 219–21.

*Epstein, Rachel. *Anne Frank.* New York: Franklin Watts, 1997.

Ergas, Yasmine. "Growing Up Banished: A Reading of Anne Frank and Etty Hillesum." In *Behind the Lines: Gender and the Two World Wars.* Ed. Margaret R. Higonnet, Jane Jenson, Sonya Michel, and Margaret Collins Weitz. New Haven: Yale University Press, 1987. 84–95.

Evert, Elizabeth Cutter. "Sexual Integration in Female Adolescence: Anne Frank's Diary as a Study in Healthy Development." *Psychoanalytic Study of the Child* 46 (1991): 109–24.

Ezrahi, Sidra DeKoven. *By Words Alone: The Holocaust in Literature.* Chicago: University of Chicago Press, 1980.

*Facing History and Ourselves National Foundation. *Facing History and Ourselves: Holocaust and Human Behavior Resource Book.* Brookline, Mass.: Facing History and Ourselves National Foundation, 1995.

Fein, Helen. "Beyond the Heroic Ethic." Rev. of Bruno Bettelheim's *Surviving and Other Essays. Transaction* 17 (Mar.–Apr. 1980): 81–86.

Fine, Ellen S. "Women Writers and the Holocaust: Strategies for Survival." In *Reflections of the Holocaust in Art and Literature.* Ed. Randolph L. Braham. New York: Columbia University Press, 1990. 79–95.

Finkelstein, Norman G., and Ruth Bettina Birn. *A Nation on Trial: The Goldhagen Thesis and Historical Truth.* New York: Henry Holt, 1998.

Flanner, Janet. "Letter from Paris." *New Yorker,* Nov. 11, 1950, 26.

*Foerstel, Herbert N. 1994. *Banned in the U.S.A.: A Reference Guide to Book Censorship in Schools and Public Libraries.* Westport, Conn.: Greenwood Press.

Frank, Otto. "Has Germany Forgotten Anne Frank?" *Coronet* 47 (Feb. 1960): 48–64.

Frank-Steiner, Vincent C. "Anne Frank's Diary: Some Critical Observations." Paper presented at the Twenty-Fourth Annual Scholars' Conference on the Holocaust and the German Church Struggle. Rider University, Lawrenceville, N.J., Mar. 6–8, 1994.

Futterman, Enid, and Michael Cohen. *I Am Anne Frank.* New York: Williamson Music. 1996. Adapted from the 1985 musical *Yours, Anne.*

*Gariepy, Jennifer, ed. "Holocaust Denial Literature." *Twentieth Century Literary Criticism* 58 (1995): 1–101.

Gies, Miep, and Alison Leslie Gold. *Anne Frank Remembered.* New York: Simon and Schuster, 1987.

Gilligan, Carol. "Joining the Resistance: Psychology, Politics, Girls, and Women." *Michigan Quarterly Review* 29 (Fall 1990): 501–33.

Gilman, Sander. "The Dead Child Speaks: Reading *The Diary of Anne Frank.*" *Studies in American Jewish Literature* 7 (Spring 1988): 9–25.

*Gold, Alison L. *No Time for Goodbye: Memories of Anne Frank: Reflections of a Childhood Friend.* New York: Scholastic Press, 1997.

Goldhagen, Daniel Jonah. *Hitler's Willing Executioners: Ordinary Germans and the Holocaust.* New York: Alfred A. Knopf, 1996.

Goodrich, Frances, and Albert Hackett. *The Diary of Anne Frank: A Random House Play.* Based on the translation by B. M. Mooyaart-Doubleday. New York: Random House, 1955.

———. *The Diary of Anne Frank.* Adapted by Wendy Kesselman. Performance manuscript. New York, 1997.

Graver, Lawrence. *An Obsession with Anne Frank.* Berkeley: University of California Press, 1995.

*Grobman, Alex, and Joel Fishman, eds. *Anne Frank in Historical Perspective: A Teaching Guide for Secondary Schools.* Los Angeles: Martyrs Memorial and Museum of the Holocaust and Jewish Federation, 1995.

Halperin, Irving. "Etty Hillesum: A Story of Spiritual Growth." In *Reflections of the Holocaust in Art and Literature.* Ed. Randolph L. Braham. Boulder, Colo.: Social Science Monographs, 1990. 1–16.

*Harris, Eugenie. *Anne Frank's The Diary of a Young Girl.* Monarch Notes and Study Guides. New York: Monarch Press, 1965.

Hayes, Peter, ed. *Lessons and Legacies: The Meaning of the Holocaust in a Changing World.* Evanston, Ill.: Northwestern University Press, 1991.

Heinemann, Marlene E. *Gender and Destiny: Women Writers and the Holocaust.* Westport, Conn.: Greenwood Press, 1986.

Hellman, Peter. "Nazi-Hunting Is Their Life." *New York Times Magazine,* Nov. 6, 1979, 34–37, 74–80.

Hile, Kevin, ed. "Anne Frank." *Something about the Author* 87 (1996): 69–74.

Hillesum, Etty. *An Interrupted Life: The Diaries of Etty Hillesum.* Trans. Arnold J. Pomerans. 1981. New York: Pantheon Books, 1983.

———. *Letters from Westerbork.* Introduction and Notes by Jan G. Gaarland. Trans. Arnold J. Pomerans. London: Jonathan Cape, 1987. Originally published in the Netherlands as *Het denkende hart van de barak.* Bussum: De Iaan/Unieboek, 1982.

Hitchens, Christopher. "History of Fools." *The Nation,* June 9, 1997, 8.

Holliday, Laurel. *Children in the Holocaust and World War II: Their Secret Diaries.* New York: Simon and Schuster, 1995.

Hondius, Dienke. "A New Perspective on Helpers of Jews during the Holocaust: The Case of Miep and Jan Gies." In *Anne Frank in Historical Perspective: A Teaching Guide.* Ed. Alex Grobman. Los Angeles: Martyrs Memorial and Museum of the Holocaust, 1995. 33–37.

*Hunter, Latoya. *The Diary of Latoya Hunter: My First Year in Junior High.* New York: Crown, 1992.

*Hurwitz, Johanna. *Anne Frank: A Life in Hiding.* Philadelphia: Jewish Publication Society, 1988.

Immer, Myra H., ed. *Readings on Anne Frank: "The Diary of a Young Girl."* San Diego, Calif.: Green Haven Press, 1998.

Jews of Holland during the Shoah. Exhibition Catalog from Beit Lohamei Haghetaot. Haifa, Israel. Oct. 21, 1996.

*Johnson, Mary, and Carol Rittner. "Anne Frank in the World: A Study Guide." In *Anne Frank in the World.* Ed. Carol Rittner. Armonk, N.Y.: M. E. Sharpe, 1997. 105–16.

Katz, Esther, and Joan M. Ringelheim, eds. *Proceedings of the Conference: Women Surviving the Holocaust.* New York: Occasional Papers from the Institute for Research in History, 1983.

*Katz, Sandor. *Anne Frank.* New York: Chelsea House, 1995.

*Kennet, John. *Anne Frank: A Story Based on Her Diary.* London: Blackie, 1974.

*Kniesmeyer, Joke, ed. *Anne Frank in the World: 1929–45.* Amsterdam: Anne Frank Stichting, 1985.

*Kopelnitsky, Raimonda, with Kelly Pryor. *No Words to Say Goodbye.* New York: Hyperion, 1994.

*Kopf, Hedda Rosner. *Understanding Anne Frank's "The Diary of a Young Girl": A Student Casebook to Issues, Sources, and Historical Documents.* Westport, Conn.: Greenwood Press, 1997.

Kops, Bernard. *The Dreams of Anne Frank.* London: Methuen, 1997.

Lagerwey, Mary D. "Reading Anne Frank and Elie Wiesel: Voice and Gender in Stories of the Holocaust." *Contemporary Jewry* 17 (1996): 48–65.

Landau, Ronnie S. *The Nazi Holocaust.* Chicago: Ivan R. Dee, 1994.

Langer, Lawrence L. *Admitting the Holocaust: Collected Essays.* New York: Oxford, 1995.

———. *The Age of Atrocity.* Boston: Beacon, 1978.

———. *Preempting the Holocaust.* New Haven: Yale University Press, 1998.

———. *Versions of Survival: The Holocaust and the Human Spirit.* Albany: State University of New York Press, 1982.

Laska, Vera, ed. *Women in the Resistance and the Holocaust: The Voices of Eyewitnesses.* Westport, Conn.: Greenwood, 1983.

Last, Dick van Galen, and Rolf Wolfswinkel. *Anne Frank and After: Dutch Holocaust Literature in Historical Perspective.* Amsterdam: Amsterdam University Press, 1996.

Lee, Carol Ann. *Roses from the Earth: The Biography of Anne Frank.* London: Viking, 1999.

*Leigh, Vanora. *Anne Frank.* New York: Boatwright, 1985.

Lester, Julius. "The Stone that Weeps." In *Testimony.* Ed. David Rosenberg. New York: Random House, 1989. 195–96.

Levin, Meyer. "The Child behind the Secret Door." *New York Times Book Review,* June 15, 1952, 1, 22.

———. *The Obsession.* New York: Simon and Schuster, 1973.

———. "The Restricted Market." *Congress Weekly,* Nov. 13, 1950, 8–9.

———. "What Happened to Anne Frank?" *Anglo-Jewish Association Quarterly* 6 (Oct. 1960): 1–10.

Levy, Alan. *The Wiesenthal File.* Grand Rapids, Mich.: William B. Eerdmans, 1993.

*Lewittes, M. H., ed. *Anne Frank: The Diary of a Young Girl.* New York: Gale Books, 1958.

Lindwer, Willy. *The Last Seven Months of Anne Frank.* Trans. Alison Meersshaert. New York: Pantheon, 1991.

Lipstadt, Deborah. *Beyond Belief: The American Press and the Coming of the Holocaust, 1933–1945.* New York: Free Press, 1986.

———. *Denying the Holocaust: The Growing Assault on Truth and Memory.* New York: Free Press, 1993.

Littell, Franklin H., ed. *Hyping the Holocaust: Scholars Answer Goldhagen.* Merion Station, Penn.: Merion Westfield Press International, 1997.

*Living Voices. *Through the Eyes of a Friend.* Seattle: Theater Works/USA, 1992. Video and interactive performance of an introduction to Anne Frank and the Holocaust.

Malkin, Peter Z., and Henry Stein. *Eichmann in My Hands.* New York: Warner, 1990.

Margulies, Donald. *The Model Apartment.* New York Dramatists Play Service, 1990.

*Martin, Christopher, ed. *The Diary of Anne Frank.* Harlow, U.K.: Longman, 1989.

*McDonough, Yona Zeldis. *Anne Frank.* Illus. Mallcah Zeldis. New York: Henry Holt, 1997.

Melnick, Ralph. *The Stolen Legacy of Anne Frank: Meyer Levin, Lillian Hellman, and the Staging of the Diary.* New Haven: Yale University Press, 1997.

Menkel, Irma Sonnenberg, with Jonathan Alter. "I Saw Anne Frank Die: At Age of One Hundred Remembers the Horrors of Bergen-Belsen Concentration Camp." *Newsweek,* July 21, 1997, 16.

*Merti, Betty. *The World of Anne Frank: Readings, Activities, and Resources.* Portland, Maine: J. Weston Walch, 1984.

Miller, Judith. *One, by One, by One: Facing the Holocaust.* New York: Simon and Schuster, 1990.

*Milnes-Smith, Philippa, ed. *Dear Anne Frank: A Selection of Letters to Anne Frank Written by Children Today.* London: Puffin Books, 1995.

Minco, Marga. *Bitter Herbs.* New York: Oxford University Press, 1960.

Muhlen, Norbert. "The Return of Anne Frank." *ADL Bulletin* 14 (June 1957): 1–2, 8.

Müller, Melissa. *Anne Frank: The Biography.* Trans. Rita Kimber and Robert Kimber. New York: Henry Holt, 1998.

Ozick, Cynthia. "A Critic At Large: Who Owns Anne Frank?" *New Yorker,* Oct. 6, 1997. 76–87.

Pate, Glen S. "Part III. The United States of America." In *The Treatment of the Holocaust in Textbooks: The Federal Government of Germany, Israel, the United States of America.* Ed. Randolph L. Braham. New York: New Social Science Monographs and Institute for Holocaust Studies of the City University of New York, 1987. 233–301.

Pipher, Mary. *Reviving Ophelia: Saving the Selves of Adolescent Girls.* New York: G. P. Putnam's Sons, 1994.

Polak, Jack. "Anne Frank's Dream Came True." Letter in *Forward,* Apr. 7, 1995, 36.

———. "A Response to Miller's 'One by One.'" In *The Netherlands and Nazi Genocide.* Ed. G. Jan Colijn and Marcia Sachs Littell. Lewiston, N.Y.: Edwin Mellen Press, 1992. 77–90.

Poupard, Dennis, and J. E. Person, Jr., eds. "Anne Frank: 1929–1945." *Twentieth Century Literary Criticism* 17 (1985): 98–122.

Presser, Jacob. *The Destruction of the Dutch Jews: A Definitive Account of the Holocaust in the Netherlands.* Trans. Arnold Pomerans. New York: E. P. Dutton, 1969.

*Prince, Eileen. *The Story of Anne Frank.* 1985. London: Maxwell Macmillan, 1991.

Readers' Companion to Anne Frank: The Diary of a Young Girl: The Definitive Edition. New York: Doubleday, 1995.

*Reiss, Johanna. *The Upstairs Room.* 1972. New York: Crowell, 1980.

Ringelheim, Joan. "Women and the Holocaust: A Reconsideration of Research." In *Different Voices: Women and the Holocaust.* Ed. Carol Rittner and John K. Roth. 1993. 373–418.

*Rittner, Carol, ed. *Anne Frank in the World: Essays and Reflections.* Armonk, N.Y.: M. E. Sharpe, 1997.

Rittner, Carol, and John K. Roth, eds. *Different Voices: Women and the Holocaust.* New York: Paragon House, 1993.

Robinson, Jacob. *Psychoanalysis in a Vacuum: Bruno Bettelheim and the Holocaust.* New York: Yad Vashem Yivo Documentary Projects, 1970.

*Rol, Ruud van der, and Rian Verhoeven, eds. *Anne Frank: Beyond the Diary (A Photographic Remembrance).* Trans. Tony Lanham and Plym Peters. Intro. Anna Quindlen. New York: Viking Press, 1993.

Romein, Jan. "A Child's Voice." *Het Parool* (Amsterdam), Apr. 3, 1946, 1.

Rosenberg, David, ed. *Testimony: Contemporary Writers Make the Holocaust Personal.* New York: Random House, 1989.

Rosenfeld, Alvin H. *A Double Dying: Reflections on Holocaust Literature.* Bloomington: Indiana University Press, 1980.

———. "Popularization and Memory: The Case of Anne Frank." In *Lessons and Legacies: The Meaning of the Holocaust in a Changing World.* Ed. Peter Hayes. Evanston, Ill.: Northwestern University Press, 1991. 243–371.

Roth, Philip. *The Ghost Writer.* New York: Farrar, Straus, Giroux, 1979.

———. *Operation Shylock.* New York: Simon and Schuster, 1993.

Rubin-Dorsky, Jeffrey. "Philip Roth's *The Ghost Writer:* Literary Heritage and Jewish Irreverence." *Studies in American Jewish Literature* 8 (Fall 1989): 168–85.

Sagan, Alex. "An Optimistic Icon: Anne Frank's Canonization in Postwar Culture." *German Politics and Society* 13 (Fall 1995): 95–107.

*Sanders, Sue. *In Holland Stands a House: A Play about the Life and Times of Anne Frank.* New York: Collins Educational, 1991.

Schloss, Eva, with Evelyn Julia Kent. *Eva's Story.* New York: St. Martin's Press, 1988.

Schnabel, Ernst. *Anne Frank: A Portrait in Courage.* Trans. Richard Winston and Clara Winston. New York: Harcourt, Brace, and World, 1958. Rpt. as *The Footsteps of Anne Frank.* London: Longmans Green, 1959.

Segal, Mark. "The Second Agony of Anne Frank." *Jerusalem Post,* June 17, 1977, magazine section.

Shapiro, Shelly. "An Investigation." In *Truth Prevails: Demolishing Holocaust Denial.* Ed. Shelly Shapiro. New York: Beata Klarsfeld Foundation, 1990. 10–28.

Shatsky, Joel. "Creating an Aesthetic for Holocaust Literature." *Studies in American Jewish Literature* 10 (Spring 1991): 104–14.

*Shawn, Karen. *The End of Innocence: Anne Frank and the Holocaust.* 2d. ed. New York: Anti-Defamation League, 1994.

*Shefer-Vanson, Dorothy. *The Diary of Anne Frank: Notes.* Lincoln, Neb.: Cliff's Notes, 1984.

*Shulman, William L., ed. *Association of Holocaust Organizations Directory.* Bayside, N.Y.: Holocaust Resource Center and Archives, Queensborough Community College, 1996.

———, ed. and comp. *Holocaust Resource Guide: A Comprehensive Listing of Media for Further Study.* Woodbridge, Conn.: Blackbirch Press, 1998.

Singer, Isaac Bashevis, *Nobel Lecture.* New York: Farrar, Straus, Giroux, 1978.

Skloot, Robert. "A Multiplicity of Annes." *The Nation,* Nov. 16, 1998, 20–25.

*Steenmeijer, Anna G., ed. *A Tribute to Anne Frank.* Garden City, N.Y.: Doubleday, 1971.

Steiner, George. *Language and Silence: Essays on Language, Literature, and the Inhuman.* New York: Atheneum, 1974.

*Stern, Kenneth. *Holocaust Denial.* New York: American Jewish Committee, 1993.

Sutton, Nina. *Bettelheim: A Life and a Legacy.* Trans. David Sharp. New York: Basic Books, 1996.

*Tames, Richard. *Anne Frank.* New York: Franklin Watts, 1991.

Thurman, Judith. "Not Even a Nice Girl." *New Yorker,* Dec. 18, 1989, 116–20.

*Tridenti, Lina. *Anne Frank.* New York: Silver-Burnett Press, 1985.

*Tyler, Laura. *Anne Frank.* Englewood Cliffs, N.J.: Silver Burnett Press, 1990.

*Van Maarsen, Jacqueline (Jopie). *My Friend, Anne Frank.* Trans. Debra F. Okenhut. New York: Vantage Press, 1996.

Verschuur, Paul. "Anne Frank, Roommate Friction Revealed." *Jewish Week,* Dec. 18, 1987, 35.

Weinstein, Jacob J. "The Betrayal of Anne Frank." *Congress Weekly,* May 13, 1957, 5–7.

*Western, Richard D. "The Case for *Anne Frank: The Diary of a Young Girl.*" In *Celebrating Censored Books.* Ed. Nicholas Karolides and Lee Burress. Racine: Wisconsin Council of Teachers of English, 1985. 12–14.

Wiesenthal, Simon. *The Murderers among Us.* Paris: Opera Mundi, 1967.

Wilson, Cara. *Love, Otto: The Legacy of Anne Frank.* Kansas City: Andrews and McMeel, 1995.

Wolff, Janet. *Feminine Sentences: Essays on Women and Culture.* Berkeley: University of California Press, 1990.

*Womack, Jack. *Random Acts of Senseless Violence.* New York: Grove Press, 1993.

Young, James E., ed. *The Art of Memory: Holocaust Memorials in History.* Munich: Presetel-Verlag, 1994.

———. *Writing and Rewriting the Holocaust.* Bloomington: Indiana University Press, 1988.

Zee, Nanda van der. *De Kamergenoot van Anne Frank* [Anne Frank's Roommate]. Amsterdam: Lakeman, 1990.

———. "The Recurrent Myth of 'Dutch Heroism' and Anne Frank as a Symbol." In *The Netherlands and Nazi Genocide.* Ed. G. Jan Colijn and Marcia Sachs Littell. Lewiston, N.Y.: Edwin Mellen Press, 1992. 1–14.

Publication Acknowledgments

Algene Ballif, "Metamorphosis into American Adolescent." Copyright © 1955 by Algene Ballif. Excerpt reprinted from *Commentary* (Nov. 1955): 464–65, by permission of Algene Ballif Marcus and *Commentary;* all rights reserved.

Algene Ballif, "Letters from Readers: The Stage Anne Frank." Copyright © 1956 by *Commentary.* Reprinted from *Commentary* (Feb. 1956): 184, by permission of Algene Ballif Marcus and *Commentary;* all rights reserved.

David Barnouw, "Anne Frank and Film." Adapted by David Barnouw from "Film and *The Diary of Anne Frank*" in *Media History Yearbook No. 7: The 1950s* (Amsterdam: Media History Yearbook, 1995), 213–39. Copyright © 1995 by David Barnouw. Reprinted by permission of David Barnouw.

John Berryman, "The Development of Anne Frank." Excerpt from *The Freedom of the Poet* (New York: Farrar, Straus, and Giroux, 1976), 91–96. Copyright © 1976 by Kate Berryman. Reprinted by permission of Farrar, Straus, and Giroux, Inc.

Bruno Bettelheim, "The Ignored Lesson of Anne Frank." Excerpt from *Surviving and Other Essays* (New York: Alfred A. Knopf, 1979), 246–57. Copyright © 1952, © 1960, 1962, 1976, 1979 by Bruno Bettelheim and Trude Bettelheim as Trustees. Reprinted by permission of Alfred A. Knopf Inc. and Raines and Raines.

Ben Brantley, "This Time, Another Anne Confronts Life in the Attic." Reprinted from *New York Times,* Dec. 5, 1997, 1, 16. Copyright © 1997 by the New York Times Co. Reprinted by permission.

Rachel Feldhay Brenner, "Writing Herself against History: Anne Frank's Self-Portrait as a Young Artist." Excerpt reprinted from *Modern Judaism* 16 (1996): 105–34. Copyright © 1996 by Johns Hopkins University Press.

G. Jan Colijn, "Review Essay: Anne Frank Remembered." Excerpt from *Holocaust and Genocide Studies* 10.1 (Spring 1996): 78–92. Copyright © 1996 by Oxford University Press. Reprinted by permission of Oxford University Press and G. Jan Colijn.

Denise de Costa, "Anne Frank and Etty Hillesum: Diarists." Adapted by the editors from "Exile and Self-Censorship in *The Diary of Anne Frank*," *Lover* 21.2 (1994): 4–7; from "Feminist Perspectives on Peace, Violence, and War," paper presented at the Peace History Society symposium, Montreal, Sept. 1–2, 1995; and from "Anne Frank and Etty Hillesum: Diarists," a summary of her published dissertation entitled *Anne Frank and Etty Hillesum: Spirituality, Authorship, Sexuality* (Amsterdam: Uitgeverij Balans, 1996). Reprinted by permission of Denise de Costa.

Judith E. Doneson, "The American History of Anne Frank's Diary." Excerpt from *Holocaust and Genocide Studies* 2.1 (1987): 149–60. Copyright © 1987 by Oxford University Press. Reprinted by permission of Oxford University Press and Judith E. Doneson.

Barbara Epstein, "Letters from Readers: The Stage Anne Frank." Copyright © 1956 by *Commentary*. Reprinted from *Commentary* (Feb. 1956): 183, by permission of Barbara Epstein and *Commentary;* all rights reserved.

Epigraphs from *The Diary of a Young Girl: The Definitive Edition* by Anne Frank. Otto Frank and Mirjam Pressler, editors, translated by Susan Massotty. Translation copyright © 1995 by Doubleday, a division of Bantam Doubleday Dell Publishing Group, Inc. Reprinted by permission of Doubleday, a division of Bantam Doubleday Dell Publishing Group, Inc., and the Anne Frank-Fonds, Basel.

Miep Gies and Alison Leslie Gold, "The Darkest Days." Excerpt from *Anne Frank Remembered* (New York: Simon and Schuster, 1987), 197–201, 231–35. Copyright © 1987 by Miep Gies and Alison Leslie Gold. Reprinted by permission of Simon and Schuster, Transworld Publishing Ltd., Miep Gies, and Alison Leslie Gold.

Lawrence Graver, "Don Quixote and the Star of David." Excerpt from *An Obsession with Anne Frank* (Berkeley: University of California Press, 1995), 234–39. Copyright © 1995 by the Regents of the University of California. Reprinted by permission of the University of California Press and Lawrence Graver.

Sylvia P. Iskander, "Anne Frank's Reading: A Retrospective." Adapted by Sylvia P. Iskander from "Anne Frank's Reading," from *Children's Literary Association Quarterly* 13 (Fall 1988): 137–41. Copyright © 1988 by Sylvia P. Islander. Reprinted by permission of Sylvia P. Iskander and the Children's Literature Association.

Lin Jaldati, "Bergen-Belsen." Excerpt from *Sag nie, du gehst de letzten Weg: Lebenserin-nerungen 1911 bis 1986* by Lin Jaldati and Eberhard Rebeling (Marburg, Germany: BdWi-Verlag, 1995), 358–63. Copyright © 1995 by BdWi-Verlag, Marburg, Germany. Reprinted by permission of BdWi-Verlag.

Lawrence L. Langer, "The Uses—and Misuses—of a Young Girl's Diary: 'If Anne Frank Could Return from among the Murdered, She Would Be Appalled.'" From the *For-ward*, Mar. 17, 1995, 1, 5. Copyright © 1995 by the *Forward*. Reprinted by permission of Lawrence L. Langer and the *Forward*.

Lawrence L. Langer, "The Americanization of the Holocaust on Stage and Screen." Origi-nally published in *From Hester Street to Hollywood*, ed. Susan Blacher Cohen (Bloo-mington: Indiana University Press, 1983), 213–17. Copyright © 1983 by Sarah Blacher Cohen. Excerpt from *Admitting the Holocaust: Collected Essays* by Lawrence L. Langer (New York: Oxford University Press, 1995), 157–77. Reprinted by permission of Lawrence L. Langer and Sarah Blacher Cohen.

Deborah E. Lipstadt, "Twisting the Truth: The Diary of Anne Frank." Excerpt from *Denying the Holocaust: The Growing Assault on Truth and Memory* (New York: Free Press, 1993), 229–35. Copyright © 1993 by the Vidal Sassoon International Center for the Study of Antisemitism, the Hebrew University of Jerusalem. Reprinted by per-mission of the Free Press, a division of Simon and Schuster.

Susan Massotty, translation of Anne Frank's handwritten table of contents for her short stories that was first published in *Anne Frank Verhaaltjes en Gebeurtenissen uit het Achterhuis* (Amsterdam: Bert Bakker, 1986). © 1949 by the Anne Frank-Fonds, Basel, Switzerland. Translation copyright © 1996 by Susan Massotty.

Harry Mulisch, "Death and the Maiden." Excerpt from *New York Review of Books,* July 17, 1966, 7–8. Reprinted by permission of the *New York Review of Books.* Copyright © 1986 by Nyrev, Inc.

Laureen Nussbaum, "Anne Frank." Excerpts from "Anne Frank" in *Women Writing in Dutch,* ed. Kristiann Aercke (New York: Garland, 1994), 513–30, © 1994 by Garland Publishing, Inc., and from "Anne Frank: The Writer," paper presented at the Confer-ence on Children in Exile, Reno, Nev., Oct. 3–6, 1996. © 1996 by Laureen Nussbaum. Reprinted by permission of Laureen Nussbaum and Garland Publishing, Inc.

Harry Paape, "The Arrest." Excerpt from *The Diary of Anne Frank: The Critical Edition,* prepared by the Netherlands State Institute for War Documentation, ed. David Barnouw and Gerrold van der Stroom, trans. Arnold J. Pomerans and B. M. Mooyaart-Doubleday (New York: Doubleday, 1989), 21–27. Copyright © 1986 by Anne Frank-Fonds, Basel/Switzerland, for all texts of Anne Frank. Copyright © 1986 by the Neth-erlands State Institute for War Documentation for preface, introduction, commentary, and notes. Reprinted by permission of Doubleday, a division of Bantam Doubleday Dell Publishing Group, Inc. and by Penguin UK.

Harry Paape, "The Betrayal." Excerpt from *The Diary of Anne Frank: The Critical Edition,* prepared by the Netherlands State Institute for War Documentation, ed. David Barnouw and Gerrold van der Stroom, trans. Arnold J. Pomerans and B. M. Mooyaart-Doubleday (New York: Doubleday, 1989), 28–48. Copyright © 1986 by Anne Frank-Fonds, Basel/Switzerland, for all texts of Anne Frank. Copyright © 1986 by the Netherlands State Institute for War Documentation for preface, introduction, commentary, and notes. Reprinted by permission of Doubleday, a division of Bantam Doubleday Dell Publishing Group, Inc. and by Penguin UK.

Hannah Elisabeth Pick-Goslar, "Her Last Days." Excerpt from *The Last Seven Months of Anne Frank,* ed. Willy Lindwer (New York: Pantheon, 1991), 7, 20–29. English translation copyright © 1991 by Random House, Inc. Reprinted by permission of Pantheon Books, a division of Random House, Inc.

Henry F. Pommer, "The Legend and Art of Anne Frank." Excerpt reprinted by permission from *Judaism* 9.1 (Winter 1960): 37–46. Copyright © 1960 American Jewish Congress.

Alvin H. Rosenfeld, "Anne Frank—and Us: Finding the Right Words." Excerpt from *Reconstruction* 2.2 (1993): 86–92. © 1993 by Alvin H. Rosenfeld. Reprinted by permission of Alvin Rosenfeld and *Reconstruction.*

Philip Roth, "Femme Fatale." Excerpt from *The Ghost Writer* (New York: Farrar, Straus, and Giroux, 1979), 125–53. Copyright © 1979 by Philip Roth. Reprinted by permission of Farrar, Straus, and Giroux, Inc., and Jonathan Cape.

Ernst Schnabel, "Visiting Hours after 9 A.M." Excerpt from *Anne Frank: A Portrait in Courage,* trans. Richard Winston and Clara Winston (New York: Harcourt, Brace, and World, 1958), 133–37. Originally published as *Anne Frank: Spur eines Kindes* (Frankfurt: S. Fischer Verlag, 1958). Copyright © 1958 by Fischer Bücherei KG, Frankfurt am Main. All other rights remain with Fischer Taschenbuch Verlag GmbH, Frankfurt am Main. Reprinted by permission of S. Fischer Verlag and Harcourt Brace and Company.

G. B. Stern, "Introduction to *The Tales from the House Behind.*" Excerpt from *Tales from the House Behind: Fables, Personal Reminiscences, and Short Stories by Anne Frank* (Kingswood, England: World's Work [1913], 1962), 9–16. Copyright © 1962 by The World's Work (1913) Ltd. Reprinted by permission of the Society of Authors as the literary representative of the estate of G. B. Stern.

Kenneth Tynan, "At the Theater: Berlin Postscript." Excerpt from the *London Observer,* Oct. 7, 1956, 13–14. © 1956 by Kenneth Tynan. Reprinted by permission of Roxana Tynan and Matthew Tynan.

Berteke Waaldijk, "Reading Anne Frank as a Woman." Excerpt from *Women's Studies International Forum* 16.4 (1993): 327–35. Copyright © 1993 by Elsevier Science Ltd. Reprinted by permission of Elsevier Science Ltd., Oxford, England.

Alfred Werner, "Germany's New Flagellants." Excerpt from *American Scholar* 27 (Spring 1958): 169–78. Copyright © 1958 by the *American Scholar*. Reprinted by permission of the *American Scholar*.

Simon Wiesenthal, "Epilogue to the Diary of Anne Frank." Excerpt from *The Murderers among Us* (Paris: Opera Mundi, 1967), 170–82. Copyright © 1967 by Simon Wiesenthal. Reprinted by permission of Simon Wiesenthal.

James E. Young, "The Anne Frank House: Holland's Memorial Shrine of the Book." Excerpt from *The Art of Memory: Holocaust Memorials in History* (New York: Jewish Museum, 1994), 131–37. Copyright © 1994 by James E. Young. Reprinted by permission of James E. Young.

Contributors

Algene Ballif (aka Gene Marcus), a native of Salt Lake City, has published reviews and critical articles in little magazines. She taught English in various colleges, has acted in theatrical productions in the United States and in England, and has been editing the diaries and letters of her parents, who were once active in the Mormon community in Provo, Utah.

David Barnouw, author and editor of more than eight books and many articles on Dutch wartime history, is one of the principal editors of *The Diary of Anne Frank: The Critical Edition* and a staff researcher of the Netherlands Institute for War Documentation. He has written on the German occupation, film history, and the Nazi Youth Movement and has lectured extensively in Europe and at colleges and Holocaust centers in the United States.

John Berryman (1914–72), winner of the Pulitzer Prize in 1965 and ten other distinguished awards for his poetry, received honorary degrees from Cambridge University and Drake University. Fifteen volumes of his poetry have been published since 1942 in addition to several collections of essays, a biography of Stephen Crane, and one novel, *Recovery.*

Bruno Bettelheim (1909–90) was released from Dachau in 1939, came to the United States, and established a school for autistic children in Chicago. Among his many books and articles, *The Uses of Enchantment,* on the benefits of violence in fairy tales, may be best known. His reputation as a brilliant, arrogant, and even brutal psychologist has been recollected by former patients since his death in 1990. Two biographies on his complex life and career were published in 1996, one by Nina Sutton and the other by Richard Pollak.

Ben Brantley is the chief drama critic for the *New York Times* and winner of the George Jean Nathan award for excellence in theater criticism. He is a graduate of Swarthmore College.

Rachel Feldhay Brenner, an associate professor of Hebrew and Semitic studies at the University of Wisconsin at Madison, is the author of *Writing as Resistance,* on Edith Stein, Simone Weil, Anne Frank, and Etty Hillesum, and books on two Canadian authors, Mordecai Richler and A. M. Klein. In addition to several chapters in edited volumes on Jewish themes, she has written reviews in many professional journals.

G. Jan Colijn, dean of general studies at Stockton State College in Pomona, New Jersey, is the coeditor of *Confronting the Holocaust* and of *The Netherlands and Nazi Genocide,* the collection of papers sponsored annually by the Scholars Conference on the Holocaust and the Churches. He is the author of many articles on the Holocaust, including "Toward a Proper Legacy—The Use and Abuse of the Anne Frank Symbol."

Denise de Costa is the author of *Anne Frank and Etty Hillesum: Spirituality, Authorship, Sexuality;* a book on the French theorists Luce Irigaray, Julia Kristeva, and Jean-François Lyotard; and articles on women's studies. She received her Ph.D. from the University of Utrecht in 1996.

Judith E. Doneson, the director of the St. Louis Holocaust Museum and Learning Center, has specialized in contemporary Jewish film history and has taught at universities in Tel Aviv, Jerusalem, Philadelphia, and St. Louis. She received a doctorate from Hebrew University in Jerusalem and worked there on a film course for the Institute of Contemporary Jewry. She is a contributor to *Spielberg's Holocaust: Critical Essays on Schindler's List* and the author of "Holocaust Revisited: A Catalyst for Memory or Trivialization?"

Bernd Elias, president of the Anne Frank-Fonds in Basel, Switzerland, since 1996, made his childhood hobbies of acting and ice skating into a professional career. His cousin Anne Frank, four years younger, joined him in those early games and wrote about them in her diary. Their correspondence began after he moved to Basel with his mother, Otto Frank's sister, in 1931. Elias has performed in many productions on stage and film in Switzerland, Germany, and England, including a starring role in Sonja Henie's ice show during the coronation of Queen Elizabeth in London in 1953. On behalf of the Anne Frank-Fonds he presented "The Anne Frank Declaration of the Millennium" at the United Nations early in 1999, a proclamation to be signed by government leaders throughout the world.

Hyman Aaron Enzer, a professor of sociology emeritus at Hofstra University and the former chairman of the Sociology and Anthropology Department, initiated the Journalism Program at Hofstra in 1950. He co-coordinated the Russell Sage Program in Sociology and Journalism at the University of Wisconsin in 1964–65. His specialty has been the sociology of literature and the arts, and he has presented several papers on Anne Frank and the Holocaust for professional conferences in the United States and Canada. His most recent publications are "Sociology of Literature" for the *Macmillan Encyclopedia of Sociology* and a review of *The Diary of Anne Frank: The Critical Edition* for *Contemporary Sociology.*

Barbara Epstein is a coeditor of the *New York Review of Books* and an essayist. She helped edit the 1952 American version of *The Diary of a Young Girl.*

Miep Gies was eleven in 1920 when she was taken with other sickly Austrian children to foster homes in Holland because her family was near starvation after World War I. By 1933 she gained health and opportunities to work in Amsterdam, where she eventually became Otto Frank's secretary at Opekta. She has been given the highest civilian honors by the Dutch and German governments and by many Jewish and Christian organizations for her role as a protector of the Frank family during the Nazi occupation of Holland.

Alison Leslie Gold, a novelist and feelance writer, is the author of a biography of Hannah Pick-Goslar as well as the co-author with Miep Gies of *Anne Frank Remembered,* which won the 1988 Christopher Award. She also received the 1987 Merit of Educational Distinction from the International Center of Holocaust Studies of the American Anti-Defamation League. Born in Brooklyn, educated in universities in North Carolina, Mexico City, and New York City, she now lives in Santa Monica, California.

Lawrence Graver is John Hawley Professor Emeritus of English at Williams College and an author and literary critic. His work has been published in major periodicals and he is editor of *Conrad's Short Fiction, Carson McCullers, Beckett: The Critical Heritage,* and *Samuel Beckett: Waiting for Godot.*

Sylvia P. Iskander is a professor of English at the University of Southwestern Louisiana in Lafayette and did much of her research on Anne Frank's reading in the local library near 263 Prinsengracht. Her three articles on Anne Frank deal with Anne's family relationships, her reading, and her autobiographical style. Iskander has taught and written extensively in children's and young adult literature since the mid-1970s.

Lin Jaldati (1912–88), born Rebekka Brilleslijper in Amsterdam, was a dancer and Jewish entertainer, who, after the war, toured throughout the world with her husband, Eberhard Rebling, a pianist and musicologist. During the Nazi occupation of Holland she and Rebling, a non-Jew, were active in the resistance movement. They could not marry until 1946 because of the Nuremberg laws. She and her younger sister, Marianne (Janny) Brandes-Brilleslijper, served as nurses in Bergen-Belsen and were direct witnesses of the last days of Anne and Margot Frank.

Lawrence L. Langer, a professor emeritus of English at Simmons College, is the author or editor of critical works on Henry James and Mark Twain. His books and essays on the Holocaust span more than thirty years. These include *Admitting the Holocaust,* a collection of his writings, *Art from the Ashes,* an anthology of poetry, essays, and sketches by Holocaust victims, and *Preempting the Holocaust.*

Deborah E. Lipstadt, a professor of modern Jewish and Holocaust studies at Emory University in Atlanta, is the author of *Beyond Belief: The American Press and the Coming of the Holocaust, 1933–1945* and *Denying the Holocaust: The Growing Assault on Truth and Memory.*

Harry Mulisch has won most of Holland's prestigious awards for his novels, poems, plays, and critical essays. His novel *The Discovery of Heaven* was published in English in 1996. His novel *The Assault,* translated in 1985, was the basis for a film that won an Academy Award for the best foreign movie of 1986. Among other notable writings is his 1962 report in Dutch on the Eichmann trial.

Laureen Nussbaum, born Hannelore Klein, knew Anne and Margot Frank in Amsterdam and remained a close friend of Otto Frank, who was best man at her wedding in 1947. She is a professor emerita of foreign languages at the University of Oregon at Portland and has written and lectured extensively on Anne Frank and the diary. Her personal recollection of the Frank family is featured in the 1995 documentary film *Anne Frank Remembered.*

Harry Paape, the author of numerous publications and a popular book about the first resistance group, the Geuzen, studied political science in Amsterdam. He started work with the Netherlands State Institute for War Documentation in 1952 and served as deputy director and then director from 1970 until his retirement in 1990.

Hannah Elisabeth Pick-Goslar, the "Hannali" and "Lies Goosens" frequently mentioned in Anne Frank's diary, was a childhood friend of Anne in Amsterdam and later met her in Bergen-Belsen just before Anne's death. Pick-Goslar's memories of Anne are the subject of a biography by Alison Leslie Gold and have been retold to many audiences in Europe and America. After the war she became a children's nurse in Israel and now lives in Jerusalem with her large family.

Henry F. Pommer (1918–82), a literary scholar and college administrator, was the author of *Milton and Melville, Emerson's First Marriage,* and numerous other publications. After teaching at Swarthmore and Cornell he taught at Allegheny College for twenty years. He served as dean and academic vice president at Ripon College in Wisconsin and later at Cedar Crest College in Pennsylvania. He was also an ordained minister and active administrator of the Universalist Church of America.

Alvin H. Rosenfeld is the director of the Roberta A. and Sandra S. Borns Jewish Studies Program at Indiana University and the author of *A Double Dying: Reflections on Holocaust Literature, Imagining Hitler,* and numerous scholarly articles on American poetry and Jewish writers. He has been honored with grants from the American Council of Learned Societies and the National Endowment for the Humanities and has served as a visiting professor at the University of Kiel, Hebrew University, and Hamburg University.

Philip Roth, winner of the Pulitzer Prize for fiction in 1997, has published more than fifteen novels, many short stories and critical essays, and several autobiographical works. Among many other honors, he won the National Book Award in 1960 for *Goodbye, Columbus* and again in 1996 for *Sabbath's Theater.* Roth has served as general editor of Penguin's series Writers from the Other Europe that introduced the work of such authors as Tadeusz Borowski, Milan Kundera, Danilo Kis, and Bruno Schulz.

Ernst Schnabel (1913–86), an author and radio-TV commentator in northern Germany and Berlin after the war years, conducted interviews with more than forty individuals to retrace the history of the Franks. He also included some of Anne Frank's unpublished works in his book that was translated under two different titles: *The Footsteps of Anne Frank* and *Anne Frank: A Portrait in Courage.* He wrote five novels, several collections of short stories, and a libretto for an opera by H. W. Henze based on the Medusa legend.

Sandra Solotaroff-Enzer, an associate professor of English emerita at SUNY Nassau Community College, has taught English literature at Hofstra University and Nassau Community College. Her doctoral dissertation at SUNY Stony Brook was entitled "George Gissing's Short Stories about Women."

Anne Frank's diary and feminist literature have been among her academic specialties. She has written a number of papers on pedagogy and literature and also teaches piano.

G. B. Stern (1890–1973), one of England's most prolific writers, produced a novel almost every year after her first one at age twenty. Like Anne, she began writing early; later she wrote witty dialogues with Sheila Kaye-Smith about Jane Austen, whom she characterized as "an experienced flirt."

Kenneth Tynan (1927–80), a noted British drama critic, had important roles in supporting the literary "Angry Young Men" movement and the establishment of the National Theater in London in association with Laurence Olivier. He published a collection of his reviews, *Tynan, Right and Left*, among other works, and was co-author of the erotic musical *Oh! Calcutta*.

Berteke Waaldijk is an assistant professor in the department of women's studies at Utrecht University. Her doctoral dissertation, a comparative study of women and social work in the Netherlands and the United States, was published in 1996. She and her colleague, Denise de Costa, are active in developing programs in feminist scholarship at Utrecht and other Dutch universities.

Alfred Werner (1911–79), an art critic and biographer, was imprisoned for almost a year in Dachau. In 1940 he came to the United States and began another career as a freelance writer and lecturer. He contributed articles on central European affairs and art history to a number of American periodicals and wrote biographies on famous artists, including Modigliani, Chagall, Munch, and Utrillo. He also was the editor of the *Universal Jewish Encyclopedia*.

Simon Wiesenthal is famous for his relentless pursuit of Nazi leaders and collaborators he identifies by analyzing news items, photographs, and official and informal documents gathered by informants throughout the world. His experience in several concentration camps, ending at Mauthausen in 1945, and the deaths of many of his family members in the Holocaust became the impetus for his postwar career. His work has been recognized by many governments as well as the United Nations, which has granted his Simon Wiesenthal Center in Los Angeles official nongovernmental organization status. The center also sponsors the Museum of Tolerance and the international journal *Response*.

James E. Young is a professor of English and Judaic studies at the University of Massachusetts at Amherst, the author of *Writing and Rewriting the Holocaust*, the recipient of many honors and fellowships, the curator of the international exhibition of Holocaust memorials in 1994–95, and the editor of *The Art of Memory: Holocaust Memorials in History*.

Index

Typeset in 10.5/13 Adobe Garamond
with Poster Bodini display
Designed by Dennis Roberts
Composed by Jim Proefrock
at the University of Illinois Press
Manufactured by Thomson-Shore, Inc.

University of Illinois Press
1325 South Oak Street
Champaign, IL 61820–6903
www.press.uillinois.edu

4604